W-Frank Brown

April '81.

ORGANIZATIONAL BEHAVIOR
An applied psychological approach

By

W. CLAY HAMNER
Duke University

and

DENNIS W. ORGAN
Indiana University

ORGANIZATIONAL BEHAVIOR

an applied psychological approach

1978

BUSINESS PUBLICATIONS, INC.
Dallas, Texas   75243

Irwin-Dorsey Limited
Georgetown, Ontario   L7G 4B3

5 6 7 8 9 0 K 5 4 3 2 1 0

ISBN 0-256-01811-1
Library of Congress Catalog Card No. 77-79388

Printed in the United States of America

To two men who have made lasting contributions to the field of organizational behavior and to our own lives:

William E. Scott, Jr.

J. Stacy Adams

and to two lovely people who are our best friends and constant companions—Ellen *and* Kay.

Preface

The last decade has witnessed an exponential growth rate of research and writing on behavior in organizations. A result of this is that organizational behavior is no longer merely a "behavioral approach to management," nor is it a superficial melange of interdisciplinary topics; it has jelled into a discipline in its own right, with a commonly shared conceptual core, a set of distinctive methodologies, and unifying points of reference. Although there are many differences of opinion with regard to certain basic issues, there is increased consensus as to what the basic issues are. The field of organizational behavior has approached the point at which it takes on its own unique paradigmatic thrust.

Our efforts in this volume have been aimed at articulating and systematizing what we perceive as the definitive conceptual core of organizational behavior as a reasonably mature discipline. Several heuristics have guided our efforts toward this end. First, we have focused our efforts at the level of individual and group behavior in organizations, or in other words, at the "micro" level; to an increasing extent, organization theory—the study of "macro" features such as organization structure, design, and development—constitutes an identifiably separate field of inquiry, and we felt that we could not do justice to both areas in one volume, just as most teachers feel that they cannot do justice to both in a single course. This choice, in turn, anchored us in psychology as the underlying discipline from which the concepts and methods for studying individual and group behavior in organizations emerged. Second, our intention has been to pursue an essentially *descriptive* as opposed to *normative* approach: to present a systematic narrative account of the empirical fund of knowledge presently available to us. Third, we have emphasized contemporary developments in this fund of knowledge without neglecting older contributions that have proved their worth over the years. Fourth, and perhaps most important, we have tried to be selective in that we have concentrated on those topics we believe to be richest in their implications for the management of people in organizations—richest not only as guides to immediate action, but in their potential for guiding a lifelong process of self-education in the dynamics of human behavior in organizations.

Our bias is that college courses in organizational behavior are doomed to failure if they attempt to provide a series of quick and easy steps to solving complex behavioral problems. Rather, the aim should be to develop "cognitive maps" or conceptual frameworks that enable the practicing administrator to make sense of his or her own behavior and the behavior of others; to provide the basis for critical reading and evaluations of prescriptive statements encountered in a variety of media; and to develop criteria for intellectual honesty and integrity in the analysis of behavioral phenomena in organizations.

The authors bear a heavy debt to Jim Erskine, who contributed significantly to the early planning of this book; to Walter Nord and Edward Morrison, who provided valuable comments on early drafts of the chapters; to Ellen P. Hamner for pilot testing the material and providing helpful feedback; and to colleagues and students, too numerous to mention without fear of slighting some, who gave us helpful feedback on some chapters. We also recognize, unfortunately without being able to cite specifically, the numerous instances in which we have unconsciously incorporated the insights of countless others in such a manner that they have become part and parcel of our own thinking. Gratitude is cheerfully if inadequately expressed to Paula Horne, Maureen LaFaive, Shirley Newman, Paula Keyser, Marla Clark, and Trina Latimer for the typing of this manuscript, and to the valuable support services of the School of Management at Boston University and the School of Business at Indiana University. All imperfections in the final product must, of course, be attributed to its authors.

December 1977   W. CLAY HAMNER
                                             DENNIS W. ORGAN

Contents

determining whether punishment is effective. The "Hot Stove Rule." The importance of explaining the rules. Case study. Styles of discipline. Concluding comment.

Chapter 5

The perceptual process   89

May 11

Characteristics and definition of perception: *The input process. The storing process. Outputs.* Interpersonal perception: *Knowing another person: A theory of inference. Uniform inference processes. Idiosyncratic processes.* The validity of judgments of others: *Characteristics of the person being judged. The judge. The situation.* Shortcuts used in judging others. Attribution and the judgment of others. Organizational implications: Judging performance: *Perceptual judgments and the performance appraisal.* Conclusions.

Chapter 6

Attitudes and behavior   107

May 11

What is an attitude? Readiness to respond and importance of an attitude. Components of an attitude: *The affective component. The cognitive component. The overt or behavioral response component.* Are attitudes (beliefs and emotions) related to behavioral responses? Where do attitudes come from? Attitude structure and consistency: *Festinger's cognitive dissonance theory. An alternative explanation of dissonance behavior.* Functions served by attitudes. Prejudice as an ego-defense attitude. The process of changing attitudes: *Arousal and change of adjustment attitudes. Arousal and change of the ego-defense attitude. Arousal and change of the value-expressive attitude. Arousal and change of the knowledge-function attitude.* Factors determining the effectiveness of persuasion. Appendix: Federal regulations covering prejudiced attitudes and behavior.

Chapter 7

Needs, goals, and motives: Theories of motivation   137

May 25

What energizes human behavior? *Need theory. Activation theory.* What directs or channels energized behavior? *Expectancy theory. Principles. Goal-setting theory.* Once behavior is channeled, how is it maintained? *Social comparison theory. Attribution theories. Two-factor theory.*

Chapter 8

Personality: Dimensions of individual differences   163

May 25

The concept of personality. Personality measurement: *Questionnaires. Ratings by observers. Other methods of personality assessment.* Personality: Dimensions of physiologically based differences: *Emotionality (neuroticism). Extraversion-introversion. The interaction between neuroticism and extraversion.* Personality: Differences in belief systems: *Locus of control. Causes of internal/external locus of control.* Personality: Differences in motive strength: *Need*

Chapter 14

15
June 22

Chapter 15

July 6

Chapter 16

July 13

Chapter 17

July 13

Chapter 18

July 20

ORGANIZATIONAL BEHAVIOR
An applied psychological approach

1

Introduction to organizational behavior

MANAGING IN A CHANGING WORLD

Although we have limited the material presented here to the psychology of work behavior within and among organizations, we do not fail to recognize that our society is always changing and that behavior within organizations must also change in order to meet the needs and demands of a changing society. Therefore, it is important to recognize that human nature does not remain the same. People develop over time, organizations develop over time, and society changes over time. We have attempted to discuss three important aspects of change in this text. First, we have attempted to describe how people change over time during their careers. As certain needs are fulfilled, as certain goals are achieved, as certain experiences are encountered, people obviously change. Second, we have attempted to describe how changes in our environment and society (for example, technology, family structure, defense needs, and laws) have induced changes in the behavior, attitudes, and needs of people within organizations. Third, we have attempted to discuss the antecedents or causes of performance and satisfaction in *dynamic* rather than *static* terms. Managers are not trying to maintain behavior, or to understand behavior only as it currently is. They are trying to change behavior (increase productivity, improve job satisfaction, meet demands, adjust to external pressures) and to understand the causes of the behavior they wish to evoke in people.

The reader should understand that as a relatively new field of study (dating from about a quarter of a century ago), the empirical science of organizational behavior is itself dynamic, like any other field of knowledge. In no sense is this book or any part of it the "last word." We hope that new developments and breakthroughs lie in the future; some of our current approaches will later be shown to be faulty or misdirected. It is therefore important that the reader develop a lifelong habit of reading and thinking about behavior and, more important, of standing ready to modify or qualify his or her own private knowledge about behavior in organizations. To this end, we have attempted to provide in this book the fundamentals requisite to a continuous self-directed study of behavior in the work environment.

OVERVIEW OF BOOK

In Chapter 2 we begin to expand on the points presented above. In that chapter we discuss where our current state of knowledge comes from and how a student of organizational behavior can interpret the results from various sources concerning this knowledge in order to determine its validity and generalizability.

In Chapters 3 through 12 we focus on the psychology of individual

No matter what you have to do with an organization—whether you are going to study what goes on in it, work in it, consult for it, sabotage it, or use it for your own purposes—you need, according to Perrow (1970), to have some view or conceptual model of it. The title of this book, *Organizational Behavior: An Applied Psychological Approach,* implies that the view we are presenting here is one that attempts to explain, in psychological terms, what goes on within the organization. In this book we look at three units of behavior—the behavior of the individual, the behavior of groups, and the effects of individual and group behavior on the organization as a whole.

Several of the reasons managers need to understand the psychology of individual human beings have been outlined by Leavitt (1972). First, the characteristics of people in general are a good base from which to build up to the characteristics of people in groups and organizations. Second, managers, unlike parents, must work with *used,* not new, human beings—human beings whom other people have gotten to first. Third, the manager is his or her own best management mechanism. An examination of his own makeup should, therefore, prove personally useful.

Psychology has many immediate applications to management, not only because it can help people to manage organizations better, but also because it can make both managers and workers more fully developed individuals. Many managers are well trained in the technical side of their job (engineering, accounting, hospital administration, law, economics), but have slighted the formal study of behavior. As managers gain more experience and are promoted to higher levels, they begin to see that most of their problems are manifested in terms of people problems—such as union-management relations, power struggles, interpersonal conflict, low job motivation, and absenteeism. Perhaps this is the reason so many middle-level and upper-middle-level managers invest so much time and money in organizational behavior training programs dealing with such topics as job motivation, communication, goal-setting, managing time, leadership development, and negotiation skills.

MANAGEMENT'S ASSUMPTIONS ABOUT PEOPLE

As we will demonstrate in later chapters of this book, managers make assumptions about how their own actions influence the performance and satisfaction of their subordinates, peers, and supervisors. Often, these assumptions are derived from many years of "trial and error" experience; many times administrators are unaware of the assumptions upon which they are basing their actions. Unfortunately, the assumptions are often wrong. Some managers, for example, assume that money is not a motivator of performance; others assume that money is the only motivator of performance. One manager will find Jane Doe's work exceptional; another will find that same work marginal. The point is that these assumptions often influence how a manager treats other people, and a faulty set of assumptions about human behavior can therefore be detrimental not only to the person being managed but also to the manager.

One purpose of this book, therefore, is to help current and future managers develop a systematic set of assumptions of what they can do to increase the satisfaction and productivity of the organizational members they influence. This systematic set of assumptions, we feel, can best be developed by learning what behavioral scientists and current managers have learned through research and experience. We attempt in this book both to describe the current state of our knowledge about behavior and to give organizational examples of the systematic application of this knowledge and of the positive and negative consequences which have resulted.

WHY ORGANIZATIONAL BEHAVIOR?

You may be asking yourself, Why study organizational behavior? Why not study psychology in general, or better yet, why not forget it altogether? Isn't it really just common sense? Don't worry. These questions should be asked, and in fact we have asked them ourselves many times. Our conclusion is this. Current and future managers should study organizational behavior or, more correctly, the behavior of individuals and groups within and among organizations, in addition to psychology in general because of the uniqueness of the rules and the environment of organizations. The rules of work are different from the rules of play. Work occurs at a period in the life cycle of people different from that in which they learn other habits and behaviors. Work is crucial to the adult self-image. Work activities take up the majority of our waking hours. Psychology in general, on the other hand, deals with behavior in all realms, at all times of life, and it attempts to explain both normal and abnormal ranges of behavior. We think that prior courses in psychology, sociology, or anthropology will help you as future managers. But it is important to realize that the work environment itself puts constraints on the generalizability of the knowledge of human behavior learned in such courses. Therefore, a more specific course, such as organizational behavior, will enable you to develop a more refined, workable set of assumptions more directly relevant to your work interactions. More important, this course should also help you destroy "incorrect" assumptions that you hold about behavior.

The question about whether organizational behavior is just common sense is easy to answer. Each of us, with or without formal training,

can influence, manipulate, control, change, and reward other people in such a way as to affect their behavior, self-esteem, and satisfaction. We have all had experiences, however, in which our influence was not in the direction we desired, and in many cases we were not even aware of what we had done that caused the negative influence. The simple fact is this: you can never learn too much about *how* your own actions affect other people. More important, even if you know *how*, it would be interesting to know *why*.

Students and researchers in the field of organizational behavior have three goals. First, they should attempt to understand *what* causes behavior. Second, they should attempt to understand *why* these particular antecedents cause behavior. Third, and most important for the future manager, they should attempt to understand *which* of these antecedents of behavior they control directly and which are beyond their control. If you fail to work toward this third goal, then you are likely to attempt to change things you don't control directly (for example, a person's need state or personality) or to overlook antecedents of behavior which you can control.

This book will attempt to help you understand what progress behavioral scientists have made toward these goals. You should realize at the outset that we cannot derive from our fund of knowledge any quick and easy answers to all complex behavioral issues in organizations. There is not, and there never will be, any substitute for the *judgment* of the practicing manager in dealing with a specific problem. What is important is that administrators use *informed* judgment. This means judgment that is derived from tenable assumptions; judgment that takes into account the important variables underlying the situation; judgment that gives due recognition to the complexity of individual or group behavior; judgment that explicitly takes into account the manager's own goals, motives, hang-ups, blind spots, and frailties. Our article of faith is that studying the psychology of organizational behavior will contribute to such an informed judgment.

TYPES OF ORGANIZATIONS

The material of this course is concerned with the psychology of work behavior. In the last century, a large percentage of jobs has moved from private sector, profit-centered organizations to public sector, cost-centered organizations. Whether you are now working for, or aspire to work for, such organizations as a union, a church, a health care facility, an educational institution, a state agency, a small business, or a large corporation, you are still involved in influencing work activities. We have attempted throughout this book to give examples from all areas of work, including the aforementioned types of organizations including all levels within those organizations.

work behavior. Chapter 3 is devoted to the acquisition of knowledge by the employer. How does a person learn correct and incorrect behavioral responses? Why is it important that managers be able to verbalize rules and relationships? How does the environment act as a motivator of performance? These and other important questions are addressed.

Chapter 4 takes up the important topic of punishment. It describes when punishment is manipulative and when punishment is a desirable motivator of future performance. Important issues relating to the ethical use of punishment are also addressed. Chapter 5 modifies the explanation of behavior presented in Chapters 3 and 4. It moves the major cause of behavior from outside the individual (the surrounding environment) to the cognitive "template" (mind) of the individual. It attempts to show how the perception of the environment varies from individual to individual, and thus it helps explain the "uniqueness" of each of us.

The uniqueness of men and women is further explained in our discussion of attitudes in Chapter 6. Here we learn what functions attitudes play for each of us and how they help us classify the information we receive from the environment. Chapter 7 discusses the important issues of the individual's needs, goals, and motives. We attempt to explain how people choose their courses of action and how each of us, facing the same set of alternatives, might rationally choose a different course of action.

In Chapter 8, on personality, we see that individuals differ in their manner of responding to identical organizational environments. In Chapter 9 we also see how the level of stress faced by individuals can also influence their responses to the work environment.

In Chapter 10 we talk about the benefit derived from work by the individual. This chapter on job satisfaction explains why it is important that both parties (that is, the organization and the individual) benefit from the exchange relationship. Obviously, the organization benefits by increased profits, reduced costs, or improved services. But how does the individual benefit? Chapter 10 attempts to answer this important question.

Chapters 11 and 12 complete the discussion of "the individual in the organization" by giving examples of worker motivation programs currently being used by organizations to increase both the productivity of organization members and their level of satisfaction with the dimensions of work found in the organizations.

Chapters 13 through 17 focus on group behavior. Even though we start the book with a discussion of the individual, managers really direct groups of individuals. Chapter 13 discusses how groups are formed; how groups, like individuals, develop; and how the properties of groups affect performance. Chapter 14 talks about how groups can influence, either positively or negatively, the quality of individual output (decisions, productivity, responses to the formal organization).

In Chapter 15 we discuss the management of conflict within and between groups which naturally arises from group interactions. This discussion talks about the need for conflict, how to manage conflict, and why some conflict is healthy while other conflict is not. Chapter 16 discusses the important topic of power and its importance to the group leader. This discussion is continued in Chapter 17, on leadership of groups. Here we consider various approaches to leadership and discuss how leadership effectiveness can be enhanced.

The last chapter, Chapter 18, deals with the environment of the organization and introduces the student to the sociology of the organization as compared to the psychology of the individual. Here we explore and develop some useful conceptual tools for understanding the structure and dynamics of relationships between the organization and its environment, and for understanding relationships of groups and individuals within the organization as they are affected by factors external to the organization.

QUESTIONS FOR DISCUSSION

1. What are the disadvantages of studying organizational behavior?
2. How would the understanding of human behavior have helped prevent the Watergate scandal?
3. Look back over the last ten years of your life. How has your life changed? Do you think you respond to people differently now than you did two years ago? If so, how?
4. Have a discussion with two or three middle-level managers about their work. Ask them to list the major problems they face. How many are technical in nature? How many are behavioral in nature?
5. Distinguish between manipulation and influence.

REFERENCES

Lawless, D. J. *Effective management.* Englewood Cliffs, N.J.: Prentice-Hall, 1972.

Leavitt, H. J. *Managerial psychology* (3d ed.). Chicago: University of Chicago Press, 1972.

Perrow, C. *Organizational analysis: A sociological view.* Belmont, Calif.: Brooks/Cole, 1970.

Theory and research in organizational behavior

What is the nature of theory in the behavioral sciences?

What are the functions of theory?

How do we evaluate theories?

What are the strengths and weaknesses of different methods used to study behavior in organizations?

Chapter 1 provided an overview of the subject matter of this book. The purpose of the present chapter is to help the reader develop a perspective for the comprehension, interpretation, evaluation, and ultimately the application of the findings described in this volume.

The contributions of psychology and other behavioral sciences to the study of organizational behavior are generated by the interaction between theory and research. The consumer of behavioral science knowledge must have a solid understanding of the functions of theory in order to derive the full appreciation and benefit of that knowledge. In addition, the student of organizational behavior needs to know something about the methods by which psychological findings relevant to organizational behavior are generated, because each method poses its own built-in limitations. Thus, it is not enough to know that "considerate leaders have productive work groups." We have to understand the theoretical rationale for our expectations that this will be the case, and the theoretical linkages between this observation and other dimensions of the leadership process. Moreover, we have to know by what method this finding was ascertained in order to assess its cause-effect implications and its generalizability.

Our aim in this chapter, then, is not so much to teach the reader how to be a theorist or how to conduct research in organizational behavior as it is to train the reader to be a relatively sophisticated consumer of behavioral science findings. It is our hope that the reader will not terminate inquiry into the psychology of organizational behavior with the final chapter of this book, but will continue to read popular magazines and books on the subject. An elementary understanding of the functions of theory and the methods of behavioral research should equip the student with the tools for a lifelong process of self-education in this field.

THEORY

The impatience of students and management practitioners with behavioral science theory is legendary. The student's ultimate put-down of a disliked course or reading assignment is "It's too theoretical"; the practitioner's response to a conceptually based argument is "That's fine in theory, but it doesn't work in practice." To the action-oriented seeker of knowledge about organizational psychology, theory is something with a capital *T* that stands totally apart from life and experience.

This attitude toward theory probably stems from a misunderstanding of what theory is and what a theory attempts to do. Moreover, it reflects an unawareness of students and practitioners that they themselves are active users of theory.

A *theory* is a set of statements about how certain concepts or constructs are interrelated. The statements are implicitly or explicitly

11

based on certain assumptions or premises, and the statements permit the logical deduction of propositions, hypotheses, or hunches which predict the occurrence of events or explain why certain events have already occurred. Neither esoteric jargon nor mathematical symbols are essential to a theory, although it will be shown later why specialized language often figures importantly in theories used by scientists.

Consider the following example. A supervisor oversees the work of several subordinates who have varying abilities, work at a number of different tasks of varying levels of difficulty, and perform at varying levels of quantity and quality. The supervisor, drawing upon observations of these workers as well as other experiences, concludes that individual performance is best when the task level is neither too far below nor too far above the abilities of the worker. If the task is too easy, the worker soon becomes bored and blasé about the job; if the task is too difficult, the worker becomes tense, anxious, or inhibited. The supervisor, whether consciously or unwittingly, has formulated a theory. The components of the theory are task difficulty, worker abilities, emotional states of the individual worker, and performance. The theory contains the statements that: (1) when a task is easy relative to the worker's ability, the emotional state of boredom results; (2) when a task is very difficult relative to the worker's ability, anxiety results; (3) both boredom and anxiety impair performance. A number of predictions about specific cases could be drawn from these statements. If several bright people are working on a humdrum task, it won't be long before they begin to indulge in a lot of horseplay—because when people get bored, they seek out stimulation to eliminate the boredom. Or one would predict that if changes have to be made in jobs which make the jobs more difficult, and if people are presently performing those jobs at an optimal level, the changes will have to be made gradually so that worker abilities can adapt.

Consider, now, a more *formal* theory about *task scope* and employee performance. For example, a theory formulated by Schwab and Cummings (1976) draws upon the larger body of *expectancy theory of motivation*. The core notion of the theory is that the motivational force upon a person to perform an act depends upon the *valence* (attractiveness or reward value) of the outcomes of the act and the *expectancy* (or subjective, privately believed probability) that those outcomes will occur. For a worker of a given level of competence, there is an ideal task scope which will maximize the product of valence × expectancy. As the task scope falls below the ideal, then the valence of successful performance declines; that is, the successful performance which results from the person's acts doesn't mean much to him or her, doesn't generate any feeling of pride, accomplishment, or achievement. As the task scope exceeds the ideal, the valence of successful performance increases. For example, a high jumper gets more satisfaction clearing a bar at seven feet than one at four feet. However, the expectancy that the person's actions will result in successful performance begins to decrease. The high jumper would feel good about successfully clearing a bar at eight feet, but no one on record has ever done this; so you won't motivate many high jumpers by putting the bar that high. Since jumping ability varies, there are many people you wouldn't motivate to jump by placing the bar at seven feet, six feet, or less. The position of the bar will maximize the motivation of different jumpers at different heights.

Space does not permit a discussion sufficient to do the Schwab and Cummings theory justice, but we hope that the reader can see how the theory addresses phenomena similar to those of interest to the hypothetical supervisor described above. The supervisor's theory is just as much a theory as that formulated by Cummings and Schwab: both contain concepts (though labeled somewhat differently) and statements about how those concepts are interrelated.

If managers and other action-oriented people use behavioral theories, then why their discomfort with theories in behavioral science? The reasons have to do, not with the intrinsic nature of theory, but rather with certain qualitative differences between theory-in-use or "informal theory" and the reconstructed theory or "formal theory" used by behavioral scientists. First of all, the concepts and the components of informal theory are usually couched at a *low level of abstraction*, close to the level of actual physical or biological entities. The behavioral scientist, on the other hand, typically works with constructs at a more abstract level. In the Schwab and Cummings theory, for example, "task scope" represents a concept sufficiently abstract to cover not only the dimension of difficulty but also complexity and the degree of ambiguity versus clarity in task operations. Second, and related to the first difference, informal theory usually addresses a very specific, sometimes unique, problem or set of problems, whereas formal theory in behavioral science encompasses a greater range of related problems. The manager theorizes about how performance is determined on a particular job; the behavioral scientist theorizes about performance in general or on a relatively broad category of jobs which share certain definitive properties. Third, the manager uses ordinary, everyday language or labels in theory construction, whereas the behavioral scientist often prefers new terms with special meanings. Finally, the manager tends to be less explicit about the assumptions on which a theory rests, whereas the behavioral scientist insists on specifying unambiguously the premises underlying a theory and the conditions within which the theory is appropriate.

Perhaps it would be helpful, then, to explain why the behavioral scientist uses abstract, general concepts with exotic or awkward labels. Behavioral science uses abstractions so that knowledge accumulated about some aspects of behavior can be applied to superficially unrelated behavioral phenomena. Consider, for example, the case of a worker who works harder and faster than the other workers in the group believe to be appropriate. To the social psychologist, this is not merely an instance of "rate-busting"—it represents the case of a *deviant* who violates a *group norm*. Thus, it is conceptually similar to the Democratic congressman who votes in line with the policy of a Republican president; to the dissenter in a discussion group which seeks consensual unanimity; to the bank loan officer who defies orthodox colleagues by sporting mod apparel; or to the commissioned officer who fraternizes easily with enlisted personnel. Moreover, research conducted by social psychologists with discussion groups supplies a fund of knowledge about how the group will react to the deviant. For example, Schachter (1951) found that if the group is not very cohesive, if the norm being violated is of marginal relevance to the group's objectives, or if the deviant occupies special status because of other contributions to group goals, the group probably won't react strongly. But if the norm is highly relevant to group values or purposes and the group is cohesive, the group will try to bring the dissident in line: first by cajolery or gentle persuasion, and if that doesn't work, then by threat and intimidation. If the latter fail, the group psychologically "amputates" the deviant from the bonds of group belongingness. (See Harold Leavitt's discussion in chapter 21 of *Managerial Psychology:* "Independence and conformity: The problem of truth in the face of pressure.")

This fund of knowledge is applicable to the case of the rate-buster only by way of the overarching, mediating links of the concepts "deviant," "group norm," "group cohesion," and "status" (the concepts are further discussed in Chapters 13 and 14 of this volume). Without those concepts, the relevance of observations of a discussion group would not be apparent. Abstract concepts, then, serve to integrate diverse phenomena so that knowledge in one sphere is cross-pollinated to other spheres. We might add that only by theories which employ concepts at a considerable level of abstraction can research findings ever be applied to the "real world." Abstract concepts are the linking pins between scientific data and practical affairs.

The reader might agree at this point, but reply: the English language of everyday life is rich with concepts; why not use the language of everyday life so that we can more easily understand what a theory is saying, rather than use such unfamiliar terms as *valence, task scope, alienation, reinforcement, cohesion,* and *initiating structure?* One reason for using specialized terms is that the more familiar concept labels have different shades of meaning in the minds of different people; by inventing a new term with a given definition, the behavioral scientist avoids the misinterpretations which would otherwise occur in scholarly discourse. A more important reason, however, is that everyday concepts often carry value-charged connotations which get in the way of detached, logical analysis. To talk about democratic as opposed to autocratic leadership is to invite preexisting prejudices or emotions into the arena of inquiry. Phrasing the issue in terms of directive versus participative supervision is less likely to trigger preconceived biases and more likely to facilitate a patient, open-minded exploration of the effects of different styles of management.

It cannot be denied that social scientists sometimes proliferate jargon needlessly to serve other purposes: to give the appearance of erudition without its substance; or merely for "brand differentiation" in order to promote the personal identification of theories advanced in competition with other colleagues for status in their professions. But after all, talented athletes have been known to "hotdog it," making easy plays look difficult or trying to project a unique style; politicians occasionally do their bit at "grandstanding," as do actors, physicians, and clergy. So, we suggest, do managers. To say that some behavioral scientists sometimes err in the direction of obsession with the attributes intrinsic to their work is merely to say that they are human. It does not change the fact that abstract, esoteric concepts are the useful tools by which they integrate knowledge for good purposes.

What functions does theory serve?

One of the functions served by theory has already been implied by the foregoing discussion. Theory helps *organize* our knowledge into a pattern whereby facts, data, and observed regularities are interconnected in such a way that they take on a new meaning not evident when viewed in isolation. Theory brings to light similarities in seemingly dissimilar phenomena.

Second, a theory is a useful means of *summarizing* in symbolic form a diverse body of knowledge. As Shaw and Costanzo (1970) state, a theory "permits us to handle large amounts of empirical data with relatively few propositions" (p. 9). Theory, then, functions as a wieldly shorthand method of stating what we have learned or believe about a class of phenomena; it relieves us of the tedium of having to attend to a cumulative record of raw observations.

Third, theory *points the way to continued research*, or the pursuit of new facts. Theory prompts us to ask new questions about the phenomenon we are studying, questions that might not otherwise have occurred to us. Indeed, a good theory may raise more questions than it answers. Furthermore, theory helps us distinguish between trivial questions and important questions. Theories do not end with the data or experiences which gave birth to them; they go beyond such data to suggest tentative inferences or predictions about what new data or experiences will look like. Without a theory, we would not know what to study, or if we did, just how to study it.

The organizing, summarizing, and guiding functions are as important in informal theories as in formal theories. The problem-solving manager stores his or her accumulated observations in an organized and symbolic form. The tentative conclusions drawn from his or her experiences then suggest new solutions to old problems or new problems to be attacked in the never-ending quest for organizational improvement. The effective manager operates in a conceptual world of assumptions, logic, and tentative conclusions about relationships among variables, and the design of activities to test the truth-value or usefulness of those conclusions.

Alfred P. Sloan, Jr., in his autobiographical *My Years with General Motors*, stated that "every enterprise needs a concept of its industry." Sloan's ensuing account makes clear that he was very much a theorist—and self-consciously so—about the automobile industry. Furthermore, he attributed much of General Motors' success to the exercise of theory construction. Theory, then, is not something that the action-oriented individual need view as alien, artificial, or barren. However, it is important, both to the behavioral scientist and the practitioner, to discriminate good theories from bad ones.

What are the criteria for evaluating a theory?

Abraham Kaplan, in his book *The Conduct of Inquiry* (1964), discusses a number of criteria by which the scientific community assesses the worth of a theory. The *norm of correspondence* is the most obvious one: how well does the theory fit the facts? How closely do predictions drawn from the theory match up with actual events? The layperson tends to think of this as the sole and ultimate acid test of a theory. But suppose that several theories all explain the data equally well. How do we decide which is better?

The *norm of coherence* enters into consideration here. A theory should be internally consistent and straightforward in its logic. It should not depend on its author for drawing out the connections between its component statements; the connections should not be so loose or imprecise that totally opposite conclusions could be drawn from the theory. According to the *principle of parsimony*, a theory should contain no more concepts or assumptions than are necessary to account for the data. A simple theory is preferable to a complex theory unless the added complexity can account for additional findings not explained by the simple theory. A new theory must also fit in with the larger body of preexisting theories in the field, assuming that there is good reason to think that these theories have validity. For example, a theory of leadership which assumes that subordinate satisfaction is a direct cause of performance does violence to fairly well-established theories about how attitudes and performance are related; such a leadership theory, then, no matter how well it fits the facts of a study or one's informal observations, would not get high marks.

The *norm of pragmatism* refers not, as the label might imply, to the practical applications of a theory in everyday affairs, but rather to how well a theory furthers the activities of scientists. This relates quite closely to the guidance function of theories. How much new research is suggested by the theory? What new puzzles or questions does the theory bring to light? To test well on the norm of pragmatism, a theory must at the very least be testable; it must be capable of being put to a test in which only certain results, and not just any conceivable results, could support the theory. A theory so flexible that it could account for results of any kind is by definition untestable and thus does not guide us in seeking new knowledge.

In evaluating theories of organizational behavior, we often make use of a fourth criterion, namely, the *intuitive appeal* of a theory. Some theories are more appealing than others because they suggest a more flattering portrait of human nature. Others are appealing because of the imagery they evoke, the analogies they use, or their diagrammatic properties. Scientists, being human, are not devoid of aesthetic sensitivities. Maslow's need hierarchy theory (see Chapter 7) has occupied a special niche in the sentiments of work motivation theorists precisely because of its intuitive appeal; it receives little support from empirical studies, and it is probably untestable as originally formulated.

It should be noted that every theory is born only to die, always serving as a way station to newer theories. Theories serve certain functions; if a particular theory has served those functions well, it goes into its grave with honor, for newer theories build upon old ones and retain the best qualities of their predecessors. No theory, however, is killed by a few discrepant facts. A theory remains alive until a rival theory is available which can do all that the old one did, and just a little bit better. Therefore, if theories encountered in the pages of this volume give up the ghost in the years ahead, this does not mean that the reader has studied them in vain; their contributions will have been well preserved by new theoretical developments.

METHODS OF RESEARCH IN ORGANIZATIONAL BEHAVIOR

Theories do not exist apart from data of some kind. Theories are stimulated by empirical observations and are tested, modified, and ultimately abandoned as a consequence of the interaction between theory and research. These statements apply to informal theory as well as formal theory. It behooves us, then, to consider the various methods of research by which we generate the lifeblood of theory.

A method of research is any procedure by which we acquire knowledge about a phenomenon. A number of research methods are used to provide us with knowledge—or, to be more precise, statements of tentative or provisional truth-value—about organizational behavior. All of these methods have their place in the ongoing pursuit of a more extensive, firmer fund of knowledge about organizational variables and human behavior. However, each of these methods has its characteristic shortcomings. Therefore, the consumer of knowledge about organizational behavior, whether behavioral scientist or manager, must be able to qualify that knowledge on the basis of the shortcomings of the method that produced it. Some understanding of the strengths and weaknesses of each method is a prerequisite to the intelligent reading, evaluation, and use of the results of informal or formal studies of organizational behavior.

Naturalistic observation

The most primitive method of research in organizational behavior is represented by the impressions we draw from simply witnessing the events around us in organizations and living in the stream of organizational experience. All of us have spent a considerable amount of time in organizations of various kinds, be they educational, voluntary, or commercial. We have some notion about how organizational size, organizational reward systems, and styles of leadership have affected our own behavior. We have also observed how certain characteristics of individual or group behavior seem to correlate or covary with changes or differences in organization characteristics. To the extent that we have voiced these impressions, we may have discovered that others agree with us. Each of us, then, has a private fund of knowledge about behavior in organizations. Furthermore, this knowledge has been supplemented by the accounts of others who have offered their observations in the form of conversations, speeches, popular magazine articles, autobiographies (for example, Sloan's *My Year at General Motors*), even fiction (as in *Executive Suite* and other business novels written by Cameron Hawley, who drew from his own experience as an executive).

A more systematic form of naturalistic observation is represented by the *case study*. In using this method, one or more researchers enter an organization—sometimes as participants, otherwise as consultants or guests—solely for the purpose of observing what goes on. Usually the researchers have some particular focus already planned for their observations. For example, Alvin Gouldner entered a gypsum plant with the intent of finding out what would happen when a new plant manager was sent in from corporate headquarters in order to tighten up bureaucratic rules and procedures (his observations are recorded in the book *Patterns of Industrial Bureaucracy*); Melville Dalton, a sociologist, became an employee on the payrolls of an industrial organization in order to examine the politics of management (his impressions formed the basis of his book *Men Who Manage*). In conducting the case study, researchers often keep diaries or journals of their daily experiences and usually supplement their own perceptions by examining company records, documents, archives, memos, and selected interviews with personnel.

The attractiveness of naturalistic observation as a method of research results mainly from the fact that it is a method which confronts its subject head-on; it deals with behavior in the raw, with the "real world." The data are rich with human drama and existence. Accounts of such studies are easy for readers to identify with; at their best, such studies enthrall and spark the imagination of the reader as well as any journalistic medium is capable of doing. Furthermore, the sensitive observer may glimpse subtle insights not obtainable from more rigorous methods, such as the laboratory experiment.

The shortcomings of naturalistic observation, however, are numerous and quite serious.[1] First of all, the "original data" are actually soon and irretrievably lost, transformed, and mangled because of the limited information-processing capabilities of human beings. When we read, say, Sloan's account of his experiences at General Motors, we are not privy to the events as they actually occurred. We are totally dependent upon Sloan's subjective frame of reference as it affected both his perceptions and his memories of events. We do not know what things he chose *not* to attend to; we do not know what part of his account represents inferential leaps of faith concerning things he did not directly experience or observe; we do not know the extent to which, or the manner in which, filtering has occurred, as it must inevitably occur in the transmission of information; we do not know whether other observers would have drawn the same conclusions.

It is precisely because naturalistic observation is so rich, colorful, and pulsating that knowledge based on it must be hedged about with qualifications and cautions. Psychological research has shown that human beings have a very limited short-term storage capacity for processing information. Our perceptions are therefore highly selective, and under conditions nonoptimal for perceiving—for example, when the stimulus field is rapidly changing, as would be the case with real-life experience in organizations—the perceiver instinctively uses econo-

---

[1] The shortcomings discussed refer to the case study as a method of formal science. This is not to deny the obvious advantages of the case study as a method of instruction, learning, and discussion.

mizing but error-prone shortcuts to overcome the limitations of channel capacity (the perceptual process is discussed at greater length in
Chapter 5). Furthermore, Jenkins and Ward (1965) have conducted
experiments demonstrating that in naturalistic observation people
make woefully inaccurate estimates of the degree of correlation among
events; typically, their subjects deluded themselves into thinking that
they discerned systematic causal relationships where in fact such relationships did not exist. Rainmakers, politicians, bookies, and fortune-
tellers exploit this weakness in naturalistic observation.

Still another shortcoming of informal observation or case studies
is that they tend to have a biased focus on dramatic, unusual, or otherwise newsworthy phenomena (Weick, 1969). Mergers, strikes, changes
in leadership, reorganizations, and the like are frequently the occasions
for starting case studies; less momentous but equally colorful incidents
provide the fare of our everyday attention and ruminations. It is far
from obvious that such "exciting" events provide the best material
for learning about organizational behavior. As Karl Weick (1965) notes,
much of organizational behavior is routine, bland, and uninspiring;
indeed, routinization is the goal if not the foundation of organization.
Yet we still have much to learn about such routine phenomena as
why most people exhibit reliable role behavior in the absence of overt
pressures to do so.

Another problem with case studies is untangling the unique properties of the host organization or its participants from more generalizable
relationships. Suppose that a case study of a beer bottling plant in a
small town finds that the introduction of automated processes is followed by a wildcat strike. Does this tell us something about a lawful
relationship between technological change and aggressive behavior?
Or do the causes of the strike stem from factors woven into the history
of the community, the ambitions of a labor leader, or the fact that
the duck hunting season had just begun? To what extent could we
generalize from this organization to a steel mill, an insurance office,
or the local grocery store?

Finally, naturalistic observation of human behavior defies quantification. Statistics are not the be-all and end-all of any science, but comparative judgments of some sort are essential, and quantification through
measurement renders such judgments much more reliable and commu-
nicable. Case studies seldom give us much to work with in estimating
the *strength* of relationships among variables or in gauging the *relative
contribution of different factors to an end result.*

These shortcomings make naturalistic observation more useful in
the exploratory rather than the advanced stages of studying a phenomenon. Case studies provide a crude sketch of the terrain we plan to
embark upon; more rigorous, sophisticated methods are essential for
producing a workable map. Naturalistic observation can be a fruitful

source of hypothesis creation, and at times it provides a corrective for the mistake of studying only trivial issues rigorously, but by itself it is a very insecure foundation for a body of knowledge about organizational behavior.

Field survey research

An alternative to naturalistic observation in organizations is the design of systematic surveys of the opinions, perceptions, attitudes, or self-reported behavior of participants in organizations. Whereas naturalistic observation relies almost totally on the perceptions of the researcher, survey research taps the perceptions of others, at least as they are reported and described by others. Whereas the naturalistic observer might conclude from watching workers perform a repetitive task, that they are bored with or "alienated" from their jobs, survey research would solicit the workers' own feelings about their work. The workers might, in fact, express considerable satisfaction with their jobs (and possibly even rejoice in their freedom from the paperwork and statistical computations of a behavioral science researcher).

One form of survey research is the *person-to-person interview*. The researcher sits down with a subject and asks questions, to which the subject responds. The interview may be *unstructured* in format, in which case the questions would be open-ended and the interviewer would selectively probe in greater depth, depending on how the respondent answered. If the interview were *structured*, the questions would all be formulated in advance so that the respondent could answer by choosing among a few response alternatives, such as "yes" or "no," "agree" or "disagree," and the same questions would be used over and over again with subsequent interviewees.

Alfred Kinsey, for example, used the interview as his basic method of researching the sexual behavior of males and females (Kinsey, Pomeroy, & Martin, 1949). David Granick interviewed Soviet and European managers in order to assess the cross-cultural similarities and differences in the role of the executive (Granick, 1961). People in different types of organizations can be interviewed to see whether they have correspondingly different experiences in their work, different levels of stress, different types of problems, and so on. People can be interviewed about the leadership style of their superiors and about whether or not their work attitudes are related to such differences in their superiors.

The chief advantage of the interview is that it offers observations independent of, and supplementary to, those of the researcher. There are problems, however, with the interview as a method of research. First of all, the person being interviewed might feel a bit awed or threatened by the presence of the interviewer. The subject might refrain from offering opinions or information which could place him or her in an embarrassing or vulnerable position. Only if the interviewer has a knack for putting subjects completely at ease and winning their confidence can he or she reliably elicit candid responses; Kinsey apparently had this knack, even with very unusual subject populations, such as prison inmates (Christenson, 1971). Second, the interviewer can unwittingly shape a certain pattern to the subjects' verbal responses merely by characterisic nods, grimaces, or other nonverbal cues (the phenomenon of "shaping" is discussed in the next chapter). Again, considerable skill and training in interviewing are necessary to avoid such biases. Finally, interviews are very expensive in terms of the researcher's time. For all these reasons, most contemporary research in organizational behavior utilizes the direct interview primarily in the initial, preliminary phases of a more elaborate project using other methods.

The questionnaire represents a more efficient means of survey research which avoids some of the pitfalls of the interview. Questionnaires, like interviews, may be unstructured or highly structured in format; increasingly, researchers attempt to use the more structured versions. Typically the researcher either mails a large number of questionnaires to potential subjects or distributes questionnaires to an assembled group. Under such conditions, the anonymity of the respondent can be guaranteed and a vast amount of data in the form of written responses can be collected and machine-processed.

One reason for the increased use of questionnaires in survey research is the recent development of a number of standardized instruments for measuring subjects' perceptions of relevant organizational attributes. Psychologists have designed scales consisting of a relatively small number of items (that is, questions) to measure job satisfaction, perceptions of supervisor's style, perceptions of organizational climate, the degree of stress experienced in work, beliefs about the kinds of rewards made contingent on performance, and a variety of other social psychological variables. Scales are scored by weighting the extremity of the answer in a given direction (for example, 5 for "strongly disagree" versus 1 for "strongly agree," or 4 for "frequently" versus 2 for "occasionally") and summing across all items in the scale. The average scores of different groups can then be compared (for example, the mean job satisfaction score for males versus females). Or scores on one scale can be compared with scores on another scale to see whether they are statistically related: Do higher scores by respondents on a scale measuring perceptions of role ambiguity tend to go along with higher scores on a scale measuring job tensions, and vice versa? In short, the use of standardized scales in questionnaires facilitates quantification.

Despite the advantages of the written questionnaire over the inter-

Questionaire
Disadvantages

1) view, the former nevertheless has its own problems. Its use presumes that respondents are both able and willing to describe their feelings or perceptions by circling a number or checking a blank space. Testing conditions that assure anonymity make this assumption somewhat plausible, but even then there is the problem that respondents might sometimes consciously or unwittingly slant their responses in a direction which is more consistent with how they would *like to see themselves* rather than with their actual behavior. Consider, for example, self-report studies of how people rank the various outcomes of their jobs (see, for example, Opsahl & Dunnette, 1966). People often do not rank money as the most important job consideration; to do so would apparently be to view themselves as materialistic. Yet, as Opsahl and Dunnette note, people apparently behave as if money were quite important: professors move to institutions that pay them more; superstar athletes play out their contract options if they don't get the salary they want; and movie stars go to court to recover commissions on the distribution of their films. One has to take into account, then, the complicating factor of *social desirability in response set* in interpreting the results of questionnaire studies.

2) Another problem with questionnaires is that people tend to structure their answers to different scales in a manner which they perceive to be consistent and logical, even if doing so inaccurately portrays life situations which in fact are not always consistent and logical. One finding from questionnaire studies of supervisory styles is that people who describe their boss as autocratic report lower job satisfaction than do those who view their boss as democratic or participative. It would be tempting to conclude from this that type of supervisory style is a determinant of subordinate satisfaction. But an alternative explanation could simply be that dissatisfied workers describe everything else in their work environment in such a way as to make it seem consistent with their dissatisfaction. This would be especially likely when they are describing something which is very subjective and open to differences in interpretation, as would be true with leadership style or "organizational climate." It would be less of a problem when respondents are asked for reasonably straightforward, more objective, or emotionally neutral information, such as their hours of work, the frequency with which they have job-related interaction with persons outside their departments, their degree of dependence on others for their own job performance, or the number of formal performance appraisals they have had in the past two years.

3) Correlational field studies using objective indices

All of the methods of research we have discussed so far are essentially *correlational* in nature. This means that they are methods which attempt to ascertain the extent to which two or more variables correlate or covary as we find them in nature. To say that job satisfaction correlates with job tenure is to say that the more satisfied people tend to be the ones with longer experience on the job and that the less satisfied people tend to be those with less tenure on the job. Analogously, we would be stating that those people who have been on the job longer tend to report a higher level of work satisfaction than do the short-timers. Note that we are not saying that either one causes the other—that staying on the job longer makes a person more satisfied, or that satisfaction makes a worker stay around longer—only that satisfaction and tenure vary in a similar fashion.

correlation
Coefficient
&
Statistical
Significance

The correlation coefficient is a statistical estimate of the degree of linear relationship between two variables—a device for expressing the degree to which two things vary together. The correlation coefficient can range from −1.00 (meaning that two variables vary in a completely opposite pattern, or that as one increases the other always decreases, and vice versa) through 0.00 (meaning that the two variables are totally unrelated, the variation in either one telling us nothing about the variation in the other) to 1.00 (meaning that the two variables change in the same direction in perfect agreement, that an increase or decrease in either is accompanied by the same relative increase or decrease in the other). Usually correlation coefficients between different variables in organizational behavior are well below 1.00 in absolute value. This is simply a reflection of these two facts: (1) that our measurement devices themselves yield a substantial amount of error; and (2) that any important aspect of human behavior—such as the level of individual job satisfaction or the group performance level—usually has a large number of causes, no one of which can fully predict or account for all of the variation in the variable we are trying to explain.

The *statistical significance* of a correlation coefficient is simply a statement about how unlikely it is that a given correlation coefficient could have been obtained by chance alone if the two variables were in fact totally unrelated. For example, the statement that a correlation of .40 between worker's age and performance is "significant at the level of .01" means that there was only 1 chance in 100 that we could have obtained such a coefficient if in fact there were no relationship at all between age and performance on that type of job. However, the statistical significance depends not only on the size of the coefficient, but also on the size of the sample studied. A coefficient of .20 in a sample of 1,000 workers is more significant in a statistical sense—less likely to be due to chance—than one of .50 in a sample of 16 workers. The latter coefficient, however, is significant at the .05 level (there is only 1 chance in 20 that it would have occurred randomly in the absence of some relationship), which has traditionally been the level of significance considered acceptable in scientific study for a relationship to be inferred. Moreover, when the .50 coefficient is squared (.50 × .50), this tells us that .25 or 25 percent of the variance in either age or performance can be predicted by variance in the other. A coefficient of .20, on the other hand, regardless of its level of statistical significance, means that only 4 percent of either variable can be accounted for by the other.

We should emphasize that a study which is correlational in design does not necessarily have to compute or report a correlation coefficient. It is correlational if it shows by tables, bars, graphs, or charts how two or more variables covary.

A correlational field study using objective indices measures at least one variable by means other than self-reports. One objective index is either correlated with another or with responses to questionnaire items. Such variables as absence rate, number of subordinates supervised by a manager, number of patents obtained by a research division, frequency of grievances processed by a bargaining unit, and attrition rate are examples of objective indices. They are "hard data" in the sense that measurements of such variables are unlikely to be distorted by subjective perceptions or emotions, although the measurements may be prone to other kinds of errors (for example, sloppiness in record keeping). Even appraisals of subordinates' performance by superiors, although subjective in nature, may be considered an objective index in a study if they were obtained *independently* of other variables in the study, such as subordinates' descriptions of their supervisors' leadership style. In that case, the performance rating would have been obtained from a source different from that of the subordinates' reported perceptions, and thus any correlation between the two would probably not have arisen because of response set tendencies of either superior or subordinate in the direction of social desirability or consistency (provided, of course, that subordinates were not aware of how they had been appraised and that superiors were not privy to subordinates' descriptions of their leadership style).

Consider, for example, a study of supervisory styles reporting the results shown in Table 2–1. The study, which took place in the home office of a large insurance company, assessed the styles of the supervisors by means of questionnaires distributed to workers in various sections of the company headquarters. From subjects' responses to questions concerning the typical behavior of their bosses, the researchers could classify the styles of the supervisors as predominantly employee-centered (a greater concern with the welfare of the employees) or job-centered (a dominant concern with getting the work out). The researchers obtained measures of productivity by consulting company records of the volume of paperwork processed by the different groups. As the findings show, employee-centered supervisors obviously tended to have more productive work units. Conclusion: The employee-cen-

Table 2–1
Correlation between style of supervisor and productivity of supervisor's section

	Job-centered supervisors	*Employee-centered supervisors*
High-producing sections	1	6
Low-producing sections	7	3

Source: Adapted from P. Hersey and K. H. Blanchard, *Management of Organizational Behavior* (Englewood Cliffs, N. J.: Prentice-Hall, 1969), p. 70.

tered style of supervision causes a higher level of group productivity than does the job-centered style. But is this the only tenable explanation for the results? No, because all correlational studies have in common the limitation that they cannot show what is cause and what is effect, and that is their major shortcoming.

Anytime we have a correlation between two variables, say, A and B, it could be that A caused B or that B caused A. In the study described above, it seems logical to think that supervisory style caused the level of productivity. But it could very well be that the level of group productivity caused the supervisor to act in a certain way. The leader of a good group does not have to be critical, punitive, or concerned about production; he or she has the luxury of attending primarily to personal relationships and promoting a comfortable work climate. The unfortunate soul who inherits a group of incompetent or foot-dragging workers does not have that luxury and must set about improving the level of work. Thus, the productivity of the section could have been the cause and supervisory style a consequence or effect due to that cause.

Yet another explanation for the correlation between two variables is that they each may have been caused by some other unknown or unmeasured variable, C. A study conducted some years ago found a strikingly high correlation between consumption of a certain soft drink and the incidence of polio (before polio vaccines were available). This was not because the drink made people more susceptible to polio, nor was it because polio made you like the taste of the pop. Both variables were caused by climate. Polio occurred more often in the summer months and in the warmer regions, and of course people drink more liquids in hot weather.

In order to infer that a correlation between A and B is due to A causing B, we have to be able to *manipulate* A at our discretion, holding other possible causes of B constant, and then see whether B changes as we manipulate A. In correlational studies, controlled manipulation has not occurred; instead, we have recorded observations of things "changing as they will."

Field experiments

In a field experiment, we change an organizational variable in one setting and observe the consequent changes as compared to the changes occurring in a similar setting where that variable was not altered, or as compared to the changes in a similar setting where the change was made in the opposite direction or to a different extent. For example, Morse and Reimer (1956) decentralized the level of decision making in some sections of a company by letting employees make more work-related decisions. In other sections of the company, they centralized decision making by restricting the number of work-related decisions an employee could make. In both situations the type of employee and the type of job were otherwise similar. At the end of 18 months, Morse and Reimer compared the two groups in terms of productivity. Both groups increased productivity over previous levels, but the increase was slightly greater in the centralized sections. Note that if the change had been made *only* in the decentralized sections, the increased productivity would have suggested that the decentralization of decision making was the cause of the increase. However, with the comparison (centralized) sections also showing an increase in productivity, we know that decentralization per se was not the causative factor.

In another field experiment, Muczyk (1976) conducted a study on the effects of a Management-by-Objectives (MBO) program on organizational performance. The site of the study was a multibranch bank, in 13 branches of which the MBO program was introduced. A comparable number of other branches—characterized by market areas, types and volumes of business, and personnel profiles similar to those in the experimental groups—served as controls, or baselines against which to assess the effects of the MBO program. Although the branches using the MBO program did show positive changes in a number of banking performance criteria 6 months and 12 months later, performance had increased by comparable levels in the control branches. In the absence of the control group, the performance improvements might have been erroneously attributed to the MBO program rather than to changes in the national or state economic climates.

In the field experiment, then, the essential features include not only the ability to change or manipulate something, but also the ability to control other relevant variables, either by using a comparison group or by holding all other factors constant. The latter is virtually impossible in a live organization, so comparison groups are usually necessary.

True field experiments are somewhat rare in the study of organizational behavior. In order to conduct them, researchers need permission to make the necessary changes and to take the steps essential for proper controls. Organizational officials are understandably reluctant to permit such changes if they regard the changes as risks to the reliability of normal operations. Those who do permit the changes may be so unusual—either in their philosophy or their tolerance for such risks—that the results obtained could not be safely generalized as applicable to other settings.

A particularly troublesome issue in field experiments concerns the time dimension. It may take months or years for the full effects of a change in an organizational variable to be felt (for example, Muczyk had reason to believe that the MBO program was just beginning to have an impact when his study was concluded). Yet the longer the experiment, the greater the opportunity for noncomparabilities between experimental and control groups to develop. In the Morse and Reimer field experiment, for example, one group (the centralized sections) experienced a higher rate of turnover in personnel than did the other. This left a smaller group with the same amount of work to do, resulting in a higher rate of production per employee work hour.

In sum, live organizations—with rare exceptions—are not the ideal places to conduct experiments because they seldom give us the desired degree of control over what we want to change or what we want to hold constant. Where they do permit such control, they represent perhaps the optimum in research methods, namely rigor plus realism.

Laboratory experiments

Undoubtedly the most misunderstood and least appreciated method of research in organizational behavior is the laboratory experiment. Since much of the knowledge base described in this volume rests on data generated by laboratory experiments, it is important that the reader comprehend the logic and rationale for studying and observing behavior in the laboratory.

The term *laboratory* denotes nothing more than a setting which makes observation easier. A laboratory does not have to be on a college campus or in a psychology department, nor does it require the presence of exotic, futuristic apparatus. An unused classroom, a vacant office, or a materials storeroom could constitute a laboratory. Nothing more awesome than tables, chairs, pencils, and paper need be used. As Weick (1965) points out, all you need for a laboratory is a setting, some subjects, and a task (that is, something for the subjects to do). With these minimal requirements satisfied, the experimenter can proceed to study a virtually unlimited range of behavioral phenomena, including many that characterize the organizational environment.

The <u>purpose of the laboratory setting</u> is, first of all, <u>to screen out</u> <u>the presence of distractions</u> which are not of immediate interest but which inevitably get in the way when one is trying to observe organizational behavior in the raw state. Suppose, for example, that you were interested in the effects of feedback on performance. You want to find out how the timeliness of feedback, the accuracy of feedback, or the positivity versus negativity of feedback affected people's work. You could probably spend a few hours or days in a real, live organization watching how people perform when they get no feedback, when it is delayed, when it is erroneous, and so on. But if you honestly appraised the limits of your knowledge thus gained, you would be forced to hedge any conclusions drawn with numerous doubts and qualifications. For example, the kind of supervisor who gives quick feedback is likely to be different in a variety of ways from the kind who delays giving feedback to subordinates; he or she may also be more considerate, a better planner, or simply more knowledgeable, and these differences obscure our observation of the effect of feedback per se. You would probably also find that positive feedback is given more quickly than negative feedback. If so, is any difference in the effect on worker performance due to the difference in timing or to the difference in positivity versus negativity? Suppose that the people who get positive feedback are simply better friends of the boss as well as better workers, or that the people who get faster feedback tend to be the ones who work on certain jobs? There is no way of unscrambling the separate effects of all these varying factors from the feedback itself.

<u>The laboratory filters out those details which, though interesting</u> <u>in their own right, are irrelevant to the question of theoretical interest.</u> In so doing, the reader is likely to argue, the laboratory makes the situation "unrealistic" or "artificial." That is precisely the purpose in taking the issue into the laboratory: to see the phenomenon for what it actually is, not as we ordinarily find it camouflaged in the natural elements. In the laboratory, the only reality that counts is the reality of the variable we are looking at, and it is just as real there as it is anywhere else.

Second, <u>in the laboratory the researcher can exert more control</u> <u>over the structure of events.</u> The experimenter makes things happen at his or her own convenience or dictates. The experimenter can also vary combinations of factors. For example, subjects can be given either positive or negative feedback, and the speed with which feedback is given after performance can also be varied. Thus, the experimenter can observe the separate as well as the additive or interacting effects of both timing and the positivity or negativity of feedback on subsequent performance. In the "real world" we would not be likely to find proportionate representation of all four combinations, or we might have to wait an inordinately long time for a particular combination—

say, quick negative feedback—to occur. Furthermore, the nature of
the task, the time of day, and the personality or the manner of the
feedback-presenter can be kept constant across all of these combinations so that those factors can be excluded as alternative explanations
of the results. If the difficulty of the task happens to be of interest,
however, that too can be systematically varied in all possible combinations of easy-difficult task, quick-delayed feedback, and positive-nega-
tive feedback. The point is that the researcher can arrange at his or
her own discretion the combinations of factors judged relevant, and
either exclude or hold constant any irrelevant variables.

Third, the researcher knows and can state in unambiguous terms
the conditions under which results were obtained. A certain task was
used, subjects were drawn from a specified population of known
attributes, certain instructions were given, and so on. These statements
are part and parcel of experimental findings, for they serve as a baseline
from which to assess the generalizability of the findings. Laboratory
experiments thus engender a healthy caution in interpreting the limits
of our knowledge. Unfortunately, this virtue is often mistaken by the
general public as a vice. The layperson's typical response to a set of
laboratory findings is "Yes, but you can't generalize from that set of
conditions to the situation in my factory." True enough, in one sense,
but neither can the results of a field study at the launderette, welfare
agency, or power plant; more important, in the latter settings we are
hard pressed to specify precisely the conditions under which the results
were obtained. In the strict sense, we cannot generalize the data obtained in a steel mill to situations in textile mills, or vice versa, any
more than we can generalize from the lab to either. Only theory can
bridge the gap, and it can do so only to the extent that idiosyncratic
features of any setting are known and can be interpreted within a
theoretical overview.

It is theory, after all—in the sense that we have defined it earlier
in this chapter—that directs experimentation, telling us what is important to vary, what should be excluded, what to hold constant. A number
of defining characteristics of organizations can be conceptualized in
abstract terms so that they can then be simulated in the lab. For example, if hierarchy is one of the intrinsic attributes of organizations, then
a group of seven subjects can be organized into a chief, two lieutenants,
and four bottom-line workers. Reward systems, indirect communication, stress, or the interdependence of workers upon one another can
all be simulated in the lab if theory suggests that these earmarks of
organization are integral to the phenomenon of interest. It is the theory
which determines what to include in the lab, not the realism of everyday life.

Some critics argue that in laboratory experiments the subjects are not sufficiently "involved" in what happens. There are, in fact, ways of increasing subject involvement (the interested reader may consult Weick, 1965, for a discussion of involvement-enhancing techniques), but we should remember that much of everyday life is also characterized by passive involvement. The frequent dependence upon college freshmen and sophomores is also cited as a shortcoming of lab studies, but once again only theory can guide us as to whether such subjects are so radically different from others in the general population on the relevant attributes that different subjects should be studied, and if that be the case, then there is no reason why laboratory experiments cannot use supervisors, sales personnel, or night watchmen as subjects.

One limitation of laboratory experiments stems from *professional ethics.* Responsible investigators are prohibited, both by conscience and professional guidelines, from subjecting persons to any conditions which might run the risk of physical or emotional injury. In real organizations, participants are occasionally cheated, humiliated, driven to nervous collapse, or otherwise unmercifully exploited. While a few psychologists have been accused of somewhat amoral conduct in the pursuit of science, all psychologists recognize that there are bounds beyond which they dare not tread in the treatment of subjects. Thus, the seamier side of organizational life, including such occurrences as brutal political infighting, lies beyond the pale of experimental methods.

A second problem often encountered in the use of the laboratory experiment concerns the *reactivity* of the method. When we say that a measurement device is "reactive," we mean that the attempt to use it to measure something automatically alters the state of that which we would measure; for example, when you apply a tire pressure gauge to the valve stem, you release air, thus changing the pressure to a level other than that recorded on the gauge. Laboratory experiments are often reactive because the subjects, being human, wonder what the experimenter's hypothesis is and try to adjust their behavior accordingly—to "help" the experimenter prove something, to behave in a light which makes the subjects look "good," or sometimes to obstinately act in a manner exactly opposite of the way they think the experimenter would predict. Experimenters, aware of this potential reactivity, then may go to extreme efforts to disguise the true purpose of the experiment, and sometimes the entire enterprise is a theater of the absurd in which experimenter and subject try to outsmart each other. The reactivity problem is a threat to the internal validity of findings from some experimental studies, but by no means all; the degree of threat depends upon the particular behavioral phenomenon under scrutiny, the craftsmanship of the experimenter, and the amount of experience the subject has had in previous experiments.

Methods of research: Concluding note

As the preceding discussion has shown, all of the available research methods used in the study of organizational behavior have their respective strengths and weaknesses. Fortunately, the weaknesses are largely offsetting. This means that we have the maximum confidence in the reliability and validity of a particular empirical generalization when it is supported by different studies using varied research methods. Laboratory experiments serve as cross-checks on the causal inferences drawn from correlational self-report or field studies; the latter, in turn, provide a means of extending the generalizability of the former. When a particular finding is "method-bound"—resulting only when a single type of method is used—our conclusions must be highly tentative, even tempered by an informed skepticism.

SUMMARY

A theory is a set of statements describing the relationships among conceptual variables. Both behavioral scientists and administrators are active users of theory; the characteristic differences between their respective theories have to do with level of abstraction, the breadth of the behavioral phenomena under study, and specialization of terminology. Theory serves the functions of organizing and summarizing existing knowledge and guiding the search for new knowledge. Theories are evaluated on the bases of conformity to empirical observations, internal consistency, parsimony, congruence with other well-established theories, utility in directing the search for new knowledge, and intuitive or aesthetic appeal. No theory ever occupies a permanent place in our knowledge; all theories are transient to varying degrees, surviving only until newer and better theories replace them, carrying forward the contributions of their predecessors.

In the study of organizational behavior, a variety of methods of research contribute to the acquisition of knowledge from theory development and theory testing. These methods include—in order of increasing rigor—naturalistic observation, field surveys, correlational field studies using objective indices, field experiments, and laboratory experiments. All of these methods have their unique advantages and disadvantages, with the result that findings from studies using any single method must be qualified to take methodological imperfections into account. Our confidence in the validity of an assertion about organizational behavior is greatest when it is supported by inquiries using a host of different methods.

CONCEPTS TO REMEMBER

norm of correspondence	field survey research
norm of coherence	social desirability in response set

principle of parsimony

norm of pragmatism

naturalistic observation

case study

reactivity

correlational field studies

statistical significance

field experiment

laboratory experiment

QUESTIONS FOR DISCUSSION

1. "Theory" is sometimes contrasted with "fact." To what extent is this a valid distinction? To what extent is it an oversimplification?

2. In mystery novels and crime movies, a detective is said to have a "theory" concerning "who done it." Is this a correct use of the term *theory?* Why or why not?

3. What properties of a theory about some organizationally relevant phenomenon (for example, worker motivation) would be likely to determine its acceptability to practicing managers?

4. What does it mean to say that a "theory has been proved"? Is such a statement misleading? If so, how could it be best restated?

5. Suppose that you have a theory which says that "people are more effectively motivated by love than by fear or hate." What would be the qualifications essential to any conclusions drawn from a study of this theory using (*a*) naturalistic observation? (*b*) interviews or questionnaires? (*c*) field experiments? (*d*) laboratory experiments?

6. Why is a more "rigorous" method of research not necessarily a better one simply because of its rigor?

REFERENCES

Christenson, C. V. *Kinsey: A biography.* Bloomington: Indiana University Press, 1971.

Cummings, L. L., & Scott, W. E., Jr. (Eds.). *Readings in organizational behavior and human performance.* Homewood, Ill.: Irwin-Dorsey, 1969.

Dalton, M. *Men who manage.* New York: Wiley, 1959.

Gouldner, A. W. *Patterns of industrial bureaucracy.* Glencoe, Ill.: Free Press, 1954.

Granick, D. *The red executive.* New York: Anchor Books, Doubleday, 1961.

Hersey, P., & Blanchard, K. H. *Management of organizational behavior.* Englewood Cliffs, N.J.: Prentice-Hall, 1969.

Jenkins, H. M., & Ward, W. C. Judgment of contingency between responses and outcomes. *Psychological Monographs: General and Applied,* 1965, *79* (1, Whole No. 594).

Kaplan, A. *The conduct of inquiry.* San Francisco: Chandler, 1964.

Kinsey, A. C., Pomeroy, W. B., & Martin, C. E. *Sexual behavior in the human male.* Philadelphia: Saunders, 1949.

Leavitt, H. J.   *Managerial psychology* (3d ed.). Chicago: University of Chicago Press, 1972.

Morse, N., & Reimer, E.   The experimental change of a major organizational variable. *Journal of Abnormal and Social Psychology,* 1956, *52,* 120–129.

Muczyk, J. P.   A controlled field experiment measuring the impact of MBO on performance data. Unpublished paper, Cleveland State University, 1976.

Opsahl, R. L., & Dunnette, M. D.   The role of financial compensation in industrial motivation. *Psychological Bulletin,* 1966, *66* (2), 94–118.

Schachter, S.   Deviation, rejection, and communication. *Journal of Abnormal and Social Psychology,* 1951, *46,* 190–207.

Schwab, D. P., & Cummings, L. L.   A theoretical analysis of the impact of task scope on employee performance. *Academy of Management Review,* 1976, *1* (2), 36–46.

Shaw, M. E., & Costanzo, P. R.   *Theories of social psychology.* New York: McGraw-Hill, 1970.

Sloan, A. P., Jr.   *My years with General Motors.* New York: MacFadden Books, Doubleday, 1965.

Weick, K. E.   Laboratory experimentation with organizations. In J. G. March, (Ed.), *Handbook of organizations.* Chicago: Rand McNally, 1965.

Weick, K. E.   *The social psychology of organizing.* Reading, Mass.: Addison-Wesley, 1969.

Management and the learning process

Using reinforcement to shape behavior

How is behavior acquired, strengthened, maintained, and changed?

How can managers design effective environments for strengthening desired behavior in organizations?

Traditionally management has been defined as the process of getting things done through other people. The succinctness of this definition is misleading in that, though it is easy to say "what" a manager does, it is difficult to describe the determinants of behavior; that is, to tell "how" the behavior of the manager influences the behavior of the employee in such a way that the latter willingly accomplishes the desired task. Human behavior in organizational settings has always been a phenomenon of interest and concern. However, only in recent years have social scientists made a concerted effort to describe the principles of reinforcement and their implications for describing the determinants of behavior as they relate to the theory and practice of management. Traditional management methods reinforce employee behavior, but in a less systematic way, and generally without the benefit of well-developed theory.

Organizational leaders must resort to environmental changes as a means of influencing behavior. Reinforcement principles are the most useful method in this regard because they indicate to leaders how they might proceed in designing or modifying the work environment in order to effect specific changes in behavior. A reinforcement approach to management does not consist of a "bag of tricks" to be applied indiscriminately for the purpose of coercing unwilling people. Unfortunately, many people who think of Skinnerian applications (Skinner, 1969) in the field of management and personnel think of manipulation and aversive control over employees. Much more knowledge of the positive aspects of conditioning as applied to worker performance is available today which should dispel these false notions.

The purpose of this chapter is to describe the determinants of behavior as seen from the standpoint of reinforcement theory, and to describe how the management of the "contingencies of reinforcement" in organizational settings is a vital key to being a successful manager. We hope that this will enable the manager to understand how his or her behavior affects the behavior of subordinates and to see that, in most cases, the failure or success of the worker at the performance of a task is in part a direct function of the manager's own behavior. Since a large portion of the manager's time is spent in the process of modifying behavior patterns and shaping them so that they will be more goal oriented, it is only natural to begin this chapter by describing the processes and principles that govern behavior.

Note: Portions of the material presented in this chapter were first published by the senior author in H. L. Tosi and W. C. Hamner, *Organizational Behavior and Management,* St. Clair Press, 1974. Reprinted here by permission of the publisher.

LEARNING AS A PREREQUISITE FOR BEHAVIOR

Learning is such a common phenomenon that we tend to overlook its occurrence. Nevertheless, a major premise of reinforcement theory is that all behavior is learned. For example, a worker's skill, a supervisor's attitude, and a secretary's manners are all learned. The importance of learning in an organizational setting is highlighted by Costello and Zalkind (1963) when they conclude:

Every aspect of human behavior is responsive to learning experiences. Knowledge, language, and skills, of course; but also attitudes, value systems, and personality characteristics. All the individual's activities in the organization—his loyalties, awareness of organizational goals, job performance, even his safety record have been learned in the largest sense of that term. (p. 205)

There seems to be general agreement among social scientists that learning can be defined as *a relatively permanent change in behavior potentiality that results from reinforced practice or experience.* Note that this definition states that there is change in behavior potentiality and not necessarily in behavior itself. The reason for this distinction rests on the fact that we can observe other people respond to their environment, see the consequences which accrue to them, and be vicariously conditioned. For example, a boy can watch his older sister burn her hand on a hot stove and "learn" that pain is the result of touching a hot stove. This definition therefore allows us to account for "no-trial" learning. Bandura (1969) describes this as imitative learning and says that while behavior can be *acquired* by observing, reading, or other vicarious methods, *"performance* of observationally learned responses will depend to a great extent upon the nature of the reinforcing consequences to the model or to the observer" (p. 128).

Luthans (1973, p. 362) says that we need to consider the following points when we define the learning process:

1. Learning involves a change, though not necessarily an improvement, in behavior. Learning generally has the connotation of improved performance, but under this definition bad habits, prejudices, stereotypes, and work restrictions are learned.
2. The change in behavior must be relatively permanent in order to be considered learning. This qualification rules out behavioral changes resulting from fatigue or temporary adaptations as learning.
3. Some form of practice or experience is necessary for learning to occur.
4. Finally it should be stressed that practice or experience must be reinforced in order for learning to occur. If reinforcement does not accompany the practice or experience, the behavior will eventually disappear.

From this discussion, we can conclude that learning is the acquisition of knowledge and that performance is the translation of knowledge into practice. The primary effect of reinforcement is to strengthen and intensify certain aspects of ensuing behavior. Behavior that has become highly differentiated (shaped) can be understood and accounted for only in terms of the history of the reinforcement of that behavior. Reinforcement generates a reproducible behavior process in time. A response occurs, is followed by a reinforcer, and further responses occur with a characteristic temporal patterning. When a response is reinforced it subsequently occurs more frequently than before it was reinforced. Reinforcement may be assumed to have a characteristic and reproducible effect on a particular behavior, and usually it will enhance and intensify that behavior (Skinner, 1938, 1953).

TWO BASIC LEARNING PROCESSES

Before discussing in any detail exactly how the *general laws* or *principles* of reinforcement can be used to predict and influence behavior, we must differentiate between two types of behavior. One type is known as *voluntary* or *operant* behavior, and the other is known as *reflex* or *respondent* behavior. Respondent behavior takes in all responses of human beings that are *elicited* by special stimulus changes in the environment. For example, when a person turns a light on in a dark room (stimulus change), the pupils of his eyes contract (respondent behavior).

Operant behavior includes an even greater amount of human activity. It takes in all the responses of a person that may at some time be said to have an effect upon or to do something to the person's outside world. Operant behavior *operates* on this world either directly or indirectly. For example, when a person presses the up button at the elevator entrance to "call" the elevator, he or she is operating on the environment.

The process of learning or acquiring reflex behavior is different from the process of learning or acquiring voluntary behavior. The two basic and distinct learning processes are known as classical conditioning and operant conditioning. It is from studying these two learning processes that much of our knowledge of individual behavior has emerged.

Classical conditioning[1]

While studying the automatic reflexes associated with digestion, Pavlov (1902) noticed that his laboratory dog salivated (unconditioned response) not only when food (unconditioned stimulus) was placed in the dog's mouth, but also when Pavlov presented the dog with other stimuli before food was placed in its mouth. In other words, by presenting a neutral stimulus (ringing of a bell) every time food was presented

---

[1] Classical conditioning is also known as respondent conditioning and Pavlovian conditioning.

to the dog, Pavlov was able to get the dog to salivate to the bell alone.

A stimulus which is not a part of a reflex relationship (the bell in Pavlov's experiment) becomes a *conditioned stimulus* for the response by repeated, temporal pairing with an *unconditioned* stimulus (food) which already elicits the response. This new relationship is known as a conditioned reflex, and the pairing procedure is known as classical conditioning.

While it is important to understand that reflex behavior is conditioned by a different process than is voluntary behavior, classical conditioning principles will not be discussed in great detail since most of the behavior that is of interest to society does not fit into the paradigm of reflex behavior. Nevertheless, the ability to generalize from one stimulus setting to another is very important in human learning and problem solving, and for this reason knowledge of the classical conditioning process is important.

Operant conditioning[2]

The basic distinction between classical and operant conditioning procedures is in terms of the *consequences* of the conditioned response. In classical conditioning, the sequence of events is independent of the subject's behavior. In operant conditioning, consequences (rewards and punishments) are made to occur as a consequence of the subject's response or failure to respond. The distinction between these two methods is shown in Figure 3–1.

In Figure 3–1, we see that classical conditioning involves a three-stage process. In the diagram, let S refer to *stimulus* and R to *response.* We see that in stage 1 the unconditioned stimulus (food) elicits an unconditioned response (salivation). In stage 2, a neutral stimulus (bell) elicits no known response. However, in stage 3, after the ringing of the bell is repeatedly paired with the presence of food, the bell alone becomes a conditioned stimulus and elicits a conditioned response (salivation). The subject has no control over the unconditioned or conditioned response, but is "at the mercy" of its environment and its past conditioning history.

Note, however, that for voluntary behavior the consequence is dependent on the behavior of the individual in a given stimulus setting. Such behavior can be said to "operate" on the environment, in contrast to behavior which is "respondent" to prior eliciting stimuli. Reinforcement is not given every time the stimulus is presented, but is *only* given when the correct response is made. For example, if an employee taking a work break puts a penny (R) in the soft drink machine (S),

---

[2] Operant conditioning is also known as instrumental conditioning and Skinnerian conditioning.

nothing happens (consequence). However, if he puts a quarter (R) in the machine (S), he gets the soft drink (consequence). In other words, the employee's behavior is *instrumental* in determining the consequences which accrue to him.

The interrelationships among the three components of (1) *stimulus* or environment, (2) *response* or performance, and (3) consequences or *reinforcements* are known as the *contingencies* of reinforcement. Skinner (1969) says, "The class of responses upon which a reinforcer is *contingent* is called an operant, to suggest the action on the environment followed by reinforcements" (p. 7). Operant conditioning presupposes that human beings explore their environment and act upon it. This behavior, randomly emitted at first, can be constructed as an operant by making a reinforcement contingent on a response. Any

Figure 3–1
Classical versus operant conditioning

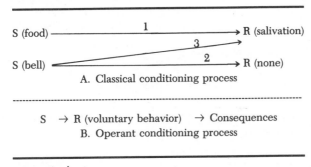

A. Classical conditioning process

S → R (voluntary behavior) → Consequences
B. Operant conditioning process

S = stimulus
R = responses
→ = leads to

stimulus present when an operant is reinforced acquires control in the sense that the rate of response for that individual will be higher when it is present. "Such a stimulus does not act as a *goad;* it does not elicit the response [as was the case in the classical conditioning of reflex behavior] in the sense of forcing it to occur. It is simply an essential aspect of the occasion upon which response is made and reinforced" (Skinner, 1969, p. 7).

Therefore, an adequate formulation of the interaction between an individual and his environment must always specify three things: (1) the occasion upon which a response occurs, (2) the response itself, and (3) the reinforcing consequences. Skinner holds that the consequences determine the likelihood that a given operant will be performed in the future. Thus, in order to change behavior, the consequences of the behavior must be changed, that is, the contingencies (the ways in which the consequences are related to the behavior) must be rearranged. For Skinner, the behavior generated by a given set of contingencies can be accounted for without appealing to hypothetical inner states (for example, awareness or expectancies). "If a conspicuous stimulus does not have an effect, it is not because the organism has not attended to it or because some central gatekeeper has screened it out, but because the stimulus plays no important role in the prevailing contingencies" (Skinner, 1969, p. 8).

ARRANGEMENT OF THE CONTINGENCIES OF REINFORCEMENT

In order to *understand* and *interpret* behavior, we must look at the interrelationship among the components of the contingencies of behavior. If one expects to influence behavior, he or she must also be able to manipulate the consequences of the behavior. Haire (1964) reports the importance of being able to manipulate the consequences when he says:

> Indeed, whether he is conscious of it or not, the superior is bound to be constantly shaping the behavior of his subordinates by the way in which he utilizes the rewards that are at his disposal, and he will inevitably modify the behavior patterns of his work group thereby. For this reason, it is important to see as clearly as possible what is going on, so that the changes can be planned and chosen in advance, rather than simply accepted after the fact.

After appropriate reinforcers that have sufficient incentive value to maintain stable responsiveness have been chosen, the contingencies between specific performances and reinforcing stimuli must be arranged. Employers intuitively use rewards in their attempts to modify and influence behavior, but their efforts often produce limited results because the rewards are used improperly, inconsistently, or inefficiently. In many instances considerable rewards are bestowed upon workers, but these rewards are not made conditional or contingent on the behavior the manager wishes to promote. Also, "long delays often intervene between the occurrence of the desired behavior and its intended consequences; special privileges, activities, and rewards are generally furnished according to fixed time schedules rather than performance requirements; and in many cases, positive reinforcers are inadvertently made contingent upon the wrong type of behavior" (Bandura, 1969, pp. 229–230).

One of the primary reasons that managers fail to "motivate" workers to perform in the desired manner is a lack of understanding of the power of the contingencies of reinforcement over the employee and of the manager's role in arranging those contingencies. The laws or principles for arranging the contingencies are not hard to understand, and if students of behavior grasp them firmly, these laws are powerful tools which can be used to increase supervisory effectiveness.

As stated previously, operant conditioning is the process by which behavior is modified by manipulation of the contingencies of the behavior. To understand how this works, we will first look at various *types* (arrangements) of contingencies, and then at various *schedules* of the contingencies available. Rachlin (1970) described the four basic ways of arranging the contingencies available to the manager—*positive reinforcement, avoidance learning, extinction,* and *punishment.* The differences among these types of contingencies depend on the consequence which results from the behavioral act. Positive reinforcement and avoidance learning are methods of strengthening *desired* behavior, and extinction and punishment are methods of weakening *undesired* behavior.

Positive reinforcement

"A positive reinforcer is a stimulus which, when added to a situation, strengthens the probability of an operant response" (Skinner, 1953, p. 73). The reason it strengthens the response is explained by Thorndike's (1911) Law of Effect. This law simply states that behavior which appears to lead to a positive consequence tends to be repeated, whereas behavior which appears to lead to a negative consequence tends not to be repeated. A positive consequence is often called a reward and is described as pleasant.

Reinforcers, either positive or negative, are classified as either (1) unconditioned or primary reinforcers, or (2) conditioned or secondary reinforcers. Primary reinforcers, such as food, water, and sex, are of biological importance in that they are innately rewarding and have effects which are independent of past experiences. Secondary reinforcers, such as job advancement, praise, recognition, and money, derive their effects from a consistent pairing with other reinforcers (that is, they are conditioned). Secondary reinforcement, therefore, depends on the individual and his or her past reinforcement history. What is rewarding to one person may not be rewarding to another. Managers should look for a reward system which has maximal reinforcing consequences to the group he or she is supervising. (See question one at the end of this chapter for an example of how individual differences affect perceptions of rewards.)

Regardless of whether the positive reinforcer is primary or secondary in nature, once it has been determined that a consequence has reward value to the worker, it can be used to increase the worker's performance. So the *first step* in the successful application of reinforcement procedures is to select reinforcers that are sufficiently powerful and durable to "maintain responsiveness while complex patterns of behavior are being established and strengthened" (Bandura, 1969, p. 225).

The *second step* is to design the contingencies in such a way that the reinforcing events are made contingent upon the desired behavior. This is the rule of reinforcement which is most often violated. Rewards must result from performance, and the greater the degree of performance by an employee, the greater should be the reward. Money as a reinforcer will be discussed in Chapter 11, but it should be noted that money is not the only reward available. As a matter of fact, for unionized employees the supervisor has virtually no way to tie money to performance. Nevertheless, other forms of rewards, such as recognition, promotion, and job assignments, can be made contingent on good performance. Unless a manager is willing to discriminate among employees on the basis of their level of performance, the effectiveness of his or her power over the employee is nil.

The arrangement of positive reinforcement contingencies can be pictured as follows:

$$\text{Stimulus} \rightarrow \text{Desired response} \rightarrow \text{Positive consequences}$$
$$(S \rightarrow R \rightarrow R^+)$$

The stimulus is the work environment which leads to a response (some level of performance). If this response leads to positive consequences, then the probability of the response being emitted again increases. Now, if the response is undesired, then the supervisor is conditioning or teaching the employee that undesired behavior will lead to a desired reward. It is therefore important that the reward administered be equal to the performance input of the employee. Homans (1961) labels this as the rule of distributive justice and states that this reciprocal norm applies in both formal (work) and informal (friendship) relationships. In other words, the employee *exchanges* his services for the rewards of the organization. In order to maintain desired performance, it is important that the manager design the reward system so that the level of reward administered is proportionately contingent on the level of performance emitted.

The *third step* is to design the contingencies in such a way that a reliable procedure for eliciting or inducing the desired response patterns is established. If the desired response patterns rarely occur, there will be few opportunities to influence the desired behavior through contingent management. If the behavior that a manager wishes to strengthen is already present, and occurs with some frequency, then contingent applications of incentives can, from the outset, increase and maintain the desired performance patterns at a high level. However, as Bandura (1969) states, "When the initial level of the desired behavior is extremely low, if the criterion for reinforcement is initially set too high, most, if not all, of the person's responses go unrewarded, so that his efforts are gradually extinguished and his motivation diminished" (p. 232).

The nature of the learning process is such that the new response patterns can be easily established. The principle of operant conditioning says that an operant followed by a positive reinforcement is more likely to occur under *similar* conditions in the future. Through the process of *generalization,* the more nearly alike the new situation or stimulus is to the original one, the more likely is the old behavior to be emitted in the new environment. For example, if you contract with an electrician to rewire your house, he is able to accomplish the task because he brings with him enough old behavioral patterns which he generalized to this unfamiliar but similar stimulus setting (the house). He has learned through his past reinforcement history that when in a new environment, one way to speed up the correct behavior needed to get rewarded is to generalize from similar settings with which he has had experience. Perhaps one reason an employer wants a person with work experience is that there is a greater probability that such a person will emit the correct behavior, and thus the job of managing the person is simplified.

Just as generalization is the ability to react to similarities in the environment, *discrimination* is the ability to react to differences in a new environmental setting. Usually when an employee moves from one environment (a job, a city, an office) to another he or she finds that only certain dimensions of the stimulus conditions change. Although not all of the responses of the employee in this new setting will be correct, by skilled use of the procedures of reinforcement, we can bring about the more precise type of stimulus control called discrimination. When we purchase a new car, we do not have to relearn how to drive a car (generalizable stimulus). Instead we only need to learn the differences between the new car and the old car so that we can respond to those differences in order to get reinforced. This procedure is called *discrimination training.* "If in the presence of a stimulus a response is reinforced, and in the absence of this stimulus it is extinguished, the stimulus will control the probability of the response in high degree. Such a stimulus is called a *discriminative stimulus*" (Michael and Meyerson, 1962).

The development of effective discriminative repertoires is important for dealing with many different people on interpersonal bases. Effective training techniques will allow the supervisor to develop the necessary discriminative repertoires in new employees.

Using the principles of generalization and discrimination in a well-designed training program allows the manager to accomplish the third goal of eliciting or inducing the desired response patterns. Training is a method of *shaping* desired behavior so that it can be conditioned to come under the control of the reinforcement stimuli. Shaping behavior is necessary when the response to be learned is not currently in the individual's repertoire and when it is a fairly complex behavior.

In shaping, we teach a desired response by reinforcing the series of successive steps which lead to the final response. This method is essentially the one your parents used when they first taught you to drive. You were first taught how to adjust the seat and mirror, fasten the seat belt, turn on the lights and windshield wipers, and then how to start the engine. When you successfully completed each stage you were positively reinforced by some comment. (You were also probably negatively reinforced when you were unsuccessful.) You were then allowed to practice driving on back roads and in empty lots. By focusing on one aspect at a time, and reinforcing proper responses, your parents were able to shape your driving behavior until you reached the final stage of being able to drive. After your behavior was shaped, driving other cars or driving in new territories was accomplished successfully by the process of generalization and discrimination. This same process is used with a management trainee who is rotated from department to department for a period of time until he or she has "learned the ropes." After the trainee's managerial behavior has been minimally shaped, he is transferred to a managerial position where, using the principles of generalization and discrimination, he is able to adjust to the contingencies of the work environment.

Avoidance learning

The second type of contingency arrangement available to the manager is called escape learning or avoidance learning. Like positive reinforcement, this is a method of strengthening desired behavior. A contingency arrangement in which an individual's performance can terminate an already noxious stimulus is called *escape* learning. When an individual's behavior can prevent the onset of a noxious stimulus, the procedure is called *avoidance learning.* In both cases, the result is the development and maintenance of the desired operant behavior.

An example of this kind of control can easily be found in a work environment. Punctuality of employees is often maintained by avoidance learning. The noxious stimulus is criticism by the shop steward or the office manager for being late. In order to avoid criticism the employees make a special effort to come to work on time. Examples of escape behavior can also be found in industry. An employee's home life is so noxious that she leaves for work early in order to escape. A supervisor begins criticizing a worker for "goofing off." The worker starts working to *escape* the criticism of the supervisor and continues working in order to avoid the employer's criticism.

The arrangement of an escape reinforcement contingency can be diagrammed as follows:

Noxious stimulus → Desired response → Removal of noxious stimulus
$$(S^- \rightarrow R \nrightarrow S^-)$$

The distinction between strengthening behavior by means of positive reinforcement techniques and by means of avoidance learning techniques should be noted carefully. In one case the individual works hard to gain the consequences from the environment which result from good work, and in the other case the individual works hard to avoid the noxious aspects of the environment itself. In both cases the same behavior is strengthened.

Extinction

While positive reinforcement and avoidance learning techniques can be used by managers to strengthen desired behavior, extinction and punishment techniques are methods available to managers for reducing undesired behavior. When positive reinforcement for a learned or previously conditioned response is withheld, individuals will continue to exhibit that behavior for an extended period of time. Under repeated nonreinforcement, the behavior decreases and eventually disappears. This decline in response rate as a result of nonrewarded repetition of a task is defined as extinction.

The diagram of the extinction process can be shown as follows:

(1) Stimulus → Response → Positive consequences
$$(S \rightarrow R \rightarrow R^+)$$
(2) Stimulus → Response → Withholding of positive consequences
$$(S \rightarrow R \not\rightarrow R^+)$$
(3) Stimulus → Withholding of response
$$(S \not\rightarrow R)$$

The behavior was previously reinforced because (a) it was desired or (b) poor reinforcement practices were used. To extinguish this behavior in a naturally recurring situation, response patterns sustained by positive reinforcement (stage 1) are frequently eliminated (stage 3) by discontinuing the rewards (stage 2) that ordinarily produce the behavior. This method, when combined with a positive reinforcement method, is the procedure of behavior modification recommended by Skinner (1953). It leads to the least negative side effects, and when the two methods are used together, it allows the employee to get the rewards he or she desires, and the organization to eliminate the undesired behavior.

Punishment

A second method of reducing the frequency of undesired behavior is punishment. Because of the complexity and controversy surrounding punishment, we have devoted an entire chapter (Chapter 4) to this topic. A brief summary of the method is presented here to introduce you to this complex conditioning procedure.

Punishment is defined as presenting an aversive or noxious consequence contingent upon a response, or removing a positive consequence contingent upon a response. Based on the Law of Effect, as rewards strengthen behavior, punishments weaken it. This process can be shown as follows:

(1) Stimulus → Undesired behavior →   Noxious consequence or withholding of positive consequence

$$\left(\begin{array}{c} S \rightarrow R \rightarrow R^{-} \\ \text{or } R^{+} \end{array} \right)$$

(2) Stimulus ↛ Undesired behavior

(S ↛ R)

Notice carefully the difference between the withholding of rewards in the punishment process and the withholding of rewards in the extinction process. In the extinction process, you withhold rewards for behavior that has previously been rewarded because the behavior was desired. In punishment, you withhold a reward from behavior that is undesired, that has never been associated with the reward, and that is in fact a noxious consequence. For example, if your young son began imitating an older boy's use of profanity and you thought this "cute," you might reinforce the behavior by laughing or by calling public attention to it. Soon the son learns that one way to get the recognition he craves is to use profanity—even though he may have no concept of its meaning. As the child reaches an accountable age, you decide that his use of profanity is no longer as cute as it once was. To stop the behavior you can do one of three things: (1) You can withhold the previous recognition you gave the child by ignoring him (extinction). (2) You can give the child a spanking (punishment by noxious consequence). (3) You can withhold the child's allowance or refuse to let him watch television (punishment by withholding of positive consequences not previously connected with the act).

It should be noted that method 2 and perhaps method 3 would be considered cruel because of the parent's own inconsistencies. Punishment should rarely be used to extinguish behavior that has previously been reinforced if the person administering the punishment is the same person who previously reinforced the behavior. However, had the parent failed to extinguish the use of profanity prior to sending the child out into society (for example, school or church), the society might punish the child for behavior that the parent was reinforcing or at least tolerating. It is often argued therefore that the failure of parents to punish a child for socially unacceptable behavior (for example, stealing, driving at excessive speeds, poor table manners) is crueler than the punishment itself, simply because the society will withhold rewards or administer aversive consequences for behavior which the parents should have extinguished.

The use of aversive control is frequently questioned on the assumption that it produces undesirable by-products. In many cases this concern is warranted. Bandura (1969) states that whether punishment or extinction should be used depends on the circumstances and on the past reinforcement history of the reinforcement agent and the reinforcement target. He says:

> Many of the unfavorable effects, however, that are sometimes associated with punishment are not necessarily inherent in the methods themselves but result from the faulty manner in which they are applied. A great deal of human behavior is, in fact, modified and closely regulated by natural aversive contingencies without any ill effects. On the basis of negative consequences people learn to avoid or to protect themselves against hazardous falls, flaming or scalding objects, deafening sounds, and other hurtful stimuli. . . . In instances where certain activities can have injurious effects aversive contingencies *must* be socially arranged to ensure survival. Punishment is rarely indicted for ineffectiveness or deleterious side effects when used, for example, to teach young children not to insert metal objects into electrical outlets, not to cross busy thoroughfares. . . . Certain types of negative sanctions, if applied considerately, can likewise aid in eliminating self-defeating and socially detrimental behavior without creating any special problems. (p. 294)

RULES FOR USING OPERANT CONDITIONING TECHNIQUES

Several rules concerning the arrangement of the contingencies of reinforcement should be discussed. Although these rules have "commonsense" appeal, the research findings indicate that the rules are often violated by managers when they design their control systems.

Rule 1. Don't reward all people the same. In other words, differentiate employees' rewards on the basis of performance as compared to some defined objective or standard. We know that people compare their performance to their peers' performance to determine how well they are doing and that they compare their rewards to the rewards of their peers in order to determine how to evaluate their rewards. Although some managers seem to think that the fairest system of compensation is one in which everyone in the same job classification gets the same pay, employees want differentiation so that they know their importance to the organization. It can be argued that managers who reward all people the same are encouraging only average performance at best. The behavior of high-performance workers is being extinguished (ignored), whereas the behavior of average-performance and poor-performance workers is being strengthened by positive reinforcement.

Rule 2. Failure to respond has reinforcing consequences. Managers who find the job of differentiating among workers so unpleasant that they fail to respond must recognize that failure to respond modifies behavior. Therefore, managers must be careful to examine the performance consequences of their inaction as well as their action.

Rule 3. Be sure to tell a person what he or she can do to get reinforced. By making clear the contingencies of reinforcement to the worker, a manager may actually increase the freedom of the individual worker. The employee who has a standard against which to measure his job will have a built-in feedback system which allows him to make judgments about his own work. The awarding of the reinforcement in an organization in which the worker's goal is specified will be associated with the performance of the worker and not based on the biases of the supervisor. The assumption is that the supervisor rates the employee accurately and that he or she then reinforces the employee on the basis of the employee's ratings. If the supervisor fails to rate accurately or to administer rewards based on performance, then the stated goals for the worker will lose stimulus control, and the worker will be forced to search for the "true" contingencies—that is, for the behavior he should perform in order to get rewarded (for example, ingratiation, loyalty, a positive attitude).

Rule 4. Be sure to tell a person what he or she is doing wrong. As a general rule, very few people find the act of failing rewarding. One behavioral assumption, therefore, is that a worker wants to be rewarded in a positive manner. A supervisor should never use extinction or punishment as the sole method for modifying behavior, but used judiciously in conjunction with other techniques designed to promote more effective response options (Rule 3), these methods can hasten the change process. If the supervisor fails to specify why a reward is being withheld the employee may associate the action with past undesired behavior instead of the undesired behavior that the supervisor is trying to extinguish. Thus the supervisor extinguishes good performance while having no affect on the undesired behavior.

Used in combination, Rules 3 and 4 should allow the manager to control behavior in the best interests of the organization. At the same time these rules should give the employee the clarity he needs to see that his outcomes are controlled by his own behavior and not the behavior of the supervisor.

Rule 5. Don't punish in front of others. The reason for this rule is quite simple. The punishment (for example, reprimand) should be enough to extinguish the undesired behavior. Administering the punishment in front of the work group, doubly punishes the worker in the sense that he is also ridiculed before his peers. This additional punishment may lead to negative side effects in three ways. First, the worker whose self-image is damaged may feel that he must retaliate in order to protect himself. Therefore, the supervisor has actually prompted undesired responses. Second, the work group may associate the punishment with the wrong behavior of the worker, and through "avoidance learning" techniques its members may modify their own behavior in ways not intended by the supervisor. Third, the work group is also being punished, in the sense that observing a member of their team being reprimanded has noxious or aversive properties for most people. This may result in a decrease in the performance of the total work group.

   Rule 6. Make the consequences equal to the behavior. In other words, be fair. Don't cheat the worker out of his or her just rewards. If he or she is a good worker, say so. Many supervisors find it very difficult to praise an employee. Others find it very difficult to counsel an employee about what he is doing wrong. When a manager fails to use these reinforcement tools, he is actually reducing his effectiveness. When a worker is overrewarded he may feel guilty, and based on the principles of reinforcement, the worker's current level of performance is being conditioned. If his performance level is less than that of others who get the same reward, he has no reason to increase his output. When a worker is underrewarded he becomes angry with the system. His behavior is being extinguished, and the company may be forcing the good, underrewarded employee to seek employment elsewhere while encouraging the poor, overrewarded employee to stay.

CURRENT THEORIES OF POSITIVE REINFORCEMENT

   Since the very heart of the conditioning process is positive reinforcement, behavioral scientists have concerned themselves with predicting whether a given stimulus will reinforce a given behavior. Rachlin reported:

> We have been talking loosely about positive reinforcers such as food for hungry organisms or water for thirsty organisms, but we have not specified any characteristic that food and water have in common to make them reinforcing. If we knew what this characteristic was we could make true behavioral predictions; we would predict that a new stimulus with the characteristics would be reinforcing (that is, it would increase the probability of behavior it followed), while a new stimulus without the characteristics would not be reinforcing. (Rachlin, 1970, p. 107)

   Four of the more influential theories of positive reinforcement that have emerged from the prolific speculation about the relation of reinforcement to the individual are: (1) *need reduction,* (2) *tension reduction,* (3) *brain stimulation,* and (4) *response as a reinforcement* (Rachlin, 1970).

   Need reduction theory says that every reinforcer ultimately satisfies some vital need of the individual, such as food or water, and that in satisfying the need, the reinforcer reduces the need. This theory argues that all reinforcers must ultimately reduce a physiological need.

The *tension reduction* theory says that every reinforcer ultimately lessens some tension in the organism and is therefore reinforcing. For example, tensions can be lessened by eating or smoking. According to Hilgard (1961), the trouble with this theory is that many things that appear to immediately increase tension (crossword puzzles, sex magazines, roller coaster rides) are reinforcing. A tension reduction theorist argues that "immediate" tension reduction is not necessary for reinforcement. All that is necessary is eventual tension reduction.

According to *brain stimulation* theory, every reinforcer ultimately stimulates or activates certain parts of the brain. Scott (1966) reports that psychologists in widely diverse fields have acknowledged the importance of activation of the brain. "In the area of work behavior, activation theory offers an explanation for performance decrements and dissatisfactions frequently observed in repetitive tasks" (p. 4). In other words, the longer a person works at a boring task, the less reinforcing is the work itself, due to a decrease in the arousal level of the worker.

The *"response as a reinforcement"* theory holds that responses are reinforced by the ability to make other responses; for example, going to law school is reinforced by the ability to practice law. Less preferred behavior is strengthened by the opportunity to engage in more preferred behavior.

The above theories, plus others which have been postulated about how positive reinforcers function, help give insight into how individuals relate to reinforcers. Rachlin (1970) states: "The point to be remembered here, though, is that none [of the theories] by itself, is sufficient to account for all known reinforcers. This means that the best way to tell if a stimulus is reinforcing is to try it out in an instrumental conditioning experiment" (p. 108).

Fortunately for managers, multiple reinforcers are available to them which have reward value to the employee in that the presence of the reward increases the probability of correct performance. The important point to remember is that, whatever the reason, different individuals and groups find different consequences rewarding and that any one reinforcer may at times lose effectiveness due to satiation. It is most important that the manager know his work group and that the contingencies of reinforcement be arranged in such a way that the consequences designed to have reward valence actually do.

SCHEDULES OF POSITIVE REINFORCEMENT

The previous discussion was concerned primarily with methods of arranging the contingencies of reinforcement in order to modify behavior. Two major points were discussed. First, some type of reinforcement is necessary in order to produce a change in behavior. Second, a combined program of positive reinforcement and extinction is more effective for use in organizations than are programs using punishment and/ or avoidance learning techniques. The previous discussion thus tells what causes behavior and why this is important information for the manager, but it does not discuss the important issues dealing with the scheduling or administering of positive reinforcement.

According to Costello and Zalkind (1963), "The speed with which learning takes place and also how lasting its effects will be is determined by the timing of reinforcement" (p. 193). In other words, the effectiveness of reinforcement varies as a function of the schedule of its administration. A reinforcement schedule is a more or less formal specification of the occurrence of a reinforcer in relation to the behavioral sequence to be conditioned, and the effectiveness of a reinforcer depends as much upon its scheduling as upon any of its other features (magnitude, quality, degree of association with the behavioral act, degree of deprivation, or satiation).

There are many conceivable arrangements of a positive reinforcement schedule which managers can use to reward their workers. Two basic types of schedules which have the most promise for motivating workers are *continuous* and *partial reinforcement* schedules.

Continuous reinforcement schedule

Under this schedule, every time the correct response is emitted by the worker it is followed by a reinforcer. With this schedule, the desired behavior increases very rapidly, but when the reinforcer is removed, performance decreases rapidly (extinction). For this reason the schedule is not recommended for use by the manager over a long period of time. It is also impossible for a manager to continuously reward the employee for emitting desired behavior. Therefore, a manager should generally consider using one or more of the partial reinforcement schedules when he administers either financial or nonfinancial rewards.

Partial reinforcement schedules

Partial reinforcement, in which reinforcement does not occur after every correct operant, leads to slower learning but stronger retention of a response than does total or continuous reinforcement. "In other words, *learning is more permanent when we reward correct behavior only part of the time*" (Bass & Vaughan, 1966, p. 20). This factor is extremely relevant to the observed strong resistance to changes in attitudes, values, norms, and the like.

Ferster and Skinner (1957) have described four basic types of partial reinforcement schedules for operant learning situations. These schedules, shown in Figure 3–2, are:

1. *Fixed interval schedule.* Under this schedule, when the desired response occurs, a reinforcer is administered only after the passage of a specified period of time since the previous reinforcement. Thus a worker paid on a weekly basis would receive a full paycheck every Friday, assuming that the worker were performing minimally acceptable behavior. This method offers the least motivation for hard work among employees.

The kind of behavior often observed with fixed interval schedules is a pause after reinforcement and then an increase in the rate of responding until a high rate of performance occurs just as the interval is about to end. Suppose that the plant manager visits the shipping department each day at approximately 10:00 A.M. This fixed schedule of supervisory recognition will probably cause performance to be at its highest just prior to the plant manager's visit, and performance will probably steadily decline thereafter and not rise to a peak again until the next morning's visit.

2. *Variable interval schedule.* Under this schedule, reinforcement is administered at some variable interval of time around some average. This schedule is not recommended for use with a pay plan, but it is an ideal method to use for administering praise, promotions, and supervisory visits. Since the reinforcers are dispensed unpredictably, variable interval schedules generate higher rates of response and more stable and consistent performance than do fixed interval schedules.

Suppose that our plant manager visits the shipping department on an *average* of once a day but at randomly selected time intervals (for example, twice on Monday, once on Tuesday, not at all on Wednesday, or Thursday, and twice on Friday, all of his visits occurring at different times during the day). As you would expect, performance will be higher and will fluctuate less than under the fixed interval schedule.

3. *Fixed ratio schedule.* Here a reward is delivered only when a fixed number of desired responses take place. This is essentially the piecework schedule for pay. The response level here is significantly higher than that obtained under any of the interval (or time-based) schedules.

4. *Variable ratio schedule.* Under this schedule, a reward is delivered only after a number of desired responses, with the number of desired responses changing around an average from the occurrence of one reinforcer to the next. Thus a person working on a 15 to 1 variable ratio schedule might receive reinforcement after 10 responses, then 20 responses, then 15 responses, and so on, for an average of 1 reinforcer per 15 responses. Gambling is an example of a variable ratio reward schedule. Research evidence reveals that of all the availa-

Figure 3–2
The effects of various schedules of reinforcement on performance

1. Fixed interval schedule of reinforcement

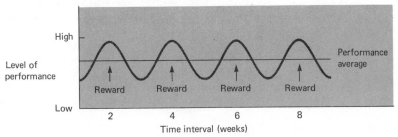

Note: Performance average lower than for a variable interval schedule and fluctuation in performance higher than under variable interval schedule.

2. Variable interval schedule of reinforcement

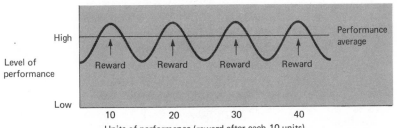

3. Fixed ratio schedule of reinforcement

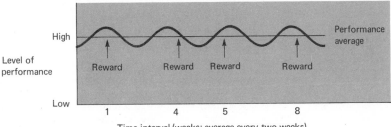

Note: Performance average lower and fluctuation greater than variable ratio schedule but superior to interval schedule.

4. Variable ratio schedule of reinforcement

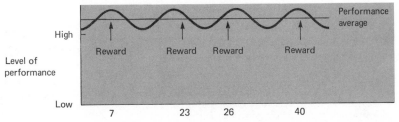

ble variations in scheduling procedures, this is the most powerful in sustaining behavior. Gamblers at a blackjack table are a classic example. In industry, it would be impossible to use this as the only plan for scheduling reinforcement. Aldis (1961) gives an example of how the variable ratio method could be used to supplement other monetary reward schedules.

> . . . Take the annual Christmas bonus as an example. In many instances, this "surprise" gift has become nothing more than a ritualized annual salary supplement which everybody expects. Therefore, its incentive-building value is largely lost. Now suppose that the total bonus were distributed at

Figure 3–3
Operant conditioning summary

Reinforcement contingencies		Effect on behavior	
Arrangement	*Schedule*	*When applied to the individual*	*When removed from the individual*
	Continuous reinforcement	Fastest method to establish a new behavior	Fastest method to extinguish a new behavior
	Partial reinforcement	Slowest method to establish a new behavior	Slowest method to extinguish a new behavior
	Variable partial reinforcement	More consistent response frequencies	Slower extinction rate
	Fixed partial reinforcement	Less consistent response frequencies	Faster extinction rate
Positive reinforcement Avoidance reinforcement		Increased frequency over pre-conditioning level	Return to pre-conditioning level
Punishment Extinction		Decreased frequency over pre-conditioning level	Return to pre-conditioning level

Source: Adapted from O. Behling, C. Schriesheim, and J. Tolliver, "Present Theories and New Directions in Theories of Work Effort,"Journal Supplement Abstract Service of the American Psychological Corporation, 1976, by permission of authors.

irregular intervals throughout the year and in small sums dependent upon the amount of work done. Wouldn't the workers find their urge to work increased? (p. 63)

An important point to remember is that to be effective a schedule should always include the specification of a contingency between the behavior desired and the occurrence of a reinforcer. In many cases it will be necessary to use each of the various schedules for administering rewards—for example, base pay on a fixed interval schedule, promotions and raises on a variable interval schedule, recognition of above-average performance with a piece-rate plan (fixed ratio schedule), and supplementary bonuses on a variable ratio schedule. The effects on worker performance of the various types of reinforcement schedules and the various methods of arranging reinforcement contingencies are shown in Figure 3–3.

The necessity for arranging appropriate reinforcement contingencies is dramatically illustrated by several studies in which rewards were shifted from a response-contingent (ratio) basis to a time-contingent (interval) basis. During the period in which rewards were made conditional upon occurrence of the desired behavior, the appropriate response patterns were exhibited at a consistently high level. When the same rewards were based on time and independent of the worker's behavior, there was a marked drop in the desired behavior. The reinstatement of the performance-contingent reward schedule promptly restored the high level of responsiveness. Similar declines in performance were obtained when workers were provided rewards in advance without performance requirements.

Source: © King Features Syndicate Inc. 1976.

Aldis (1961) encourages business leaders to recognize the importance of a positive reinforcement program. He also says that experimentation with various schedules of positive reinforcement is the key to reducing job boredom and to increasing worker satisfaction. He concludes:

Most of us fully realize that a large proportion of all workers hold jobs that are boring and repetitive and that these employees are motivated to work not by positive rewards but by various oblique forms of threat. . . . The challenge is to motivate men by positive rewards rather than by negative punishments or threats of punishments. . . . Businessmen should recognize how much their conventional wage and salary systems essentially rely on negative reinforcement.

Thus the promise of newer methods of wage payments which rely on more immediate rewards, on piece-rate pay, and greater randomization does not lie only in the increase in productivity that might follow. The greater promise is that such experiments may lead to happier workers as well. (Aldis, 1961, p. 63)

MANAGEMENT AND THE DISSEMINATION OF KNOWLEDGE

Previously we defined *learning* as the acquisition of knowledge (by the process of operant conditioning), and performance as the translation of knowledge into behavior (depending on the consequences). It can be argued, therefore, that what managers do is disseminate knowledge to those they manage in order to gain the desired level of performance. The question that remains to be answered is, what is knowledge?—that is, What information should one disseminate in order to control behavior?

There are two types of knowledge, according to Skinner (1969). *Private knowledge* is knowledge established through experience with the contingencies of reinforcement. Skinner says, "The world which establishes contingencies of reinforcement of the sort studied in an operant analysis is presumably 'what knowledge is about.' A person comes to know that world and how to behave in it in the sense that he acquires behavior which satisfies the contingencies it maintains" (p. 156). The behavior which results from private knowledge is called *contingency-shaped* behavior. This is the knowledge which one must possess in order to perform correctly and be rewarded. Such knowledge does not assume any awareness on the part of the person, but is based entirely on the person's past reinforcement history. A person can "know how" to play golf, for example, as indicated by a series of low scores—but it is an entirely different thing to be able to tell others how to play golf. A machine operator may be an excellent employee but make a poor supervisor. One reason may be that, while he possesses private knowledge about his job, he is unable to verbalize the contingencies to other people.

Public knowledge, then, is the ability to derive rules from the contingencies in the form of injunctions or descriptions which specify occasions, responses, and consequences (Skinner, 1969, p. 160). The behavior which results from public knowledge is called *rule-governed* behavior.

The possession of public knowledge is important to the manager because the employee looks to the manager for information about what behavior is required, how to perform the desired behavior, and what the consequences of the desired behavior will be. Before a manager can give correct answers to these questions, he must understand the true contingencies himself, since his business is not doing but telling others how to do. He must be able to analyze the contingencies of reinforcement found in the organization and "to formulate rules or laws which make it unnecessary to be exposed to them in order to behave appropriately" (Skinner, 1969, p. 166).

After living in a large city for a long time, a person is able to go from point A to point B with little trouble. The person's knowledge of how to get around in the city was shaped by his past history with the environment. This behavior is an example of contingency-shaped behavior. If a stranger arrives in the same city and desires to go from point A to point B, he too will have little trouble. He will look at a map of the city and will follow the path specified by the map. This behavior is an example of rule-governed behavior. Whether or not the person will continue to follow the map (rule) in the future is dependent on the consequences of following the map in the past. If the rule specified the correct contingencies, he will probably continue to use the map, but if the person found the map to be in error, then he will probably look to other sources of information (for example, asking someone with private knowledge).

The same sort of thing happens in industry. If a manager is correct in the specification of the rules—that is, the new worker follows the rules and receives a reward—then the worker will probably follow the other rules specified by the manager. If the manager specifies incorrect rules, then the worker may look to his peers or to other sources for information (for example, the union steward) for the specification of rules which describe behavior that will be rewarded.

There are two kinds of rules that the manager can specify to the employee. A command or *mand* is a rule that specifies behavior and consequences of the behavior, where the consequences are arranged by the person giving the command. The specified or implied consequences for failure to act are usually aversive in nature, and the judgment of the correctness of the behavior is made by the person giving the command. A supervisor who tells the worker to be on time for work is giving the worker a command. The implied consequence is that if the employee fails to report on time, the supervisor will take action.

Advice and warnings, called *tacts*, involve rules which specify the reinforcements contingent on prior stimulation from rules, or laws. They specify the same contingencies which would directly shape behavior (private knowledge). The specification of a tact speeds up the conditioning process. If a secretary tells the boss that he should take an umbrella when he goes to lunch, the secretary is tacting. The secretary has no control over the consequences (getting wet) of the behavior (not carrying the umbrella). Those are determined by the environment itself (the weather). Skinner (1969) says:

> *Go west, young man* is an example of advice (tacting) when the behavior it specifies will be reinforced by certain consequences which do not result from action taken by the advisor. We tend to follow advice because previous behavior in response to similar verbal stimuli has been reinforced. *Go west, young man* is a command when some consequences of the specified action are arranged by the commander—say, the aversive consequences arranged by an official charged with relocating the inhabitants of a region. When maxims, rules, and laws are advice, the governed behavior is reinforced by consequences which might have shaped the same behavior directly in the absence of the maxims, rules, and laws. When they are commands, they are effective only because special reinforcements have been made contingent upon them. (Skinner, 1969, p. 148)

Although a manager must possess public knowledge as well as private knowledge in order to accomplish his task of "getting things done through other people," in keeping with a plea for positive reinforcement and unbiased reward systems, tacting is the method of rule specification recommended. Skinner (1969) argues that by specifying the contingencies in such a way that the consequences are positive in nature and that failure to respond is met with the withholding of a reward rather than with aversive stimuli, "the 'mand' may be replaced by a 'tact' describing conditions under which specific behavior on the part of the listener will be reinforced" (p. 158). Instead of saying "Give me that report," say "I need the report." "The craftsman begins by ordering his apprentice to behave in a given way; but he may later achieve the same effect simply by describing the relation between what the apprentice does and the consequences" (Skinner, 1969, p. 158). Thus, the technique managers use to direct the employee can make a lot of difference in the acceptance of the rule by the employee. A mand operates from an avoidance learning base while a tact operates from a positive reinforcement base. A tact is more impersonal and gives the employee freedom in that it does not "enjoin anyone to behave in a given way, it simply describes the contingencies under which certain kinds of behavior will have certain kinds of consequences" (Skinner, 1969, p. 158).

CONTROVERSIES SURROUNDING A SKINNERIAN APPROACH TO MANAGEMENT

The reinforcement approach to the study and control of human behavior has met with resistance and criticism, primarily because of a lack of understanding of its recommended uses and limitations. Goodman (1964) wrote, "To be candid, I think operant-conditioning is vastly overrated." Henry (1964) said, "Learning theory has two simple points to make and does so with talmudic ingenuity, variability, intricacy, and insistence. They are reinforcement and extinction. What has to be left out . . . is thought."

Although the criticisms are too numerous to mention here, an attempt will be made to examine three of the major objections that have been advocated against an operant approach to the management of people in organizational settings.

1. *The application of operant conditioning techniques ignores the individuality of man.* Ashby (1967) said, "Now the chief weakness of programmed instruction is that it rewards rote learning, and worse than that—it rewards only those responses which are in agreement with the programme." Proponents of an operant approach to contingency management recognize that a *poorly* designed program can lead to rigidity in behavior. This is one of the major reasons that they recommend a program of reinforcement which best fits the group or the individuals being supervised. It is *untrue*, however, that Skinner and his followers ignore the individuality of people. Each person is unique because of past reinforcement history. When personnel psychologists build sophisticated selection models to predict future performance, they are actually trying to identify those applicants who will perform well under the contingencies of a particular organization. This does not mean that a rejected person cannot be motivated; it only means that the current contingencies of a particular organization are better suited to another applicant [3]

In other words, the problem a manager faces is not to design contingencies that will be liked by all men, "but a way of life which will be liked by those who live it" (Skinner, 1969, p. 41). As Hersey and Blanchard (1972) point out, "Positive reinforcement is anything that is rewarding to the individual being reinforced. Reinforcement, therefore, depends on the individual" (p. 22). What is reinforcing to one person may not be reinforcing to another person because of the latter's past history of satiation, deprivation, and conditioning operations. A manager can do two things to ensure that the contingencies of reinforcement are designed to increase the *individuality* of the worker. First, as noted earlier, he can strive to hire the worker who desires the rewards offered by the firm, that is, the worker who can be happy or satisfied with the firm. Second, if it seems that the contingencies are ineffective, the manager can change the contingencies by using a democratic process—letting the employees design their own reward structure, within the limits set by the organization. "Democracy is

---

[3] This is true because the criterion variable is some measure of performance, and performance is directly tied to the reinforcement consequences for the current employees used to derive the selection model.

an effort to solve the problem by letting the people design the contingencies under which they are to live or—to put it another way—by insisting that the designer himself live under the contingencies he designs" (Skinner, 1969, p. 43).

In summary, therefore, it can be concluded that in a voluntary society, where persons are free to move from one organization to another, operant methods of control need not ignore human individuality. Instead, people should seek work where their individuality can best be appreciated, and industries should select employees who can best be motivated by the contingencies available to them. It should be noted, however, that through the unethical application of conditioning principles, some employers may exploit workers. The overall evidence would seem to indicate that this is not due to the weaknesses of Skinnerian theory but to the weakenesses of human beings.

2. *The application of operant conditioning techniques restricts freedom of choice.*

> Discussion of the moral implications of behavioral control almost always emphasize the Machiavellian role of change agents and the self-protective maneuvers of controllers. . . . The tendency to exaggerate the powers of behavioral control by psychological methods alone, irrespective of willing cooperation by the client, and the failure to recognize the reciprocal nature of interpersonal control obscure both the ethical issues and the nature of the social influence processes. (Bandura, 1969, p. 85)

Kelman (1965) noted that the primary criterion that one might apply in judging the ethical implications of social influence approaches is the degree to which they promote freedom of choice. If individualism is to be guaranteed, it must be tempered by a sense of social obligation on the part of both the individual and the organization.

Bandura (1969) noted that a person is considered free insofar as he can influence future events by managing his own behavior. A person in a voluntary society can, within limits, exert some control over the variables that govern his own choice. Skinner (1969) noted that "men are happy in an environment in which active, productive, and creative behavior is reinforced in effective ways" (p. 64). One method of effectively reinforcing behavior is by allowing the employee some determination in the design of the reinforcement contingencies. Another method is to design self-control reinforcement systems in which individuals regulate their own activities.

Although it cannot be denied that reinforcers which are "all too abundant and powerful" (Skinner, 1969) can restrict freedom of choice, it is not true that a behavioral or Skinnerian approach has that effect. As a matter of fact, just the opposite is true. As Bandura has noted, "Contrary to common belief, behavioral approaches not only support a humanistic morality, but because of their relative effectiveness in establishing self-determination these methods hold much greater promise than traditional procedures for enhancement of behavioral freedom and fulfillment of human capabilities" (p. 88).

3. *Operant theory, through its advocacy of an external reward system, ignores the fact that individuals can be motivated by the job itself.* Deci (1971), 1972), among others, criticizes behaviorists for advocating a system of employee motivation that only utilizes externally mediated rewards, that is, rewards such as money and praise administered by someone other than the employee himself. In utilizing such measures, according to Deci, management is attempting to control the employee's behavior so that he will do what he is told. For Deci, the limitations of this method of worker motivation are that it only satisfies the "lower-order" needs (Maslow, 1943) of human beings and does not take into account their "higher-order" needs for self-esteem and self-actualization. Deci states, "It follows that there are many important motivators of human behavior which are not under the direct control of managers and, therefore, cannot be contingently administered in a system of piece-rate payments" (1972, p. 218).

Deci recommends that we move away from a method of external control and toward a system in which individuals can be motivated by the job itself. He says that this approach, in which the rewards are mediated by the employee himself (intrinsically motivated), will allow managers to focus on higher-order needs. To motivate employees intrinsically, tasks should be designed which are interesting and creative and demand resourcefulness, and workers should have some say in decisions which concern them "so they will feel like causal agents in the activities which they engage in" (Deci, 1972, p. 219). He concludes his argument against a contingency approach to management by saying:

> It is possible to pay workers and still have them intrinsically motivated. Hence the writer favors the prescription that we concentrate on structuring situations and jobs to arouse intrinsic motivation, rather than trying to structure piece-rate and other contingency payment schemes. Workers would be intrinsically motivated and would seek to satisfy their higher-order needs through effective performance. The noncontingent payments (or salaries) would help to satisfy the workers and keep them on the job, especially if the pay were equitable. (Deci, 1972, p. 227)

Deci levels four criticisms at a positive reinforcement contingency approach: (1) advocating that rewards be administered externally; (2) ignoring the importance of the task environment; (3) ignoring the importance of internal rewards; and (4) favoring a contingent payment plan. However, only one of these criticisms is applicable to the behaviorist approach—the payment plan, as with an effective reinforcement plan, must be contingent on performance if it is to have a positive effect on behavior. From the standpoint of reinforcement theory, Deci makes two major errors when he advocates noncontingent equitable pay plans. First, equity requires that rewards be based on performance. If they aren't, then the pay is equal, not equitable. Second, and more crucial, is Deci's assumption that a pay plan can be noncontingent. Bandura (1969) notes that "all behavior is inevitably controlled, and the operation of psychological laws cannot be suspended by romantic conceptions of human behavior, any more than indignant rejection of the law of gravity as antihumanistic can stop people from falling" (p. 85). Homme and Tosti (1965) made the point that "either one manages the contingencies or they get managed by accident. Either way there will be contingencies, and they will have their effect" (p. 16). In other words, if managers instituted a pay plan that was "noncontingent," they would, in fact, be rewarding poor performance and extinguishing good performance (see Rules 1, 2, and 6).

Deci's criticism that a contingency approach advocates that rewards always be administered externally is false. Skinner (1969, p. 158) specifically recommended that manding behavior of the type criticized by Deci be replaced by tacting methods for achieving the same effect. Skinner suggested that one safeguard against exploitation is to use "noncontrived" reinforcers and make sure that the designer of the contingencies never controls them. In addition to recommending that contingencies be so designed that they are controlled by the environment (tacting), operant theorists have advocated self-control processes in which individuals regulate their own behavior by arranging appropriate contingencies for themselves. Bandura (1969) concluded:

> *The selection of well-defined objectives,* both intermediate and ultimate, is an essential aspect of any self-directed program of change. The goals that individuals choose for themselves must be specified in sufficiently detailed behavioral terms to provide adequate guidance for the actions that must be taken daily to attain desired outcomes. . . . Individuals can, therefore, utilize *objective records of behavioral changes* as an additional source of reinforcement for their self-controlling behavior. (p. 255)

Studies which have explored the effects of self-reinforcement on performance have shown that allowing workers to keep a record of their own output to use as a continuous feedback system and for reinforcement purposes helped the workers to increase their performance (Kolb, Winter & Berlew, 1968; Fox, 1966). The Michigan Bell Telephone Company and the Emery Air Freight Corporation are among the firms which are currently using self-reinforcement programs in order to increase worker motivation and performance. Both programs have been immensely successful (see Chapter 11).

It should be noted that even though the individual determines his or her own reward in the self-feedback program, the reinforcers are both externally mediated (money, recognition, praise) and internally mediated (self-feedback). According to Skinner (1969) and Bem (1967), the self-report feedback is a tact or description of an internal feeling state. In *both* cases, the rewards must be contingent on performance for effective control of the behavior to take place.

Deci's recommendation that jobs be designed so that they are interesting and creative and demand resourcefulness is wholeheartedly supported by proponents of a positive reinforcement program. Skinner (1969) warns managers that too much dependence on force and a poorly designed monetary reward system may actually reduce performance, whereas designing the task so that it is automatically reinforcing can have positive effects on performance.

As we will discuss later in this book, this means that rewards from the task itself as well as monetary rewards must be considered by a manager in designing a motivating work environment. When a job or task is enjoyable to the person performing the task, the person finds the task *intrinsically* motivating. When a higher level of productivity at that task leads to a higher level of monetary reward than when there is a lower level of productivity, the job is *extrinsically* reinforcing. Whereas Deci recommends that intrinsically motivating jobs are better for people than extrinsically motivating jobs, Skinner recommends (1969, pp. 18–19) that, to be highly motivating, the jobs should be both intrinsically pleasurable as well as extrinsically rewarding.

It is true that there will be times where money will have a negative impact on job motivation. For example, if a person is performing a task out of loyalty or friendship, offering money may be insulting. Likewise overcompensating for a boring or repulsive task may cause resentment of the job even more. What one employee finds repulsive (nonintrinsically motivating) another employee may find challenging and exciting (intrinsically motivating). Therefore, it is important that the manager do two things when designing a motivating work environment: (1) match the person with the job, and (2) make sure that the monetary reward system (such as a piece rate system) is not one that compensates for an extremely negative job.

Skinner (1969) also agrees with Deci that the piece rate may actually reduce performance because it is so powerful that it is most often misused, and "it is generally opposed by those concerned with the welfare of the worker (and by workers themselves when, for example, they set daily quotas)" (p. 19).

It appears, therefore, that the critics of operant conditioning methods misunderstand the recommendations of Skinner and his followers in the area of worker motivation. Skinnerian theory does advocate interesting job design and self-reinforcement feedback systems, where possible. It does not advocate the use of force or trying to control the employee's behavior by making the employee "do what he is told." It is not against humanistic morality. Instead it advocates that workers be rewarded on the basis of their performance and not on the basis of their needs alone.

Although other controversies about operant conditioning could be reviewed, the examination of these three issues should give the reader the flavor of the criticisms and misunderstandings which surround the use of a contingency approach to behavioral control. Most of the legitimate criticisms of operant conditioning stem from the fact that managers have either devised crudely applied incentive programs or have used unethical methods to obtain control over workers.

ETHICAL IMPLICATIONS OF WORKER CONTROL

The deliberate use of positive and negative reinforcers often gives rise to ethical concern about harmful effects which may result from such practices. Poorly designed reward structures can interfere with the development of spontaneity and creativity. Deceptive and manipulative reinforcement systems are an insult to the integrity of human beings. The employee should be a willing party to efforts by the employer to influence him, with both parties benefiting from such efforts.

The question of whether efforts should be made to control human behavior is covered in a classic paper by Rogers and Skinner (1956). The central issue of the paper concerns personal values. Rogers contends that "values" emerge from the individual's "freedom of choice," a realm unavailable to science. Skinner, in rebuttal, points out that the scientific view of man does not allow for such exceptions and that, like all behavior, choice and the resulting values are a function of the individual's biology and environment. Since biology and environment lie within the realm of science, "choice" and "value" must be accessible to scientific inquiry. Skinner and Rogers are both concerned with abuse of the power held by scientists, but Skinner is optimistic that good judgment will continue to prevail. Krasner (1964) agrees with Skinner that we should apply scientific means to control behavior, but warns that behavioral control can be horribly misused unless we are constantly alert to what is taking place in society.

Probably few managers deliberately misuse their power to control behavior. Managers should realize that the mismanagement of the contingencies of reinforcement is actually self-defeating. Workers will no longer allow themselves to be pushed around, but instead will insist that the work environment be designed in such a way that they have a chance at a better life. The effective use of a positive reinforcing program is one of the most critical challenges facing modern management.

The first step in the ethical use of behavioral control in organizations is the understanding by managers of the determinants of behavior. Since reinforcement is the single most important concept in the learning process, managers must learn how to design reinforcement programs that will foster creative, productive, satisfied employees. This chapter has attempted to outline the available knowledge which is needed by managers in this endeavor.

SUMMARY

This chapter has dealt with the basic learning theory approaches to understanding behavior. We have described the differences between classical and instrumental conditioning. Because instrumental conditioning deals with voluntary behavior, it has been given greater attention.

In instrumental or operant conditioning, reinforcement is the critical construct. When behavior is reinforced, there is a change in the likelihood that it will occur again in response to a particular cue. If a behavior is positively reinforced, the probability of its recurrence is increased, but if it is punished, the likelihood that it will recur is decreased.

In this chapter we have also discussed how to increase the probability that an act will recur or fail to recur and when reinforcement should be scheduled. In addition, the chapter contains a set of guidelines for applying the concepts presented in a practical operational context.

CONCEPTS TO REMEMBER

operant behavior	extinction
respondent behavior	discriminative stimulus
classical conditioning	schedules of reinforcement
conditioned stimulus	contingency-shaped behavior
operant conditioning	rule-governed behavior
positive reinforcement	mand
contingency	tact
avoidance learning	

QUESTIONS FOR DISCUSSION

1. In a recent study, bonuses were given to people who planted seedlings for the Weyerheuser Corporation. Most of the planters were older women from rural southern areas with strong moral and religious backgrounds and norms. Those in the first crew were told that in addition to their regular base pay, they would receive a $2 bonus contingent upon planting each bag of seedlings. Those in the second crew were told that they would receive their base pay and a $4 bonus contingent upon planting each bag of seedlings and correctly guessing the outcome of a coin toss. Those in the

third crew were told that they would receive their base pay and an $8 bonus contingent upon planting each bag of seedlings and correctly guessing the outcome of two coin tosses. A fourth, control crew, isolated geographically from the first three, was paid only hourly base wages.

    a. What were the various types of reward schedules used?

    b. What do you predict the results of this study were?

2. If all people are unique, how is it that managers are expected to predict performance? Is this possible? Why or why not?

3. Define the concept of "merit."

4. Distinguish between "manding" and "tacting."

5. Why is a reinforcement approach to work control criticized by many managers and academics?

REFERENCES

Adams, J. S. Inequity in social exchange. In L. Berkowitz (Ed.), *Advances in experimental psychology*. New York: Academic Press, 1965.

Aldis, O. Of pigeons and men. *Harvard Business Review,* July–August 1961, 59–63. Copyright © by the President and Fellows of Harvard College; all rights reserved.

Ashby, E. Can education be machine made? *New Scientist,* February 2, 1967.

Ayllon, T., & Azrin, N. H. The measurement and reinforcement of behavior of psychotics. *Journal of the Experimental Analysis of Behavior,* 1965, *8,* 357–383.

Baer, D. M., Peterson, R. F., & Sherman, J. A. The development of imitation by reinforcing behavioral similarity to a model. *Journal of the Experimental Analysis of Behavior,* 1967, *10,* 405–416.

Bandura, A. *Principles of behavior modification.* New York: Holt, Rinehart and Winston, 1969.

Bandura, A., & Perloff, B. The efficacy of self-monitoring reinforcement systems. *Journal of Personality and Social Psychology,* 1967, *7,* 111–116.

Bass, B. M., & Vaughan, J. A. *Training in industry: The management of learning.* Belmont, Calif.: Wadsworth, 1966.

Behling, O., Schriescheim, C., & Tolliver, J. Present theories and new directions in theories of work effort. (Journal Supplement Abstract Service of the American Psychological Corporation, 1976.)

Bem, D. J. Self-perception: An alternative interpretation of cognitive dissonance phenomena. *Psychological Review,* 1967, *74,* 183–200.

Bridgman, P. W. *The way things are.* Cambridge, Mass.: Harvard University Press, 1959.

Costello, T. W., & Zalkind, S. S. *Psychology in administration.* Englewood Cliffs, N.J.: Prentice-Hall, 1963.

Deci, E. L. The effects of externally mediated rewards on intrinsic motivation. *Journal of Personality and Social Psychology.* 1971, *18,* 105–115.

Deci, E. L.   The effects of contingent and noncontingent rewards and controls on intrinsic motivation. *Organizational Behavior and Human Performance*, 1972, *8*, 217–229.

Ferster, C. B., Nurenberger, J. I., & Levitt, E. B.   The control of eating. *Journal of Mathetics*, 1962, *1*, 87–109.

Ferster, C. B., & Skinner, B. F.   *Schedules of reinforcement.* New York: Appleton-Century-Crofts, 1957.

Festinger, L.   A theory of social comparison processes. *Human Relations*, 1954, *7*, 117–140.

Fox, L.   The use of efficient study habits. In R. Ulrich, T. Stachnik, & J. Mabry (Eds.), *Control of human behavior.* Glenview, Ill.: Scott, Foresman, 1966.

Goffman, E.   *The presentation of self in everyday life.* New York: Doubleday, 1959.

Goodman, P.   *Compulsory mis-education.* New York: Horizon Press, 1964.

Haire, M.   *Psychology in management* (2d ed.). New York: McGraw-Hill, 1964.

Henry, J.   Review of human behavior: An inventory of scientific findings by Bernard Berelson and Gary A. Steiner. *Scientific American,* July 1964.

Hersey, P., & Blanchard, K. H.   The management of change: Part 2. *Training and Development Journal,* February 1972, pp. 20–24.

Homans, G.   *Social behavior: Its elementary forms.* New York: Harcourt, Brace and World, 1961.

Homme, L. E., & Tosti, D. T.   Contingency management and motivation. *Journal of the National Society for Programmed Instruction,* 1965, *4*, 14–16.

Jablonsky, S., & DeVries, D.   Operant conditioning principles extrapolated to the theory of management. *Organizational Behavior and Human Performance,* 1972, *7*, 340–358.

Kelman, H. C.   Manipulation of human behavior: An ethical dilemma for the social scientist. *Journal of Social Issues,* 1965, *21*, 31–46.

Kolb, D. A., Winter, S. K., & Berlew, D. E.   Self-directed change: Two studies. *Journal of Applied Behavioral Science,* 1968, *4*, 453–471.

Krasner, L.   Behavior control and social responsibility. *American Psychologist,* 1964, *17*, 199–204.

Likert, R.   *New Patterns of Management.* New York: McGraw-Hill, 1961.

Lovaas, O. I., Berberich, J. P., Perloff, B. F., & Schaeffer, B.   Acquisition of imitative speech for schizophrenic children. *Science,* 1966, *151*, 705–707.

Luthans, F.   *Organizational behavior.* New York: McGraw-Hill, 1973.

Michael, J., & Meyerson, L.   A behavioral approach to counseling and guidance. *Harvard Educational Review,* 1962, *32*, 382–402.

Pavlov, I. P.   *The work of the digestive glands.* (W. H. Thompson, Trans.) London: Charles Griffin, 1902.

Polanyi, M.   *Personal knowledge.* Chicago: University of Chicago Press, 1960.

Rachlin, H.   *Modern behaviorism.* New York: Freeman, 1970.

Rogers, Carl R., & Skinner, B. F.   Some issues concerning the control of human behavior: A symposium. *Science,* 1956, *124*, 1057–1066.

Scott, W. E.   Activation theory and task design, *Organizational behavior and human performance,* 1966, *1,* 3–30.

Skinner, B. F.   *The behavior of organisms.* New York: Appleton-Century, 1938.

Skinner, B. F.   *Science and human behavior.* New York: Macmillan, 1953.

Skinner, B. F.   *Contingencies of reinforcement: A theoretical analysis,* © 1969. Reprinted by permission of Prentice-Hall, Inc., Englewood Cliffs, New Jersey.

Thorndike, E. L.   *Animal intelligence.* New York: Macmillan, 1911.

Tosi, H. L. & Hamner, W. C. (Eds.).   *Organizational behavior and human performance: A contingency approach.* Chicago: St. Clair Press, 1974.

Vroom, V. H., & Deci, E. L.   An overview of work motivation. In V. H. Vroom & E. L. Deci (Eds.), *Management and motivation.* Baltimore: Penguin Books, 1970, 9–19.

Punishment and discipline in organizations

What are the pros and cons of using punishment to eliminate undesired behavior?

What is the process by which punishment affects behavior?

Under what conditions is punishment most likely to have desirable effects on behavior?

It is remarkable how little is written or said about the topic of punishment in organizational settings. About the only attention the topic receives in textbooks is either a brief denunciation of its use, after lengthy description of the "positive approach" of using rewards and motivators, or, in personnel texts, a discussion of the implications of disciplinary actions for management-union relationships. Extended discussions about job motivation illustrate the methods of *eliciting desired* behavior but lead one to forget that organizations also have the task of *eliminating undesired* behavior.

Yet surely punishment and disciplinary measures are, in fact, very frequently used in organizations. For many first-line supervisors and managers who have little control over organizational rewards (such as salary raises, promotions, and benefits), punishment and discipline (or their threat) are the most immediately available tools for shaping the behavior of subordinates. Indeed, one could plausibly argue that, day in and day out, punishment is used (whether intentionally or unintentionally, effectively or ineffectively) far more often than reward in attempts to influence behavior.

Why, then, the relative silence on this seemingly important topic? There are probably several reasons. First of all, punishment is a rather controversial topic. Few people debate the issue of whether to reward people for good behavior or performance, but heated arguments are touched off by the question of whether to punish ineffective or undesirable behavior. This controversy is reflected in popular discussions about child-rearing, the penal system, our "permissive" society, and even in theoretical dialogues among psychologists. Second, punishment is not as pleasant a topic as rewards or positive reinforcement. It tends to suggest or connote problems, disagreements, tensions, tyranny, and a host of other unpleasant things. Finally, as we shall soon see, punishment is considerably more complex and unpredictable than rewards in its effects on behavior. There are more qualifications that have to be specified before the general application of punishment can be predicted to have a beneficial, undesirable, or perhaps inconsequential effect on behavior.

PUNISHMENT AND DISCIPLINE DEFINED

As you recall from Chapter 3, punishment can be defined as the presentation of an aversive consequence contingent upon a certain response in a certain set of stimulus conditions:

$$S \rightarrow R \rightarrow R^-$$

Here S refers to the stimulus situation in which the undesired behavior occurs (most types of behavior are not regarded as absolutely "good" or "bad" but as "good" or "bad" depending on the time and place);

R is the unwanted behavior ("unwanted" from the perspective of the controlling agent, for example, the manager); and R⁻ is the aversive consequence—such as a verbal rebuke, an official reprimand, suspension, loss of privileges, or even a stern gaze.

Discipline is an official organizational attempt to punish. By "official" we mean recorded, documented, or specified by formal organizational policies and procedures. Thus punishment and discipline are not necessarily one and the same. A manager's verbal rebuke to a tardy employee may be aversive to the latter, but the incident is an informal use of punishment and not *discipline* in the sense that we have defined the term. On the other hand, some so-called disciplinary measures may not be aversive at all. For example, in some organizations (particularly those with unions), excessive unexcused absenteeism is "disciplined" by suspending the individual from work for a few days—the person is disciplined for what he did by having him do more of it! The discipline is presumably not too aversive, since the person was already freely doing what he is now compelled to do.

THE PSYCHOLOGICAL DYNAMICS OF PUNISHMENT

Psychologists are in general agreement about the *process* by which punishment affects behavior, even though they disagree about the desirability or utility of the effects. The aversive stimulus becomes classically conditioned to early parts of the undesired response and/or to the stimulus situation in which the undesired response takes place. This classically conditioned association may be labeled fear, guilt, or anxiety. Such feelings are aversive or uncomfortable in themselves, and also act as a cue to "do something"—whether it be to escape (by leaving the situation or terminating the disapproved response), do absolutely nothing (as a way of escape), do something incompatible with the punished response (for example, bite one's lip instead of laughing in a formal, dignified setting), or take measures to prevent punishment from occurring (such as "covering up" one's transgression or lying). The effect of any one of these responses may be to dispel the uncomfortable feelings, and this effect then reinforces whatever one has done in response to the cue produced by unpleasant emotions.

The punishment process is somewhat complex, and because of this there are several points in the process where things can "go wrong" in the sense that the punisher may not produce the effect that was intended. The aversive stimulus may not really be aversive to the person to whom it is applied—as in the case of excessive absenteeism being dealt with by allowing more absenteeism, or of a teacher giving attention to a classroom rowdy who enjoys being in the spotlight before his peers. Or the aversive stimulus may be too late or too mild to generate a strongly associated, classically conditioned emotional response. Or the "punished" person may simply learn to refine the S a bit—to discriminate between situations in which he may be caught and those in which he can respond with impunity. Or the "escape response"—in reaction to the emotional associations—may be far worse than the response for which a person is originally punished. Lying, generalized avoidance of the punisher, counteraggression, fear of doing anything because it may be considered wrong and punishable, can all have serious long-run adverse consequences for organizational functioning.

THE CASE AGAINST PUNISHMENT

Many people, including quite a few psychologists, argue that punishment should be avoided as a means of trying to influence behavior. Their objections to punishment are prompted, at least in part, by humanistic considerations or ideology, but also include the following arguments:

1. For punishment to be at all effective, there must be continued monitoring or surveillance, which is a very wasteful use of high-priced managerial time.

2. Punishment never really extinguishes or eliminates undesirable response tendencies, but only temporarily suppresses them. These tendencies reappear with full force when the threat of punishment is removed.

3. Punishment has undesirable side effects. It may cause resentment and hostility toward the punisher, with a motive of trying to "get even" later through sabotage, output restriction, or doing things that make the punisher "look bad" or cause him inconvenience. The fear associated with the punishing agent may lead the punished person to avoid his very presence; this, in turn, makes it more difficult for the manager to play the desired role of coach, teacher, or counselor. Or the reaction to punishment may be more extreme, resulting in generalized inhibition and rigidity or stereotyped behavior in the punished person; this can make it more difficult for the person to learn new behavior, including very desirable behavior, or to adapt to change.

If punishment is so ineffective in changing behavior and has such undesirable side effects, why, then, do people make so much use of it? Why haven't they learned over the centuries to make more frequent use of other methods in place of punishment? Skinner (1953) believes that punishment is still used mainly for one reason: its use is reinforcing to the punisher. Since the application of an aversive stimulus does *immediately, although temporarily,* suppress the undesired behavior which is noxious to the punisher or controlling agent, the punisher himself is reinforced in an "escape learning" sort of process. Since the immediate consequences of one's behavior are the most influential in shaping it, the punisher continues to punish when confronted by subordinate behavior that is disapproved.

One could also argue that if the controlling agent feels angry and frustrated by subordinate performance, the act of punishment may be reinforcing to the agent by letting him "blow off steam" and ventilate his feelings; that punishment gives some people a feeling of power, which is reinforcing; and that in many cases punishment is the "easiest" thing to do, since it does not require a great deal of thought.

If punishment is to be avoided, what do the critics suggest that we use in its place? They offer several possibilities:

1. Try extinction. Find out what reinforcers (sometimes subtle ones) are sustaining the undesired behavior. What does he "get from doing that"? The unruly pupil or subordinate may be getting praise and recognition from peers. Then get those peers to cooperate with you (sometimes easier said than done) by ignoring the unruly behavior. When such behavior is not reinforced, it will eventually lose strength and extinguish.

2. Use environmental engineering—rearrange the features of the environment so that the stimulus situation doesn't evoke the undesired response but some other response.

Skinner (1953) tells the story of a manager who had a traffic problem caused by women hurrying down the corridor as soon as the end of the workday was signaled. The manager solved his problem by placing wall mirrors along the corridor. The stimulus situation that had evoked stampeding down the hallway was transformed into one which encouraged a more leisurely and orderly walk-and-stop sequence.

One of the authors was once in a cafeteria and had to use the rest room facilities while waiting for lunch to be prepared. On the inside of the door to the toilet stall was a small blackboard, with a piece of chalk attached by a string. Apparently, the owner was trying to use environmental engineering to encourage behavior less costly and troublesome than the usual obscene graffiti semipermanently etched on the walls and doors.

3. Along lines similar to the strategy offered above, reward either desirable or neutral behavior which is *physically incompatible* with the undesired behavior. If children are rewarded for exercising or for performing light outdoor chores before dinner, they are prevented from excessive snacking and TV-watching.

4. Simply allow adjustment, development, or maturation to take its course. With biological maturation, young children eventually learn not to throw fragile objects, cry, or wet the bed; punishing such behavior may not speed up this process at all, and may cause emotional problems if it is applied to behavior over which the child has insufficient biological control or discrimination. Similarly, new or inexperienced employees make many mistakes and do many wrong things that they

will learn to avoid, given a reasonable period of adjustment; punishment may not hasten this process, and if it causes undue anxiety, it can actually retard the process.

These, then, are the suggested alternatives to the wholesale use of aversive control. Skinner's novel, *Walden Two,* presents a vision of a utopian society in which punishment has been made obsolete by the effective use of nonaversive procedures.

REBUTTAL TO THE CASE AGAINST PUNISHMENT

It has probably already occurred to the reader that, however desirable the use of nonaversive control may be, there are nevertheless some possible weaknesses in the case against punishment.

1. As Bandura (1969) points out, much of our healthy behavior is in fact acquired due to *naturally punishing* contingencies. We learn how to ride a bike, not to run on slick floors, not to drive fast on icy roads, not to wear heavy clothing in the summer, not to run immediately after a heavy meal, all because nature punishes us. Furthermore, we learn these things rather quickly and without any resultant emotional scars, hang-ups, or neuroses. Apparently, then, nature uses punishment very effectively, and as we shall soon see, there may be some clues in natural punishments for the effective use of punishment and discipline in organizations.

2. Some of the recommended alternatives to punishment are not always feasible, economical, or equitable. For example, if the undesired behavior is *intrinsically* reinforcing, it will be difficult, if not impossible, to use the extinction procedure. There is no way you can allow the response to occur without its being reinforced. If a kid plays with matches or a worker goes to sleep on the night shift, it is hard to imagine how these things can be allowed to occur in the absence of reinforcement, for in a sense such activities are *their own* reinforcement. Rearrangement of the physical environment may be out of the question due to technological constraints or economic considerations. Singling out the frequent offender and rewarding him for doing other things may appear inequitable to the majority of subordinates who have been conscientious all along. And the maturation or adjustment period may simply take too long for the manager who is pressed for immediate results.

FACTORS DETERMINING WHETHER PUNISHMENT IS EFFECTIVE

Solomon (1964) contends that the critics of punishment have sometimes been too dogmatic in their denunciation of its use. While punishment *may* sometimes be ineffective in changing behavior or may produce unwanted by-products, there is nevertheless considerable evidence that punishment *can* be an effective tool *under certain con-ditions.* What are the conditions which make for efficacious punishment?

1. Punishment is more effective if it is applied before an undesired response has been allowed to gain strength. The longer an undesired response is allowed to occur unpunished, the stronger it becomes, and thus the more resistant it becomes to *any* method of behavioral control. The irony is that many well-intentioned managers will "look the other way," or "try to be patient," or forestall any kind of confrontation, when they witness a rule violation. Their hope is that "things will take care of themselves" and that the subordinate will stop doing it. When the subordinate doesn't stop but persists in repeating the offense, the manager finally runs out of patience and "moves in" to correct the situation with discipline. Unfortunately, the offense may now be a strongly ingrained response and highly resistant to external control. The manager should have "moved in" earlier.

2. Other things equal, punishment is generally more effective when it is *relatively intense* and *quick,* that is, administered as soon after the undesired response as possible. When punishment is applied in a program of gradually increasing intensity, people can adapt to the punishment. Ironically, many official disciplinary programs—well intentioned and apparently based on very humanitarian considerations—begin with very mild and sometimes delayed punishment, with gradually severer punishment (culminating in dismissal) after repeated occurrences of the offense. This may be much less effective (and ultimately less humanitarian) than moderately severe punishment of early instances of the offense.

Punishment should quickly follow the undesired response in order to maximize the association between the behavior and its consequences. The speedier the punishment, the greater information value it has to the recipient and the more it seems like a natural and automatic result of his behavior.

3. Punishment should focus on a specific act, not on the person or on his general patterns of behavior. Punishment should be dispensed in an impersonal manner, not as a means of "revenge" for the manager or as a way of venting his own frustrations. The more impersonal the administration of discipline, the less likely is the person punished to experience the kind of humiliation or rage which strains the relationship between manager and subordinate.

Unfortunately, the tactic frequently used by supervisors—ignoring early offenses, trying to be patient in the hope of preventing an "incident"—almost guarantees that when the offense occurs repeatedly, the manager will finally run out of patience and that when he finally does discipline, he will do so in an emotional, personal manner. He himself is likely to feel resentment at having his patience tried, and discipline then has all the overtones of arbitrariness and pique. No wonder, then, that the person punished feels a need to "even the score" or to reassert his strength and status. On the other hand, if the manager takes some disciplinary action—however mild—when a violation first occurs, he is more apt at that point to be in control of his own emotions and to be able to punish in an impersonal manner.

4. Punishment should be consistent across persons and across time. The more consistently discipline is administered, the less it will appear to be prompted by ulterior motives. Unfortunately, as Rosen and Jerdee (1974) have found, organization officials tend to be inconsistent. They tend to let minor infractions pass unnoticed when things are running smoothly otherwise, when there is a big push to speed up production, or when the supervisor is not experiencing much pressure from above. Also, managers quite understandably (though often regrettably) apply different patterns of enforcement against those with longer job tenure as opposed to those with shorter job tenure, or against employees with hard-to-replace skills as opposed to employees who are easy to replace. The net effect of such selectivity in discipline, whether across persons or time, is that when persons are punished, they believe "It's not what I did, it's who I am." Consequently, it is not surprising that there are unwanted emotional side effects of punishment.

5. Punishment should have information value. In part, this is accomplished when discipline meets the above criteria—is administered following early instances of undesired behavior; follows quickly after such behavior; is intense; is consistent. In addition, disciplinary measures should ideally be accompanied by explanation of why the behavior is not desired, how it can be corrected, and the expected consequences of continued violations (this does not imply that discipline should be carried out either apologetically or threateningly). Again, the importance of supervisors or managers acting *before* losing patience is emphasized: they are better able to make discipline an educational experience if they have control over their own emotions.

Another ingredient of the information value desired in discipline is guidance of the offender into acceptable modes of behavior that will be rewarded. One of the criticisms cited earlier against punishment is that it only suppresses rather than extinguishes unwanted behavior. The answer to this criticism is that punishment can be used to temporarily suppress an unacceptable response in order to create an opportunity for guiding the person into different behavior that will then be strengthened by rewards (Solomon, 1964).

6. Punishment is most effective when it occurs in the context of a warm or nurtured relationship. Among other things, this means that the manager should be a source of rewards (for example, good feedback, friendly interaction) as well as punishment. This offsets the tendency for punishment to cause avoidance of the punishing agent. If the man-

ager's behavior is generally such that it represents <u>fairness and personal</u> <u>consideration and concern for subordinates</u>, and <u>if it is consistent and</u> <u>focused on people's specific responses rather than their personalities</u> or their general worth as human beings or employees, punishment is less likely to cause festering emotional problems.

7. <u>Punishment should *not* be followed by *noncontingent rewards*.</u> How often have you seen a parent discipline a small child, then feel remorse when the kid cries, and end up showering the tot with all manner of goodies to assuage the remorse? This is, of course, especially likely to happen when the person doing the disciplining does so in an emotionally aroused state. The person probably feels more guilty about his or her manner of punishing than about the punishment itself. In any case, when noncontingent reinforcers systematically follow punishment, the punishment can have the effect of strengthening the very behavior it was designed to weaken—because the aversive stimulus can become a conditioned reinforcer by virtue of its temporal relationship with other reinforcers.

THE "HOT STOVE RULE"

Much of what we have said about the factors maximizing the effectiveness of punishment can be summarized in Douglas McGregor's "Hot Stove Rule" of discipline (see Strauss and Sayles, 1967). McGregor observed that nature, as we noted earlier in this chapter, seems to apply punishment very effectively to our behavior. We learn quickly from nature, and we learn without serious emotional problems. If we get too close to the hot stove and accidentally touch it, the reaction is immediate. What is it about the hot stove that makes it such a good teacher? It is <u>swift</u>: the association between our behavior and its consequences is undeniable. It is <u>relatively intense on the very first instance</u> of our improper response. It is <u>impersonal</u>: the hot stove has nothing against us as persons and doesn't lose its temper; our behavior, our specific response, is singled out. The hot stove is unerringly <u>consistent</u>: regardless of who touches it or when, the result is the same. Finally, <u>an alternative response is available</u>: move away from the stove.

The point, then, is to strive to emulate nature in carrying out disciplinary measures.

THE IMPORTANCE OF EXPLAINING THE RULES

A study by Walters and Cheyne (1966) demonstrates that *cognitive structuring*—providing a clear, cogent rationale for the punishment contingencies—determines to a great extent the effectiveness of punishment procedures. In their study, 84 first-grade boys were given some toys to play with. Some of the boys were told beforehand that there were some toys they should not handle; others *were given reasons* why they should not play with them. In addition, the boys were punished either "early," as soon as they began to reach for the prohibited toys, or "late," three seconds after they had picked a prohibited toy off the table. The intensity of the punishment was also varied: the punishment was either a 54-decibel noise or a 96-decibel noise. When *no* cognitive structuring had been provided—when no reasons were given why the boys should refrain from playing with certain toys— then late punishment or low-intensity punishment had little effect on the subjects' behavior, compared to early/high-intensity punishment. However, when cognitive structuring had been provided, even late/ low-intensity punishment was highly effective.

The implications of the Walters-Cheyne study for punishment in organizational settings should be obvious. High-intensity punishment is often ruled out for practical reasons arising from labor contracts, legal constraints, and other factors; in addition, there are numerous reasons why punishment cannot be administered as quickly as theory would suggest. It becomes all the more important, then, for administrators to provide, in advance, clear and persuasive reasons why certain rules exist or why certain behaviors cannot be tolerated. If this step is taken, the study by Walters and Cheyne suggests that mild, delayed aversive stimuli can be quite effective in reducing the frequency of undesired responses.

CASE STUDY

In an article published in the *Harvard Business Review* in 1964, John Huberman recounts the experiences of a large plywood mill with disciplinary measures. His narrative nicely illustrates some of the points discussed above. The company had originally been a small one, but over a period of years it experienced a gradual increase in the size of its operations and in its work force. As increased size led to greater distance between top management and first-line foremen, many policy issues became uncertain. One of these was the issue of how to deal with work performance and disciplinary matters.

1. As a result of the uncertainty, foremen had a "tendency to delay action." They would "let minor infringements of the rules go by." Presumably, their underlying motive was to avoid unnecessary confrontations in the hope that their benign inaction would be appreciated and reciprocated with good behavior. Of course, the opposite effect occurred. "A few individuals . . . would then start to test just how far they could go."

2. "After several annoying incidents, a foreman would get sufficiently angry to decide on immediate discharge." When failure to discipline early offenses led to repeated offenses, the foreman lost patience

and felt personally wronged; when he finally took disciplinary action, he did so without having control over his own emotions. Predictably, the reaction of the individual being disciplined (usually he was reinstated with no loss of benefits, since the union successfully contested the suspension or discharge) was by this time certainly not one of mending his ways but an altogether different reaction.

3. "Vigilant supervision was required to make sure that the . . . individual [who had been disciplined] would not act out his annoyance over the punishment by lowering production or quality. . . . Upon return from suspension, the man obviously had to save face . . . to inform everyone how pleasantly and usefully he spent the 'time off.'" The disciplined person sought vengeance at being treated in a way he perceived as arbitrary, personal, and capricious. Discipline was non-contingently followed by reinforcement: first, from the union, in the form of full benefits and, in effect, a paid vacation; and later from being able to tell peers how he had given the company its come-uppance.

Eventually the company turned to a program that Huberman calls "discipline without punishment." Actually, the program was more like "punishment without discipline." Essentially it was a series of steps involving, on a first offense, a casual reminder and a note of correction (except for such severe violations as theft and fighting); on a second offense, a discussion with the individual in the foreman's office; on a third offense, a repetition of step two, but with the shift foreman also present and posing questions about alternative placement through vocational counseling provided by the personnel office. If unsatisfactory work behavior persisted, the offender was sent home for the day, with full pay—the latter being an expression of the company's sincere wish to see him become a productive member of the organization. If this measure proved unavailing, any future incident within a reasonably short time period would result in dismissal, not as a punitive act but as a realistic recognition that the individual and the organization did not have a viable relationship with each other.

The results in the first few years following the introduction of this program were considered highly satisfactory by plant management. Only three workers had experienced the fourth stage of being sent home with pay, and no workers had to be terminated (though two of the three left voluntarily a few weeks after returning to work from the suspension).

Several features of the new program should be noted. The program made very clear what steps foremen had to take at each stage of worker violations; they had a definite, company-wide policy to follow. Thus there was no reason for foremen to let early incidents go by without taking some action. The steps could be taken without the need for emotional involvement by the disciplining parties. The basis for re-

venge and one-upmanship was rendered rather hollow by giving suspended workers their day's pay in advance. The possibilities for subsequent noncontingent rewards from the union and peers were largely
eliminated.

And yet the steps prescribed for countering employee infractions
were, in fact, aversive. Being reminded of an offense, conducted to
the boss's office (some unions will not allow this unless the union steward
is also present), counseled to consider other employment possibilities,
sent home (even at cost to the company) are hardly cause for rejoicing.
When your rationale for hostility and recrimination are cut out from
under you, you can focus your negative feelings only on yourself.

STYLES OF DISCIPLINE

Shull and Cummings (1966) found evidence of considerable variation
among managers in their philosophy and style of discipline. The authors
presented a number of executives with a written case in which four
workers all committed the same infraction—arriving late for work for
the third time—but had different lengths of service, previous work
performance records, and reasons for being late. The executives responded to the question of whom they would dock (the plant rule
was a $5 fine for three late shows within a six-month period) and why.
Some of the respondents—dubbed "pure humanitarian" by the authors—would fine none of the men. Others—the "pure legalistic"—
would follow the rule to the letter, fining all four workers, regardless
of the extenuating circumstances. These two groups accounted for
most of the responses. A few executives, however, believed in a more
clinical or judicial approach to discipline. They seemed to recognize
the need for maintaining standards, but could not accept a mechanical
enforcement of rules, which they regarded primarily as general principles that were not necessarily applicable to every individual case. The
violations were interpreted in the context of the worker's probable
intentions, past service, and the probability of repeated offenses considering what was known about the worker's character.

With such a diversity of managerial codes of justice, it is no wonder
that disciplinary judgments are so frequently matters of controversy.
Depending on one's orientation, one can cite disciplinary precedents
based on *parity* (all violations treated alike, whether all enforced or
all glossed over) or *equity* (a person's outcomes should correspond to
his or her inputs in the form of service, effort, and value). Either standard can be eloquently defended or vigorously challenged, because
our legal system and cultural norms seem to endorse both. Since neither
standard will be universally accepted as fair by all parties, the
administration of discipline is never likely to be a favorite managerial responsibility.

CONCLUDING COMMENT

The reader should not conclude that we are advocating the indiscriminate use of punishment to whip subordinates into shape. As we implied in Chapter 3, wherever and whenever there are feasible alternatives to its use (for example, the positive approach of rewarding acceptable behavior or of changing the conditions which evoke the undesired response), these are much to be preferred to punishment. Punishment, despite the best efforts of well-intentioned managers to follow the principles outlined in this chapter, remains a risky and still unpredictable enterprise because of the complex manner in which aversive stimuli affect behavior.

A basketball coach was asked why he chose to emphasize defense rather than offense. His answer was, "Offense is very complicated, whereas defense is basically simple; and I'm not too smart, so I emphasize the simple things." If a manager keenly feels the limitations of human intelligence in administrative matters, he is well advised to emphasize the "simpler" positive reinforcement strategies (although it often requires considerable thought and planning to discover ways of using the simple methods).

For obvious reasons, empirical research on the effects of punishment on human behavior has been somewhat limited. The professional ethics which govern the conduct of research on human subjects rule out the use of anything but mild, innocuous punishment in experiments. Thus, what we know about the effects of punishment—aside from our naturalistic observations—derives mainly from studies with lower organisms and studies which use mild electric shock, loss of bonus money accumulated during the experimental period, verbal rebuke, or similar aversive stimuli in experiments with children and college students.

Nevertheless, the fact remains that administrators do use punishment and sometimes have to, even if only as a last resort. For some time to come, discipline in organizations is likely to be one of the responsibilities of managers. If the administrator can closely imitate the hot stove, the exercise of discipline can have a constructive effect on the behavior of organization participants and *need not* result in hostility, rigidity, or the alienation of subordinates from organization goals.

SUMMARY

Punishment of a response occurs when the response is followed by aversive consequences. The processes by which punishment affects behavior are quite complex, and thus the overall effects of punishment on behavior are harder to predict than are the effects of reward. Critics of aversive conditioning techniques argue that punishment requires surveillance to be effective, that punishment only suppresses rather than extinguishes undesired response tendencies, and that it frequently causes destructive side effects. These critics suggest that the prevalence of punishment is sustained primarily by its immediate but temporary reinforcement of the punisher. Alternatives to punishment in eliminating undesired behaviors include extinction, environmental engineering, reinforcing competing but acceptable responses, and allowing maturation to occur at its natural pace.

Punishment tends to be more effective when it is applied to weak responses, when the aversive stimulus is relatively intense and quickly follows the response, and when punishment is focused on the act rather than the person, is consistent across time and persons, contains or is accompanied by information, and occurs in the presence of a warm relationship. These conditions are summarized in McGregor's Hot Stove Rule of discipline in organizations.

CONCEPTS TO REMEMBER

Hot Stove Rule

cognitive structuring

pure humanitarian

pure legalistic

clinical/judicial

disciplinary style

parity

equity

QUESTIONS FOR DISCUSSION

1. Some behaviors in organizations are rewarded by one set of reinforcing agents (such as peer groups) and punished by another set of agents (superiors). What determines whether the behaviors in question will be maintained, strengthened, or weakened?

2. Some individuals seem to respond positively (in the desired direction) to disciplinary measures, some negatively, others to "shrug it off." How can we account for these differences?

3. What does the label "permissiveness" as applied to the home, the courts, the schools, or other institutions imply to you? Is an agent who forswears the use of punishment necessarily "permissive"?

4. List examples of how instructors *inadvertently* punish the very behaviors which educational programs are intended to foster.

5. "In the long run, punishment, unlike reinforcement, works to the disadvantage of both the punished organism and the punishing agency" (Skinner, 1953, p. 183). Discuss.

6. Unions, legislation, and the bureaucratization of organizations have limited or proscribed the use of a number of punitive measures by managers. What techniques of punishment—what kinds of aver-

sive stimuli—are generally available to managers? Which of these techniques can be tailored to fit the Hot Stove Rule?

7. *The Case of the New Supervisor.* * (A case study in human relations involving leadership, for discussion and analysis.)

Adam Force had just been appointed supervisor in a plant manufacturing knitted rayon underwear. Before his elevation to the ranks of management, he had been a loom fixer for five years. His work on that job had been of consistently superior caliber.

Except for a little good-natured kidding, Adam's co-workers had wished him well on his new job. And for the first week or two most of them had been cooperative—even helpful—while Adam was adjusting to his supervisory role.

Late Friday afternoon of Adam's second week as a supervisor, a disturbing incident took place. Having just made the rounds of his department, Adam stopped in the men's washroom. There he saw two of his old buddies—Mick and Bob—washing up.

"Say, fellows. You shouldn't be cleaning up this soon. It's at least another 15 minutes until quitting time," said Adam. "Get back on the floor, and I'll forget I saw you in here."

"Come off it, Adam," said Mick. "You used to slip up here early yourself on Fridays. Just because you've got a little rank now, don't think you can get tough with us." To this Adam replied, "Things are different now. Both of you get back on the job, or I'll make trouble." Mick and Bob said nothing more, and they both returned to the shop.

From that time on, Adam began to have trouble as a supervisor. Mick and Bob gave him the silent treatment. The loom operators seemed to forget how to do the simplest things. Every few minutes there was a machine shutdown. By the end of the month, Adam's department was showing the poorest record for production.

REFERENCES

Bandura, A. *Principles of behavior modification.* New York: Holt, Rinehart and Winston, 1969.

Cummings, L. L., & Scott, W. E., Jr. (Eds.). *Readings in organizational behavior and human performance.* Homewood, Ill.: Irwin-Dorsey, 1969.

Huberman, J. Discipline without punishment. *Harvard Business Review,* 1964, *42*, 62–68.

Reese, E. P. *The analysis of human operant behavior.* Dubuque, Iowa: William C. Brown, 1966.

---

* From L. R. Bittel, *What Every Supervisor Should Know,* 3d ed. (New York: McGraw-Hill, 1974), p. 130.

Rosen, B., & Jerdee, T. H.   Factors influencing disciplinary judgments. *Journal of Applied Psychology,* 1974, *59,* 327–331.

Shull, F. A., & Cummings, L. L.   Enforcing the rules—How do managers differ? *Personnel,* 1966, *43,* 33–39.

Skinner, B. F.   *Walden two.* New York: Macmillan, 1948.

Skinner, B. F.   *Science and human behavior.* New York: Macmillan, 1953.

Solomon, R. L.   Punishment. *American Psychologist,* 1964, *19,* 239–253.

Strauss, G., & Sayles, L.   *Personnel: The human problems of management.* Edglewood Cliffs, N.J.: Prentice-Hall, 1967.

Walters, R. H., & Cheyne, J. A.   Some parameters influencing the effects of punishment on social behavior. Paper presented at the Annual Meeting of the American Psychological Association, New York, 1966.

The perceptual process

What is the role of perception in individual behavior?

What are the antecedents and consequences of perception?

How are impressions of other persons formed?

How do perceptual mechanisms influence evaluations of the performance of others?

In Chapters 3 and 4 we discussed how a person's environment shapes his or her behavior. To be technically correct, we should have said that the manner in which a person *perceives* the environment affects his or her behavior.

Perception is a basic cognitive or psychological process. Differences in perceptual frameworks lead people to behave differently in the face of common circumstances. Thus, the study of perception is prerequisite to the understanding and explanation of work behavior in all of its variety and complexity.

In Chapter 3 on learning, the model or framework was based upon the principles of reinforcement contingencies. As you will recall, a reinforcement contingency involves the specification of the setting in which behavior is to take place, the behavior that occurs, and the consequences of the behavior (the $S \rightarrow R \rightarrow R^+$ model). This model can be expanded to include a number of psychological concepts or intervening processes, such as perception: $S \rightarrow O \rightarrow R \rightarrow R^+$. The expanded model is easy to diagram, but the implications are most important. In the expanded model, O represents the processes and variables that lie inside the organism or person, mediating the relation between the environment (S) and the resulting behavior (R). In later chapters, a number of other organismic (O) variables, such as attitudes, motivation, frustration, anxiety, and conflict, will be discussed.

CHARACTERISTICS AND DEFINITION OF PERCEPTION

The world and its reality are what individual people want them to be or make them be. Thus, what is seen through the "eyes of each beholder" is not always isomorphic with the real world. People are not cameras or tape recorders. People do not take in or process exactly what is "out there." Each person wears a different set of "rose-colored glasses." The critical question in the study of perception is: Why is the *same* world viewed *differently* by *different* people? The answer is that, psychologically, the world is *not* the same for different people. As we will discuss in Chapter 7, the relationship between the environment and the response is at least partially determined by individual need states. People selectively perceive those things that will help satisfy their needs. For example, we see what we want or need to see in order to defend ourselves or to advance our aims. We do not see people as they are; we see them for what they mean to us. In a similar vein, Leavitt (1972) suggests that people perceive what they think will help satisfy their needs; ignore what is mildly disturbing; and, again, pay attention to things that they feel or know are dangerous to them.

Perception is defined as *the process by which people organize, interpret, experience, and process cues or material (inputs) received from the external environment.* The characteristics of the object or person being perceived influence how a person receives the cues (the input process); organizes, interprets, and processes the cues received (the storing process); and uses the cues in choosing behavioral responses to the object or person (the output process).

The input process

The process of perception must begin with a consideration of the multitude of cues and stimuli both external and internal to the person that continually affect perceptual interpretations and evaluations, and hence resulting behavior. These input cues and stimuli can be classified into five broad categories.

Input Stimuli 1) A first and obvious input category is the physical *environment.* This category includes the variety of sights, sounds, colors, and physical objects "out there" that provide sensory input cues to the "beholder." From a broader perspective, the environment may also be seen as comprising the business and economic system, the variety of communications media, the direction and control of the governmental system, and the developments and impacts of science and technology. In sum, the environmental situation provides various customs, changes, or factual information for each beholder to interpret and evaluate.

2) A second input category comprises the *opinions, beliefs,* or *"concepts of others"* that the beholder uses to order, classify, and evaluate the people he or she encounters. Every person has or develops certain feelings, assumptions, or judgments concerning the actions of others. Examples of perceptual judgments (often inaccurate) that beholders make while interacting with others include the following: "People with red hair have quick tempers"; "some ethnic groups are lower-class citizens"; "car salesmen are hard to deal with."

3) A third input category concerns the *"concept of self."* Self-concept may be discussed in terms of a centrality of beliefs. As an analogy, picture a smooth body of water. If a stone is dropped into the water, a series of concentric circles appears. The circles are most stable and permanent at the point where the stone first entered the water. Farther and farther away from the center, the circles become less stable, less permanent, and more peripheral. Using this analogy, the most central and stable aspects of self-concept are the primitive self-beliefs. These are the beliefs that say "I am a man," or "I am a woman," or "Today I am 20 years old." These are the things we believe or know to be definite and unchangeable. Next in centrality are ideological beliefs. These include such things as the family unit, the culture, and the political system. Such beliefs are more changeable, although they cannot be changed without difficulty. Beliefs in authority are even farther removed from the central notions. Beliefs which are still more change-

able involve religion, laws, and the immediate society. Last, there are inconsequential beliefs. Such things as jobs, residence, and the clothes people wear are undoubtedly important, but they are relatively easy to change. From this discussion it is clear that self-concept embraces these questions to which all people seek answers: Who am I? What am I? How good am I? In sum, self-concept concerns the moral codes by which people live, the principles upon which people act, and the core beliefs that provide people with a sense of individuality.

Perceiving oneself accurately may be the first step in being able to judge other people accurately. As Leavitt (1972) noted, "One of the things we perceive is ourselves and other people. To protect and enhance ourselves, we try to manipulate the picture other people have of us by putting up a front that will make them think we are what we want to be. The problem of our act, and getting it across successfully, depends mostly on our ability to pick up audience reactions accurately. And accurate audience reactions are hard to come by because the audience is acting too" (p. 27).

The fourth and fifth input categories include motives or goals and past experience. *Motives* or *goals,* discussed in detail in Chapter 7, can be viewed in terms of present circumstances and future orientations. The relevance of past *experience* to the perceptual process has been presented in the discussion of learning and conditioning principles in Chapter 3.

The storing process

In the storing process, the material or cues received in the input process are selected and organized in order to provide the beholder with a degree of perceptual coherence and stability. The selection of cues for input to the perceptual process is dependent upon both the characteristics of stimuli and the personal characteristics of the beholder.

A basic principle of selective perception is that stimuli having relevance, value, or meaning to the beholder are more likely to be attended to than are stimuli that do not have these characteristics. The values of incoming stimuli include the following:

Distinctiveness: A female in a crowd of males is highly visible.

Frequency: Slogans frequently repeated are more likely to be attended to than infrequently mentioned slogans.

Intensity: A shout is more attention-getting than the normal speaking voice.

Movement and change: Animated neon signs are likely to attract more attention than roadside billboards.

Number: The more stimulus objects there are, the greater the selectivity.

Uncertainty: News that OPEC nations will raise oil prices by some undisclosed amount has more impact than does knowledge that gasoline prices will rise by one cent per gallon.

Novelty: A professor who stands on the desk to conduct a lecture is likely to get attention from students because such behavior is unexpected and surprising—even weird.

With respect to the personal characteristics of the beholder, Krech, Crutchfield, and Ballachey (1962) report three conclusions.

1. Personal factors (for example, the capacity to attend to cues during a specified period of time) limit the number of objects that can be perceived at any one moment.
2. Personal factors (for example, a person's prior experience level) selectively sensitize the perceptual mechanism of the individual and lower his or her threshold for recognizing and attending to relevant stimulus objects and aspects of objects.
3. Personal factors (for example, a person's need state) may distort cognitions of relevant objects so that they "fit" the requirements of the individual (p. 21).

The interaction of stimulus characteristics and personal characteristics leads to the development of the cognitive system. Two factors are involved in the organization of the cognitive system. First, there is the grouping of stimuli in terms of proximity in time and space and the similarity or dissimilarity between incoming stimuli and stimuli already existing in the cognitive structure. Second, there is the previous learning history of the individual, which produces interconnections among stimulus events, provides a capacity for assimilating and contrasting perceptions, and allows the individual to organize multiple perceptions in a coherent manner.

Outputs *(attitudes + Opinions + Behaviors.*

The final feature in a theoretical overview of the process of perception concerns the outputs. How do the inputs, selectively organized within a cognitive framework or structure, influence resulting behavior? This question can be addressed, first, in terms of the beliefs or the private feelings that individuals develop and hold while attempting to maintain contact with their reality. On the basis of these beliefs and feelings, attitudes and opinions are expressed to test the accuracy of perceptual interpretations and evaluations of events. A more detailed discussion of attitude formation, development, and change is the subject matter of the next chapter. Finally, there are the social behaviors engaged in as a consequence of what our perceptions "tell us" is appropriate. This final output from the process of perception is the subject matter of the following section on interpersonal perception.

INTERPERSONAL PERCEPTION

The general comments presented on the nature of perception and the theoretical overview of the perceptual process cannot completely answer the question of how one person knows or understands another. Interpersonal relationships begin with the perception of another person, an awareness and appraisal of his or her attributes, intentions, and likely reactions to our actions. Expectations about the actions of others are either confirmed, smoothing the path of social interaction, or disconfirmed, resulting in embarrassment and stress. Interpersonal experiences stimulate efforts to be more realistic in appraising others, with a consequent improvement in judgmental accuracy.

Research in the field of person perception has taken two major directions. First, questions have been raised concerning the process of *knowing* another person—forming an impression and considering the characteristics of both the *perceiver* and the *perceived* and their *situational* interactions. The second focus concerns the accuracy or the *validity* (objective reality) of the judgment and the general ability to be accurate in judging others.

Knowing another person: A theory of inference

Underlying both the process and the judgmental accuracy of interperson perception is a theory of inference. When we form an impression of another person, our initial information is usually incomplete—a grimacing face, a stern rebuke, a phrase ("she's bright" or "he's OK"). These partial bits of evidence generate a host of inferences with varying degrees of certainty. Some inference rules are common to all perceivers and promote a high level of agreement among judges in arriving at a common impression. Other inference rules are unique and private to each perceiver, thereby tending to break down agreement among judges. Secord (1958) offered two compelling reasons to suggest that perceivers must use inference in order to arrive at conclusions concerning a person. First, perceivers are always striving for cues on the basis of which to formulate an internally consistent frame of reference. Second, in a relatively ambiguous situation with respect to the perceived person's covert characteristics, it is expected that perceivers will use whatever cognitive processes are at their command to achieve their goals.

Uniform inference processes

Secord (1958) proposed five inference rules or uniform processes relevant to all perceivers.

1. *Temporal extension:* The perceiver regards a momentary characteristic of the person as if it were an enduring attribute. This uniform process underlies, in varying degrees, virtually all judgments of other persons. Because a person is seen wearing a smile, it is inferred that he is constantly good-natured and easy-going. Because a person is unshaven, it is assumed that he is always careless of his personal appearance. Temporal extension based on limited samples of behavior from different situations often leads to wide discrepancies among judges in perceiving a person.

2. *Parataxis:* The perceiver generalizes from a previous interpersonal situation with a "significant other" to an interpersonal situation with a new person. Because my last boss was friendly and fair to me, I assume that my new boss will also be friendly and fair to me. Attributes belonging to the significant other are perceived in the new person whether or not they are appropriate. More often than not, the perception does not fit the new person.

3. *Categorization:* The perceiver uses cues to place the person in a category with which the perceiver associates certain personality attributes. Because of the person's accent, it appears that he is French. Since the perceiver believes that Frenchmen are amorous and love wine, the perceiver attributes these characteristics to the person. This is the basic process in stereotyping. Categorization may lead to error because of false stereotypes, or it may help in deriving an accurate judgment if stereotypes are well founded.

4. *Functional inference:* The perceiver infers that some aspect of the person functions in a particular manner, and from this the perceiver assumes that the person possesses an associated attribute. Because a person is a good organizer, he must be a good leader. Because a person has already shown a few favorable (or unfavorable) characteristics, even more favorable (or unfavorable) characteristics are attributed to him. This is the basic process operating in what is known as the "halo effect."

5. *Metaphorical generalization* (inference through analogy): The perceiver makes an abstract generalization based upon an analogy between some denotable characteristic of the person and a personality attribute. If the person has cold blue eyes, she must be cold and insensitive. A jutting chin makes its owner belligerent. If the person is a poor dresser, he must be uncouth.

Allport (1961) has compiled the following list of some uniform processes or judgmental tendencies that people have about others. Can you relate these examples to Secord's five rules?

Faces with wrinkles at the eye corners are seen as friendly, humorous and easy-going. People wearing spectacles are perceived as studious and industrious ("they have strained their eyes through study"). Those with high foreheads are seen as more intelligent and dependable ("they have more room for brains"). Women with thicker than average lips are considered sexy, those with thin lips asexual. Facial expression, gesture, posture in sitting and standing, and even the firmness or flabbiness of a handshake convey information from which judges make broad generalizations. Long faces are considered sad; smiling faces are considered intelligent.

Allport, with tongue in cheek, suggests that if you are applying for a job you should submit a smiling photograph and that if you are an employer you should pay no attention to it. A pair of "wide, intelligent" eyes could also be helpful in landing a job. Voice "qualities," such as timbre, inflection, and stress, provide information about the speaker's state of confidence or nervousness. Perhaps with some justification, people who have a high proportion of personal pronouns in their speech are regarded as self-centered. With little justification, people with loud, powerful voices are considered persuasive. There is a high degree of agreement in the expression of stereotypes about ethnic groups, professions, and classes of people. The Italians are regarded as artistic and impulsive, the Irish as pugnacious and quick-tempered. Fat men are jolly; older women are motherly; dark and swarthy people are villainous; and Chinese are inscrutable.

Idiosyncratic processes

In contrast to uniform inference rules, which are common to most people, idiosyncratic inference processes are based on personal generalizations derived from experiences that "fit in" with an individual's views of the world. Mann (1969) discusses two major idiosyncratic inference processes. The first he labels *implicit personality theory*. The perceiver has a "theory" about what other people are like. Perceivers are widely different in their implicit personality "theories," or their assumptions about human behavior. For example, the belief that short people have inferiority complexes leads to the subsequent inference that Mickey Rooney and all midget wrestlers must have inferiority complexes. The assumption that redheaded women are aggressive is another example of an implicit "theory" of personality. Mann labels the second idiosyncratic inference process *response set* (general evaluative set). In appraising others, perceivers have the tendency to respond favorably or unfavorably, to be hard or soft. Depending upon his opinions about human nature, the perceiver's response set determines whether he looks for socially desirable or undesirable traits in others and whether his judgment is lenient or harsh.

THE VALIDITY OF JUDGMENTS OF OTHERS

We have noted that the accuracy of judgments of others depends on (1) the characteristics of the person being judged, (2) the characteristics of the person doing the judging, and (3) the situation or environment in which the judgment takes place.

Characteristics of the person being judged

Several characteristics of the person being judged can bias our evaluations or perceptions. The physical appearance of the person, whom the person reminds us of, the attitudes expressed by the person, the race and sex of the person, the physical characteristics of the person, and our prior knowledge about the person can play an important role in how we "perceive" and thus evaluate the person.

Through stereotyping we learn shortcuts for classifying people. Often these stereotypes are taught to us in school. For example, in a 1917 edition of *The Circle of Knowledge* (Ruoff, 1917), a well-respected resource book of its day, we learn that the temperaments of people vary according to their race. This work contained the following observations about racial temperament:

Caucasian or white race: Serious, steadfast, solid in the North; fiery, impulsive, fickle in the South; active, enterprising, imaginative everywhere; science, art, and letters highly developed.

Mongolian or yellow race: Sluggish, somewhat sullen, with little initiative but great endurance; generally frugal and thrifty; moral standards low; little science; art and letters moderately developed.

Negro or black race: Sensuous, indolent, improvident, fitful, passing lazily from comedy to tragedy; little sense of dignity, hence easily enslaved; slight mental development after puberty.

American or red race: Moody, taciturn, wary, impassive in presence of strangers; science and letters slightly developed, art moderately developed (p. 275).

In a management text of the same period (Fish, 1920), we learn that the stereotyping of women as managers was equally simplistic. Fish noted:

There is always a class of women who are man-crazy and who will go into shops or any other places where the chances of picking up an acquaintance seem good, but there is nothing to indicate that this number is increased by the fact that they go into shops. In fact, the greater danger is that good girls will be unjustly given a bad name. . . .

Another topic which always comes up is that of the sex of the foreman. It seems natural to the masculine mind that a room filled with women workers should have a woman as a foreman. This is the custom in some industries but not in many, for it seems to be a fairly well-established fact that women prefer to work under a man rather than one of their sex. Whether this is because they expect to be able to fool him more effectively in case of necessity or whether it is aversion to see another woman outrank them is a question. . . .

A matron [female supervisor] should be a woman in whom the other women in the shop have confidence. She must not be the "doll" type and yet she should not be so homely that the other girls will say, "If working in this shop makes women look like *that* I'll work somewhere else.". . .

The matron should not be responsible to the foreman, though she should cooperate with him so far as he will allow her to do so. She should not cooperate to the extent of trying to transmit his orders and directions to the girls. If he appears to be having trouble making them understand, she might "listen in" and find out why they do not understand or if they are bluffing him. All cases of illness should come through her hands, though accident cases should not wait for her. Many of these cases are mental disturbances only and can be cured by a few minutes' rest and being let alone. A Christian Scientist would make an excellent matron if she could only realize that the laws of chemistry are just as much laws of nature as the laws of the mind. Whether there are such Christian Scientists or not the author does not know. (pp. 149–153)

We know that many of these stereotypes have vanished from our teachings, and in fact most organizations are vigorously pursuing women and minorities for managerial positions. Yet, even in current management and personnel textbooks (for example, see Miner, 1969) we still find perceptual judgments of this nature being made. Miner for example notes:

Finally a very important difference between the sexes occurs in the area of emotional adjustment. There is good reason to believe that many more women than men experience emotional distress. (p. 16)

The highest level of ability [among blacks] has constantly been found in the three West Coast states. Other areas of the country do not appear to differ a great deal, except for the Deep South, where studies have repeatedly indicated that the general level of intelligence is well below the national average. (p. 22)

The traits identified as typical of Southern Negroes seemed to suggest considerable personality disorganization. (p. 24)

The incidence of emotional disorders among Negroes does appear to be considerably higher than for whites. Even more important from the personnel viewpoint, a great many more cases go untreated and remain in the labor force. (p. 25)

We hope that present-day students of personnel and organizational behavior are able to see that many of the stereotypes held of people are based on studies whose results are group averages which say nothing about particular individuals. In addition, many of the statements discussed here use old sources as a basis of support and are descriptive in nature.

The judge

There are two different types of ability to judge others. As Mann (1969) has suggested, one is the "sensitivity to the generalized other" which is based on knowledge of general behavior in people. This ability involves accuracy in perceiving social norms and major social trends, such as the public's preferences in food, music, and fashions and its attitudes and moods. A second, independent ability has been termed "interpersonal sensitivity." This is the ability to perceive how a given person feels in a specific situation. A person possessing this ability is usually described as "a good judge of people" or "able to read character." Sensitivity in judging specific individuals is of major interest to managers, as we will show in our discussion of judging performance.

Our own values, needs, expectations, attitudes, past experience, and personality play a part in how we judge other people, independently in many cases of the actual performance of the person being judged. If, for example, a person whom you respect tells you something positive about a person you have not met previously, you would probably tend to rate that person higher than you would have had you not had this prior information.

Costello and Zalkind (1963) note that our own strengths and weaknesses play a role in how we meet other people. For example, people with "authoritarian" tendencies are more likely to view others in terms of power and are less sensitive to the psychological or personality characteristics of other people than are nonauthoritarians. Alas, the relatively few categories we use in describing other people tend to be the same ones we use in describing ourselves. Thus, in forming impressions of others, we place excessive stress on traits that are important to us. For example, we see more problems in other people in those areas in which we ourselves are more insecure. We are more likely to like those who have the traits we accept in ourselves, and to reject those who have the traits we do not like in ourselves.

The situation

A third major factor which determines how we perceive other people is the situation in which we perceive them. If we meet a person at church, we are probably going to judge the person differently than if we meet him or her at the racetrack. If we meet a person in the company of a high-status individual, we are likely to judge the person differently than if we meet him or her in the company of a poorly regarded individual. If we interact with a person for the first time in a competitive situation, we will probably judge the person differently than if we meet him or her in a cooperative situation. The reason for these situational effects, of course, is that people are accustomed to showing only selective parts of their personality or behavioral repertoire in specific situations. The perceiver, nevertheless, is apt to generalize from such situationally bound observations and to infer that the behavior shown reflects more durable traits and tendencies.

SHORTCUTS USED IN JUDGING OTHERS

As we have noted, we tend to use perceptual shortcut techniques or rules to help us reduce the data we receive. The use of these rules, sometimes called perceptual sets, generally produces a tendency not only to judge persons in a particular, predictable way but also to behave toward those persons in a particular, predictable way. Many of the rules have been discussed earlier in this chapter. They include such devices as stereotyping, halo effect, expectancy, projection, selective perception, and perceptual defense. Before we present the positive and negative implications of these shortcuts, let us consider these devices.

Stereotyping. As discussed in the last section, stereotyping is evaluating an individual on the basis of our perception of the group to which he or she belongs.

Halo effect. This is the process of using one favorable or unfavorable trait to color everything we know about a person. Asch (1946) was one of the first to demonstrate that judges are influenced by certain salient traits of the person being judged. In one experiment, Asch read a list of character traits to two groups of students. The list was identical for both groups, except that the term *warm* was used with one group and the term *cold* with the other. The following words were used: intelligent, skillful, industrious, *warm*, determined, practical, cautious. The students in each group, after having heard the list of descriptive adjectives, wrote a brief sketch of the person described and then selected from 18 pairs of different adjectives the one of each pair that they thought best described the person. The results indicated that the "warm" group wrote more positive sketches than did the "cold" group. In addition, the "warm" group selected such attributes as wise, humorous, and popular, whereas the "cold" group tended to select opposite attributes. Thus we see that one bipolar pair of traits—warm-cold—seems to convey a number of meanings, more positive, or acceptable, meanings being associated with "warm" than are associated with "cold." In fact, another study showed that students reacted more warmly to an instructor who was described as warm than did students who were told that the instructor would be cold.

Expectancy. Sometimes called the *self-fulfilling prophecy*, expectancy is the process whereby the person doing the evaluating makes happen that which he expects will happen. Rosenthal (1966) demonstrated this process with a number of experiments. For example, after intelligence tests had been administered to two groups of students, their teachers were told that some of their students were much more intelligent than others. In actuality, however, the research had randomized the groups so that both groups represented the same level of intelligence. Nevertheless, those children that the teacher thought were more intelligent actually showed gains on intelligence test scores. It appears that teachers spent more time teaching those they thought were bright, gave them more opportunity to demonstrate what they had learned, and rewarded their efforts with expressions of warmth.

Projection. This is a process by which we attribute our own feelings or characteristics to others. For example, you have probably often observed two friends arguing over a controversial subject, say, politics or religion. One of the parties to the argument may accuse his opponent of being rigid, bigoted, unreasonable, and so forth. Yet those may be the very characteristics that you would have attributed to him rather than to his opponent. Or you negotiate with a friend to buy her car. She wants $50 more than you are willing to pay. You may feel that she is "only after money," that "she is cheap," and so forth. Those are probably the same characteristics that she would use to describe you. We often project (or blame) our negative traits on others.

Selective perception. Here we draw unwarranted conclusions from an ambiguous situation. We see what we want to see. You see your boyfriend having lunch with another woman, and you immediately conclude that he is "running around."

Perceptual defense. Once we have established characteristic ways of perceiving the world, we have a difficult time changing our perceptions, or viewing the world in a different light. All of the previous shortcuts, such as stereotyping, halo effect, and projection, are included in this process of perceptual defense. They help us classify and organize the world in ways that make sense to us. We thus tend to attribute to others things which will help us maintain consistency with our view of the world. Often, however, we should probably examine our view of the world to see whether it needs to be changed as we receive contradictory information.

ATTRIBUTION AND THE JUDGMENT OF OTHERS

Attribution theory has been developed by psychologists to describe and explain the process of judging the actions of others. We attempt to judge from a person's current behavior whether or not that behavior reflects the "true person," or what the person is "really like," or what the person "really feels." According to Jones and Nisbett (1971), behavior which is truly reflective of a person's motives or feelings depends on three things. First, the behavior must be a matter of *free choice.* That is, the person must perform the behavior for "internal" reasons, such as enjoyment or interest, rather than for "external" reasons, such as social norms, social pressure, or money. If we can find strong external reasons for a person's actions, then we can assume that those actions do not really reflect that person's "true self." We judge not only the act but also its motive. Our criminal justice system, for example, has always made *intent* the criterion for distinguishing between murder and manslaughter.

A second determinant of whether a person's motives or feelings are assessed correctly is the extent to which the behavior of the person being judged leads to positive or negative *consequences* for the judge. An action which has strong reward consequences for you is judged as being more relevant than one that is of little or no consequence to you. For example, if a friend insults a stranger, that behavior may be of little consequence to you, and you may not attribute negative traits to your friend because of it. However, if the friend insults you, you will probably be more confident about attributing a personal cause to the behavior, and thus evaluate it more critically. Likewise, a drunken driver is regarded with more disfavor when he maims a child than when he knocks down a signpost, even though the behavior is the same.

Third, acts of strong *personalism* are more likely to be utilized as bases for inference. Personalism refers to acts which are intentionally directed toward you. If, for example, a friend is always late for appointments with you, you might not attribute her latenesses to personal causation if she is also late for appointments with others. That is, you might blame her latenesses on her parents, her biorhythms, and so forth. However, if you find that the friend is late only when she is to meet you, you might see this behavior as being directed toward you, and you will have more confidence in making interpretations about the behavior.

Attribution theory suggests, therefore, that when we have confidence that a person's actions are based on free choice, are consequential to us, and/or is intentionally directed toward us, we have more confidence in making an attribution or judgment, either positive or negative about that person. However, when the person's behavior is explained by external causes, has no consequences for us, and/or is not intentionally directed toward us, then we are not as willing to make attributions or judgments about that person's actions.

ORGANIZATIONAL IMPLICATIONS: JUDGING PERFORMANCE

Unfortunately, the state of measuring current and future levels of performance is not as objective as managers would like it to be. In fact, in most cases it is very subjective and therefore subject to the types of perceptual problems we have noted throughout this chapter. Nevertheless, the subjective measurements or judgments made by managers in a work situation are critical to the success or failure of the people being judged. Two major organizational examples of situations in which such judgments are crucial are the employment interview and the supervisor's annual performance appraisal.

Perceptual judgments and the employment interview

There is considerable evidence that although a particular interviewer will exhibit consistency in successive evaluations of the same individual, different interviewers are likely to come to quite different conclusions. Studies have shown that most interviewers are much more influenced by unfavorable information than by favorable information. Selection interviewers tend to compare job candidates against stereotypes, in the sense of looking for deviant characteristics, and this leads to negative results with regard to hiring.

In order to overcome the perceptual deficiency of the interview process, Carlson, Thayer, Mayfield, and Peterson (1971) made two recommendations. First, the selection interview should be made an integral part of an overall hiring procedure, and to accomplish this new and additional materials should be used. The new materials should include: a broad-gauge, comprehensively structured interviewer guide; standardized evaluation and prediction forms that aid the interviewer in summarizing information from all steps in the selection process; and an explanation system that provides feedback to the interviewer in language similar to the preemployment job behavior predictions he or she must make. Second, an intensive training program for interviewers is necessary to increase the probability that interviewers will make generally valid judgments in the selection interview.

Perceptual judgments and the performance appraisal

Evaluating the performance of employees has presented a severe challenge to managers, personnel officers, and organizational behaviorists. It is difficult to condense an employee's performance over a period of six months or a year into a relatively concise and meaningful appraisal. Measures of performance can be objective (sales, scraprate, words typed per minute) or judgmental (general impressions of a person's work). Most organizational jobs do not lend themselves to objective measurement, and subjective, perceptually based ratings are therefore the rule rather than the exception.

Goodale (1977) describes three types of rating scales found in use today. The *trait* appraisal form is designed to allow the manager to judge a person on more permanent characteristics ("what he or she is"), such as initiative, maturity, and personality. Unfortunately, this method opens the door to perceptual bias, since each manager has his or her own definition of these terms. Furthermore, these *traits* may not even be related to current levels of actual performance on the job.

The *behavior* rating scale measures performance in terms of specific job requirements ("what he or she does") and is rich in behavioral detail. This method has the advantage of being understood by both the rater and the employee being rated and is clearly superior to the trait approach.

The *goal-oriented* performance appraisal focuses on employee goals ("what he or she achieves"). Goals are set either by the superior alone or jointly by the supervisor and his or her employee. Such appraisal systems have the advantage of relative precision of standards. They represent by far the most valid and reliable subjective measures available, but we must still remember that our perceptions are influencing the appraisal process. Managers must attempt to understand this process and train others to understand it so that important judgments of subordinates are as free of bias as possible.

CONCLUSIONS

In this chapter we have attempted to explain how our perception of the environment determines, in part, our responses to that environment. We defined perception as the process by which we organize, interpret, experience, process, and use stimulus materials in the environment. Three distinct units of the perceptual process were described. The *input* process involves the manner in which we attend to the cues we see. The *storing* process involves the organization of the cues received and processed in the mind. The *output* process involves the impact of the information received and stored on our responses.

The processing of information is simplified by many shortcut techniques, such as stereotyping, which can seriously distort our perceptions and judgments of others. Considerable attention was given in this chapter to making perceptual judgments more accurate, especially in job-related situations. As Costello and Zalkind (1963) have suggested,

Significant interaction between two or more people would seem to be the very heart of administrative action. Literally hundreds of times during the day, the administrator is perceived and his behavior interpreted by people around him. He, in turn, perceives others and interprets their behavior. This perceiving is not usually a slow and deliberate process of observation. Often, such activities are fleeting and barely conscious, but they help to make up the human atmosphere in which the person lives and functions and, moreover, are crucial for administrative success. (p. 3)

Based on these potential shortcomings, Costello and Zalkind leave us with two suggestions for raising the probability of more effective administrative action.

One suggestion is that the administrator become aware of the intricacies of the perceptual process and thus be warned to avoid arbitrary and categorical judgments and to seek reliable evidence before judgments are made. A second suggestion grows out of the first—increased accuracy in one's self-perception can make possible the flexibility to go slowly, to seek evidence and to shift positions as time provides additional evidence about others. The danger (of too complete reliance on formal training for perceptual accuracy) is that a little learning encourages the perceiver to respond with increased sensitivity to individual differences, without making it possible to gauge the real meaning of the differences he has seen. (p. 53)

CONCEPTS TO REMEMBER

self-concept   stereotyping
implicit personality theory   self-fulfilling prophecy
response set   projection
halo effect   attribution

QUESTIONS FOR DISCUSSION

1. Does a person have to be aware of (be able to verbally describe) stimulus inputs in order to perceive or process information?
2. When can stereotyping be beneficial to an individual?
3. Why do you think initial perceptions of people are weighted more heavily than later pieces of information? What does this say about our storage process?
4. Why are some people better judges of people than others?
5. If the interview is so unreliable, why is it the single most frequently used method of hiring people?
6. List as many perceptual defense mechanisms as you can (for example, the halo effect), and define each.
7. Visit a company, and look at its interview guide and managerial appraisal forms. Based on what you have learned here, what changes would you make, and why?

REFERENCES

Allport, G. W. *Pattern and growth in personality.* New York: Holt, Rinehart and Winston, 1961.

Asch, S. E. Forming impressions of personality. *Journal of Abnormal and Social Psychology,* 1946, *41,* 258–290.

Carlson, R. E., Thayer, P. W., Mayfield, E. C., & Peterson, D. A. Improvements in the selection interview. *Personnel Journal,* 1971, *50,* 268–275.

Costello, T. W., & Zalkind, S. S. *Psychology in administration.* Englewood Cliffs, N.J.: Prentice-Hall, 1963.

Fish, E. H. *How to manage men.* New York: Engineering Magazine Company, 1920.

Goodale, J. G. Behaviorally-based rating scales: Toward an integrated approach to performance appraisal. In W. C. Hamner & F. L. Schmidt (Eds.), *Contemporary Problems in Personnel* (2d ed.). Chicago: St. Clair Press, 1977.

Jones, E. E., & Nisbett, R. E. *The actor and the observer: Divergent perceptions of the causes of behavior.* New York: General Learning Corporation, 1971.

Krech, D., Crutchfield, R. S., & Ballachey, E. L. *Individual in society.* New York: McGraw-Hill, 1962.

Leavitt, H. J. *Managerial psychology* (3d ed.). Chicago: University of Chicago Press, 1972.

Mann, L. *Social psychology.* New York: Wiley, 1969.

Maslow, A. H. *Motivation and personality.* New York: Harper, 1954.

Miner, J. B. *Personnel psychology.* New York: Macmillan, 1969.

Rosenthal, R. *Experimenter effects in behavioral research.* New York: Appleton-Century-Crofts, 1966.

Ruoff, H. W. *The circle of knowledge.* Boston: Standard Publishing, 1917.

Secord, P. F. Facial features and inference processes in interpersonal perception. In R. Tagiuri & L. Petrullo (Eds.), *Person perception and interpersonal behavior.* Stanford, Calif.: Stanford University Press, 1958.

Attitudes and behavior

How closely are attitudes related to behavior?

How and why are attitudes developed?

How and why do attitudes change?

I n Chapter 3 we noted that behavior is determined *in part* by the interrelationships of the contingencies of reinforcement, for example, the *environment,* the *response,* and the *consequence* of the response. However, in Chapter 5, in our discussion of the *perceptual* process, we noted that the cognitive states of people also play an important part in determining their response patterns, as shown in Figure 6–1.

As seen in Figure 6–1, the physical properties of the stimulus or environmental cues are received by the person and ordered by means of cognitive processes. As explained in Chapter 5, the interpretation and classification given to an object or cue are determined partially by the perceptual process. In addition to perceptions, a second cognitive property which determines our classification scheme is our *attitude* toward the object being perceived.

Figure 6–1
Mediating role of cognitive processes

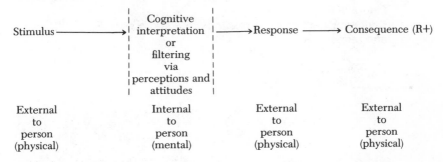

WHAT IS AN ATTITUDE?

An attitude can be defined as an individual's *predisposition* to *evaluate* a stimulus (object, person, and so on) in a favorable or an unfavorable manner. We assume that this evaluation reflects a person's *readiness to respond* to that stimulus object. An attitude can also be defined as an enduring organization of motivational, emotional, perceptual and cognitive processes with respect to some aspect of the individual's world. An attitude is considered as an entity or a process which exists in a person, even though we are unable to observe it directly. (This is what the psychologist calls a *hypothetical construct,* in that it is measured indirectly through observing behavior, questionnaire responses, or physiological reactions.)

READINESS TO RESPOND AND IMPORTANCE OF AN ATTITUDE

When we say that a person has a readiness to respond in a certain way toward a certain object, or the symbol of that object, we are actually referring to a prediction we can make about the person's behavior. In addition to knowing the nature of the attitude a person holds toward an object (Katz 1960), we also need to understand the importance of that particular attitude in order to determine the person's predisposition to behave in a particular manner toward the object. The more *central* the attitude is to a person, the greater is the probability that the intense feeling will be linked with external response patterns.

Before we attempt to discuss the centrality of attitudes and their relationship to behavior, it is appropriate to consider and discuss the three components of attitudes. As stated earlier, an attitude is the predisposition of the individual to evaluate some object in a favorable or an unfavorable manner. This evaluation can be expressed in one of three ways.

A common feature of attitudes is that they involve emotional reactions, a verbal or belief component, and an action component. That

Figure 6–2
Conceptual scheme for relating attitudes to stimuli and responses

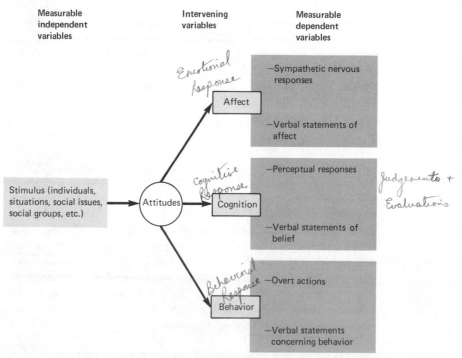

Source: From M. J. Rosenberg and C. I. Hovland, "Cognitive, Affective, and Behavioral Components of Attitude," in M. J. Rosenberg, C. I. Hovland, W. J. McGuire, R. P. Abelson, and J. H. Brehm (Eds.), *Attitude, Organization, and Change* (New Haven: Yale University Press, 1960).

is, a person may think one thing, say a second, and do a third. Thus the structure of a person's attitude comprises these three components (affects or emotions, beliefs or opinions, and behaviors or responses). A scheme for relating attitudes to stimuli and responses can be seen in Figure 6–2.

COMPONENTS OF AN ATTITUDE (Three)

1) The affective component

McGinnies (1970) states that the emotional component of an attitude develops as a *conditioned response* by association with stimuli that have either rewarding or punishing effects. Thus, affective components are learned through classical conditioning methods (see Chapter 3). For example, McGinnies points out that expressions of warmth and affection from one's parents are probably among the earliest unconditioned stimuli for positive affective responses and that the stimuli for many negative affective responses are probably derived from parental disapproval or neglect. Any behavior by either parent or child that immediately precedes these rewarding or punishing stimuli gains some measure of control over the elicited reaction. Thus the term *love,* because it is often preceded by physical demonstrations of affection, becomes a conditioned stimulus to reactions that most persons would describe as pleasant. On the other hand, a word such as *hate* elicits other reactions, generally reported as unpleasant because they have characteristically preceded some aversive event. Thus certain words become cues for emotional reactions, and we may assume that the context in which the words are used comes to serve the same functions. In addition, the words help us understand our *feelings* about the object in question.

In 1966 Dickson and McGinnies used questionnaires to survey the attitudes of a sample of university students toward the church. They then presented these students with tape-recorded statements that either praised or disparaged the church, while simultaneously recording their emotional responses (as measured physiologically with the galvanic skin response, or GSR). Both prochurch and antichurch students responded with greater emotion (as shown by elevations in GSR) to statements that contradicted their attitudes than to those that reflected their attitudes.

2) The cognitive component

The cognitive component of a social attitude consists of the individual's perceptions, beliefs, and *ideas* about an object. For example, your attitude toward Nixon's record as president may include your understanding of the history of the Vietnam War, your beliefs about corruption among politicians, your understanding of the Republican party, your conception of the foreign policy at that time, and so on. According to Krech, Crutchfield, and Ballachey (1962), the most critical cognitions incorporated into the attitude system are *evaluative* beliefs which involve the attribution of favorable or unfavorable, desirable or undesirable, "good" or "bad" qualities to the object.

The term *opinion* is often used as a substitute for the cognitive component of an attitude, especially when it is relevant to some question or issue. For example, politicians often base their decision to run or not to run on the opinion (belief about a particular candidate) of a constituency and their view that the attitudes of people as measured in opinion research are highly correlated with behavior (that is, how the people will *actually vote* in the future). Thus, according to *U.S. News & World Report* (April 5, 1976, p. 11), "The real reason Representative Wilbur Mills decided not to run for re-election was a private poll, taken just before his decision to step down, which showed the Arkansas Democrat running far behind one of his potential opponents."

The overt or behavioral response component

The behavioral component of attitudes consists of the tendency to act or react toward an object in certain ways. This action orientation is measured by noting what an individual actually does in a given environmental situation.

During the early 1930s a sociologist named Richard LaPiere traveled throughout the United States in the company of a young Chinese couple. Unknown to the young couple, LaPiere maintained a record of their travels, noting especially how the two Chinese were received by clerks in hotels and restaurants. In a 1934 article, LaPiere reported that only once was the couple not treated hospitably.

In addition to recording how the Chinese couple was treated, LaPiere obtained information about attitudes toward Chinese. Six months after visiting each establishment, he sent a letter to the hotel or restaurant asking whether Chinese clientele would be accepted. Over 93 percent of the responses said no—Chinese would not be accommodated.

LaPiere thus obtained extremely discrepant information about prejudice toward the Chinese. People *acted* one way (friendly, hospitably) but reported that they would respond to Chinese in a different manner (negative affect and beliefs about Chinese).

ARE ATTITUDES (BELIEFS AND EMOTIONS) RELATED TO BEHAVIORAL RESPONSES?

The study by LaPiere poses the important question of whether or not internal attitude components (beliefs and emotions) are related to behavior. According to Calder and Ross (1973), "It would seem to be a theoretical necessity that attitudes operate in both modes. But in terms of a person's awareness of his attitudes, the perceptual aspect may be more salient than the behavioral. It follows that a person's report of how his attitudes affect his perceptions should be trusted more than his report of how his attitudes affect his behavior. He is more likely to be unaware of the impact of his attitudes on his behavior" (p. 8).

Organizational Behavior is a subject in which there is a great deal of interest in the attitude-behavior relationship. The central concern is whether job attitudes (usually operationalized as job satisfaction) are related to job performance. Vroom (1964) reviewed more than 20 studies conducted on individuals in a variety of occupations. In general the results showed correlations between job satisfaction and measures of job performance which were small and often insignificant. There was, however, a relatively consistent negative relationship between job satisfaction and the probability of resignation. That is, less satisfied workers tended to be more likely to resign. We will have more to say about the relationship between worker satisfaction, attitude, and performance in Chapter 10. What should be obvious to the reader here is that while an attitude may be related to a behavior, it is not the sole determining factor. Attitudes interact with situational influences to produce behavior.

Mann (1969) noted that the discrepancies between attitudes and behavior are not really surprising and should be expected. He offers three reasons for these discrepancies. First, Mann agrees that behavior is determined not only by attitudes but also by external factors in the immediate social situation. Mann says, "Consider the non-prejudiced behavior of the seemingly prejudiced proprietors in LaPiere's study. Perhaps at the time of the visit of the Chinese the proprietors needed the money, were reluctant to become involved in an argument, or were impressed with LaPiere; these factors may have prevented the prejudiced attitude from influencing their behavior" (p. 111).

Wicker (1969) examined the relationship between verbally expressed attitudes and overt behavior. After reviewing a sizable portion of the research evidence, he concluded that there is little evidence to support the assumption that verbally expressed attitudes correlate highly with the overt behaviors implied by those attitudes. One reason, of course, is that noted by Mann—people refrain from behaving in a manner consistent with their attitudes when such behavior would be socially undesirable.

A second reason given by Mann as to why attitudes and behavior are often discrepant is that many different attitudes are relevant to a single action. Rokeach (1966) contends that attitudes toward the object as well as attitudes toward the situation in which the object is encountered determine the individual's behavior. Attitude objects are almost always encountered in situations in which there are already strong, overriding attitudes toward other components of the situations. Therefore, inconsistency between behavior and internal attitudes might be a function of orientation to a situation. Mann noted, "In public places, such as restaurants and hotels, there are socially defined and regulated codes of conduct. One is not supposed to make a scene, embarrass the guests or scream racist obscenities in the foyer of a hotel. The attitude that politeness and decorum is the appropriate behavior in a hotel supersedes the attitude of prejudice toward Chinese, and LaPiere's companions are made welcome" (p. 112).

A third factor, according to Mann, is the type of attitude underlying the prejudice. He notes that "intellectualized" attitudes are rich in beliefs and stereotypes but have no real action tendencies. "Just because the proprietor expresses a negative evaluation or intention about Chinese in general, it cannot be assumed that he has committed himself to a corresponding form of behavior to every Chinese he might encounter. . . . If there is no action orientation in a particular attitude there is little reason to expect consistency among beliefs, feelings, and behavior" (p. 112).

This last reason for the inconsistent attitude-behavior relationship brings us back to an earlier point made in this chapter. The centrality or importance of an attitude determines to some extent our readiness to respond. The *centrality* of an attitude refers to its role as part of a value system which is closely related to the individual's self-concept. Other dimensions which determine our readiness to respond, according to Katz, include the *intensity* of an attitude (the strength of the emotional reaction), the *specificity or generality* of the attitude (I dislike Chiang Kai-shek versus I dislike Chinese), and the *differentiation* of the belief structure (how strongly the specific belief is tied to a related value system). Therefore, the more central, intense, generalizable, and differentiated the attitude, the greater the likelihood is that behavior will be consistent with beliefs and emotions.

WHERE DO ATTITUDES COME FROM?[1]

Attitudes reflect a person's previous reinforcement history. As such, attitudes are *learned.* The determinants of a person's attitude system include societal influences, major group memberships, the family, peer groups, and prior work experience.

Societal influences. Our culture and language provide us with the experiences and boundaries for our initial attitudes. We are taught at a very early age that certain attitudes and beliefs are more acceptable

---

[1] Adapted from T. W. Costello and S. S. Zalkind, *Psychology in Administration* (Englewood Cliffs, N.J.: Prentice-Hall, 1963), pp. 260–263.

than others. The attitudes of Americans toward communism are very different from those held by the average Russian.

In the area of international management and multinational organizational exchanges, it is important to understand the value system (attitude framework) of the society or culture one is in before making judgments or taking action. What seems appropriate in one's own culture may be totally unacceptable in another culture. For example, in South America attitudes toward punctuality are not nearly as intense as they usually are in urban North America.

Major group memberships. Within our own society, each of us is strongly influenced by the major groups to which we belong. Our geographic region, religion, educational background, race, sex, age, and income class all strongly influence how we view the world. Students familiar with marketing surveys will readily point out that *target* markets are generally based on these categories. *Playboy,* for example, claims to be the magazine of highest readership among males between the ages of 18–30 with incomes over $15,000 annually. If one were interested in influencing the attitude of young adult males toward a new product, then *Playboy* might well be a good place to advertise the product.

The family. The family is the major influence on the initial core attitude system held by a person. Obviously the family influences early learning patterns and controls the groups and culture to which a person is initially exposed.

Peer groups. As we approach adulthood, we rely increasingly on our peer groups for approval. Initially other children, acquaintances, playmates, and friends influence our attitudes. As we enter the world of work, our co-workers and others whom we seek out for approval influence what we say, how we feel, and how we respond. How others judge us determines to a certain extent our self-image and our approval-seeking behavior. We often seek out others who share attitudes similar to our own, or else we change our attitudes to conform to the attitudes of those in the group (fraternity, dorm, club) whose approval is important to us.

Prior work experience. According to Costello and Zalkind (1963), when a person starts to work, he takes with him the host of attitudes he has developed and acquired from the culture, the family, and the peer group. By the time the person goes to work in a specific organization, he or she will hold many attitudes toward the type of job which is acceptable, the pay expected, working conditions, and supervision. As noted in Chapter 3, the manager will have to understand these individual differences when administering rewards and punishments and when assigning jobs.

In a study of the attitudes of skilled and semiskilled workers to job enrichment (the process of increasing a person's responsibility at the jobsite—see Chapter 12), Davis and Werling (1960) surveyed a West coast plant employing 400 operating personnel and 250 clerical and administrative personnel. The interests of skilled workers, which were similar to those of management, included company success, self-improvement, and improvement of operations. Semiskilled workers, on the other hand, lacked concern for company goals and attached little importance to job content. Blood and Hulin (1967) suggested that workers in large cities were alienated from the "work" norms of the middle class (positive affect for occupational achievement, a belief in the intrinsic value of hard work, a striving for the attainment of responsible positions, and a belief in the work-related aspects of Calvinism and the Protestant ethic). Rather, they adopted the norms of their own particular group (for example, extrinsic job need, alienation from work, seeing work as a necessary evil, and emphasizing fulfillment away from work).

ATTITUDE STRUCTURE AND CONSISTENCY

In our examination of the relationships among the components of attitudes, we noted that people strive to maintain consistency among these components (beliefs, feelings, and actions) but that apparent contradictions often occur. In addition to the question of the internal structure of attitudes, there is the question of the structure of attitude *systems*—clusters of attitudes about a set of related objects which fit together in an interconnected, integrated whole. Social scientists have spent a considerable amount of time studying the extent to which consistency exists among the attitudes in a cognitive system, what happens when attitudes become inconsistent with one another, and how adjustments are made to restore consistency to the system.

In seeking answers to these questions, a number of theories of cognitive consistency have been developed. The reference in these theories goes beyond attitudinal consistency to a more generic cognitive consistency. This is due to the concern with the internal cognitive process in its broadest sense, that is, with the image or map of the world held by the individual. That image includes thoughts, values, and actions as well as attitudes about some object or some set of events. At the core of the interest in cognitive consistency is the assumption that people need to attain harmony and congruity among their cognitions of objects and persons in the environment. Brown (1965) observed that "the human mind expects good things to cluster together and to be opposed to the cluster of bad things. . . . positively valued objects should be linked by associative bonds and, similarly, negatively valued objects should be linked by associative bonds. Between positively valued objects and negatively valued objects there should be only disassociative bonds" (p. 553). Whenever these rules are violated, a state of disequilibrium exists and a tension is generated that is reduced only when equilibrium is restored.

Given that an individual has formed an attitude and has engaged in some behavior, what are the psychological implications of any discrepancy between the attitude and the behavior? Like Brown, Festinger (1957) notes that a state of disequilibrium, which he calls *dissonance*, sets in when there is a discrepancy between the attitude and the behavior of an individual. Although several other theories have been advanced to explain the psychological processes employed in reaching equilibrium, Festinger's cognitive dissonance theory will be discussed here since it relates to *both* the attitude-behavior consistency argument and to the more generic problem of cognitive consistency mentioned earlier.

Festinger's cognitive dissonance theory

The term *dissonance* refers to a psychological inconsistency among cognitions associated with internal attitudes and behaviors. Two cognitions are in a dissonant relation if one implies the opposite of the other. For example, the cognition "I smoke a pack of cigarettes a day" is psychologically inconsistent with "Cigarette smoking is extremely hazardous to one's health, and I could die of cancer!"

Cognitive dissonance theory predicts that a person will experience discomfort or tension (dissonance) when two cognitions are psychologically inconsistent. Because the occurrence of cognitive dissonance is unpleasant, the individual acts to reduce or eliminate it. Dissonance is thus conceptualized as a drive state that, when aroused, elicits actions designed to return the individual to a state in which the drive is at a lower level of arousal.

The individual reduces dissonance arousal by restoring consistency between cognitions. This may be done in several ways. The person may alter personal behavior, change beliefs, change feelings, or add new cognitions that explain the previous inconsistency (Calder & Ross, 1976). The smoker may reduce dissonance by giving up smoking, or if he or she is unwilling to do this, the person can choose to believe that "smoking is not dangerous if you don't inhale," or believe that "when your number is up, it's up."

When a behavior is fully justified by external circumstances (for example, the avoidance of pain or the acquisition of rewards), little or no dissonance is aroused by an inconsistency between that behavior and the person's attitude. On the other hand, if the behavior cannot be explained by a reference to external circumstances, the person will experience dissonance and be motivated to reduce the inconsistency. For example, Staw (1974) studied male students enrolled in the ROTC in 1969–71. Many of these men had joined the ROTC, in part, to avoid being drafted and sent to Vietnam. When they joined the ROTC they signed a contract requiring them to continue in it for the remainder of their stay at the university and to become reserve officers in the Army if such appointments were offered. After these students had made their commitment to ROTC, the Selective Service System conducted a draft lottery, and each of the ROTC cadets received a number that would have been his had he not joined ROTC. The number indicated a high, medium, or virtually no chance of being drafted.

Staw reasoned that students who won numbers that would have allowed them to avoid the draft should have experienced cognitive dissonance. They had made an irrevocable commitment to the ROTC for what turned out to be no gain on their part. In other words, they did not need to join the ROTC to escape the draft. One way these students could reduce dissonance was to decide that they enjoyed the ROTC, that the ROTC was a valuable experience in its own right. Accordingly, Staw had the cadets complete questionnaires that assessed their satisfaction with the ROTC. As dissonance theory predicted, those students who had the least to gain by being in the ROTC (those with high draft numbers and little probability of being drafted) indicated the most satisfaction. Interestingly enough, those students also averaged the highest grades in the ROTC.

Cognitive dissonance theory has important implications for the relationship between the effort a person exerts to attain a goal and the person's attitude toward the goal once it is achieved. Specifically, any undesirable aspects of the goal are dissonant with the knowledge that a considerable amount of effort was exerted to attain it. The more effort, in any form, an individual exerts to achieve a goal, the more dissonance is aroused if the goal is less valuable than was expected. The individual may reduce this dissonance by concentrating on the positive aspects of the goal, by coming to the conviction that the goal is truly desirable.

One study (Doob, Carlsmith, Freedman, Landauer, & Tom, 1969) tested this justification of effort hypothesis by varying the initial selling price of a product and measuring the subsequent sales of that product. The "introductory low price offer" is a selling tactic in which a distributor introduces a new product at a lower price and subsequently raises it to its normal level. The assumptions underlying this technique are that the low price will lead many consumers to try the new brand and that the customers will like the brand enough to continue to buy it when the price rises.

According to the effort-dissonance principle, if effort is translated into the amount a person pays for a product, it becomes evident that the higher the price, the more the purchaser should appreciate the product. This would be true since not liking the product would be dissonant with the cognition that it was obtained at a higher cost. If greater liking is associated with continued purchases of a product, a greater proportion of customers should continue to buy a product purchased at a high initial price than one purchased at a low initial price, even though the low initial price may at first attract more customers. In the long run, however, the increased liking produced by the dissonance involved in paying a higher price may yield greater sales.

Doob and his associates tested this proposition in a chain of discount stores that sold a variety of products (mouth wash, toothpaste, and so on). Pairs of stores, matched in gross sales, were randomly assigned to one of two experimental conditions. The same product was sold at either a discounted price or at the regular price for a short period of time, after which the prices were standardized at the regular price at all stores. As expected, sales were initially higher at the stores that discounted the product. However, subsequent sales (following the price change) were higher at the stores whose initial price was high, a result consistent with predictions from dissonance theory.

Thus we see that Festinger's (1957) cognitive dissonance theory not only explains the psychological processes employed in reaching *attitude* equilibrium but also explains postdecision conflicts in *choice* behavior. In the latter, the amount of dissonance that exists after a choice decision has been made is a direct function of the number of things the person knows that are inconsistent with the particular decision. That is, the greater the conflict before the decision, the greater the dissonance afterward. Thus, the more difficulty the person had in making the decision, the greater would be his or her tendency to justify the decision (reduce the dissonance) afterward. According to Festinger, the decision can be justified by increasing the attractiveness of the chosen alternative and decreasing the attractiveness of the rejected alternative, and one would expect a postdecision cognitive process to occur that accomplishes this by spreading apart the attractiveness of the alternatives (for example, the low-price versus high-price purchases in the example above).

An alternative explanation of dissonance behavior

Cognitive dissonance theory portrays people as strongly motivated to avoid and reduce tensions caused by inconsistencies among cognitions. Bem (1967) offered an alternative explanation of cognitive dissonance phenomena. Bem's *self-perception theory* suggests that people are generally not aware of their own cognitions, let alone inconsistencies among the cognitions. According to Bem's nonmotivational interpretation, a person who wants to "know" his or her own feelings or beliefs will study his or her own behavior and, in essence, ask, "What must my attitude be if I am willing to behave in this fashion in this situation?" (Bem & McConnell, 1970, p. 24). If a person were asked whether he liked brown bread, according to this theory, the person might reply, "Since I am always eating it, I guess I do" (Bem, 1968).

Bem therefore offers a conflicting explanation of the relationship between internal states and overt actions. While this debate may at first seem trivial to the student, the issues it raises are important when one is trying to predict behavior. According to Bem, the model of behavior-attitude interaction is as follows:

$$S \rightarrow R \rightarrow R+ \rightarrow \text{Attitude discovery}$$

According to some cognitive theorists, the model of behavior-attitude interaction is as follows:

$$S \rightarrow \text{Attitudes} \rightarrow R \rightarrow R+$$
$$\text{(Cognitions)}$$

Therefore, according to Bem and other reinforcement theorists, one would have to change behavior in order to change attitudes. For some cognitive theorists, however, changes in attitudes affect future behavioral responses. While this dispute may still seem trivial, it brings up an interesting question when we examine attitude change. Suppose that you are interested in achieving racial integration of your work force. If the members of your work force are predominantly white and have never worked with or lived near members of the black community, how should you go about introducing this change? Should you try to change the beliefs of the white employees first, through persuasion and propaganda? Or should you select qualified blacks and put them in the work force, under the assumption that the white workers will find interaction with blacks to be a positive experience and that their attitudes will then shift as a matter of course? We will not attempt an answer here, but will have more to say about this when we discuss strategies of attitude change. However, the astute reader should see that a strategy based on a cognitive explanation of behavior would probably be different from a strategy based on a reinforcement (noncognitive) explanation of behavior.

FUNCTIONS SERVED BY ATTITUDES

Regardless of how attitudes are formed, there is little dispute among psychologists that people do have attitudes and that it is important to understand those attitudes. Organizations, especially their personnel and marketing departments, spend millions of dollars to measure the attitudes of employees and consumers. Why? Because attitudes influence other important psychological processes, such as the formation of simple social judgments, the perception and interpretation of ambiguous stimuli, the learning and retention of controversial material, and receptivity and openness to new information. Moreover, attitudes confer considerable stability and consistency to behavior—knowing that a person holds a certain attitude enables the observer to anticipate and predict that person's behavior with a fair amount of accuracy and confidence. Costello and Zalkind (1963) say, "An administrator who is seeking to influence behavior of others—whether these others are subordinates, superiors or colleagues in his own organization, or those he deals with in other organizations—soon becomes aware of the importance of their attitudes" (p. 247).

In addition to helping us predict the behavior of others, attitudes, according to Katz (1960), serve functions for the personality and help us adapt to our environment. Katz suggests that four personality functions are served by the maintenance and modification of social attitudes: *adjustment, value expression, knowledge,* and *ego-defense*. Unless we understand the psychological need which is met by holding an attitude, states Katz, we are in a poor position to predict when and how the attitude will change. The same attitude may perform different functions for the different people who express it. Let us see how Katz perceives the differences in the various functions served by attitudes.

The adjustment function. This function is a recognition of the fact that people strive to maximize the rewards and to minimize the penalties in their external environment (the hedonistic principle discussed in Chapter 3). Attitudes acquired in the service of the adjustment function are means for reaching desired goals or for avoiding undesirable results, or are associations of sentiments based on experiences in attaining motive satisfactions. How expressing the wrong attitude (belief about the most qualified candidate for president) can lead to negative reactions was illustrated in a story in *U.S. News & World Report*. "Since the Governor of South Carolina, James B. Edwards, rebuffed Mr. Ford by endorsing Reagan for President, federal grants for his state have practically dried up. An embittered South Carolina official quoted a White House source as saying: 'Tough, but that's the way the game is played' " (April 5, 1976, p. 11).

The ego-defensive function. People expend a great deal of their energy learning to live with themselves. Many of our attitudes have the function of defending our self-image. When we cannot admit to ourselves that we have feelings of inferiority, we may project those feelings onto some convenient minority group and bolster our egos by attitudes of superiority toward this minority group.

The value-expressive function. Although many attitudes have the function of preventing the individual from revealing his true nature to himself and others, other attitudes have the function of giving positive expression to his central values and to the type of person he conceives himself to be. Katz (1960) says, "Value-expressive attitudes not only give clarity to the self-image but also mold that self-image closer to the heart's desire" (p. 170). In a recent interview, John M. Johnson, editor and publisher of *Ebony* magazine and one of the most successful black businessmen in the country, talked about his self-image and his attitude toward failure.

> **Q:** Mr. Johnson, an admirer of yours quotes you as saying, "Success in business is a time-honored process involving hard work, risk-taking, money, a good product, maybe a bit of luck and most of all a burning commitment to succeed." . . . What do you mean by a burning desire to succeed?
>
> **Mr. Johnson:** I don't see, never did see, failure as an option. When *Life* went out of business, the guys who made the decision to discontinue it knew that it was not going to disturb their lives. As a matter of fact, Time, Inc.'s stock went up that day. But if *Ebony* didn't succeed, it was going to destroy my life. So I had total commitment; my whole life depended on *Ebony*. I had no options. So I had to learn the rules of the game to win. (*Harvard Business Review*, March–April 1976, p. 79)

The knowledge function. This function is based on the need to understand, make sense of, and give adequate structure to the universe. Attitudes are maintained that deal with situations adequately and that structure experiences meaningfully. Attitudes which are inadequate for dealing with new and changing situations are discarded because they lead to contradictions and inconsistency. Beliefs about such matters as the Vietnam War, the energy crisis, and the corruption of big business are modified as more meaningful information comes to hand. A very important function of knowledge is its satisfaction of the need for meaningful cognitive organization and for cognitive consistency and clarity. During his campaign for the Democratic presidential nomination in 1976, Representative Morris Udall, congressman from Arizona, said that his earlier support of the Vietnam War had been a "mistake" (*Chicago Tribune*, March 31, 1976, p. 1). During the same campaign, Udall stopped labeling himself a "liberal," a designation he had previously chosen to describe himself, since the term *liberal* "is associated with abortion, drugs, busing, and big-spending wasteful government" (*Chicago Tribune*, March 31, 1976, p. 4).

PREJUDICE AS AN EGO-DEFENSE ATTITUDE

As noted in the previous section, one function of an attitude is to act as an ego-defense. One method of building up the group to which one belongs is to ascribe undesirable traits and characteristics to other groups. Social scientists have defined "prejudice" in a number of ways. It is generally expressed through "stereotyping," and both terms, *prejudice* and *stereotyping*, have negative connotations. Stereotyping refers to an overgeneralization—the attribution of identical characteristics to all persons in a group, regardless of the actual variations among the members of that group. Thus, to believe that Southerners are dumb, that Jews are materialistic, that blacks are lazy, that Italians belong to the Mafia, and that older citizens are senile is to label all members of those subgroups on the basis of a limited experience or a lack of experience with members of those groups. Often we classify certain groups on the basis of very limited information (seeing a movie, reading a novel, listening to our parents talk about an event that happened 30 years ago, and so on). However, we all engage in stereotyping. It is frequently merely a way of simplifying our view of the world. Aronson (1972) states, "To the extent that the stereotype is based on experience and is at all accurate, it is an adaptive, shorthand way of dealing with the world. On the other hand, if it blinds us to individual differences within a class of people it is maladaptive and potentially dangerous. Moreover, most stereotypes are not based on valid experience, but are based on hearsay or images concocted by the mass media or are generated within our own heads as ways of justifying our own prejudices and cruelty" (p. 173).

Unfortunately, unfavorable attitudes held by people in one group often cause the "self-fulfilling prophecy" to occur in the behavior of the stereotyped group. The self-fulfilling prophecy, in turn, provides a justification for actions toward the stereotyped group. If you, as a male, say that women are unqualified for top management positions and that therefore you won't train them for such positions, sure enough, women remain unqualified for the positions, and they know it as well as you do. Women thus may come to believe that they are unqualified because they have been discriminated against, and both men and women are then justified in their attitudes—the men for believing that women are inferior at certain tasks and the women for feeling that men are biased and prejudiced. The research of Rosen and Jerdee (1976) has shown that older people are perceived to be significantly less capable of effective performance with respect to creative, motivational, and productive job demands, even though the actual performance of older people does not support this belief.

Another example of the self-fulfilling prophecy's impact on people was demonstrated by Kenneth and Mamie Clark in 1947. They showed that black children only three years old were already convinced that black skin was inferior. When asked to choose between a black doll and a white doll and to describe which doll was nice, which looked bad, and which had the nice color, black children overwhelmingly rejected black dolls, feeling that white dolls were prettier and generally superior. This experiment played a major role in the Supreme Court decision (*Brown* v. *Board of Education,* 1954) that declared the segregation of schools to be unconstitutional.

Goldberg (1968) conducted an experiment which demonstrated that women have been taught to consider themselves the intellectual inferiors of men. In the experiment he asked a number of female college students to read scholarly articles and evaluate them in terms of their competence, style, and so on. Female students rated the articles much higher if they were attributed to a male author than if they were attributed to a female author.

Bem and Bem (1970) argued that the prejudice against women that exists in our society is an example of a *nonconscious ideology*—that is, of a set of beliefs that we accept implicitly but of which we are unaware because we cannot conceive of alternative conceptions of the world, such as, role reversal. Jean Lipman-Blumen (1972) reported that women who acquired a traditional view of their sex role in early childhood (for example, "women's place is in the home") choose not to seek advanced education as often as women who acquired a more egalitarian view of sex roles.

On the basis of evidence concerning the damage that prejudice can have, Aronson (1972) says: "It should be plain, moreover, that stereotyping can be painful to the target, even if the stereotype would seem to be neutral or positive. For example, it is not necessarily negative to attribute 'ambitiousness' to Jews or a 'natural sense of rhythm' to blacks; but it is abusive, if only it robs the individual Jew or black person of his right to be treated as an individual with his own individual traits, be they positive or negative" (p. 174).

THE PROCESS OF CHANGING ATTITUDES

Managers are faced with the task of making sure that prejudiced attitudes do not interfere with equal opportunity for stereotyped group members. (See the appendix to this chapter for a detailed view of federal regulations covering equal employment opportunity.)

According to Katz (1960), an attitude that no longer serves its function will cause the individual holding that attitude to feel blocked or frustrated. Modifying an old attitude and replacing it with a new one is a process of learning, and learning always starts with a sense of being thwarted in coping with a situation. However being thwarted is a necessary, but not a sufficient, condition for attitude change. See Figure 6–3 for an overview of the growth and change dynamics of attitudes serving different functions.

Arousal and change of adjustment attitudes *Max Reward & min Penalties.*

Katz states that the two basic conditions for the arousal of existing attitudes are the activation of their relevant need states and the perception of the appropriate cues associated with the content of the attitude. To change attitudes which serve an adjustment function, one of two conditions must prevail: (1) the attitude and the activities related to

Figure 6–3
Determinants of attitude formation, arousal, and change in relation to type of function

Function	Origin and dynamics	Arousal condition	Change condition
Adjustment	Utility of attitudinal object in need satisfaction; maximizing external rewards and minimizing punishments	1. Activation of needs 2. Salience of cues associated with need satisfaction	1. Need deprivation 2. Creation of new needs and new levels of aspiration 3. Shifting rewards and punishments 4. Emphasis on new and better paths for need satisfaction
Ego-defense	Protection against internal conflicts and external changes	1. Posing of threats 2. Appeal to hatred and repressed impulses 3. Rise in frustrations 4. Use of authoritarian suggestion	1. Removal of threats 2. Catharsis 3. Development of self-insight
Value expression	Maintenance of self-identity; enhancing favorable self-image; self-expression and self-determination	1. Salience of cues associated with values 2. Appeal to individual to reassert self-image 3. Ambiguities which threaten self-concept	1. Some degree of dissatisfaction with self 2. Greater appropriateness of new attitude for the self 3. Control of all environmental supports to undermine old values
Knowledge	Need for understanding, meaningful cognitive organization, consistency and clarity	Reinstatement of cues associated with old problems or of old problems themselves	1. Ambiguity created by new information or by change in environment. 2. More meaningful information about problems

Source: From T. W. Costello and S. S. Zalkind, *Psychology in Administration* (Englewood Cliffs, N.J.: Prentice-Hall, 1963), p. 274.

it no longer provide the satisfactions they once did; or (2) the individual's level of aspiration has been raised.

Since the prejudices of employees serve the function of meeting *current needs* by following the rewards and avoiding punishment, one way to change such attitudes is to change the environment and its rewards. Changes in attitudes occur more readily when people perceive that they can accomplish their objectives by revising their existing attitudes. Hovland, Janis, and Kelley (1953) state that attitude change is contingent upon some incentive that is provided by the communicator or is implied as a consequence of accepting the communicator's message. Kelman (1961) refers to this acceptance as *compliance;* that is, the individual accepts influence because he hopes to achieve a favorable reaction from another person or group. In face-to-face situations in which an individual is put under group pressure to adopt an opinion contrary to what he believes, yielding to the influence attempt is based on the desire to conform to the expectations of others in order to receive rewards or avoid punishment. For Kelman, this is an instance of compliance in which the opinion is adopted publicly without actual inner acceptance. In such instances, as soon as the group releases its arousal pressure, the individual reverts to his initial opinion.

An example of compliance change can be seen in the following quotation from John M. Johnson, editor and publisher of *Ebony* magazine. He says:

> ". . . once I was trying to get a second-class [postal] permit for *Tan*, which had some suggestive stories in it. When I went to the post office, the man said he didn't like *Tan*, he couldn't approve it. I tried all kinds of ways to get him to approve it, including saying, 'Well, gee, you must be prejudiced because I'm black, and you've okayed similar magazines like *True Story*, *True Confessions*, and so on. Why do you want to do this to me?' But the man just kept rejecting my application. So finally, I went down to see him again, and I said, 'Mr. So-and-So, I've got to have this second-class permit. I can't survive without it. You're in charge, and I've concluded that the only thing I can do is to do what you want. Will you please tell me what you want me to do?' He said, 'Now you're talking, Johnson.' And then, really, he told me to do what I was doing right then, namely, being persistent but not hostile. I learned the rules of the game. It wasn't easy, but I learned them." (*Harvard Business Review*, March–April 1976, pp. 79–80)

Arousal and change of the ego-defense attitude

Katz (1960) notes that attitudes which help protect the individual from internally induced anxieties or from facing up to external dangers are readily elicited by any form of threat to the ego. As implied in Figure 6–3, the threat may be external, as in the case of a highly competitive situation, a failure experience, or a derogatory remark. Prejudice, as noted earlier, is a major type of ego-defense attitude. Most prejudices are maintained because the group to which one belongs gives support to them. Since many prejudiced attitudes are learned through classical conditioning (association) and are *emotional* in basis, they are harder to change than are attitudes based on information (beliefs) and learned by instrumental conditioning methods.

Katz lists three factors which can help change ego-defensive attitudes. First, the source of threat, real or imagined, must be removed. Social approval is important to the individual's self-image, and people have less need of ego-defensive attitudes in a supportive climate. Second, catharsis, or the ventilation of feelings, can help set the stage for attitude change. Third, ego-defensive behavior can be altered as the individual acquires insight into his or her own mechanisms of defense. Stotland, Katz, and Patchen (1959), for example, found that involving people in the task of understanding the dynamics of prejudice helped arouse self-insight and reduce prejudice. The manager who is faced with the need to hire more women could *involve* the biased foreman in their selection. Instead of saying "You must hire Sally Jones," the manager might allow the foreman to interview five or six qualified women and to select the one he thinks is suitable for the job.

Arousal and change of the value-expressive attitude

Katz (1960) suggests two conditions which are relevant to changes in an aroused value-expressive attitude. First some degree of dissatisfaction with one's self-concept or its associated values is the opening wedge for fundamental change. Dissatisfaction with the self can result from failure or from the inadequacy of one's values in preserving a favorable image of oneself in a changing world. Second, dissatisfaction with old attitudes as inappropriate to one's values can also lead to change. Such dissatisfaction with old attitudes may stem from new experiences or the suggestions of other people. These two conditions for attitudinal change were the bases for F. Lee Bailey's defense of Patty Hearst.

Kelman (1961) labels this process of change "identification." Identification occurs when an individual adopts the attitudes of a person or a group because his or her relationship with the person or group is satisfying and forms part of his or her self-image. An illustration of the role reference groups play in changing value-expressive attitudes is provided by observations made at Bennington College in the 1930s by Newcomb. Questionnaires measuring political-economic progressivism were given to members of the student body each year to determine how these attitudes changed during their four years at Bennington. A steady decrease in conservatism, with a concurrent increase in progressivism, was found in students as they advanced from the freshman through the senior years. For example, 62 percent of the freshmen, 43 percent of the sophomores, 15 percent of the juniors, and 15 percent of the seniors favored Alfred Landon, the conservative Republican presidential candidate of 1936. Interestingly, 66 percent of the students' parents favored Landon, a figure most closely associated with the results for the freshmen. It was apparent that the political-economic attitudes of the students became increasingly divorced from the attitudes of their parents as the students proceeded from freshman to senior (Newcomb, 1943).

Arousal and change of the knowledge-function attitude

The knowledge-function attitude should be the easiest attitude to change since it is based on information and beliefs which are open to examination and dispute. The means for changing this attitude are persuasion and the use of new sources of information. Kelman (1961) sees the knowledge-function attitude as being based on the *internalization* of attitude-related information contained in persuasive communication delivered by reliable and trustworthy sources. The central idea is that an opinion or attitude becomes accepted because its adoption and expression satisfy a desire for consistency and structure in one's framework of knowledge.

FACTORS DETERMINING THE EFFECTIVENESS OF PERSUASION

As noted above, persuasion is a primary method for changing a person's existing attitudes, especially if those attitudes serve a knowledge function. A great deal of research has been devoted to find out "who says what to whom and with what effect." In a series of studies at Yale University, Hovland, Janis, and Kelley (1953) established many interesting things about the persuasion process. The communicator is more likely to induce attitude change if he has high credibility. The influence agent will be more successful if he seeks a moderate degree of attitude change than if he seeks either a small degree of change or such a great degree of change that defensiveness is aroused. In addition, the change agent will have more influence on the attitude change if both sides of an issue are discussed than he will have if only one side is presented—particularly if the audience is above average in intelligence. Emotional appeals that arouse fear or anxiety are more effective with less informed or less intelligent people than with better informed or more intelligent people. In some instances, however, the emotional appeal can "boomerang" and lead to initial defensive reactions that prevent the message itself from being heard.

One of the most effective agents of attitude change is the "opinion leader"—a key high-status person in the community who is a particularly attentive monitor of the mass media and who interprets and relays information to a circle of friends. This process is known as the "two-step flow of communication," since information and ideas flow first from the mass media to local opinion leaders (the priest, the union leader, the politician, and so on), and from these opinion leaders by word of mouth to rank-and-file members of the community. If the manager is an opinion leader, he may have a great effect on the attitudes developed by employees who hold him or her in high regard. It is important to note, however, that in order to maintain credibility a manager, should be open, flexible, and willing to change his own attitudes when valid information from subordinates and other respected sources is presented to him.

SUMMARY

An attitude is an individual's predisposition to evaluate an object in a favorable or an unfavorable manner. Attitudes are learned from our parents, friends, society, peer groups, and from our experiences with our environment. Attitudes have identifiable emotional, cognitive, and behavioral components. A person's behavior in a given environmental situation, however, does not necessarily correspond to his or her belief or emotions. Situational and social approval factors play a major part in controlling attitudinal behavior.

Attitudes serve ego-defense, adjustment, value-expressive, and knowledge functions for individuals. Attitude change processes vary according to the centrality of the attitude to one's value system and to the function it serves. Prejudice, an ego-defense attitude, was singled out for emphasis, since organizations are mandated by Congress to eliminate bias in the treatment of people in organizational settings.

APPENDIX: FEDERAL REGULATIONS COVERING PREJUDICED ATTITUDES AND BEHAVIOR[2]

In both educational and work organizations, the Congress of the United States has mandated *behavioral acts* which must take place to compensate for the inequities which have resulted for minority groups due to the shared stereotypes previously held.

The *5th Amendment* to the U.S. Constitution, which became effective in 1791, specified that no free person shall "be deprived of life, liberty, or property, without due process of law." The *13th Amendment,* ratified in 1865, abolished slavery. The *Civil Rights Act of 1866* stated that all people, regardless of race, had the right to enter into a contract. In 1868, the *14th Amendment* granted equal protection to all persons under state laws. The *Civil Rights Act of 1871* said that state laws must grant equal rights to all persons regardless of race, national origin, or sex.

Although discrimination was mandated as illegal in 1866, labor statis-

---

[2] Adapted from W. C. Hamner, "The Supervisor and Affirmative Action," in M. G. Newport, *Supervisory Management: Tools and Techniques* (St. Paul: West Publishing), pp. 1235–1250.

tics show that from 1900 to 1965 little progress was made in the advancement of minorities and females in employment situations. Many reasons for this lack of progress can be given. The industrial revolution had reduced the proportion of highly skilled workers. Blacks and women were less educated than white males. Many companies were family-owned, and only family members became managers. War and depression diverted attention from the problem. Congress was busy enacting laws to guarantee minimum wages, maximum hours, and the right to unionize—all three of which were more pressing issues of the day.

Nevertheless, in the early 1950s the emphasis began to shift. The armed forces were integrated. In 1954 the Supreme Court (*Brown* v. *Board of Education*) ruled that the segregation of schoolchildren was illegal. From 1954 to 1964 the major shift in minority benefits took place in the schools and colleges.

Due to the pressure brought to bear by several special interest groups (for example, the NAACP), the president and Congress began to focus on the employment rights—selection, promotion, termination, and training—of previously denied groups of employees. In 1961 President Kennedy established the Commission on the Status of Women to draw up recommendations for improving the progress women could make in employment and other areas. Partially as a result of this commission's work, Congress passed the Equal Pay Act of 1963. This act was an amendment to the Fair Labor Standards Act of 1938, which established minimum wages and maximum hours and protected women and children from certain physical abuses in the work setting. Under the Equal Pay Act, Congress guaranteed equal pay for equal work for jobs which required equal skills, efforts, responsibility, and performance levels. In other words, supervisors could no longer pay women a wage scale different from that of men for approximately equal jobs. Today, this act covers all employees covered by the minimum wage law plus executive, administrative, professional, and academic employees and outside salespersons. From 1964 through 1972 more than $55 million was found owing under the Equal Pay Act to 129,000 employees (mostly women). In 1970, for example, Wheaton Glass Company paid more than $900,000 in back wages and interest to 200 female employees. Other companies have also paid money to women as a result of this act (AT&T, $68 million; Pittsburgh Plate and Glass, $1 million; Delta Airlines, $700,000; Corning Glass, $600,000; and so on). Nevertheless, the U.S. Department of Labor's Women's Bureau noted in 1972 that "women who work at full-time jobs the year round earn, on the average, only $3 for every $5 earned by *similarly* employed men." Ironically, the ratio was the same in 1939.

It became evident to Congress and the president that federal and state laws had not achieved equal employment opportunity, even though our American heritage encouraged the right of all persons to work and to advance on the basis of merit, ability, and potential. Therefore, Congress provided for federal legal enforcement of equal employment in Title VII of the Civil Rights Act of 1964, and amendments strengthening this change were added in 1967 and 1972.

Title VII of the Civil Rights Act prohibits discrimination because of race, color, religion, sex, national origin, or age (40–65 age range, 1967 amendment) in hiring, firing, promotion, compensation, and other terms, privileges, and conditions of employment. The U.S. Equal Employment Opportunity Commission (EEOC) was created to administer Title VII and to assure equal treatment for all employees.

Discrimination or job bias under Title VII can take place through conscious, overt *action* against individuals. However, the courts have begun to realize that few firms are guilty of such willful discrimination (based on beliefs) and have redefined discrimination to include "systemic" or practical discrimination. In 1971 U.S. Supreme Court Chief Justice Warren Burger stated, "What is required by Congress is the removal of artificial, arbitrary, and unnecessary barriers to employment when the barriers operate invidiously to discriminate on the basis of racial or other impermissible classification. . . . [Title VII of the Civil Rights Act] proscribes not only overt discrimination but also practices that are fair in form but discriminatory in operation." (*Griggs* v. *Duke Power Co.*, 1971, p. 424)

In other words, employers are required not only to cease overt discrimination but also to "make up for past sins" by taking specific remedial actions to remove "systemic" discrimination which has resulted from prior acts of discrimination. Systemic *discrimination is said to occur when one or more protected groups are adversely affected. For example, if an organization has no female supervisors, then there is discrimination in fact (statistically shown systemic discrimination) even though the organization may be an equal employment opportunity employer.* When discrimination can be confirmed by the statistics of underemployment, nonemployment, unemployment, and income of minorities and women as compared to other employees, Title VII provides that a court may "order such affirmative action as may be appropriate" to eliminate such discrimination.

Title VII of the Civil Rights Act of 1964, as amended in 1972, covers all employers with 15 or more employees, including unions, educational institutions, state and local governments, joint labor and management committees, and employment agencies. Thus, almost all supervisors are faced with the enforcement of equal employment opportunity personnel practices.

In order to ensure that all people, regardless of group affiliations, are hired on the basis of merit, Title VII established the EEOC and empowered this body to investigate charges of discrimination, to persuade employers to restore the rights of parties discriminated against, and if necessary, to bring civil actions directly into federal courts in order to enforce the provisions of Title VII and to remedy instances of their violation. The EEOC bases its decisions to bring charges of discrimination on the answers to two questions: First, do the records kept by supervisors indicate discrimination or adverse effect? Second, is adverse effect (a disproportionately small number of black employees, for example) based on artificial barriers (emotions and beliefs) or factual barriers (valid)?

In resolving both questions, the EEOC uses *statistics*. If an employer is charged with discrimination, *it is up to the employer to prove that discrimination did not take place.* He can do this by following the two principles used by the EEOC. First, he can show that there is no discriminatory treatment of people (that is, no adverse effect). Second, if he is unable to do this, he can show that his decisions were based on valid criteria as established by the EEO guidelines (1970, as amended in 1976). A complete discussion of these guidelines is beyond the scope of this chapter. It should be noted that the guidelines require an employer to show statistically that information used in making personnel decisions was related to levels of job performance. An employer who cannot show that one of the two principles has been followed will probably be forced to make restitution, in dollars, positions, and the establishment of an affirmative action program to avoid the same problems in the future.

Policies determined to be unlawfully discriminatory because of their effects on minority groups *and* because they cannot be shown to be related to job performance include:

1. Refusing to hire because of an arrest record.
2. Refusal to hire because of a conviction record.
3. Discharging because of garnishment.
4. Refusing to hire persons with poor credit ratings.
5. Hiring through unions whose admission preference is to friends and relatives.
6. Using word-of-mouth recruiting by present employees as the primary source of new applicants.
7. Refusing to hire men wearing beards, goatees, or mustaches.
8. Using a transfer rule (change of jobs) which does not allow carryover seniority so as to perpetuate discrimination.
9. Using high school diploma requirements which cannot be shown to be job-related.
10. Using inquiries about charge accounts, home ownership, or car ownership (unless the car is required for job use). (See Equal Employment Opportunity Commission 7th Annual Report, 1972.)

These are some of the areas of information that a manager should avoid in a job interview or in forming an opinion about a prospective employee. Sex discrimination is another sphere in which managers should avoid problems. The following policies and practices by supervisors have been held illegal because of their impact on women *and* because they could not be shown to be job-related.

1. A job candidate cannot be asked questions about number and age of children.
2. It is a violation of the law for employers to require preemployment information on child-care arrangements from female applicants only.
3. Height and weight requirements violate the law if they screen out a disproportionate number of Spanish-surnamed persons, Asian-Americans, or women, and if the supervisor cannot show these standards to be job-related.
4. It may be illegal to discharge or refuse to hire males with long hair if similar restrictions are not imposed on females.
5. State "protective" laws limiting the occupation, hours, and weight which can be lifted by women should be ignored if they deny jobs to women.
6. It is illegal to exclude applicants or employees from a job because of pregnancy, or to require pregnant women to stop work at a specified date.
7. A supervisor cannot blame his or her failure to take affirmative action on barriers in the union contract.
8. A company cannot use "male-female" ads. (Anaconda Aluminum Company was ordered to pay $190,000 in back wages and court costs to 276 women who alleged that the company maintained sex-segregated job classifications.)

As you can see from this listing of areas that should be avoided in discussions with employees, the manager is in a very sensitive position, since he comes in direct contact with the employee and, in many cases, the job applicant. All workers are protected by equal employment opportunity laws. The EEOC received 45,000 individual complaints of discrimination from July 1, 1974, through April 1975. It has negotiated settlements bringing 44,000 minority workers more than $46 million in back pay.

After reading this section, you may be asking yourself whether the manager has any remaining decision-making powers. Well, the answer is yes. An affirmative action program is designed to bring more *qualified* applicants into the job pool. It doesn't mean that you can't discriminate against an incompetent worker. It only means that you must show that your discrimination is based on *job performance,* not on attitudes, speech patterns, dress, mannerisms, age, sex, or skin color. As a matter of fact, having an efficient affirmative action program should make it easier for the manager to discharge or discipline minority and female employee without fear of being charged with job bias. Nothing in the EEO guidelines requires you to hire or promote inferior members of your work force. Instead, you are left with the challenge of developing your work force in such a way that *all* people are given the chance to become qualified.

FRANK AND ERNEST   **by Bob Thaves**

I'VE GOT GOOD NEWS FOR YOU, HOTCHKISS. AS PART OF OUR AFFIRMATIVE ACTION PLAN, I HAVE TO PROMOTE SOMEONE WHO IS TOTALLY INCOMPETENT.

Source: Reprinted by permission of Newspaper Enterprise Association.

CONCEPTS TO REMEMBER

hypothetical construct	adjustment function
affective component	value-expressive function
cognitive component	ego-defensive function
behavioral component	knowledge function
attitude centrality	stereotyping
attitudinal consistency	identification
cognitive dissonance	internalization
self-perception theory	two-step flow of communication

QUESTIONS FOR DISCUSSION

1. If attitudes are not observable, how can we know what another person's attitude really is?

2. Sears, Roebuck and Company has had a department for employee attitude research since 1939. This department surveys the attitudes of all employees every three years. As you can imagine, this is a very costly project, requiring many man-hours of labor. Sears feels that the program is very beneficial. Why do you think Sears is willing to spend millions of dollars to measure employees' attitudes? How do you think it uses this information?

3. Why do politicians use opinion polls?

4. Who are Harris, Gallup, Yankelovich, and Nielsen? How large a business does each of these people represent? To what do you attribute their success?

5. Millions of dollars are spent each year to make sure that managers are not biased in their treatment of women and minorities. Why?

6. Do attitudes cause behavior? How do you know?

7. Why is the two-step flow of communication important for group leaders interested in motivating high levels of performance?

REFERENCES

Aronson, E. *The social animal.* New York: Freeman Press, 1972.

Bem, D. J. Self-perception: An alternative interpretation of cognitive dissonance phenomena. *Psychological Review,* 1967, *74,* 183–200.

Bem, D. J. Attitudes as self-descriptions: Another look at the attitude-behavior link. In A. G. Greenwald, T. C. Brock, & T. M. Ostrom (Eds.), *Psychological foundations of attitudes.* New York: Academic Press, 1968.

Bem, D. J., & Bem, S. We're all non-conscious sexists. *Psychology Today,* November 1970, pp. 22–26; 115–116.

Bem, D. J., & McConnell, H. K. Testing the self-perception explanation of dissonance phenomena: On the salience of premanipulation attitudes. *Journal of Personality and Social Psychology,* 1970, *14,* 23–31.

Blood, M. R., & Hulin, C. L. Alienation, environmental characteristics, and worker responses. *Journal of Applied Psychology,* 1967, *51,* 284–290.

Brehm, J., & Cohen, A. *Exploration in cognitive dissonance.* New York: Wiley, 1962.

Brown, R. *Social psychology.* New York: Free Press, 1965.

Calder, B. J., & Ross, M. *Attitudes and behavior.* Morristown, N.J.: General Learning Press, 1973.

Calder, B. J., & Ross, M. *Attitudes: Theories and issues.* Morristown, N.J.: General Learning Press, 1976.

Clark, K., & Clark, M. Racial identification and preference in Negro children. In T. M. Newcomb & E. L. Hartley (Eds.), *Readings in Social Psychology.* New York: Holt, 1947.

Cook, S. W., & Selltiz, C. A multiple-indicator approach to attitude measurement. *Psychological Bulletin,* 1964, *62,* 36–55.

Costello, T. W., & Zalkind, S. S. *Psychology in administration.* Englewood Cliffs, N.J.: Prentice-Hall, 1963.

Davis, L., & Werling, R. Job design factors. *Occupational Psychology,* 1960, *34,* 109–132.

Dickson, H. W., & McGinnies, E. Affectivity and arousal of attitudes as measured by galvanic skin responses. *American Journal of Psychology,* 1966, *79,* 584–589.

Doob, A. N., Carlsmith, J. M., Freedman, J. L., Laundauer, T. K., & Tom, S.   Effect of initial selling price on subsequent sales. *Journal of Personality and Social Psychology*, 1969, *11*, 345–350.

Equal Employment Opportunity Commission 7th Annual Report, EEOC, Washington, D.C., 1972.

Festinger, L.   *A theory of cognitive dissonance*. Evanston, Ill.: Row-Peterson, 1957.

Goldberg, P.   Are women prejudiced against women? *Trans-Action*, April 1968, pp. 28–30.

Griggs v. *Duke Power Co., 401 United States Reports*, 1971, p. 424.

Hammond, K. R.   Measuring attitudes by error-choice: An indirect method. *Journal of Abnormal and Social Psychology*, 1948, *43*, 38–48.

Heider, F.   Attitudes and cognitive orientation. *Journal of Psychology*, 1946, *21*, 107–112.

Hovland, C. I., Janis, I. L., & Kelley, H. H.   *Communication and persuasion: Psychological studies of opinion change*. New Haven: Yale University Press, 1953.

An interview with J. M. Johnson. *Harvard Business Review*, March–April 1976, pp. 78–85.

Katz, D.   The functional approach to the study of attitudes. *Public Opinion Quarterly*, 1960, *24*, 163-204.

Katz, D., & Stotland, G.   A preliminary statement to a theory of attitude structure and change. In S. Koch (Ed.), *Psychology: A study of science* (Vol. 3). New York: McGraw-Hill, 1959.

Kelman, H. C.   Processes of opinion change. *Public Opinion Quarterly*, 1961, *25*, 57–78.

Kidder, L. H., & Campbell, D. T.   The indirect testing of social attitudes. In G. F. Summers (Ed.), *Attitude measurement*. Chicago: Rand McNally, 1970.

Krech, D., & Crutchfield, R. S.   *Theory and problems in social psychology*. New York: McGraw-Hill, 1948.

Krech, D., Crutchfield, R. S., & Ballachey, E. L.   *Individuals in society*. New York: McGraw-Hill, 1962.

LaPiere, R. T.   Attitudes vs. actions. *Social Forces*, 1934, *14*, 230–237.

Lawless, D. J.   *Effective management: Social psychological approach*. Englewood Cliffs, N.J.: Prentice-Hall, 1972.

Lipman-Blumen, J.   How ideology shapes women's lives. *Scientific American*, January 1972, pp. 34–42.

Mann, L.   *Social psychology*. New York: Wiley, 1969.

McGinnies, E.   *Social behavior: A functional analysis*. Boston: Houghton Mifflin, 1970.

Newcomb, T. M.   *Personality and social change*. New York: Dryden Press, 1943.

Newcomb, T. M.   An approach to the study of communicative acts. *Psychological Review*, 1953, *60*, 393–404.

Rokeach, M.   Attitude change and opinion change. *Public Opinion Quarterly,* 1966, *30,* 529–548.

Rosen, B., & Jerdee, T. H.   The nature of job-related age stereotypes. *Journal of Applied Psychology,* 1976, *61,* 180–183.

Rosenberg, M. J., & Abelson, R.   An analysis of cognitive balancing. In C. I. Hovland & M. J. Rosenberg (Eds.), *Attitude organization and change.* New Haven: Yale University Press, 1960.

Rosenberg, M. J., & Hovland, C. I.   Cognitive, affective, and behavioral components of attitude. In M. J. Rosenberg, C. I. Hovland, W. J. McGuire, R. P. Abelson, & J. H. Brehm (Eds.), *Attitude, organization, and change.* New Haven: Yale University Press, 1960.

Staw, B.   Attitudinal and behavioral consequences of changing a major organizational reward: A natural field experiment. *Journal of Personality and Social Psychology,* 1974, *29,* 742–751.

Stotland, E., Katz, D., & Patchen, M.   The reduction of prejudice through the arousal of self-insight. *Journal of Personality,* 1959, *27,* 507–531.

Udall no longer a liberal. *Chicago Tribune,* March 31, 1976, pp. 1,4.

Vroom, V. H.   *Work and motivation.* New York: Wiley, 1964.

Wicker, A. W.   Attitudes versus actions: The relationship of verbal and overt behavioral responses to attitude objects. *Journal of Social Issues,* 1969, *25,* 41–78.

Needs, goals, and motives
Theories of motivation

How is behavior energized?

How is behavior directed?

How is behavior maintained?

When organizational behaviorists discuss motivation, they are primarily concerned with: (1) what energizes human behavior; (2) what directs or channels the behavior; and (3) how the behavior is maintained or sustained. As Steers and Porter (1975) note, each of these three components represents an important factor in our understanding of human behavior at work. First, we see that an energizing force within individuals "drives" them to behave in certain ways. Second, there is the notion that a goal orientation of individuals directs their behavior *toward* a goal object. Third, this way of viewing motivation considers the fact that, as noted in previous chapters, forces in individuals and their environments either reinforce the intensity of their drive and the direction of their energy or discourage them from their course of action and redirect their efforts. Building on these three components of motivation, we can now present a general description of the motivational process.

WHAT ENERGIZES HUMAN BEHAVIOR?

As noted above, one of the things that managers need to understand about the motivation of their subordinates is what energizes human behavior. A comprehensive review of all motivational theories is clearly beyond the scope of this text. There are, however, two popular theories that can provide the student with an understanding of what energizes a worker's performance. These are need theory (Maslow, 1943; Alderfer, 1969) and activation theory (Scott, 1966).

Need theory

Maslow has suggested that the underlying needs for all human motivation can be organized in a hierarchical manner on five general levels, as shown in Figure 7–1.

At the lowest-order level are *physiological needs*, which include the need for food, water, sex, and shelter. For a human being who lacks everything, the major motivation would be such physiological needs. For example, an extremely hungry man would define Utopia as a place where there is plenty of food. Human beings live by bread alone when there is no bread.

When the physiological needs are satisfied, the *safety needs* become the most important in the hierarchy. These are the needs for protection against danger, threat, and deprivation. McGregor (1960) has aptly summarized the potency of the safety needs:

Arbitrary management actions, behavior which arouses uncertainty with respect to continued employment or which reflects favoritism or discrimination, unpredictable administration of policy—these can be powerful motivators of the safety needs in the employment relationship at every level,

137

Figure 7–1
Maslow's need hierarchy

Note

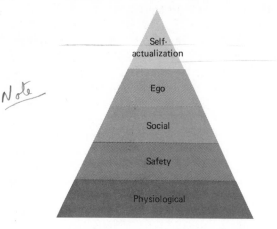

from worker to vice president. In addition, the safety needs of managers are often aroused by their dependence downward or laterally. This is a major reason for emphasis on management prerogatives and clear assignments of authority.

The third level in the hierarchy comprises the *social needs*, that is, the giving and receiving of love, friendship, affection, belonging, association, and acceptance. If the first two levels are fairly well gratified a person becomes keenly aware of the absence of friends, or of a sweetheart, and will be motivated toward affectionate relations with people in general and toward a place in his or her primary group relations in particular.

Identical to Herzberg Motivators

At the fourth level in the hierarchy are the *ego needs*, which are generally classified into two subsets. The first subset includes the needs for achievement, adequacy, strength and freedom. In essence this is the need for autonomy or independence. The second subset includes the needs for status, recognition, appreciation, and prestige. In essence this is the need for self-esteem or self-worth.

The fifth and highest level in the hierarchy is the *self-actualization need*. This is the need to realize one's potentialities for continued self-development and the desire to become more and more of what one is and what one is capable of becoming. For example, a musician must create music, an artist must paint, a poet must write in order to achieve ultimate satisfaction. Unfortunately, the conditions of modern industrial life afford only limited opportunity for the self-actualizing need to find expression.

Several characteristics are derived from Maslow's hierarchy. (1) The hierarchy is dynamic in the sense that the most prepotent need takes precedence in motivating behavior. For example, to the extent that one has been deprived of food, physiological needs become more important than all other needs. But when a given need is fairly well satisfied, the next higher need emerges to motivate behavior. (2) Any behavior tends to be determined by several or all of the basic needs simultaneously rather than by only one of them. For example, eating may be partially for the sake of filling the stomach and partially for the sake of comfort and the amelioration of the other needs; or one may make love not only for sexual release but also to convince oneself of one's sexual prowess, to make a conquest, or to win more basic affection. (3) The basic needs are only one class of behavioral determinants. While behavior is almost always motivated, it is also almost always biologically, culturally, and situationally determined as well. (4) There are relative degrees of satisfaction in these basic needs, and the hierarchy should not be interpreted in an all-or-none sense. In 1943 Maslow arbitrarily suggested that in our society the physiological needs are generally 85 percent satisfied, the safety needs 70 percent satisfied, the social needs 50 percent satisfied, the ego needs 40 percent satisfied, and the self-actualization need 10 percent satisfied.

Two major postulates can be derived from Maslow's need hierarchy. (1) A satisfied need is not a motivator of behavior. (2) To the extent that lower-order needs become satisfied, the next higher-order level of needs becomes the most prepotent determinant of behavior.

A second need theory, similar to the one offered by Maslow, has been presented by Alderfer (1969). Alderfer argues for three levels of needs: *existence, relatedness,* and *growth.* Like Maslow, he argues that the extent to which a lower-level need is satisfied influences its importance and the importance of higher-level needs. He agrees with Maslow's hypothesis that the satisfaction of growth needs makes them more important to people; however, he also predicts that the lack of satisfaction of higher-order needs can make lower-order needs more important to people.

Need theory is very difficult to test empirically, and only a few studies have attempted to either prove or refute the model. Some support has been found for the following conclusions. (1) In the United States and Great Britain there tends to be the hierarchical satisfaction of needs that Maslow postulates. (2) Across all managerial levels there is a tendency for the least satisfied needs to be seen as most important. (3) Security and social needs tend to be better satisfied in higher-level managerial jobs than in lower-level jobs. (4) Higher-order needs are usually activated and satisfied after lower-order needs are fulfilled.

Hall and Nougaim (1968) conducted a five-year study designed to establish how needs affect work performance. In the course of the study 49 young managers employed by American Telephone and Telegraph participated in five annual three-hour interviews with consulting psychologists. Hall and Nougaim concluded from their data that the changes they had found could be explained only in terms of developing career concerns rather than in terms of prepotent need gratification. Accordingly they indicate that the early stages of a career are characterized by concern with security—gaining recognition and getting established in a profession or an organization. During the first five years, concern shifts to achievement and autonomy. Given success during this intermediate level, the individual reaches a terminal plateau and turns to other means of gratification, such as helping younger executives to grow and to strengthen the organization.

On the basis of this and other work, Hall (1976) claims that people's

Figure 7–2
An integrative model of career stages

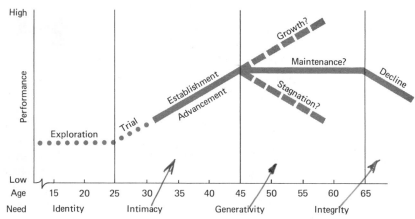

Source: Adapted from D. T. Hall, *Careers in Organizations* (Pacific Palisades, Calif.: Goodyear, 1976), p. 57.

needs change as their stages of career development change. Hall defines a career stage as a period of time in a person's life characterized by distinctive needs and activities. The stages of a person's career development and his or her corresponding need state are shown in Figure 7–2. In the first career stage, known as the *exploration* stage, a person displays a need for identity formation. In this stage, self-examination, role tryouts, and trial periods of work are experienced. The next stage (between approximately ages 25 and 44) is called the *establishment* stage, and it is during this stage that people display a need for intimacy. Intimacy refers to the forming of attachments and the making of commitments both to organizations and to co-workers. During the third stage, known as the *maintenance* stage, a need for generativity is present. Generativity refers to the concern for producing something meaningful to be left to the next generation. The last stage of career development is termed the *decline* stage. This stage is characterized by a need for integrity, which is the person's feeling of satisfaction with his or her life, choices, and actions.

Thus Hall believes that the energizing force of behavior shifts over a person's work life. A need for identity (security, existence) is followed by a need for intimacy (social relatedness), then a need for generativity (ego, self-actualization, growth), and finally a need for integrity (relatedness, ego).

Regardless of which theory of needs we subscribe to, it seems obvious that we all have motives or reasons for our actions. One of the primary motives seems to be our current need state. Thus managers who are attempting to motivate increased productivity among workers being supervised should be careful to relate to the needs of the workers rather than to the needs of the supervisor. Otherwise the energy source of the workers' behavior may not be tapped.

Activation theory

A number of researchers (most notably Scott, 1966) have presented the view that the *degree of activation* of a person is a major determinant of the power to perform. The term *activation* refers to the degree of general excitation of the brain from stimulation by all sources. For example, bright colors, variety, noise, and caffeine tend to increase the activation level; dull colors, quietness, and routine tend to lower it. The relationship between a person's performance and his activation or arousal level is generally described by an inverted *U*. (See Figure 14–1 for a diagram of this relationship.) At low activation levels, performance is handicapped by a low level of alertness, a decrease in sensory sensitivity, and a lack of muscular coordination; at intermediate levels of activation, performance is optimal; and at high levels, performance is again handicapped, this time by hypertension, loss of muscular control, "implosion to action," and in the extreme, total disorganization of responses. For example, "jet lag" is partially caused by fatigue which interferes with proper mental alertness and functioning. John Foster Dulles once complained that one of his biggest mistakes as secretary of state—failure to back Egypt in the Aswan Dam project—came after a long overseas flight. He stated that he was fatigued and disoriented when he made his decision.

Thus we see that not only does the internal need state of a person energize a person but the variety and complexity of the stimulus setting can also determine the level of energy a person possesses at any point in time. If the internal need is great and/or the stimulus configuration is complex (challenging), we would expect more activity on the part of a person than if the need is small and/or the stimulus configuration simple (boring).

WHAT DIRECTS OR CHANNELS ENERGIZED BEHAVIOR?

Once the environmental and internal cues are such that a person is aroused to act, why does that person choose a particular act or level of action? According to Tolman (1932), a person's energy level is channeled toward a goal-object based on the person's value system. The channeling function of a person's value system is explained by the *expectancy theory* of motivation, and the challenging function of a goal-object is explained by *goal-setting theory.*

Expectancy theory

The expectancy theory of motivation (often referred to as instrumentality theory) was originally proposed by Tolman in 1932 as a part of his *purposive psychology of behavior.* In essence, he argued that a person's purpose in behaving must be analyzed with respect to the person's *perceived likelihood* that an action will lead to a certain outcome or goal and with respect to the stated *value* or *attractiveness* of the outcome or goal. Several theorists subsequently offered further conceptual additions to this theory (see, for example, Porter and Lawler, 1968). Vroom (1964) was the first to specifically relate the theory to motivation in the work environment. Among today's industrial and organizational psychologists, expectancy theory is a widely accepted theory of motivation.

Vroom defines motivation as a process governing choices made by persons among alternative forms of voluntary activity. "Although some behaviors, especially those that are not under voluntary control, are defined as unmotivated, these probably constitute a rather small proportion of the total behavior of adult human beings. It is reasonable to assume that most of the behavior exhibited by individuals on their jobs as well as their behavior in the 'job market' is voluntary and consequently motivated" (Vroom 1964, p. 9).

We will describe a number of independent concepts associated with the theory before depicting their interrelations in terms of principles. These concepts include first- and second-level outcomes, valence, instrumentality, expectancy, force (or motivation), and ability.

First- and second-level outcomes. The first-level outcomes resulting from behavior are those associated with the work itself. Such outcomes include job performance, productivity, turnover, and absenteeism. Second-level outcomes are the events (rewards) which first-level outcomes are likely to produce, such as money, promotion, supervisor support, group acceptance, and fringe benefits.

Valence. The concept of valence is based on the assumption that a person has preferences or affective orientations toward various outcomes or states of nature. For example, a person may prefer outcome *x* over outcome *y* or outcome *y* over outcome *x* or be indifferent toward outcomes x and y but prefer outcome z. An outcome is positively valent when a person prefers attaining it to not attaining it (that is, prefers x to not x). An outcome has a valence of zero when the person is indifferent to attaining or not attaining it (that is, is neutral to x and not x). An outcome is negatively valent when a person prefers not attaining it to attaining it (that is, prefers not x to x). The concept of valence applies to both first- and second-level outcomes. For example, people may desire to join a group (group membership = first-level outcome) because they believe that membership will enhance their status in the community (status = second-level outcome), or people may desire to perform their job effectively (performance = first-level outcome) because they believe that good performance will lead to a promotion (promotion = second-level outcome).

Instrumentality. This concept refers to the individual's perception of the relationship between first-level outcomes and second-level outcomes. In the example offered above, instrumentality is the extent to which status in the community will, in fact, result from membership in a particular group. Vroom (1964) suggests that instrumentality "can take values ranging from -1, indicating a belief that attainment of the second outcome is certain without the first outcome and impossible with it, to $+1$, indicating that the first outcome is believed to be a necessary and sufficient condition for the attainment of the second outcome" (p. 18).

Expectancy. The specific outcomes attained by a person are dependent not only on the choices that the person makes but also on events beyond his or her control. For example, the student enrolling in a program of business studies is seldom certain that the program will be successfully completed. Vroom defined expectancy as a momentary belief concerning the likelihood or subjective probability that a particular act or behavior will be followed by a particular outcome (that is, what the probability of success is if I choose a certain course of action). As such, expectancy relates the action — outcome relationship and has a value ranging from 0, indicating total doubt that an act will be followed by an outcome, to $+1$, indicating certainty that the act will be followed by a particular outcome.

Force. Vroom equates motivation to a force which serves to direct and allocate behavior among various alternative actions available to the individual. The predictive potential of expectancy theory derives from assessing the magnitude and direction of all the forces acting on the individual. That is, among all potential acts the one having the highest strength will be predicted to be directed either toward or away from a particular outcome.

Ability. The term *ability* usually denotes a potential for performing some task or a "capacity to work" which may or may not be utilized. It refers to what a person can do rather than to what a person will do.

Principles

When these concepts are interrelated, three major principles are derived: (1) $P = f(M \times A)$; (2) $M = f(V_t \times E)$; and (3) $V_t = f(V_R \times I)$.

1. $P = f(M \times A)$. This equation suggests that performance is a multiplicative function of motivation and ability. That is, performance is dependent upon both the "willingness" and the "capacity" to behave. It follows from this formulation that "when ability has a low value, increments in motivation will result in smaller increases in performance than when ability has a high value. Furthermore, when motivation has a low value, increments in ability will result in smaller increases in performance than when motivation has a high value" (Vroom, 1964, p. 203).

2. $M = f(V_t \times E)$. The motivation for a given action, in turn, is a multiplicative function of the valence for each first-level outcome (V_t, or valence for task action) and the believed expectancy that a given behavior will be followed by a particular first-level outcome. It follows from this formulation that "an outcome with high positive or negative valence will have no effect on the generation of a force unless there is some expectancy (i.e., subjective probability greater than zero) that the outcome will be attained by some act. Similarly, if the valence of an outcome is zero (i.e., the person is indifferent to the outcome), neither the absolute value nor variations in the strength of expectancies of attaining it will have any effect on forces" (Vroom, 1964, p. 19).

3. $V_t = (V_R \times I)$. The valence associated with various first-level outcomes is a multiplicative function of the sum of the valences attached to all second-level outcomes (valence of the reward, V_R) and the instrumentality that achievement of the first-level outcome has for attaining each of the second-level outcomes.

As an illustration of how the model works, consider the information contained in Figure 7–3. The hypothetical situation involves an undergraduate student faced with various first- and second-level outcomes. On the basis of the numbers arbitrarily selected and the principles stated above, one would predict that the strongest force or motivation for the student would be directed toward behavior leading to a B average. The resulting performance, in turn, would depend not only on the strength and direction of the motivation but also on the student's ability to perform.

Since Vroom's (1964) conceptualization of expectancy notions of motivation and work behavior, several modifications and extensions have been offered by various researchers. Three reviews of empirical research based on expectancy theory have been published recently. Mitchell and Biglan (1971) reviewed 6 studies in the area of industrial psychology; Heneman and Schwab (1972) reviewed research design and measurement issues connected with 9 field studies in managerial settings; and Wahba and House (1972) reviewed 14 empirical studies. These reviews indicate that some propositions of expectancy theory have been supported. However, a fully developed test incorporating force, expectancy, and instrumentality measures as well as ability assessment has not yet been offered. Thus the predictive potential of this theory is still largely untested.

Although the motivations of employees cannot always be reduced to a simple formula, the concepts of expectancy theory do suggest

Figure 7–3
Expectancy model illustration

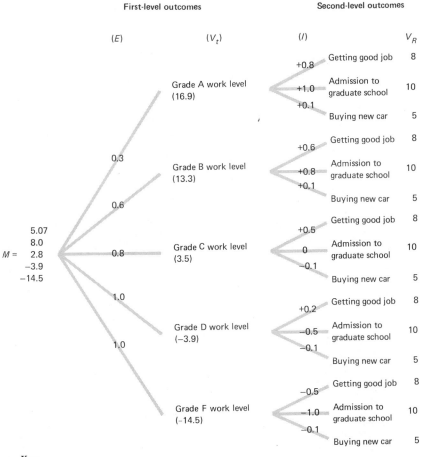

Key:
  M = Force to perform. If a person has ability, then M = expected level of performance, since
      performance = motivation X ability (expectancy times valence of task performance)
  E = Expectancy of success if this is path of action chosen
  V_t = Valence of task action (the sum of the cross products of I and V_R)
  I = Instrumentality (degree of contingency relationship between task performance and reward)
  V_R = Valence of reward offered

several prescriptions for managers in dealing with individuals and groups. Galbraith and Cummings (1967) suggest the following: (1) The components of an organizational reward system, such as money, fringe benefits, and promotion, must be desired by the employee; that is, they must be positively valent in the employee's ordering of preferences. (2) The employee must perceive that variations in performance level will lead to variations in the amount of reward received; that is, the instrumentality between performance and reward must be significantly different from zero. (3) Given (1) and (2), the technology, union contract, and other environmental factors constraining the effectiveness of the reward system must be such that managers can vary the magnitude of the reward component sufficiently to evoke variations in employee behavior.

Goal-setting theory

Although expectancy theory has been the most popular explanation of worker motivation (see, for example, Lawler, 1973) it has not had as much impact in on-the-job settings as has goal-setting theory. According to Locke (1976), expectancy theory as currently formulated is nothing more than a theory of cognitive hedonism which posits that the individual cognitively chooses the course of action that leads to the greatest degree of pleasure or the smallest degree of pain. Locke criticizes expectancy theory for failing to see that hedonistic cognitions alone are insufficient to determine a person's value system, but he also notes that values alone are insufficient to determine a person's behavior. Following the teaching of Tolman (1932), he states: "If individuals cannot properly be described as pursuing pleasure, then what does guide their action? With respect to motivation, it would be more accurate to say that individuals strive to attain goals, values or purposes than to say that they strive for pleasure. Even when pleasure is a causal factor in choice, an individual's focus in acting is typically on the object of the action (the goal) rather than on pleasure" (Locke, 1976, p. 2).

Thus, in goal-setting theory there seem to be two cognitive determinants of behavior: *values* and *intentions* (goals). Locke offers two definitions of values: "A value is that which one acts to gain and/or keep" (Rand, 1964); "It is that which one regards as conducive to one's welfare" (Branden, 1966). Locke goes on to state that the form in which one experiences one's value judgments are emotions. For Locke, therefore, the most fundamental effects of goals on mental or physical action are directive in nature. They guide people's thoughts and overt acts to one end rather than another. Locke goes on to state that not every goal leads to an activity or end specified by the goal. A particular goal may not lead to an efficacious action because it conflicts with the individual's other goals. Moreover, the situation at a given time may be perceived as inappropriate for action. An individual may not have sufficient knowledge, ability, or determination to carry out his plan of action. Even abortive action, however, is typically initiated and guided by conscious goals, and such action may be highly correlated with the action intended. Schematically, a goal-setting model of performance appears as shown in Figure 7–4.

A considerable amount of work has been carried out to test the linkage between goal setting and action. Although this work has been confined to a few investigators and some rather constrained settings, the support is impressive. Locke and his associates (see Locke, 1968) conducted a series of laboratory experiments to test the effects of goals on performance. They found that the higher the intended level of achievement among their subjects, the higher the level of performance. Even individuals who tried for goals so high that the goals were rarely, if ever, reached, performed better than did individuals who set relatively easy goals.

Figure 7–4
Goal-setting model of motivation

Values → Emotions ——→ Intentions——→ Responses or——→ Consequences,
        and desires   (goals)   performance   feedback, or reinforcement

Researchers have found that goal setting not only affects performance levels but also has a direct effect on satisfaction. Foa (1957) described satisfaction as a function of a cognitive comparison between an individual's perceptions of his outcome at a task and his expectations about that outcome. In this and other research, satisfaction is shown to be a monotonically increasing function of the algebraic difference between an individual's perceptions about an outcome and his prior expectations about that outcome. According to Ilgen and Hamstra (1972), when a situation is perceived as yielding less than expected, the individual will be less satisfied than when it is perceived as yielding as much as expected. When the situation is perceived as yielding more than expected, the individual will be more satisfied than when it is perceived as yielding as much as expected.

Although most of the support for goal-setting theory has come from laboratory experiments, work by Carroll and Tosi (1973), Latham and Kinne (1974), Latham and Baldes (1975), and Kim and Hamner (1976) has also established the external validity of goal setting as an important motivational tool.

Thus there seems to be no dispute that goal setting is a cause of performance. If a manager knows what a person expects or values, what goals the person has, and what rewards the person finds reinforcing, then the manager has the tools needed to channel the energy of the person in a given direction.

ONCE BEHAVIOR IS CHANNELED, HOW IS IT MAINTAINED?

You will recall that at the beginning of this chapter we said that the study of motivation implies an understanding of how to *energize, channel,* and *maintain* behavior. Just as there are several theories which explain how behavior is energized and channeled, there are also several theories which explain how behavior is maintained. These theories are all similar in nature since they deal with the internal and external reward structure. They include reinforcement theory, social comparison theory, attribution theory, and two-factor theory. Since we discussed reinforcement theory in detail in Chapters 3 and 4, we will focus our discussion here on social comparison theory, attribution theory, and two-factor theory.

Social comparison theory

Another cognitive approach to explaining worker motivation is that of social comparison. An early social comparison framework was developed by Festinger (1954). Festinger hypothesized that people possess a drive to evaluate their opinions and attitudes (that is, their cognitive state). People prefer to use objective criteria for this purpose if such criteria are available. Festinger went on to suggest that when no objective criteria are available, people compare themselves with other persons having similar ability and opinions.

The effect of Festinger's writings on worker motivation theory is evident in the writings of Adams (1961). According to Adams' equity theory, individuals compare the ratio of their inputs and outcomes to the input-outcome ratios of another person. The crucial element is the individual's perception of inequality in the following relationship:

$$\frac{\text{Outcomes}}{\text{Inputs (own)}} = \frac{\text{Outcomes}}{\text{Inputs (other's)}}$$

If an inequality is seen in the above comparison, individuals will act to reduce the perceived deprivation or overpayment. An individual may alter his inputs or outcomes, may attempt to alter the comparison person's inputs or outcomes, or may cognitively distort any of these four factors. The individual may also choose a different comparison person, or perhaps even leave the work situation. Some research suggests that individuals will increase their inputs if they perceive that they are overrewarded (see, for example, Adams & Rosenbaum, 1962; Goodman & Friedman, 1969). There are also data showing that overrewarded individuals may actively lobby to increase the outcomes of others (for example, Staw, Notz, & Cook, 1974). However, the data on the actions of individuals who perceive that they are underrewarded are much more definitive. According to Adams (1963), individuals will generally take that course of action which is least costly to them, but typically will reduce their level of inputs—put forth less effort, make fewer personal sacrifices, or leave the organization if corrective increases in outcome are not obtained.

One of the weakest elements of equity theory is its analysis of the process by which individuals choose a comparison other. Fortunately, there is beginning to be some systematic research and theory development on this problem (Goodman, 1976). Goodman suggests that a stimulus event triggers a search program. After an individual finds a comparison person, a testing procedure is enacted and comparisons take place. The referents may be the individual himself at an earlier period, other individuals in his organization, or the system as a whole.

Ilgen and Hamstra (1972) and Hamner and Harnett (1974) have shown the level of satisfaction or dissatisfaction (deprivation) with the outcomes received to be a function of two comparisons. The first involves a person's comparison of his or her actual performance with his or her expected level of performance (cognitively determined through goal setting). The second involves the comparison of actual performance to the perceived performance of a reference person (an equity comparison).

In regard to the first comparison, Hamner and Harnett (1974), for example, found that subjects who exceeded their goals were significantly more satisfied than subjects who failed to meet their goals. In regard to the second comparison, Hamner and Harnett found that subjects whose outcomes exceeded their comparison person's outcomes were significantly more satisfied than subjects whose outcomes fell short of their comparison person's outcomes.

This same study showed that there was little difference in satisfaction among individuals who exceeded their goal, individuals who exceeded their reference person's performance, and individuals who did both. The least satisfied individuals by far were those who failed to exceed either their goals or their reference person's performance. This result suggests that many individuals may have a flexible standard of comparison for determining satisfaction with a reward—either exceed their personal goal (an internal comparison, Smith, Kendall, & Hulin, 1969) or exceed the performance level of their reference person (an external comparison, Smith et al., 1969), but not necessarily both.

Thus we see that whereas goal-setting theory and expectancy theory discuss the determinants of performance levels, social comparison theory explains how a person can use external comparisons to determine the *appropriateness* of that performance level and the resulting reward.

We also see, from the work of Ilgen and Hamstra (1972) and Hamner and Harnett (1974), how a person can use internal comparisons (expectancies and goals) to make these same judgments of appropriateness.

Therefore, instead of conflicting with other motivational theories that we have discussed previously, social comparison theory extends our ability to predict the worker's level of performance and satisfaction. Indeed, the theory, especially as formulated by Adams (1963), brings into clearer focus the important determinants of satisfaction with rewards.

It seems, therefore, that people determine the appropriateness of their performance and its consequences on the basis of both internal and external comparisons. Thus, for practitioners, the message should be that future performance is determined, to a great extent, by the way in which goals are set and rewards are administered. When employees perceive failure in their own performance and/or reward inequity, their satisfaction is predicted to be reduced. If this situation is not corrected, the employees' feeling of dissatisfaction with self or others is likely to have a negative impact on future perceptions of valences and goals, and thus, eventually, on performance itself.

Obviously, the most problematic form of inequity for practitioners is some form of perceived underpayment or relative deprivation. Unfortunately, this type of inequity is also the most prevalent. It may be virtually impossible to remove the perception of deprivation for all the members of a given social organization. Nevertheless, it may be possible to manage the consequences of perceived deprivation more effectively.

Some practical recommendations can be made from equity formulations. First, it would seem that the entire process of performance evaluation must be made an explicit, public process, perhaps even with some form of adjudication or appeal. At the very least, it would seem essential that organizations make explicit exactly what inputs are valued highly for individual employees. Similarly, outcomes within organizations should be overtly tied to such inputs. Lawler (1973), for instance, reports that employees tend to overestimate the pay others receive. From a social comparison point of view this may be harmful if it leads individuals to reduce their own inputs in order to remedy perceived inequity. Thus policies of pay secrecy should be reexamined (see Chapter 11). Managers should also be attuned to the fact that different types of employees select different comparison others. Salaried individuals tend to compare themselves to values that they themselves have established. Professionals, on the other hand, compare their inputs and outcomes to those of other professionals (Goodman, 1976). The fact that an individual may be well rewarded by intraorganizational standards does not ensure high employee inputs if the comparison others are much better rewarded professional referents.

Attribution theories

Another class of motivation theories which has gained prominence of late is the attribution approach. The most well developed theoretical notion of this approach is what Kelley (1971) has termed the "discounting principle." Simply stated, "the role of a given cause in producing a given effect is discounted if other plausible causes are also present" (Kelley, 1971, p. 113). There have been many demonstrations of this principle within both interpersonal and individual task situations.

Within the interpersonal area, Heider (1958) noted that the causes of another's actions are a function of personal and environmental forces, and that one will infer personal causation to the extent that environmental forces are absent.

More recently, Bem (1972) extrapolated the discounting principle of causal attribution to the study of self-perception—or how one views his own behavior—within a social context. Bem hypothesized that the strength of external pressures will determine the likelihood that a person will attribute his own actions to external or internal causes. Thus, a person who acts under strong external rewards or punishments is likely to assume that his behavior is under external control. However, if extrinsic contingencies are not strong or salient, the person is likely to assume that this behavior is due to his own interest in the activity or that his behavior is intrinsically motivated. De Charmes (1968) has made a similar point in his discussion of individuals' perception of personal causation: "As a first approximation, we propose that whenever a person experiences himself to be the locus of causality for his own behavior (to be an Origin), he will consider himself to be intrinsically motivated. Conversely, when a person perceives the locus of causality for his behavior to be external to himself (that he is a Pawn), he will consider himself to be extrinsically motivated" (p. 328).

Although such a distinction between intrinsic and extrinsic motivation may be of academic interest, the impetus for increased concern by organizational psychologists stems from the practical possibility that intrinsic and extrinsic motivation may not be strictly additive. Deci (1971), for instance, suggested that the use of extrinsic rewards may lower intrinsic motivation on a positively perceived task activity. His studies show that if you pay people for doing something they already enjoy doing, they will soon enjoy it less, and that if the pay is later withdrawn, they will expend less effort in doing it.

Some boundary conditions have been established for the negative relation between intrinsic and extrinsic motivation. Deci (1972) suggests that extrinsic rewards may not lower intrinsic motivation if the rewards are not contingently administered according to individual level of performance. Ross (1975) claims that external rewards must be salient in the task situation. Staw, Calder, and Hess (1976) maintain that external rewards must be inappropriate or counter to situational norms in order to find an inhibitory effect.

Although the above moderating variables would appear to lessen the concern of managers intent on organizational motivation, the attribution approach remains troublesome to organizational psychologists. It is probably evident to the reader by now that the causal attribution theory of Deci (1972) and de Charmes (1968), known as "cognitive evaluation" theory, is somewhat in disagreement with reinforcement theory, expectancy theory, goal-setting theory, and social comparison theory as regards the impact of contingent reinforcement (especially monetary rewards) on worker motivation. While the latter four theories differ greatly on the origins of behavior and/or the reasons why contingent reinforcement has a positive impact on future performance, they do agree that contingent rewards, including money, enhance the motivational level of a person involved in an interesting task assignment. This is not the case with cognitive evaluation theory. As de Charmes (1968) notes:

> Intrinsically motivating tasks are those in which a person feels that he is in control, that he originated the behavior (as an Origin) with the concomitant feelings of free choice and commitment. Introduction of extrinsic reward, however, places the person in a dependent position relative to the source of the reward. To the extent that the person expects a reward for his task he is unfree and has not chosen the task for its own sake alone. The source of the reward is an external causal locus for his behavior. When rewards are important, dependence on the source of reward places a person in the position of a Pawn. Put in a more commonplace way, the highly paid employee is less free to dissent. (p. 329)

Although there is some anecdotal support for the theory that money is not a motivator of performance or is a negative motivator of performance, there is little empirical support. Indeed, as we have discussed in this chapter and in Chapter 11, contingently administered rewards are positively related to high levels of performance. It is possible, however, that money and other external rewards can be so strong that the intrinsic aspects of the task itself are ignored, to the detriment of future performance. It is also possible that offering strong external rewards, such as money, is inappropriate in certain situations (for example, in return for friendship, to obtain sexual favors, and so on). In those situations, offering such rewards may have detrimental effects on the performance and the relationship. However, cognitive evaluation theory seems to relate only to those special circumstances. In work situations, it seems to have less relevance. It does make a contribution, however, in that it highlights the need to understand both the rewards of the task (intrinsic rewards) and the rewards of the outcomes (extrinsic rewards).

Two-factor theory

A theory of work motivation which has aroused a good deal of comment, support, and controversy in recent years and one whose terminology is now ingrained in modern management literature is Herzberg's (1959) two-factor theory (also known as the motivation-hygiene theory). The theory is based on the assumption that dissatisfaction leading to the avoidance of work and satisfaction leading to attraction toward work do not represent the end points of a single continuum. Rather, two separate, unipolar continua are required to reflect people's dual orientation to work; hence, the two-factor theory. On the one hand, people seek to avoid anything painful or unpleasant. Hence, unpleasant factors which cannot be avoided produce degrees of increasing job dissatisfaction. That is:

−	0
Increasing job dis-satisfaction Negative orientation to work	No dissatisfaction Neutral orientation to work

On the other hand, people are attracted toward anything agreeable or pleasant. Hence, pleasant or attractive factors which are potentially attainable lead to degrees of increasing job satisfaction. That is:

0	+
No satisfaction Neutral orientation to work	Increasing job satisfaction Positive orientation to work

As discussed below, the independence of these two scales results from two distinctive sets of job factors that apply to only one continuum or the other.

Herzberg's theory was derived from a study of need satisfactions and the reported motivational effects of those satisfactions on 200 engineers and accountants employed by firms in the Pittsburgh area. Each of these employees was asked to recall an event or a time personally experienced at work when he felt particularly and exceptionally *good* about his job. Interviews were then conducted to determine why the employees felt as they did, and whether their feelings of satisfaction had affected their performance, their personal relationships, and their feelings of well-being. The same respondents were then asked to recall an event or a time personally experienced at work when they felt particularly and exceptionally *bad* about their jobs. Interviews followed to determine the nature of the events which led to the negative expressions.

On the basis of the data provided by the employees' recall (known as the "critical incident" method), by the subsequent interviews, and by a content analysis of the information obtained, the following conclu-

Figure 7–5
The components of
Herzberg's two-factor theory

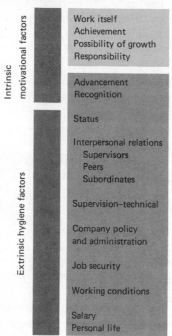

sions were derived: (1) Factors associated with the job itself (intrinsic, content, or psychological factors) tend to lead to job satisfaction (on the positive side, or to the right of zero, as noted above). The intrinsic factors associated with job satisfaction are achievement, recognition for work well done, the work itself, responsibility, and advancement. (2) Factors associated with the environment surrounding the job (extrinsic, context, or physical factors) tend to lead to job dissatisfaction (on the negative side, or to the left of zero, as noted above). As shown in Figure 7–5, the extrinsic factors associated with job dissatisfaction are company policy and administration, supervision, salary, interpersonal relations, and working conditions. (3) Job satisfiers are generally determiners of long-term changes, and job dissatisfiers are generally determiners of short-term positive changes of attitude. (4) <u>Job satisfiers</u> <u>are called</u> *motivators* <u>since they fulfill an individual's need for psycho-</u> <u>logical growth. Job dissatisfiers are called</u> *hygienes* <u>since they merely</u> <u>serve to prevent an individual from getting "sick of work"; hence,</u> the motivation-hygiene theory.

Herzberg's theory has been one of the most researched theories in organizational behavior. Evidence refuting the theory is almost as extensive as the evidence confirming it. Herzberg himself, in a review of 10 studies of 17 populations through 1966, all of which used the "critical incident method," found general confirmation for the theory. However, House and Wigdor, in a review of 31 studies through 1967, some of which did not use the "critical incident method," found a general lack of confirmation for the theory. In their own reinterpretation of Herzberg's original data, House and Wigdor (1967) found that lack of achievement and recognition were more frequently identified as job dissatisfiers than were working conditions and relations with supervisors.

Even though the evidence does not uniformly support the theory, it would be foolish to suggest that hygiene factors are not important. They *are* important. Salary, company policy, administration, and working conditions must not be neglected, but they must be held in perspective. The hygienes have always been—and probably always will be— easier to measure, control, and manipulate than the motivators. The motivators are more complex and subjective, and often too elusive to measure. But to the extent that management concentrates on hygienes, while at the same time neglecting motivators, then workers are probably going to seek more of the hygienes—higher salaries, better working conditions, more fringe benefits, shorter hours, and so on.

It seems that both cognitive evaluation theory and Herzberg's two-factor theory point out the need to examine the rewards of the task itself as a sustainer of performance. We will have more to say about this in Chapter 11 on worker motivation programs. We should note here, however, that both task rewards (how pleasant is my task? how challenging is my job?) and outcome rewards (praise, promotion, pay) should be used by management as a tool for maintaining channeled behavior.

SUMMARY

Motivation is a concept used to explain why a person performs in the manner and on the level that he or she does. Since performance is assumed to be a function of motivation and ability, if an able person fails to perform as we expect, then we tend to attribute the lack of performance to low motivation. This low motivation can stem from a lack of drive, inadequate goals, or a negative task assignment. A major point made in this chapter is that a manager needs to understand, from the point of view of the employee, (1) what energizes behavior, (2) what directs or channels behavior, and (3) how channeled behavior can be maintained. A manager can partially influence all three of these dimensions; therefore, when a worker is "unmotivated" in a task situation, the low productivity which results is partially the fault of the manager.

Figure 7–6
General model of performance

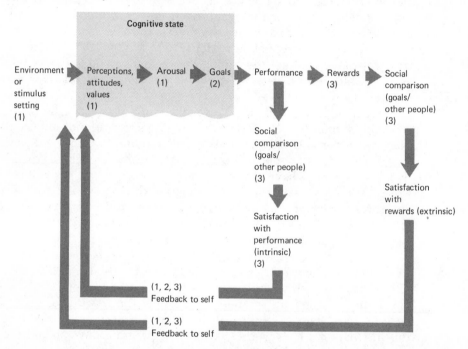

If we draw upon the material presented thus far in this text, we can now depict a general model of performance as shown in Figure 7–6.

In Figure 7–6 we see that a person's cognitive state and environmental situation influence current and future levels of performance. Number one (1) items are "drive-producing" (energizing) motivators. Number two (2) items are "channeling" motivators. Number three (3) items are "maintaining" motivators. Thus, although motivation is a complex phenomenon, by directly or indirectly controlling these various components, a manager can have a great influence on a worker's performance level. However, since the worker is also influenced by persons other than the manager, the manager can never expect to be able to exercise complete control over the motivation of the worker.

CONCEPTS TO REMEMBER

need hierarchy   expectancy
career stages   social comparison
activation   equity
first- and second-level outcomes   two-factor theory
valence   attribution
instrumentality   hygienes
critical incident method

QUESTIONS FOR DISCUSSION

1. How does a motivated person differ from an unmotivated person?
2. What contribution do Herzberg's two-factor theory and cognitive evaluation theory make to our understanding of motivation? That is, even though the research does not support these theories, why do both of these theories imply sound management principles?
3. How are a person's perceptions (Chapter 5) and attitude (Chapter 6) related to the person's motivation level?
4. Bill Butterfield, marketing manager of the Topeka Manufacturing Company, had just completed a two-week trip during which he audited customer accounts and prospective accounts in the northeastern states. His primary intention was to do follow-up work on prospective accounts contacted by sales staff members during the previous six months. The prospective clients were usually dealers or large department stores.

   To his amazement, Mr. Butterfield discovered that almost all of the so-called prospective accounts were fictitious. The sales staff had obviously turned in falsely documented field reports and expense statements. Company sales personnel had actually called upon only 6 of 32 reported dealers or department stores. Thus Mr. Butterfield surmised that the sales staff had falsely claimed approximately 80 percent of the goodwill contacts. Further study showed that all members of the sales staff had followed this general practice and that not one had a clean record.

   a. How would reinforcement theory, expectancy theory, goal-setting theory, and equity theory be used to explain this situation?
   b. How would two-factor theory and cognitive evaluation theory explain this situation?

    c. How do you explain the fact that *all* sales personnel followed this practice?

REFERENCES

Adams, J. S.   Wages inequities in a clerical task. Unpublished study, General Electric Company, New York, 1961.

Adams, J. S.   Toward an understanding of inequity. *Journal of Abnormal Social Psychology.* 1963, *67,* 422–436.

Adams, J. S., & Rosenbaum, W. B.   The relationship of worker productivity to cognitive dissonance about wage inequities. *Journal of Applied Psychology,* 1962, *46,* 161–164.

Alderfer, C. P.   An empirical test of a new theory of human needs. *Organizational Behavior and Human Performance,* 1969, *4,* 142–175.

Bem, D. J.   "Self-perception theory." In L. Berkowitz (Ed.), *Advances in experimental social psychology* (Vol. 6). New York: Academic Press, 1972.

Branden, N.   Emotions and values. *Objectivist,* 1966, *5,* 1–9.

Calder, B. J., & Staw, B. M.   Interaction of intrinsic and extrinsic motivation: Some methodological notes. *Journal of Personality and Social Psychology,* 1975.

Carroll, S. J., & Tosi, H. L.   *Management by objectives.* New York: Macmillan, 1973.

De Charmes, R.   *Personal causation.* New York: Academic Press, 1968.

Deci, E. L.   Intrinsic motivation, extrinsic reinforcement, and inequity. *Journal of Personality and Social Psychology,* 1972, *22,* 113–120.

Festinger, L.   A theory of social comparison processes. *Human Relations,* 1954, *7,* 117–140.

Foa, V. E.   Relations of worker's expectation to satisfaction with the supervisor. *Personnel Psychology,* 1957, *10,* 161–168.

Galbraith, J., & Cummings, L. L.   An empirical investigation of the motivational determinants of past performance: Interactive effects between instrumentality, valence, motivation, and ability. *Organizational Behavior and Human Performance,* 1967, *2*(3), 237–257.

Goodman, P. S.   Social comparison processes in organizations. In B. M. Staw & G. R. Salancik (Eds.), *New directions in organizational behavior.* Chicago: St. Clair Press, 1976.

Goodman, P. S., & Friedman, A.   An examination of quantity and quality of performance under conditions of overpayment in piece rate. *Organizational Behavior and Human Performance,* 1969, *4,* 365–374.

Hall, D. T.   *Careers in organizations.* Pacific Palisades, Calif.: Goodyear, 1976.

Hall, D. T. & Nougaim, K. E.   An examination of Maslow's need hierarchy in an organizational setting. *Organizational Behavior and Human Performance,* 1968, *3*(1), 12–35.

Hamner, W. C., & Harnett, D. L.   Goal setting, performance, and satisfaction in an interdependent task. *Organizational Behavior and Human Performance,* 1974, *12,* 217–230.

Heider, F.   *The psychology of interpersonal relations.* New York: Wiley, 1958.

Heneman, H. G., III, & Schwab, D. P.   Evaluation of research on expectancy theory predictions of employee performance. *Psychological Bulletin,* 1972, *78,* 1–9.

Herzberg, F.   *Work and the nature of man.* Cleveland: World Publishing Company, 1966.

Herzberg, F., Mausner, B., & Snyderman, B.   *The motivation to work* (2d ed.). New York: Wiley, 1959.

House, R. J., & Wigdor, L. A.   Herzberg's dual-factor theory of job satisfaction and motivation: A review of the evidence and a criticism. *Personnel Psychology,* 1967, *20*(4), 369–389.

Ilgen, D. R., & Hamstra, B. W.   Performance satisfaction as a function of the difference between expected and reported performance at five levels of reported performance. *Organizational Behavior and Human Performance,* 1972, *7,* 359–370.

Johnson, J. H.   " 'Failure is a word I don't accept.' " *Harvard Business Review,* March–April 1976. Copyright © 1976 by the Presidents and Fellows of Harvard College; all rights reserved.

Kelley, H. H.   *Attribution in social interaction.* New York: General Learning Press, 1971.

Kim, J., & Hamner, W. C.   The effect of goal setting, feedback, and praise on productivity and satisfaction in an organizational setting. *Journal of Applied Psychology,* 1976, *61,* 48–57.

Latham, G. P., & Baldes, J. J.   The practical significance of Locke's theory of goal setting. *Journal of Applied Psychology,* 1975, *60,* 122–124.

Latham, G. P., & Kinne, S. B.   Improving job performance through training in goal setting. *Journal of Applied Psychology,* 1974, *59,* 20–24.

Lawler, E. E.   *Motivation in work organizations.* Monterey, Calif.: Brooks/ Cole, 1973.

Locke, E. A.   Toward a theory of task motivation and incentives. *Organizational Behavior and Human Performance,* 1968, *3,* 157–189.

Locke, E. A.   Personnel attitudes and motivation. Working paper, University of Maryland, 1976.

Maslow, A. H.   A theory of human motivation. *Psychological Review,* July 1943, 370–396.

McGregor, D.   *The human side of enterprise.* New York: McGraw-Hill, 1960.

Mitchell, T. R., & Biglan, A.   Instrumentality theories: Current uses in psychology. *Psychological Bulletin,* 1971, *76*(6), 432–454.

Porter, L. W., & Lawler, E. E.   *Managerial attitudes and performance.* Homewood, Ill.: Irwin-Dorsey, 1968.

Rand, A.   The objectivist ethics. In A. Rand (Ed.), *The virtue of selfishness.* New York: Signet, 1964.

Ross, M.   Salience of reward and intrinsic motivation. *Journal of Personality and Social Psychology,* 1975, *32,* 245–254.

Scott, W. E., Jr.   Activation theory and task design. *Organizational Behavior and Human Performance,* 1966, *1,* 3–30.

Smith, P. C., Kendall, L. M., & Hulin, C. L.   *The measurement of satisfaction in work and retirement.* Chicago: Rand McNally, 1969.

Staw, B. M., Calder, B., & Hess, R.   Intrinsic motivation and norms of payment. Working paper, Northwestern University, 1976.

Staw, B. M., Notz, W. W., & Cook, T. D.   Vulnerability to draft and attitudes toward troop withdrawal from Indochina: Replication and refinement. *Psychological Reports,* 1974, *34,* 407–417.

Steers, R. M., & Porter, L. W. (Eds.).   *Motivation and work behavior.* New York: McGraw-Hill, 1975.

Tolman, E. C.   *Purposive behavior in animals and men.* New York: Century, 1932.

Vroom, V. H.   *Work and motivation.* New York: Wiley, 1964.

Wahba, M., & House, R.   Expectancy theory in work and motivation: Some logical and methodological issues. Working paper, Baruch College, City University of New York, 1972.

8

Personality
Dimensions of individual differences

What are the important dimensions of personality?

How can the organization accommodate diverse personalities in an effective manner?

As we pointed out in Chapter 2, theories and concepts of organizational behavior are usually pitched at a rather high level of abstraction. The reasons for this include: the aim for generality in relating findings from one area of study to another; the effort to achieve economy and elegance in language (a theory that incorporates a great many details becomes awkward and unwieldy in presentation); and the attempt to filter out irrelevant issues from the questions that have broader and more recurrent significance.

One consequence of this high level of abstraction is that "organizational behavior" in these theories seems to refer to the behavior of nameless, dimensionless entities rather than to that of real people. Predictions drawn from the theories refer to "tendencies" of behavior—the idea being that, given a large enough number of persons, some proportion of them, much of the time, will behave as the theories predict. The theories, then, have the flavor of dealing with some standardized, homogenized raw material which is pumped into organizations, and convey the notion that out of this malleable material the organizational environment and processes will shape identifiable products.

In the classroom, of course, students and practitioners are quick to point out gaps in behavioral theories by observing, "But some people won't react that way—it depends on the personality of the individual." And this observation is correct, as far as it goes (to be of value to theories of organizational behavior, it must go farther than that). Individuals come to organizations with rich and widely differing histories, exposure to differing previous (and concurrent) environments, different physiological and biochemical makeups, different behavioral repertoires, and different perceptual styles. Although the organizations (if they are to survive at all) will limit to some degree this natural variance as it is reflected in behavior, individual differences will still be abundantly manifest. Therefore, some account has to be taken of the psychology of individual attributes and, more specifically, of personality, to increase the explanatory and predictive power of our theories.

This chapter will explore some of the dimensions in personality which have been found to be useful for understanding individual differences. It is not in any way intended to be a complete account of our knowledge about personality or other individual attributes. There are many approaches and schools of thought in the study of personality, and a single chapter could not possibly do justice to the insights of such prolific theorists as Sigmund Freud, Gordon Allport, Carl Rogers, Erich Fromm, Karen Horney, Henry A. Murray, Kurt Lewin, and others. Also, there are individual differences along dimensions which are not explicitly addressed here, such as age, sex, intelligence, education, and ethnic origin.[1]

---

[1] The interested reader is referred to *The Psychology of Individual Differences*, by Leona E. Tyler (1965), for a more comprehensive account of this field.

THE CONCEPT OF PERSONALITY

"Personality" has been defined in different ways by those who study it, but these definitions usually include the notion of *stable differences in manner of responding to one or more classes of situations.* Take, for example, the situation in which a superior chastises three subordinates for sloppy work. Subordinate A may react by conscientiously attempting to improve his work; subordinate B may react in a resentful manner by deliberately becoming sloppier; subordinate C may simply "shrug it off" and not change at all. Since the environmental situation is the same for all three subordinates, the differences in behavior could be explained by differences in personality. If continued observation revealed that A, B, and C characteristically responded in these different ways to other punitive measures, our inferences about differences in personality would be strengthened. When we describe persons by using such terms as *honest, shy, aggressive, ambitious,* and *conservative,* we are not talking about specific episodes but about stabilities over time and across specific situations in how they characteristically behave. Some traits are, of course, likely to be more stable or resistant to change than others, but in our intuitive as well as our scientific habits of thinking, we regard personality (or simply "the person," as defined by his or her personality) as being stable over short time intervals.

In using individual personality traits to enrich our theories of behavior in organizations, we soon run into a problem—there are so many traits that it is an impossible task to use all of them (in theory or practice). In a search through the dictionary Allport and Odbert (1936) found that there are from 3,000 to 5,000 words for describing personal qualities. So we must either choose a small number of traits which we think are more important than the rest, or we must choose some dimensions which are so broad in meaning that each subsumes a greater number of more specific "surface" traits. Psychologists have generally opted for the latter course; and since theories of organizational behavior should build on the spadework of the basic disciplines, we will largely follow the lead of the psychologists.

At this point it should be clear that even though we hoped to make our theories less abstract by adding personality variables to them, a personality trait or dimension is itself an abstract concept. People do not really "have" honesty or aggressiveness. The trait names are shorthand fictions which enable us to describe economically someone's characteristic and somewhat consistent pattern of responding to certain classes of situations; and to use, as we must, a limited number of broad personality dimensions necessarily means that even the description of a single trait will allow for differences in the way that trait is manifested or in the particular situations in which an individual's behavior is described by that trait.

PERSONALITY MEASUREMENT

People are not simply honest or dishonest, active or passive, impulsive or restrained—they are honest, active, or impulsive in varying degrees. To use personality variables in either a scientific or practical manner in our theories, we need some means of measuring, however crudely, the extent to which people differ on the personality dimensions or traits we choose to study. Basic and applied studies of organizational behavior have found several methods (all of them crude and imperfect, but with more or less offsetting error tendencies) to accomplish at least some relative ordering of individuals on personality attributes.

Questionnaires

The most frequently used method is probably the "inventory" approach. This requires the individual to answer (usually in written form, but sometimes orally) a series of questions about himself—what he thinks, what he likes, what he often does. Usually the question is in a very specific form (for example, "Do you daydream a lot?"), and the person can answer either "Yes" or "No," or along a wider continuum, "Very often," "Somewhat often," "Sometimes," "Very rarely," "Almost never." The questions are also designed to refer to very specific manifestations of a broad, underlying trait. The greater the number of questions a person answers in a way consistent with the underlying trait, and/or the more emphatically he does this, the greater his score.

This measurement approach has several limitations. First, it assumes that people will be candid in answering such questions. Even if the questionnaire is anonymous and a pencil and paper format is used, people are not always willing to answer questions in ways that they think would make them appear lacking in virtue or other socially desirable qualities. Some personality inventories have "lie" scales built into them in order to identify scorers who are "faking," and others have irrelevant "buffer" items to disguise the intended use and meaning of the measure, but these devices do not completely eliminate the problem of answering in socially desirable rather than individually descriptive terms. Second, these types of measurement methods assume that a person is *able* (as well as willing) to view his own behavior in an objective, detached manner. People may have self-concepts biased in positive, or negative fashions, due to different frames of reference, differences in the groups to which they compare themselves, or differences in level of aspiration. Quite often, people express the feeling that they simply and honestly don't know how to respond to questions in the inventory, and that to give any answer would be arbitrary or misleading.

Ratings by observers

A second measurement approach is to have others who are familiar observers of a subject's behavior (friends, family, work associates) rate that behavior on some trait—for example, sociability—on a scale from 1 (very unsociable) to 7 (very sociable). The assumptions behind this approach are that the trait in question is likely to be made manifest frequently to such persons and that these persons can be more objective in observing and describing the behavior than can the subject himself. Nevertheless, there are still problems with this method. Persons who interact with the same individual will do so in different role relationships, and thus each person will probably be exposed to only a specialized sample of the individual's behavior. The boss, the spouse, the brother, the golf partner, and the secretary may be interacting with the same physical individual, but their own responses will elicit different response repertoires from the individual. Furthermore, our own personalities are likely to affect how we perceive or rate another person's behavior (see Chapter 5), and it is still a moot question whether the ability to judge people is general or specific.

The questionnaire and rating methods, despite their limitations, are the ones most often used by, and most easily accessible to, researchers and practitioners of organizational behavior. Even when used in a rough way, these devices can help identify those individuals within a given population who are at the extreme ends of the personality dimension considered—for example, the top and bottom quartiles. It should be noted that the *construction* of such devices, as opposed to their use and interpretation, is a job for personnel who have specialized training along those lines. Also, some background in personnel or industrial psychology or consultation with a psychologist is needed to find, select, score, and interpret the appropriate measures.

Other methods of personality assessment

The *projective* test, a measure seldom used by anyone other than clinical or research psychologists, requires that a person respond to some unstructured stimulus (such as an inkblot, a cartoon, or a photograph) by describing his thoughts about the stimulus, telling what it looks like to him, or making up a story about it. The guiding assumption here is that the more ambiguous the stimulus, the more a person reads his own values, habits, and temperament into the stimulus. This approach has been used by McClelland (1961) in trying to gauge an individual's needs for achievement, power, and affiliation. The scoring of such tests typically corresponds to the frequency with which certain themes are mentioned or the strength with which certain kinds of imagery are evoked. Usually a very experienced or highly trained specialist is needed to quantify an individual's responses to such items.

The *behavioral* test—also used primarily for research purposes—introduces the individual to a highly controlled situation (often in a psychological laboratory). The situation is then varied or manipulated in some predesigned way, and the individual is forced to respond overtly (that is, not merely verbally). For example, he can be asked to solve a puzzle which is, in fact, insoluble. The length of time he works on the puzzle before quitting or showing anger may be taken as an index of persistence, frustration tolerance, or some other personality construct.

There are, of course, other measures, even cruder and less systematic, that organizational officials can use (at their own risk) for measures of personality. For example, the application blank or biographical inventory of an employee can be studied for hobbies, interests, educational background, affiliations, career history, or other items which (when they are actually a matter of individual choice) may have been found in past studies to *correlate* with more formal personality measures and thus provide a means for drawing some inference, however tentative, about where the person is located along some personality dimension.

Regardless of the types of personality measures chosen, these measures should *not* be used for the purpose of selecting among applicants for a job. Very little evidence exists to show that personality measures are good predictors of future job performance, particularly in managerial or administrative positions. Rulings by court and federal government officials have therefore discouraged their use in making hiring decisions. The purpose of this chapter is not to help the prospective manager screen out individuals with particular personality profiles, but rather to demonstrate the manner in which stable dimensions of individual differences combine with properties of the immediate organizational environment in affecting behavior.

A complete discussion of the different personality dimensions identified and researched to date would take us far beyond the scope of this book. What follows is a selective discussion of a number of such dimensions. The reasons for including these particular dimensions are that they seem to account for a considerable degree of variance in individual behavior, that they have been shown to have immediate relevance for behavior in organizations, and that they are currently attracting attention from teachers and researchers in the field of organizational behavior.

Emotionality and *extraversion* represent two dimensions of personality which are believed to have their ultimate basis in genetic or physiological differences. *Locus of control* is a dimension based on belief systems. *Need for achievement, need for affiliation,* and *need for power* are based on differences in motive strength. The description of these dimensions of individual differences and discussion of their relevance to performance in organizations follow.

PERSONALITY: DIMENSIONS OF PHYSIOLOGICALLY BASED DIFFERENCES

Emotionality (neuroticism)

Perhaps the first broad, underlying dimension of personality to be identified by empirical research methods was that of *neuroticism.* This is sometimes labeled emotionality or anxiety, which are perhaps more judicious terms, since among general audiences the word *neuroticism* tends to evoke the unpleasant connotations of mental illness or maladjustment. A number of different researchers—for example Eysenck, Cattell, French, and Guilford—have independently converged on this dimension as one which ties together the common features of many surface traits in behavior. Neuroticism underlies such individual differences as those pertaining to emotional instability; changeability in mood; sensitivity to environmental stress; tendencies toward guilt, worry, anxiety, and lower self-esteem; feelings of fatigue and, more generally, concern about physical health; and experience of tension. Although most of the various measures of neuroticism were validated by research on clinical patients, neuroticism is a continuous variable along which all persons range, including normal and well-adjusted persons; it is not something one "has" or doesn't have in an all-or-nothing fashion.

What is the significance of neuroticism in theories of organizational behavior? In order to answer this question, we must refer to the Yerkes-Dodson law, first formulated by those two researchers in 1908. In their experiments with rats, using electric shock and later food deprivation to manipulate motivational levels, Yerkes and Dodson (1908) found that there is an optimal level of emotional arousal for learning and performance, which tends to decrease as the task becomes more difficult or complex. For example, in their experiments on discrimination learning, Yerkes and Dodson found that performance on easy discriminations was greatest at high levels of shock, but that as discriminations became more subtle and difficult, performance was better at intermediate shock levels and declined at higher levels. Similar relationships have been found among human subjects with whom various kinds of motivational techniques have been employed. The Spence-Hull theory also predicts a curvilinear, inverted-U-shaped relationship between emotional arousal and performance (see Chapter 3 for an example). Increases in *generalized drive*—emotional arousal—make dominant responses stronger relative to responses lower in the habit hierarchy. The more routine, familiar, or simple the task, the more likely that dominant responses are correct; thus, on such tasks, increases in emotional arousal should improve task performance. At extremely high levels of emotionality, of course—as in stark fear or panic—primitive responses come into play, and then performance may break down even on simple tasks. As the task becomes more novel and complex, requiring finer discriminations, dominant responses are likely to be inappropriate; the correct responses are much weaker and lower in the habit hierarchy. On such tasks, moderate increases in emotional arousal may facilitate performance, due to a general energizing effect, but high levels of motiviation elicit dominant, incorrect responses which interfere with new learning. There is also evidence that heightened levels of motivation (in the emotional sense) cause "tunnel vision"; the person loses the ability to pick up nonobvious cues and relationships and glosses over subtle distinctions among stimuli (Silverman & Blitz, 1956).

The suggestion that people can be "too motivated," may sound strange at first, but the adverse effects of extremely high "motivation" of the avoidance kind—motivation to escape pain or avoid injuries to the ego—are well documented in everyday life. Forgetting one's lines because of stage fright, jumping from windows rather than looking for the fire escape, drawing a blank on the final exam even though one "knows" the material, all illustrate this phenomenon. Even motivation of a more positive variety can be too great—witness the number of fumbles and penalties incurred by the underdog football team as it nears the goal for a go-ahead touchdown, or the plethora of turnovers by two fine basketball teams in the opening game of a postseason tournament.

Individual neuroticism can be regarded as a source of generalized drive or as an *index of emotional arousability* which interacts with motivational pressures exerted by the environment. Persons who score higher on neuroticism will require less externally induced motivation to reach the level of emotional arousal optimal for performance. Along the same line of reasoning, they can withstand less intense external motivational pressure before their performance deteriorates (see Figure 8–1). Persons low in neuroticism may require considerable amounts of external pressure before they "get going" and may not reach their best performance until they are really "under the gun." The differences between the two types is usually most evident when the motivational pressures are of the aversive kind—such as threat or punishment.

Figure 8–1
Relationship between externally induced motivational pressure and performance for persons of high and low neuroticism

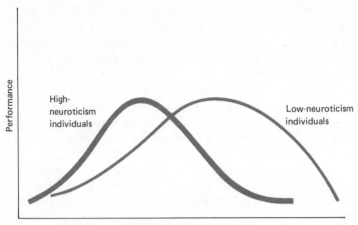

To illustrate this point, let us consider two hypothetical persons, Alice and Mary. Alice scores in the upper third of the distribution of scores on neuroticism, Mary in the lower third. Assume that they both work on a task which is moderate in terms of difficulty and complexity. Assume also that little pressure is exerted upon them by their immediate superior and that no important immediate consequences are contingent on performance. If they are roughly equal in aptitude and intelligence, Alice will probably outperform Mary. Why? Since the surrounding social or physical environment induces minimal drive, energy mobilization will be largely accounted for by internal emotional arousal, and since Alice scores higher on this dimension, she is apt to be closer to the level of drive optimal for task performance.

Now assume that their superior threatens the two women with punishment unless performance is increased, that he or she keeps close watch over them, and that co-workers are also putting pressure on them. Now Mary will probably perform more effectively than Alice. The greater pressure from the environment compensates for her lower innate drive level, and she has now reached the optimal level of drive associated with performance, whereas Alice, because of the combined effects of high innate arousability and high environmentally induced drive, has gone past the optimal drive level. Alice is now coping with internal stimuli, such as worry, fear of failure, consciousness of rapid heartbeat, muscle tautness, and self-reproach. Contending with these symptoms disrupts the smooth efficiency of her instrumental behavior.

In brief, then, individual neuroticism is a factor that has to be taken into account in any sweeping generalizations or prescriptions concerning the effects of external motivation or pressure on performance.

Studies indicate that persons high in neuroticism are particularly susceptible to the stressful effects of role conflict (Kahn, Wolfe, Quinn, Snoek, & Rosenthal, 1964) and ambiguity, particularly when the latter is also associated with job pressure (Organ, 1975a). Under conditions of low role conflict, high-neuroticism persons experience as high a level of job satisfaction as do their opposites, but under conditions of high role conflict, high-neuroticism individuals drop considerably more in satisfaction than do low-neuroticism individuals. Neuroticism is related to feelings of emotional stress when the task is very unstructured, but not when the work role is well defined and articulated.

Perhaps it should be emphasized here that high neuroticism is not in any absolute sense an undesirable characteristic of organization members and that neuroticism-prone individuals should not be systematically selected out of important jobs (Kahn et al., 1964). Such individuals do not suffer in intelligence or other general aptitudes relative to other persons, and they are certainly no less loyal or conscientious (if anything, they are sometimes conscientious to a fault, in the sense that they may "press too hard"). The point, rather, is that their maximum effectiveness and satisfaction are tapped by supervisory orientations (they generally require more nurturance and support and more frequent positive feedback, especially under stressful conditions) and incentive systems different from those which are most effective for their opposites.

One cannot help wondering about the origins of high neuroticism and whether or not organizational attempts to reduce it would be fruitful. One school of thought, supported by some empirical evidence, suggests that neuroticism is linked to hereditary biochemical and physiological factors. An hypothesis advanced by Eysenck, which seems to fit a number of findings but has not been demonstrated by direct test, is that differences in neuroticism are related to differential thresholds of arousal in the visceral brain, which integrates the autonomic functions of the sympathetic nervous system (Eysenck, 1967).

If neuroticism in behavior is indeed a product of physiologically based factors, then it would seem that organizational environments could not appreciably change this personality dimension (this is not to say, of course, that organizational environments would not interact with a given level of neuroticism in affecting individual behavior). On the other hand, Kahn and his colleagues argue that the "presence of environmental stress seems to produce 'neurotic' emotional reactions in those who score low on the neurotic anxiety scale" (Kahn et al., 1964, p. 260). Such symptoms, they admit, may be temporary rather than chronic. Nevertheless, they regard it as plausible that persistent organizationally derived stress may amplify the individual's tendencies toward the generalized trait of neuroticism, whether or not this trait is mediated by changes in body chemistry.

There is some speculation that susceptibility toward neurotic anxiety is a function of early reinforcement histories (that is, in childhood) emphasizing threat, aversive conditioning, and avoidance learning, the effects of which extend into and generalize to adult behavior. If this argument has validity, then one could argue that organizational environments which are noncontingently supportive and nurturant could over a long period of time reduce levels of neuroticism for those who are located at the extreme upper ends of the distribution. Whether such environments would have a beneficial effect, a dysfunctional effect, or no effect at all on low-neuroticism individuals is another question. In any case, any changes in neuroticism that could be effected would seem to require rather long periods of time. However, the organization official can add to his understanding of organizational behavior by recognizing the present effects of neuroticism without having to decide whether his attempts to change levels of neuroticism would be efficacious.

How can the manager identify subordinates or other organization members who may be quite high on the dimension of neuroticism? One way, of course, is to have people take one of the various available questionnaires for measuring this trait.[2] A more direct, but cruder judgment may be made by observing in people's behavior or self-descriptions the qualities which have been associated with high neuroticism. Frequent references to guilt feelings about trivial matters, expressions of worry about health that seem exaggerated or unconfirmed by medical examination, a habit of working feverishly to complete minor projects long before their deadlines, obsessive concern with possible traumatic events in the distant future, inability to shrug off past mistakes or failures, are all possible clues. The perceptive executive can notice when a patterning of such symptoms suggests an individual relatively high in neurotic emotionality and then make reasonable predictions about how such a person would react to various types of motivational systems, leadership styles, or environmental stressors.

Extraversion-introversion

The dimension of extraversion-introversion is a second broad, underlying trait which historically has figured very prominently in the theo-

---

[2] A note of caution: even the best of these instruments yield scores with a sizable error component and therefore, these instruments are likely to be useful only for identifying the extreme ends of the distribution, such as the upper or lower quartiles; or they are applicable primarily to comparisons of relatively large groups, say, 25 or more persons, in terms of average level of emotionality.

retical and empirical work on personality. The dimension has had a stormy history, however, and there has been more confusion and disagreement about its meaning than has been the case with neuroticism.

In everyday parlance, we typically use the terms *extravert* and *introvert* in a manner that relates primarily to sociability: extraverts are more outgoing and gregarious, introverts shier and more retiring. The meaning of extraversion in the psychological literature has been broader than this, although sociability may be one of a cluster of surface traits related to extraversion. Jung used the concept "extraversion" to refer to "the kind of outward orientation that makes a person highly aware of what is going on around him and causes him to direct his energy toward objects and people outside himself" (Tyler, 1965). "Introversion" referred to the opposite tendency—sensitivity to one's own feelings, memories, consciousness, and inner life.

A contemporary interpretation of extraversion as a personality dimension, as typified in the writings of Hans J. Eysenck (1967), is that extraversion represents and relates to individual differences in the need or quest for external sensory stimulation. In general, extraverts have a greater need for such stimulation—in the form of social activities, crowds, novel or exciting adventures, frequent change or stimulus variation in the environment, intensity of colors or noises, or drugs. Introverts need less stimulation, and are more often concerned with reducing stimulation from the environment than increasing it.

Of course, this dimension is a continuous one, and the terms *introvert* and *extravert* are used only in a relative or comparative sense. Most of us experience both needs, but at different times or in different proportions; that is, there are occasions when we need to shut out stimulation in order to avoid overstimulation and other occasions when we feel a bit starved for stimulation. We try to regulate the flow of stimulation in order to maintain some comfortable level of "subjective excitement." Quiet, restful vacations at secluded spots appeal to us when we are being bombarded by the events of a hectic workday; but usually after a few days or weeks of escape to such havens, we become restless or bored and our appetite for stimulation reasserts itself. Furthermore, the level of "subjective excitement" that is comfortable for us tends to vary with the time of day (receptivity to stimulation for most of us being greater in the late morning or the early afternoon than in the early morning hours or late in the evening) and with the task that preoccupies us.

Eysenck believes that differences in the need for external sensory stimulation correspond to individual differences in the functioning of the reticular brain stem formation. The latter is a dense nerve network in the lower central part of the brain. It acts as a gatekeeper by which external stimulation "sprays" the entire brain cortex with the energy to function—to see, hear, think, or react (French, 1957). The reticular formation is somewhat like a battery for the working parts of the brain, and it extracts from stimulation only the "juice"—not information about what *kind* of stimulation it is or what the source of stimulation is—for altering the wakefulness of the more sophisticated structures that actually direct the senses, bones, and muscles. Two components within the reticular formation work in antagonistic functions to regulate this generalized current: a facilitator, which "amplifies" the stimulation; and an inhibitor, which tends to "muffle" it. Eysenck suggests that the extravert's "muffler" is stronger than the "amplifier," and that the reverse is true for introverts. Thus, extraverts need more generalized stimulation to overcome the inhibitory or muffling tendencies, whereas introverts have a greater need for holding stimulation within bounds due to the stronger excitatory tendencies of the facilitator. Eysenck's hypothesis has not been directly proved, but he has traced the converging lines of a host of different studies to this appealing explanation.

Of what importance is the extraversion-introversion dimension to the study of behavior in organizations? Some implications are perhaps obvious. On repetitive tasks or on tasks performed in environments that offer very little sensory stimulation, the introvert will usually do better; the extravert will spontaneously engage in task-irrelevant behaviors designed to provide the necessary variation to increase stimulation. On tasks performed in environments in which sensory overload threatens (for example, variable noise, random stimulus changes that require unpredictable shifts in the focus of attention, distractions), the extravert will get along better. In short, extraverts are more apt to suffer—either in terms of lower satisfaction or deterioration in performance—from sensory deprivation or understimulation; introverts more often fall prey to overstimulation, sensory overload, and excitation. As with other dimensions of personality, the differences do not become striking until one compares groups at opposite ends of the distribution.

There is a less obvious—though ultimately perhaps much more important—implication of this personality variable for the theory and practice of organizational behavior. Research findings have shown that introverts may be *more conditionable* than extraverts, especially when conditioning occurs on variable (as opposed to continuous) schedules of reinforcement and when the reinforcing stimulus is low in intensity (this would exclude strong aversive stimuli). The issue is not completely settled, but the evidence points in this direction, and it is a crucial issue for organizations. Organizations are very much involved in the conditioning process, inasmuch as they seek to shape individual behavior toward designated ends. Much of this conditioning is, of course, unplanned, subtle, unsystematic, and uses the mildest reinforcers; these, however are precisely the conditions under which, according to Eysenck, introverts demonstrate greater conditionability. Furthermore, as more and more organizations turn toward explicit operant techniques for shaping such participant behavior as attendance, quality control, safety, and consistency of performance, it becomes important to be able to predict what groups will respond most sensitively to the contingencies. One study showed that introverts had longer job tenure and fewer unexcused absences, and were generally rated as better adjusted to the job (Cooper & Payne, 1967). Another study found that introverts in graduate business courses reacted more positively to small bonuses contingent on maintaining day-to-day preparation for classes (Organ, 1975b).

To date, extraversion has received little attention in studies investigating such topics as motivation, performance, and leadership in ongoing organizations. Perhaps future research integrating this variable into theories of organizational behavior will increase their explanatory power.

Figure 8–2
Trait patterns related to combinations of levels of neuroticism and extraversion

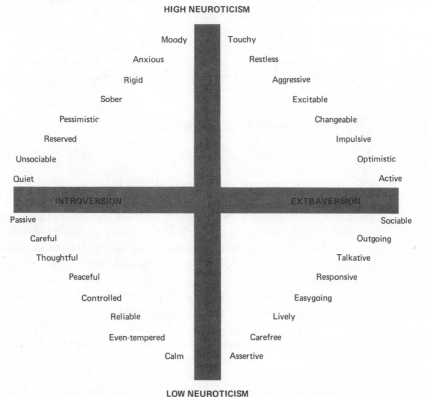

Source: Adapted from H. J. Eysenck, *Eysenck on Extraversion* (New York: Wiley, 1973), p. 27.

The interaction between neuroticism and extraversion

If neuroticism and extraversion are basic yet separate and independent dimensions of personality, one might wonder what sorts of surface-trait personality profiles might result from a combination of high neuroticism and extraversion, low neuroticism and extraversion, high neuroticism and introversion, and low neuroticism and introversion. Eysenck (1973) suggests that Figure 8–2 presents a plausible classification of traits that emerge. For example, persons high in neuroticism will display different patterns of behavior, depending on whether they are introverts or extraverts. The highly emotional introvert copes with psychic turbulence by turning inward on it—withdrawing from social relationships and dwelling on his or her fears and anxieties. The unstable extravert copes by expressing his or her emotions, snapping at people, or becoming hyperactive.

Eysenck (1970) has found that a common profile among criminals is a very high level of neuroticism coupled with extreme extraversion. Managers and administrators tend toward moderate introversion and low neuroticism, with some variations on the introversion dimension, depending on the field of work—for example, sales and personnel executives score higher on extraversion, closer to the norm of the general population, than do managers in finance or in research and development. This is *not* to suggest that such makeups cause a person to be a *better* manager in those areas, but rather that those kinds of personalities are attracted to and remain in such positions more often.

PERSONALITY: DIFFERENCES IN BELIEF SYSTEMS

Locus of control

Neuroticism and extraversion are dimensions of personality that are thought to be based ultimately on physiological variables. What about differences in behavior that might be explained by corresponding differences in *cognitive* variables—belief systems, attitude structures, perceptual styles? We take it for granted that cognitive variables underlie or precede much of our behavior, but many of these variables—expectancies, assumptions, intentions—are highly specific in nature and fluctuate from situation to situation. We typically do not think of such variables as representing stable dimensions of difference among individuals. Are there, in fact, any belief systems which, once acquired, resist change in the short run and also help predict differences in behavior?

Julian B. Rotter (1966) seems to have isolated such a belief system and has developed an instrument for measuring it. It is *locus of control:* the degree to which a person believes that his actions can influence his outcomes in life. *Internals* believe their behavior to be relatively decisive in determining their fate. *Externals* believe their behavior to be less decisive in this respect; they believe that chance, luck, or powerful agencies (persons or institutions) exert a very strong influence on what happens to them, an influence which supersedes any effects due to their own actions. Note that the issue here is *not* differences in the amount of reinforcements, success, or rewards experienced. The external may consider himself very well off in terms of what he is actually getting out of life. Nor do the differences lie in the perceptions people have of the amount of power possessed by other entities in the environment. Rather, the differences refer to beliefs about whether outcomes (good or bad) are *contingent on one's behavior* (even if made contingent by powerful others).

Since the development of Rotter's instrument, internals and externals (again, the labels refer to somewhat extreme ends of the distribution of scores on Rotter's scale) have been found to differ reliably in numerous ways. Internals seem to have better control over their own behavior, as suggested by the finding that internals are more successful at giving up smoking. They are more likely to be activists on political and social issues and more successful at persuading other people. On the other hand, they are less persuadable themselves (Phares, 1973). Internals make greater attempts to seek information relevant to their situation. One study (Seeman & Evans, 1962) found that internals hospitalized because of a physical illness made more persistent inquiries to the medical staff about the nature, origins, causes, and treatment of the illness. Valecha (1972) found internals to be better informed about their respective vocations, and Organ and Greene (1974) reported internals to experience less ambiguity about their jobs than did externals.

It seems logical that internals would search more actively for strategic kinds of information and knowledge. If a person believes that rewards are contingent upon a specific class of responses, he is likely to place more instrumental value on information concerning the type of response that is appropriate and the means of acquiring or executing that response. If a person believes that his outcomes are determined by events beyond his control and unrelated to his behavior, then he will regard much information as not being of sufficient instrumental value to be worth the costs of search. On the other hand, we should be cautious before drawing conclusions about what is cause and what is effect. It could be that individuals who have acquired the habit of searching for information become internals—believe that they can influence their outcomes—because they find that a store of practical information enables them to affect the course of events in their lives. It is also plausible, of course, that the relationship between internal-external locus of control and information-search habits is dynamic and reciprocal. Internals may initiate searches to a greater extent because of the instrumental value they place on information, but the acquisition and subsequent effective use of such information strengthen their beliefs that their behavior can significantly influence their rewards.

Internals seem to be highly attracted to situations that offer possibilities for individual achievement. For example, internals often experience greater academic success than do externals, and they do so by a margin not explainable in terms of purely intellectual abilities. Internals are more highly motivated and better performers on tasks that are presented as skill-related, but just the opposite is true when the same tasks are said to depend on luck or chance (Watson & Baumol, 1967). A number of studies have found internals to be more efficient at processing information (Wolk & DuCette, 1974).

Other correlates of locus of control include anxiety (externals being more anxious and emotional), clarity of self-concept (internals being more subjectively certain, though not necessarily more accurate, in their image of who they are and what they are like), trust (internals being more trusting), reactions to failure (internals being more likely to block out remembrance of failures), style of supervision preferred (externals preferring a more structured, directive style), and conditionability (internals being more sensitive to organizational uses of operant attempts to shape behavior). Not all of these relationships are conclusive, however, since attempts to replicate original findings have not always been successful.

Recent studies have produced evidence that locus of control is not a unitary dimension but is made up of qualitatively different components. Collins (1974) identifies four: beliefs about the *difficulty,* the *justice,* the *predictability,* and the *political responsiveness* of one's environment. Thus, a person might regard his organizational environment as very demanding, yet just (only a small percentage of people get promoted, but the few who do get promotions deserve them). Similarly, the mood of one's boss might be very predictable, yet not influenceable.

Others have argued that the locus of control variable is best viewed as made up of two belief systems—one pertaining to control over one's personal life (that is, over the events that have direct and particular significance for the person as a private individual) and the other pertaining to beliefs about the ability of society in general to control large-scale economic and political phenomena. According to this argument, an individual's beliefs about the extent to which his behavior shapes personal outcomes could be totally unrelated to political opinions concerning the responsiveness or rigidity of government, corporations, and national affairs. Nevertheless, the research of Rotter and others suggests that some common denominator links these various belief systems, at least to some degree.

Causes of internal/external locus of control

Although researchers have identified a host of correlates of locus of control, little evidence has been found that addresses the more specific question of what precedes or causes the belief system covered by this construct. One can speculate by drawing tentative inferences from the correlational studies that have been conducted, but only longitudinal studies that trace the changes in subjects' belief systems over a considerable period of time—ideally from childhood into the early adult years—will shed much light on the origins of internal and external locus of control. Nevertheless, the question is worthy of attention for the theory and practice of organizational behavior, for several related reasons: (1) Locus of control, being a cognitive variable, is presumably amenable to alteration, even if the process requires months or years. Unlike neuroticism and extraversion, which are probably rooted in relatively permanent physiological factors, belief systems are necessarily acquired and are the product of exposure to some type of social and physical environment. (2) Many of the behavior patterns that go along with internal locus of control—the search for information, achievement orientation, trust, attempts to control the environment, conditionability—would appear to be positively related to the effectiveness of organizational functioning. If internal locus of control is the *cause* (rather than the effect) of these behavior characteristics, and if the organization can learn how to influence people's locus of control beliefs (for example, by the reward contingencies or other components of the organizational climate), our understanding of organizational effectiveness could be enriched considerably.

In all probability, there are a variety of causal antecedents of locus of control. The simplest explanation would be to assume that internals and externals are rather accurate in their perceptions, that is, that internals are simply products of an environment in which their behavior has actually been the determinant of their outcomes and that externals have experienced futility in trying to determine their own lots. Some support for this argument comes from studies showing that minority groups and disadvantaged socioeconomic classes score more external on the Rotter questionnaire than do white middle-class groups. It certainly seems plausible that such individuals actually do exert less leverage in the way of choice or voluntary behavior for affecting their fates. Nevertheless, economic, social, and political disadvantages do not seem to tell the whole story, for even within relatively homogeneous demographic groups there is considerable variation in locus of control, from extreme internal to extreme external.

A number of researchers have focused on parental antecedents of locus of control as a causal explanation. Predictability and consistency of parental discipline, parental support and involvement, and parental encouragement of autonomy and self-control have been hypothesized as causes of internal locus of control. However, the evidence is sketchy, and it is derived from retrospective descriptions by college students of what their parents' behavior was like.

Wolk and DuCette (1974) have presented evidence in favor of a radically different explanation of the origins of locus of control. Their studies indicate that internals display a significant superiority over externals in amount of *incidental learning*—that is, in the ability to pick up incidental, apparently unrelated cues and relationships while concentrating on material relevant to some other task for which they have been given instructions. Internals seem to be blessed with a cognitive style that organizes stimuli into structures or chunks preserving maximal amounts of the originally embedded information. Wolk and DuCette apparently regard this ability as a cause rather than an effect of locus of control, although their evidence is still of a correlational nature.

Nevertheless, their explanation fits well with operant concepts. Recall that the three important components of a contingency are the S (the discriminative stimulus), the R (the response), and the R+ (the consequence). In real-life situations, a given R never gets rewarded under all conditions, but only in certain stimulus situations—in other words, when certain stimuli are present. Furthermore, the nature of the stimulus, the elements which define it and which differentiate it from stimulus situations in which the response is not rewarded, can be very subtle and elusive. It could be that externals habitually use a cognitive style which often fails to capture subtle differences in stimuli. As a result, an external sees only that he is sometimes rewarded and sometimes unrewarded for certain behavior, on a seemingly random basis; if this is true for a large number of classes of behavior, he draws the generalization that this behavior does not have a large influence on his outcomes. On the other hand, the internal—due to his different method of processing information—picks up the subtleties of the different stimuli and concludes that, *under certain conditions,* a systematic relationship does exist between his behavior and his rewards.

An alternative explanation of Wolk and DuCette's findings derives from the frequent association between high external locus of control and high neuroticism, emotionality, or anxiety. There is considerable evidence to show that when we become more aroused—due to important motivational inducements, fear, or stress—we tend to get "tunnel vision," in the sense that our cognitive or perceptual focus becomes increasingly narrow. Thus, if locus of control affects emotionality, and emotionality in turn affects the breadth of perceptual scanning, then the latter is an indirect *effect* of locus of control rather than an explanation of its origins.

In any case, much work remains to be done before we can answer the question of whether the organization can alter the locus of control of its participants, and if so, which, if any, of the correlates of locus of control also change. In the absence of conclusive evidence, one prescription can be strongly urged. Organization officials should try to make reward systems as sensitive as possible to individual differences in behavior, to communicate the reward contingencies as clearly as possible, and to train or nurture individuals to enable them to meet those contingencies. To the extent possible, individuals should also have input into the formalizing of contingencies that apply to important areas of their work behavior.

Martin Seligman (1973) has called attention to what at first glance seems a paradoxical observation. Clinical psychologists have found an increasing incidence of depression among college students. Yet these students have had a greater abundance of reinforcers—purchasing power, cars, sex, music, fewer restrictions on personal behavior—than has any previous generation of students. What could be the reason for the depression? Seligman suggests that the noncontingent nature of the reinforcers, "goodies from the sky" that are independent of the students' behavior, has undermined the students' belief in the instrumental effectiveness of their behavior. Such "learned helplessness" induces depression. Not too incidentally, Rotter (1971) found externals to be more susceptible to learned helplessness. The foregoing observations seem to support Skinner's (1966) assertion that "men are happy in an environment in which active, productive, and creative behavior is reinforced in effective ways" (p. 166). It is not sufficient to satisfy "needs"—need satisfaction must also be coupled with behavior in such a way that the individual realizes that he or she is an effective human being.

Argyris (1957) notes that the expected normal development of the individual personality from infancy to mature adulthood is characterized by certain important trends. These include the tendency to develop from a state of passivity to one of activity, self-initiative, and self-determination; from a state of dependence on others to a state of relative independence; from having a short time perspective to having a longer time horizon (for example, the capacity to forgo immediate gratification of impulses or wants in order to realize more significant future gains); from a subordinate status in the family and society to a status that is predominantly one of equality; and from lack of self-awareness to an ever clearer self-concept and increasing control over self. Perhaps we can sum up Argyris' observations by saying that healthy human development proceeds from an external locus of control orientation along a continuum toward increased internal locus of control.

Argyris contends that this growth trend is stunted in many individuals by the effects of bureaucratic organizations which rely on intimidation, coercion, autocratic leadership, and hierarchy to manage individual behavior. The effects of such controls, he argues, are that lower-level participants can adapt only by regressing to a state of dependence, passivity, and a shorter time perspective. This is unfortunate, since as a result potential long-run contributions by such persons to organizations never materialize. Argyris does not deny the need for certain basic control mechanisms in formal organizations, but he believes that there are viable alternative forms of control which are more compatible with the continued psychological growth of the participants.

Before we leave the topic of locus of control, we should voice a note of caution. The abilities and behavioral patterns that correlate with internal locus of control (as scored by Rotter's measure) seem to suggest that the internal is a "better person" than the external, and that the more internal one is, the better one is. One could argue, however, that *very extreme* internals are no better—perhaps less well adjusted—than their counterparts. If we live in a world in which forces beyond the control of the individual do exist, then the very extreme internal may be overrigid, defensively overestimating his ability to control events in his life.

PERSONALITY: DIFFERENCES IN MOTIVE STRENGTH

Some motives or needs—such as those for food, water, sleep, and shelter—are quite temporary in nature. Our need for food persists only until we have ingested enough of it to satiate ourselves, and then our behavior is directed toward other goals until hunger pangs strike again or until some delicacy (for example, chocolate cream pie) appears in our perceptual field. There seem to be other motives, however, which are more enduring, more chronic, and less likely to be quickly satiated. The persistence and stability of such motives suggest yet another approach to studying personality. A stable motive is by definition a preoccupation with certain types of goal objects and thus a predisposition to respond in certain directions.

Atkinson (1958) and McClelland (1961), among others, have discovered a technique for identifying such motives in human subjects. Their technique, called the thematic apperception test, consists of presenting the subject with a still picture and asking the subject to make up a story about that picture. For example, the picture might show an architect seated at a desk, with blueprints, drafting materials, and a photograph of the architect's family on the desk. The subject is asked to make up a story explaining what has led up to that scene, what the architect is thinking, and what will happen later.

The use of this projective technique is based on the assumption that, given such an ambiguous stimulus, people will *project* into it their own longings, desires, and goals. Motives are identified by the kinds of imagery or themes which emerge strongly in the subject's story.

Need for achievement

A strong achievement motive is identified by themes in the subject's story which relate to striving for some standard of excellence in task accomplishment. Need for achievement (or *n Ach*, as abbreviated by McClelland) reflects a strong goal orientation, an obsession with a job or task to be done. Someone with strong n Ach, making up a story about the picture mentioned above, would talk about a challenging assignment that the architect is working on, such as the need to design a bridge which would withstand strong winds, yet also meet other criteria.

McClelland (1961) has identified a number of reliable behavioral manifestations of this need. People with high n Ach are attracted to tasks which challenge their skills and their problem-solving abilities; they have little interest in games in which luck is a major determinant of success. These persons set difficult but realistic goals which present an objective prior probability of about .3 to .5 of success. They avoid setting goals that they believe are almost impossible to achieve or that guarantee a virtual certainty of success. They prefer tasks whose outcomes depend on their own individual efforts; if help is needed, they select people on the basis of competence in the task rather than people who are socially congenial. They have a compulsive need for quick, concrete feedback on how well they are doing, and they especially like feedback in quantitative form, such as percentages, number of units, and so forth.

"Achievement," then, has a special meaning in this context. Scientists, teachers, and artists do not score high in n Ach, even though they may realize substantial achievement in a more general sense. They neither need nor obtain quick, unambiguous feedback about their efforts.

McClelland finds that entrepreneurs and managers are especially likely to have high n Ach. Whether in a socialist or a capitalist country, in private business or in government, the more effective managers tend to have a sharply focused goal orientation, a drive to compete either with peers or according to some standard of excellence. They make moderately risky decisions in settings in which they believe they can exert some control over the outcomes, and they constantly gauge the effectiveness of their decisions and effort by some unambiguous index. McClelland suggests that it is no accident that most cartoons set in a business office show in the background a chart with a curve depicting sales, profits, or production.

McClelland believes that the need for achievement is shaped rather early in life—in part by the culture, through such media as children's readers, and in part by parental styles which encourage children to take responsibility, promote independence in action, and reinforce achievement. He further asserts that the economies of entire nations rise or fall over the years as a consequence of the culture's influence on the need for achievement, reflected in the development of the entrepreneurial instinct.

Need for affiliation

A second motive identified in subjects' stories is the need for establishing, maintaining, or restoring pleasant emotional relationships with other people. Persons with strong needs for affiliation (n Aff) want primarily to be liked by others; "getting along" with co-workers is more important to them than how much the group accomplishes. In response to the picture of the architect, such persons would emphasize the architect's thoughts about the family in the portrait on the desk: the good times they have had together, how much they mean to one another. Persons with high n Aff would be more sensitive to other people's feelings than would persons with high n Ach. They would be attracted to tasks involving groups, while the high n Ach person would prefer being a loner with a job that depends on him or her alone. As managers, high n Aff persons might avoid task decisions that would engender emotional or social conflict.

It would be tempting to infer that high n Ach persons make the best managers and that high n Aff individuals would make ineffective managers. However, some concern for affiliation is important if the manager is to develop the group structure and climate necessary for long-run effectiveness.

Need for power

A third motive is the desire to exert control or influence over people. Unfortunately, this need tends to suggest, to most people, something sinister or malevolent about a person's motives, to make people think of the person as a budding Napoleon or Hitler. However, a strong need for power does not necessarily result in an autocratic or tyrannical leadership style. Winter (1967) found that this need (n Pow) could take either an *unsocialized* or a *socialized* expression in college students. In the former case, it was reflected in a desire for sexual conquest or physical aggression. In its socialized form, it was manifested by active membership in, or leadership of, student and community groups or organizations which sought constructive ends, such as civil rights, campus reform, and student government.

There is reason to believe that a manager should have at least a moderate level of n Pow in order to be effective. Otherwise, he or she would shrink from making decisions and would allow the group to develop in an aimless, uncharted direction. As Chapter 3 pointed out, managers must inevitably accept the responsibility for influencing the behavior of the people who work for them. A manager's need for power has been shown to be quite compatible with a leadership style which stresses the development and participation of subordinates; it is not the exclusive mark of the bully or the manipulator.

Finally, it should be noted that the actual expression in behavior of these various motives depends to a large extent on the stimulus cues in the environment. For example, even a very strong need for achievement will not be manifested in an environment in which there is little opportunity for achievement (as we have defined it). *Motives are latent or dormant unless aroused* by *salient stimulus cues.*

THE PERSONALITY IN THE ORGANIZATION

At one time psychologists leaned toward the view that the adult personality was essentially static, having been largely determined by early childhood events, and capable of changing only superficially once biological maturity was reached. Increasingly, this view is being questioned. Recent trends in research and theory suggest that personality is much more plastic and dynamic, with development occurring throughout the life span if such development is stimulated or supported by the immediate social and cultural environment. Though it may indeed be true that numerous persons "freeze" into a roughly constant personality, the reasons are likely to be either that they maintain an unvarying role in life or work or that people close to them act in such a way as to discourage any behavior not "expected" of them.

Argyris (1957) suggested that personality consists of two interrelated balancing processes. One is an *internal, adjustment* process, in which the various personality components tend to reach a kind of working harmony and to avoid conflicts or contradictions. The other is an *external, adaptation* process, in which the person seeks to respond effectively to the demands of the environment. A person may *adapt* successfully while failing to experience total *adjustment;* for example, he or she may be successful as a salesperson, yet plagued by insomnia or ulcers, because the individual cannot reconcile his or her internal life with the behavior required by the job. On the other hand, a person may realize the state of adjustment—in the form of inner tranquillity— yet not be competent to deal with the requirements posed by the objective environment. Generally, however, the two sets of balancing processes are coordinated. When adaptation to an environmental challenge is managed, it is usually at the expense of disrupting the prior equilibrium in the internal personal world. To reestablish that equilibrium, some further adjustment is required in the constellation of personal motives, values, and temperament.

Argyris believes that many large, formal organizations stunt the personal growth of most of their participants. By blocking the expression of certain needs (for example, the needs for competence and achievement), participants *adapt* to this kind of environment by *adjusting* internal personal forces so that those needs are no longer felt or no longer create tension. The result is that—except for a minority of people, usually in the upper reaches of the hierarchy—persons in organizations reach a compromise state of placid complacency, even "happiness" of a sort, by becoming passive and dependent.

At the other extreme, of course, would be an environment changing so rapidly and fundamentally that successful adaptation would rip apart the internal fabric of a person's identity without giving adjustment a chance to occur. As discussed in the next chapter, some observers believe this to be the more serious threat in the contemporary Western world.

Clearly, the desired state of affairs would be some golden mean between these extremes—one in which people could experience a variety of life or work roles, whose succession would be ideally paced according to the individual's unique tolerance level for change in adaptation and adjustment. A number of current trends may reflect the search for this golden mean. More and more women are seeking, not to choose between the mother-housewife role and a career role, but rather to choose a course which will enable them to experience both roles and thus to give full expression to different, but complementary, needs. Men are discovering that when economically feasible, changing their career in middle age contributes to a more satisfying concept of self. There have always been men and women who did this, of course, but whereas earlier they were regarded as exceptional cases, today it is recognized that theirs may actually be the healthier or more "normal" development.

THE INDIVIDUALIZED ORGANIZATION

One fact which is undeniable in light of decades of research is that "individual differences *moderate* the way people respond to various aspects of organizations and to the practices of organizations" (Porter, Lawler, & Hackman, 1975, p. 520). No single type of management style, job design, or pay system can be truthfully said to be the "best" for all persons. To cite just a few of the dimensions along which people differ with respect to the world of work:

1. *People differ in the importance they attach to intrinsic job rewards.* At one time, and not very long ago, "job enrichment" was

touted as a prescriptive panacea for increasing morale and productivity. The assumption was that everyone preferred a "challenging" job which afforded scope for the expression of high-level skills and abilities. We now realize that a substantial minority of people seek primarily security and material benefits from work and actually prefer a job with routine operations from which they can disengage psychologically for extended intervals of time.

2. *People differ in the style of supervision they prefer.* While many people welcome opportunities to provide input into important decisions and like to be their own boss as much as possible, quite a few individuals seem to want the clarity and protection of a benevolent autocrat who makes the decisions, specifies in detail what is to be done and how to do it, and extends a helpful, if heavy, guiding hand.

3. *People differ in the type of compensation plan they want.* Some people respond enthusiastically to incentive systems which base part of one's pay on the amount or the quality of the work done, others prefer a straight salary system—and appear to work as hard or harder under such a system as under piece-rate pay.

To these differences among people we might add that people differ in their tolerance for stress, their need for stimulation, even in their preferred schedule of work hours. In fact, one of the authors of this book is an "early bird," who likes to start work before seven in the morning; the other likes the hours after midnight for serious work and panics at the thought of beginning the day before 9:30 or 10:00 A.M.

Given the growing recognition that enormous individual differences exist and the growing appreciation of their importance, Porter, Lawler, and Hackman (1975) visualize the organization of the future as one that will be increasingly "individualized." Organizations will exhibit much greater variety in internal management and structure so as to accommodate individual differences. Texas Instruments has already embarked upon a program to diagnose different types of "work personalities" and to match these types with appropriate work environments within the larger organization. Some individuals, for example, are classified as "tribalistic"—people who want strong, directive leadership from their boss; some are "egocentric," desiring individual responsibilities and wanting to work as loners in an entrepreneurial style; some are "sociocentric," seeking primarily the social relationships that a job provides; and some are "existential," seeking full expression of growth and self-fulfillment needs through their work, much as an artist does. Charles Hughes, director of personnel and organization development at Texas Instruments, believes that the variety of work that needs to be done in his organization is great enough to accommodate these different types of work personalities in such a manner that individual and organizational goals are fused.

SUMMARY

Because of differences in personality, individuals differ in their manner of responding to organizational environments. Methods of measuring and predicting these differences include questionnaires, ratings by observers, projective tests, and behavioral tests. Some dimensions of personality, such as emotionality (or neuroticism) and extraversion, are probably derived at least in part from physiological factors. Internal-external locus of control represents a personality dimension that is based on a person's beliefs about the determinants of one's fate or one's outcomes in life. Needs for achievement, affiliation, and power are dimensions defined by the strength of enduring motives in a person's thoughts and actions. Recent studies suggest that people do not necessarily freeze into a fixed personality profile at early adulthood, but have the potential for change throughout the life cycle. The growing appreciation of the diversity of individual needs, values, and motives suggests that in the future organizations will be more pluralistic and more differentiated in their internal structure and their internal environment.

CONCEPTS TO REMEMBER

projective test	thematic apperception test
neuroticism	n Ach
extraversion-introversion	n Aff
reticular brain stem	n Pow
internal-external locus of control	adjustment process
incidental learning	adaptation process
work personalities	

QUESTIONS FOR DISCUSSION

1. Is it accurate to say that personality is a *cause* of behavior? Why or why not?
2. It was noted in this chapter that measures of personality dimensions have generally not been shown to be valid predictors of success or performance on most jobs. How would you account for this?
3. Does a manager have to be a "good judge of people" to be effective? Why or why not?
4. Describe some person you know who is probably high in neuroticism. What characteristic of his or her behavior leads you to believe that this is so?
5. Would introverts or extraverts be more likely to thrive on interpersonal conflict?

6. Would applications of operant principles to organizational settings (refer to Chapters 3 and 11) tend to make people more internal or more external in locus of control? Explain.

7. Would a very strong need for achievement ever be dysfunctional for a manager's performance?

8. What situational factors might affect the level of a person's need for affiliation?

9. How are internal locus of control, need for achievement, and need for power related?

REFERENCES

Allport, G. W., & Odbert, H. W. Trait-names: A psycholexical study. *Psychological Monographs*, 1936, *47*(1).

Argyris, C. *Personality and organization*. New York: Harper, 1957.

Atkinson, J. W. *Motives in fantasy, action, and society*. Princeton, N.J.: Van Nostrand, 1958.

Collins, B. E. Four components of the Rotter internal-external scale: Belief in a difficult world, a just world, a predictable world, and a politically responsive world. *Journal of Personality and Social Psychology*, 1974, *29*, 381–391.

Cooper, R., & Payne, R. Extraversion and some aspects of work behavior. *Personnel Psychology*, 1967, *20*, 45–57.

Eysenck, H. J. *The biological basis of personality*. Springfield, Ill.: Charles C Thomas, 1967.

Eysenck, H. J. (Ed.). *Readings in extraversion-intraversion* (Vol. 3). London: Staple Press, 1970.

Eysenck, H. J. (Ed.) *Eysenck on extraversion*. New York: Wiley, 1973.

French, J. D. The reticular formation. *Scientific American*, May 1957. Reprinted in T. J. Teyler, (Ed.), *Altered states of awareness*. San Francisco: W. H. Freeman, 1972.

Joe, V. C. Review of the internal-external control construct as a personality variable. *Psychological Reports*, 1971, *28*, 619–640.

Kahn, R. L., Wolfe, D. M., Quinn, R. P., Snoek, J. D., & Rosenthal, R. A. *Organizational stress*. New York: Wiley, 1964.

McClelland, D. C. *The achieving society*. Princeton, N.J.: Van Nostrand, 1961.

Organ, D. W. Locus of control and clarity of self-concept. *Perceptual and Motor Skills*, 1973, *37*, 100–102.

Organ, D. W. Effects of pressure and individual neuroticism on emotional responses to task-role ambiguity. *Journal of Applied Psychology*, 1975, *60*, 397–400. (a)

Organ, D. W. Extraversion, locus of control, and individual differences in conditionability in organizations. *Journal of Applied Psychology*, 1975, *60*, 401–404. (b)

Organ, D. W., & Greene, C. N.   Role ambiguity, locus of control, and work satisfaction. *Journal of Applied Psychology,* 1974, *59,* 101–102.

Phares, E. J.   *Locus of control: A personality determinant of behavior.* Morristown, N.J.: General Learning Press, 1973.

Porter, L. W., Lawler, E. E., III, & Hackman, J. R.   *Behavior in organizations.* New York: McGraw-Hill, 1975.

Rotter, J. B.   Generalized expectancies for internal versus external control of reinforcement. *Psychological Monographs,* 1966, *80*(1, Whole No. 609).

Rotter, J. B.   External control and internal control. *Psychology Today,* June 1971, pp 28–33.

Runyon, K.   Some interactions between personality variables and management styles. *Journal of Applied Psychology,* 1973, *57,* 288–294.

Seeman, M., & Evans, J. W.   Alienation and learning in a hospital setting. *American Sociological Review,* 1962, *27,* 772–783.

Seligman, M.   Fall into helplessness. *Psychology Today,* June 1973, 43–48.

Silverman, R. E., & Blitz, B.   Learning and two kinds of anxiety. *Journal of Abnormal and Social Psychology,* 1956, *52,* 301–303.

Skinner, B. F.   Contingencies of reinforcement in the design of a culture. *Behavioral Science,* 1966, 159–166.

Tyler, L. E.   *The psychology of human differences.* New York: Appleton-Century-Crofts, 1965.

Valecha, G. K.   Construct validation of internal-external locus of reinforcement related to work-related variables. *Proceedings of the 80th Annual Convention of the American Psychological Association,* 1972, *7,* 455–456.

Watson, D., & Baumol, E.   Effects of locus of control and expectation of future control upon present performance. *Journal of Personality and Social Psychology,* 1967, *6,* 212–215.

Winter, D. G.   *Power motivation in thought and action.* Unpublished doctoral dissertation, Harvard University, 1967.

Wolk, S., & DuCette, J.   Intentional performance and incidental learning as a function of personality and task dimensions. *Journal of Personality and Social Psychology,* 1974, *29,* 90–101.

Yerkes, R. M., & Dodson, J. D.   The relation of strength of stimulus to rapidity of habit formation. *Journal of Comparative and Neurological Psychology,* 1908, *18,* 459–482.

Psychological stress in organizations

What are the major forms of psychological stress?

What are the major sources of stress in organizations?

How does stress affect performance?

How can managers maximize the positive effects of stress while minimizing the negative effects?

Organizations are built on the assumption that the instrumental, purposeful, goal-striving behavior of a collectivity of individuals can be harnessed and coordinated toward some ultimate organizational objective or objectives. The preceding chapters have, for the most part, been concerned with describing this instrumental behavior in organizations and the effects of environmental factors on this behavior. As we observe work activities in an office, a factory, a city government building, a hospital, or a school, it is the instrumental character of people's behavior that seems to dominate our impressions: people using "plans," or drawing upon a well-defined repertoire of response sequences, in order to accomplish some end, or satisfy some need, or attain some short- or long-term goal. If, while observing these places of work, we suddenly notice someone "stalled"—repeating the same motions with no effect, thrashing around in an aimless fashion, or totally taken up with nervous mannerisms—the instrumental character of behavior seems to be lacking. Behavior is disorganized and either going nowhere or going in all directions at once. The study of psychological stress is concerned with those events that lead to a breakdown in instrumental behavior and with how people react to such breakdowns.

THE CONCEPT OF STRESS

Stress is defined by a set of circumstances under which an individual cannot respond adequately or instrumentally to environmental stimuli, or can so respond only at the cost of excessive wear and tear on the organism—for example, chronic fatigue, tension, worry, physical damage, nervous breakdown, or loss of self-esteem. Stress is therefore a *relational* concept, since it involves factors in the environment combined with factors in the individual. Some environments are stressful for all or most persons, and some persons are highly susceptible to stress in almost any environment; but between these extremes it is the particular match-up between certain characteristics of the environment and certain individuals or certain individual attributes that produces stress.

It should be noted at the outset that stress is a fact of life, beginning at the moment of our entry into this world and recurring until we leave it. Thus, stress is inevitable in organizations. Administrators cannot completely eliminate stress either for others or for themselves. Furthermore, a certain degree of stress seems to be a precondition for psychological growth, achievement, and the development of new skills; although stress always involves at least some temporary degree of discomfort, it is frequently the occasion for the emergence of creative solutions to personal or organizational problems. On the other hand, inordinate or prolonged stress can cause apathy, breakdowns

193

in performance, and psychological or physical withdrawal from the organization.

Hans Selye (1956), who has studied the effects of physiological stress for several decades, has formulated a description of the organism's response to stress, called the *general adaptation syndrome* (see Figure 9–1). This syndrome includes three stages, the first of which is the *alarm reaction.* This represents a temporary impairment of physiological functioning, often manifested by headaches, fever, or other symptoms. In this stage the defenses of the body are rallied and consolidated

Figure 9–1
Stages of the organism's response to stress

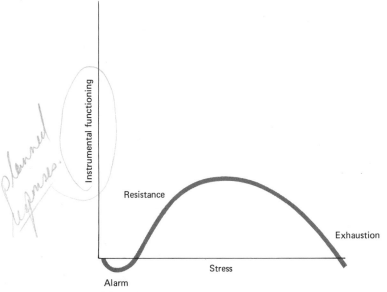

Source: From H. Selye, *The Stress of Life* (New York: McGraw-Hill, 1956) p. 87.

for *resistance,* the second stage. If stress continues past some point, the organism's defenses wear out and the body succumbs to the stress, in the third and final stage—*exhaustion,* or collapse, or even death.

The individual's response to psychological stress seems to follow much the same pattern. The initial reaction to psychological stress is a temporary lapse in instrumental responding and a surge of emotional arousal. This arousal acts to rally various coping mechanisms to defend against the stress. These coping mechanisms are learned, a product of past experiences in handling stress, and may be either functional or dysfunctional for problem solving. If they are functional, the resistance stage may bring forth the development of new skills, creative insights, and enhanced self-esteem and self-confidence. If the stress is unremitting and chronic, and all forms of coping behavior are of no avail in reducing it to manageable proportions, the exhaustion stage is reached. This may take the form of acute depression, in which almost all of the person's instrumental responding has been extinguished and he drifts into a state of extreme passivity. The result may be incapacitating physical illness. In less pathological forms, the exhaustion stage takes the form of apathy, resignation, uninvolvement, and a profound sense of futility.

Thus, the administrator's function is not to eliminate stress, but to promote functional and constructive patterns of coping with stress (in the resistance stage), and to keep stress within bounds to avoid instances of the exhaustion stage. Since individuals differ in their preferred methods of coping with stress as well as in their endurance and tolerance of stress, the administrator cannot successfully manage stress unless he is well aware of differences in individual psychological profiles.

FORMS OF PSYCHOLOGICAL STRESS

Many psychologists have found it useful to distinguish among different kinds of stress. The most preferred classification considers stress as *frustration, anxiety, or conflict.* The treatment of these concepts has not, however, always been consistent, as Costello and Zalkind (1963) have observed. These concepts have been defined in subtly different ways by different writers, and sometimes the definitions of the three concepts overlap to a considerable degree. As used by various authorities, the concepts may refer to visible and objective conditions in the environment, to overt patterns of behaving or responding, or to unobserved but intuited feelings or emotions within the person; and as applied by some authorities, the concepts have been flexible enough to signify any of these three referents. It is little wonder, then, that still other authorities consider the distinctions more confusing than helpful and would rather deal with the more general idea of psychological stress, since it captures many of the important common characteristics of frustration, anxiety, and conflict as they are usually defined.

Our preference, nevertheless, is to treat frustration and anxiety separately. We believe that the differences between them are worth noting because they are apt to be related to qualitatively different kinds of organizational behavior. However, we think that conflict can be treated as a special case of frustration without any significant loss of understanding.

Frustration

The term *frustration* applies to any obstruction between instrumental behavior and its goal or to any interference with or disruption of ongoing instrumental behavior. Specific types of frustration include the following (Lawson, 1965):

1. Nonreinforcement after a history of reinforcement. For example, a student who has been consistently rewarded for studying in a certain way (such as rote memorizing) suddenly finds himself in a course where such behavior is no longer rewarded by good marks.

2. A delay in reinforcement. An advertising writer accustomed to receiving quick feedback about his work finds that he now has to wait days or weeks before hearing anything.

3. A change in the value of reinforcement. Office workers accustomed to receiving a $10 gift certificate for a month's perfect attendance are told that, due to the need to trim labor costs, they will now get only a $5 gift certificate.

4. Sheer failure. A salesperson does all the right things, all the things he or she is used to doing, but experiences a long string of unsuccessful calls.

5. Obstruction of a response that is otherwise strong. A welder on an automobile assembly line has a full bladder, and the urge to go to the rest room is very strong, but is obstructed due to shop rules concerning rest pauses.

6. Punishment, since it temporarily suppresses a response that is otherwise strong.

7. Conflict between two or more strong but incompatible responses. Role conflict is thus a special case of frustration. So is a period of indecision when some decision has to be made quickly. Even having to choose between two equally valued alternatives (such as a Buick versus a Cadillac or a vacation in the mountains versus a vacation at the seashore) is somewhat stressful. More stressful, however, are "approach-avoidance" conflicts (desiring a promotion for its status and salary, yet being afraid of the accompanying pressure and overload) and "avoidance-avoidance" conflicts (a supervisor torn between the need to punish unacceptable performance and the desire to avoid conflict).

Frustration is obviously endemic in organizational life. The existence of a hierarchy, of competition, of constraints on behavior in order to coordinate collective action toward a goal, and often, of conflicting or competing organizational functions or goals, all guarantee that frustration will be frequent. This need not be the occasion for lamentation, however, since frustration often has very desirable effects on behavior.

1. Frustration adds color and complexity to behavior. Our repertoire of instrumental responses would never change or grow if we were never frustrated; we would more nearly resemble robots than persons. We would not experiment with new methods unless the old ones were occasionally found to be unsuccessful or obstructed.

2. Frustration is a precondition for *perceptual* as well as behavioral change (Cantril, 1957). Our unexamined assumptions and built-in biases

in viewing a situation are not recognized until actions based on them prove ineffectual. Reinterpretations of the world around us and different perspectives on our experience are evoked by the inability to use our accustomed behavior plans in transactions with the social and physical environment. A marketing executive may conceptualize a product in a radically different manner when the unprofitability of present methods of promotion or present target markets forces reexamination.

3. Frustration usually acts to arouse reserves of energy for use in dealing with the problem at hand. While arousal can sometimes be so great as to interfere with task performance (particularly when the task is very novel or complex), moderate arousal usually has the beneficial effect of focusing our attention more sharply, maintaining or improving vigilance, and toning our readiness for action.

These positive consequences are more likely to occur when frustration is temporary or intermittent; when alternative responses are available or substitute goals can suffice; or when the person's past reinforcement history, upbringing, training, and socialization have led him to develop at least a moderate level of *frustration tolerance* with regard to life in general or to that part of his or her life which is affected by the frustration. When frustration is prolonged, when increased energy in responding proves futile, when a number of attempted alternative responses prove useless, when no alternative responses are available, or when the limit of frustration tolerance has been reached and passed, then stress has gone beyond the alarm and resistance stages and is approaching the point of exhaustion. It is then that we are likely to apply the word *frustration* to an *inner emotional state* rather than to an observed condition or to overt behavior (of course, overt behavior itself may be of such a character that we immediately infer it to be governed by emotional factors rather than rational or instrumental considerations). For example, a person who prepares to leave his office and finds that he can't open the door (let's say it's stuck or possibly locked from the outside) is frustrated in an objective sense: instrumental behavior is being obstructed or is unsuccessful. Initially, however, the person may not experience a sense of frustration in the inner, emotional sense. If the person coolly tries to push or pull a little harder, to pick the lock with a paper clip, or to slip a plastic ruler between the door and the jamb, he appears to be acting rationally, and we don't usually describe him as frustrated in an inner, emotional sense. If his behavior then degenerates into kicking the door, banging it with his fist, or cursing (forms of aggression), stress seems to have taken a quantum jump, and the person's behavior reflects a noninstrumental, expressive, emotional state. If he finally gives up—decides to spend the night in the office or to waste away from hunger, crouching in a corner in a state of torpor, the stage of resistance has given way to exhaustion, apathy, and resignation.

When people repeatedly experience frustration in many different facets of life and work, and when their repeated efforts to use all available alternative methods are not rewarded, *extinction* (see Chapter 3) on a grand scale occurs. Not just one instrumental response, but instrumental responding in general undergoes a profound loss of strength. The energy to try to do *anything* other than subsist or vegetate doesn't seem to exist. The clinician calls this *depression*. Even if the person can still muddle through life or work on a day-to-day basis without requiring psychiatric assistance, some form of significant intervention—from boss, co-workers, family, or friends—is needed to guide him out of this state, to help steer him back to instrumental modes of behavior that can be reinforced and strengthened.

Frustration and aggression

The link between frustration and *aggression,* or behavior directed toward the harm of another person or object, has attracted the attention of psychologists for quite some time. Early in the century aggression was thought to be caused by some built-in instinct in animals and humans, but this explanation soon proved unsatisfactory, especially when ethological studies of animals in their natural habitats showed aggression to be quite rare, except in order to obtain food. Later, Dollard argued that frustration is always a cause of aggression, and that aggression is always preceded by frustration. This position seemed to be extreme since (*a*) people appear to be able to endure a variety of frustrating events daily without showing aggressive behavior, and (*b*) aggression, like other types of behavior, can be instrumental and can be strengthened by reinforcing consequences that are at best only remotely related to frustration—for example, killing people for their money or, in organizations, being an intimidating browbeater in order to gain a psychological advantage over others.

The currently held view is that frustration generates a *predisposition* to aggress (often labeled anger), but that other factors determine both whether aggression takes place and the form of aggression that is manifested if it does. It may be helpful here to relate aggressive tendencies to the three stages of reaction to stress. It seems plausible to locate the maximum tendency toward aggression near the end of the resistance stage—a sort of "last resort" after alternative methods of coping have failed but before exhaustion has occurred. Thus, up to a point, the tendency to aggress will vary directly with the duration of frustration, the number of responses that are blocked or unsuccessful, and the strength of the responses interfered with, and will vary inversely with the number of substitutive instrumental responses in one's behavioral repertoire for dealing with the situation. When aggression itself is unsuccessful or completely blocked, apathy or withdrawal follow.

In this light, the milder forms of aggression are a healthy sign, since they reflect a will to struggle with the environment rather than to submit resignedly to failure. Military officers have long recognized that troop morale is not at its lowest level when grumbling and griping are frequent, but rather when such bitching has given way to apathy and passive acceptance of the "inevitable."

Among the factors that determine whether or not aggression will actually take place are whether or not punishment for aggression is anticipated, whether or not one's peer group or another closely related social group approves of the aggression (and offers possible support in resisting punishment or counteraggression), and the extent to which aggression has been strengthened by reinforcement in the past. The last factor is a subtle but important one, because organization officials sometime unwittingly reinforce aggressive behavior. When noisy outbursts or verbal abuse by subordinates threaten an administrator's control over organizational functioning or make his or her life difficult, the administrator may be inclined to "give in"—remove the source of frustration. This means, of course, that when confronted by further frustrations, these subordinates are more likely to use aggression as an instrumental response. On a smaller scale, the same thing happens when we get our Coke or our quarter after some hefty slaps and kicks at the vending machine. Aggression sometimes "gets the job done."

There is some evidence that fixed ratio schedules of reinforcement— particularly when the ratio of the reinforcements to the number of responses is very low—is associated with a greater propensity to aggress when frustrating events occur (Harrell & Moss, 1974). Many reinforcers in organizations, particularly those to lower-ranking participants, are dispensed in a manner that resembles such schedules. Rest pauses, lunch periods, and smoke breaks are permitted only after relatively long and fixed periods of responding (although these are formally fixed interval schedules, the correlated work flow renders that pretty much fixed ratio also). It would seem that industry could do far more to vary the length of reinforcement intervals, yet hold the total amount of rest pauses or other reinforcers to their current levels. Although in some instances technological constraints rule out variable schedules of work breaks, more often it is the weight of tradition and administrative preferences for elegant structure that fix breaks rigidly at 9:30 A.M., 12:00 A.M., 2:30 P.M., and so forth. Recently, some organizations have experimented with the concept of "flexitime"—allowing the individual to set not only his break schedule, but even the hours of work, subject to the constraint that some fixed number of weekly hours or some fixed amount of daily output be met (see Chapter 12).

Aggression is also more likely to occur when frustration is *unanticipated* or is *perceived as arbitrary*. The emphasis here is on the point of view of the person or persons being frustrated. For very good and compelling reasons, administrators are often forced to institute changes or to take steps that are frustrating to lower-ranking participants. If the rationale behind such measures is not communicated, or if adequate lead time between the announcement and the implementation of the measures is not provided, measures are more likely to instigate aggression than would otherwise be the case. Lead time allows persons to plan and activate alternative instrumental response sequences for coping with the environment. Changes are less likely to be perceived as arbitrary if participants have had some form of input (whether direct or representational) into the reasons for introducing them and are told what considerations led to the changes, or if it is obvious that the decision makers themselves are sharing the burdens imposed by the changes.

As noted above, the anticipation of punishment can inhibit aggression. Even a severely frustrated factory worker usually doesn't punch his supervisor in the nose because the consequences may be quite costly. However, both the target and the form of aggression can be *displaced*. The frustrated worker may throw an oily rag at the boss when the latter's back is turned. He may use verbal abuse. He may try sabotage—deliberately "gum up the works." Automobile assembly line workers, for example, have ripped car upholstery or done things that caused the line to be halted. He may vent his aggression on a co-worker or do things that make the co-worker's job difficult (in assembly line or "serially interdependent" technology, this can start a vicious circle, as each person passes problems on to the next). He may "take it out on the wife and kids." He may direct the aggression *intropunitively*, in the form of self-incrimination, self-mutilation, or neurotic guilt. A more accepted mode of aggression would be filing a grievance with the union steward. This is a form of institutionally legitimate aggression which is channeled toward constructive purposes.

At this point we can describe the administrator's real task with respect to aggression. On the one hand, he must avoid reinforcing illegitimate, unconstructive forms of aggression; otherwise, he will only ensure that he will have to face more and more of it in the future, particularly as those who have been more "reasonable" learn by observation that "it pays to get tough" or that "the squeaky wheel gets the grease." On the other hand, the administrator must be careful not to bottle up direct aggression only to have it displaced onto other persons or take the form of destructive sabotage. What is the way out of this dilemma? Levinson (1959) suggests that the answer is for the organization to provide official channels for the discharge of aggression. One example is the grievance procedure of unionized organizations. Other forms could include such things as a "corporate ombudsman" or an official flak-catcher. A Japanese firm has life-sized dummies, made to look like the boss, that disgruntled workers can clobber during breaks or the lunch hour. Ultimately, of course, such devices are of little value unless organizational officials make a sincere and determined effort to keep participants' frustration within manageable bounds, take steps to reduce frustrations when it is feasible to do so, communicate the rationale for their frustrating changes in advance, and show a willingness to help bear the cost of organization frustrations. Grievances that never get fully processed, ombudsmen who carry no real clout, and defenseless dummies are not likely to succeed if they are intended to be used as manipulative control values that can be turned on and off like a steam radiator, nor can they stretch to infinity the frustration tolerance of lower-ranking members. If frustrated persons *never* or *very seldom* get any substantive relief by using such channels, their aggression will take other, less desirable channels.

Anxiety

Psychologists have found it difficult to reach agreement on a succinct definition of anxiety as a type of psychological or emotional stress. Attempts to define anxiety have often taken the form of distinguishing between anxiety and fear or between anxiety and frustration. Whereas fear is the reaction to immediate, present danger, anxiety is the reaction to anticipated harm, whether it be physical or psychological (such as loss of self-esteem or loss of status). Whereas frustration is blockage or interference with ongoing instrumental behavior, anxiety is the feeling of *not having* appropriate responses or plans for dealing with anticipated harm. Obviously, it is very difficult to make these distinctions, since the time interval that separates fear of present danger from anxiety due to future threat is subtle and only arbitrarily identified, and the feeling of not having adequate responses for dealing with real or imagined threat may come on slowly as attempted responses to deal with it prove unsuccessful. Nevertheless, most people seem to understand quite well what they mean when they say that they are experiencing anxiety: the sense of dread, foreboding, and apprehension that gnaws at their insides and darkens their outlook on things in general. Sometimes the source or cause of anxiety is uncertain or hard to define; the threat is vague, and the potential danger is itself unstructured or ambiguous. This, of course, renders anxiety all the more unsettling, since it makes any instrumental coping response harder to select or organize. In fact, one frequent reaction to uneasiness about impending threat is to arbitrarily and erroneously focus the threat on some identifiable person or thing so that "something can be done." Thus, Hitler used this scapegoating technique to reassure his followers by focusing their anxieties on the Jews. Allport and Postman (1947) found that one function served by rumors is to enable people to pinpoint their uneasiness, to give it form and structure. One suspects that the grapevine in organizations serves a similar purpose, in addition to serving the more rational and instrumental objective of facilitating information flow.

What are the causes of anxiety in organizations? Differences in power in organizations, which leave people with a feeling of vulnerability to administrative decisions adversely affecting them; frequent changes in organizations, which make existing behavior plans obsolete; competition, which creates the inevitability that some persons lose "face," esteem, and status; and job ambiguity (especially when this is coupled with pressure). To these may be added some related factors, such as lack of job feedback, volatility in the organization's economic environment, job insecurity, and high visibility of one's performance (successes as well as failures).Obviously, personal, nonorganizational factors come into play as well, such as physical illness, problems at home, unrealistically high personal goals, and estrangement from one's colleagues or one's peer group.

There is evidence that anxiety is a "trait" concept as well as a "state" reaction to a specific situation (Spielberger, 1966). Some individuals seem particularly vulnerable to the potential of psychological threat and can be said to *overreact* with anxiety symptoms even to relatively harmless stimuli. Such persons have been characterized as possessing "free-floating" anxiety, which is activated to a dominant role in consciousness whenever any stimulus can in any way be interpreted as threat-suggestive. It is not known whether this free-floating anxiety is the product of physiological differences, unresolved guilt, or a reinforcement history marked by severe punitiveness. Nevertheless, it seems to be a stable dimension of personality. Persons high on this dimension can be very effective performers if their job is well structured or if the job emphasis is on clear-cut tasks; but when they are placed in unstructured tasks in which failure is damaging to the ego, their performance is likely to suffer in comparison to that of low-anxiety persons.

Of course, all causes of anxiety cannot be eliminated in our imperfect world of imperfect organizations managed by imperfect people, nor is all anxiety deleterious to health or performance. Moderate anxiety mobilizes and focuses our energy, sharpens our sensitivity to information in the environment, and is often a prelude to the formulation of innovative, creative solutions to problems. Successful executives have been found to be almost chronically motivated by mild to moderate anxiety (Henry, 1949); they cope with it instrumentally by making phone calls, researching for technical or business-related information, formulating a priority of attempted solutions, assessing trade-offs or positions to fall back on, and identifying "secondary targets"—steps that minimize the damage if no feasible solutions are able to eliminate the threat.

When anxiety is severe and prolonged—either because of factors in the organizational environment, individual differences in susceptibility to anxiety-triggering circumstances, or a lack of available instrumental responses—dysfunctional coping mechanisms are resorted to. The individual begins to direct his attention to the internal sensations of anxiety at the cost of dealing rationally with the source of the anxiety. This may lead to alcoholism, drugs, excessive absenteeism, or a host of other forms of escapism. Since such responses do temporarily alleviate emotional stress, they are reinforcing and can become chronic habits when anxiety is elicited by any characteristic stimulus that usually precedes threat.

A complicating variable in the optimal handling of anxiety is either an unwillingness to admit to it or, even if one admits to it in one's own mind, a tendency to avoid its expression. Particularly among men, there seems to be the attitude that it is a sign of weakness to talk about the experience of anxiety. This is unfortunate, for many causes of apprehension could undoubtedly be laid to rest if they were voiced, either to one's boss or to one's colleagues.

What can administrators do to help keep anxiety within moderate, manageable bounds? One thing they can do is simply reinforce its expression, so that if it is groundless it can be dispelled. They can, where possible, avoid initiating changes that uproot people from cohesive groups. The Hawthorne studies (Roethlisberger & Dickson, 1964) showed that nagging personal worries were much less debilitating when female workers were allowed to coalesce into natural work groups (we discuss this landmark study in more detail in Chapter 13). Administrators can also give attention to individual differences, either by placing high-anxiety persons in jobs that do not combine pressure with high job ambiguity or by providing special nurturance to highly anxious individuals when efforts at optimal placement fail. Increasing job performance feedback, providing advance communication prior to significant planned organization change, and avoiding unnecessary competitive stimulation are all obvious means for mitigating stressful anxiety.

ORGANIZATIONAL STRESSORS

Given our definition of stress, any organizational problem or task which temporarily exceeds the individual's capacities for responding adequately is a stressor. However, several characteristics of organizations in general seem to act as chronic stressors.

Perhaps the most universal cause of organizational stress is the simple fact that in order to exist, organizations must contain the natural variance in human behavior. An organization is a system of roles, and any organizational role taps only a limited set of an individual's interests, wants, skills, and traits. Put another way, only that part of the individual which fits the requirements and prescriptions of his or her role is relevant to the organization. Yet the organization has to take the whole person; it cannot carve out the portion it wants and leave out the rest. Floyd Allport (1933) called this dilemma the problem of *partial inclusion.* The struggle of the full-blown person within the confines of the psychological box we call role is inherently stressful, and this conflict constantly threatens to disrupt the smooth flow of instrumental behavior.

Some recent critics of bureaucracy and business have made a major issue of this dilemma. They indict large organizations for trying to mold the person into a stereotyped form, and thus reducing him to a hollow character, stripped of his or her complexity and color. For the most part, this indictment is unfair. The conflict between the complete person and the role is not unique to business or even to large organizations of any kind; it takes place in all kinds of social groups, including families, clubs, teams, or even friendship groups. In this sense, the conflict is, as Strauss (1963) notes, a reflection of the more general, inescapable one between "individual and society, individual and environment, desire and reality, id and super ego." Moreover, individuals tend to self-select themselves into the roles they are most comfortable with, the roles which place the least restraint on their natural behavior and inclinations. Furthermore, organizational roles are not rigid boxes. To varying degrees, organizational roles are flexible in their demands and permit variations in their interpretation and enactment by the individuals who fill them. True, some organizations are more demanding (and within organizations, some roles) or have more demanding specifications than do others, and thus the conflicts with instrumental behavior are greater. Although the need of organizations to contain human behavior is the most universal cause of organizational stress, the stress is usually of manageable proportions. The exceptions usually arise from mistakes in the selection and placement process, and these mistakes can be rectified by transfer within the organization or voluntary withdrawal.

The hierarchical nature of organizations is a second very general source of stress. Again, this problem is not unique to business. The political philosopher Robert Michels and the experimenters with utopian communes in the early 19th century discovered that the evolution of hierarchy is inevitable in organizations that contain more than a handful of participants (Hampton, Summer, & Webber, 1968). Nevertheless, when differences in power lead to autocratic control by a few over the many, the former are able to make demands on behavior that exceed the capacities of individuals to respond instrumentally without undue cost.

A third general cause of stress in organizations is competition for scarce rewards, and this is probably more likely to be a stressor in business organizations. Although hierarchy (power and status distinctions) and scarce rewards guarantee a certain minimum of competition, many business organizations seem to be based on the premise that competition is not a necessary evil that should be minimized but a *Note* positive force that should be maximized in order to induce people to perform at their highest possible levels. For some individuals this is undoubtedly effective. Nevertheless, competition ensures that many will lose, some repeatedly, and that even those who win may pay a heavy price for their victories. The superior performance attained by the winners is highly visible and captures our attention; but the accomplishments of the winners may be more than offset by the cost to the organization of the effects on the losers, who are carried by unremitting competitive stress to the exhaustion stage. This cost, unfortunately, is often less visible and less easy to evaluate. Furthermore, the winners are usually the ones who wind up in privileged positions in the hierarchy. Their success confirms them in their philosophy that competition is healthy and functional and enables them to maintain a competitive climate.

Cherrington (1973) cites the view of the philosopher Bertrand Russell that the excessively stressful effects of competition might be avoided if the losers were protected from undue hardships. This might involve limiting competitive contests to bonus- or fringe-type rewards. Another possibility would be a modification of the "up or out" philosophy practiced by some organizations—throwing young managers into the race with the understanding that if they don't progress continually they are out. Taking a cue from the Peter Principle (Peter, 1969), which states that in a hierarchy people are eventually promoted to their level of incompetence, less emphasis might be placed on promotions (which are inherently competitive, given the pyramidal shape of corporations and the decreasing number of positions as one nears the apex). Some managers have assumed too long that everybody worth his or her salt lusts for repeated promotions, and often good performers have been afraid to decline promotions which they really didn't want because of fear that this would make them appear complacent.

Robert Kahn and his research colleagues at the Survey Research Center of the University of Michigan (Kahn, Wolfe, Quinn, Snoek, & Rosenthal 1964) have found *role conflict* and *role ambiguity* to be significant sources of stress in large organizations. They define role conflict as the "simultaneous occurrence of two (or more) sets of pressures such that compliance with one would make more difficult," or impossible, compliance with the other. For example, a supervisor may be pressed by superiors to maximize production from subordinates, yet at the same time to avoid morale problems that may lead to absenteeism, turnover, or grievances processed by the union. The worker may be pushed by his supervisor to maximize productivity, yet also be pressured by engineering staff to reduce materials waste or rejects due to careless workmanship. Sales executives are sometimes put in the position of having to violate the law or business ethics in order to achieve the product market penetration demanded by superiors.

Kahn et al. found role conflict to be associated with greater levels of interpersonal tension, lower job satisfaction, lower levels of trust and respect for persons exerting the conflicting role pressures, and decreased confidence in the organization. Although role conflict cannot be totally eliminated from organizations, Kahn suggests that it could perhaps be kept within reasonable bounds if administrators view the *role set*—the interlocking dependences, expectations, and coordinative requirements of a given number of interacting participants—rather than the individual as the basic building block of organizations.

Another form of role conflict is represented by *role overload*, in which the different expectations from or role pressures on a person are not inherently or logically incompatible, but the sheer number of expectations either exceeds the person's capacity or forces him to do some jobs more hastily and less carefully than he believes he should. In executive, administrative, or professional roles that do not have well-defined job descriptions, this form of stress is exacerbated by the apparent inability of some individuals to say no to any request for service, either because of extremely high achievement aspirations or for fear that a refusal will be looked upon negatively and thus be detrimental to their career advancement. This process is further compounded by the fact that individuals who do accept such ad hoc responsibilities and stretch themselves to do a conscientious job are all the more likely to be the target of increased requests for service—because they have, by their cooperation and performance, reinforced others for turning to them. The development of role overload can be an insidious and deceptive process due to the gradual accumulation of obligations, commitments, and short- and long-term goals that add up over time. The person then finds his organizational role crowding into other life roles (such as family or community roles) as he stews over the disarray of unfinished business on the "back-burner" or becomes obsessed with the items still on his "guilt shelf." It would be useful if organizations could provide occasional short periods of time for taking inventory of one's accumulated commitments, pruning the less essential items away, and leaving a manageable set of high-priority tasks.

Role ambiguity is the uncertainty surrounding one's job definition: uncertainty concerning the expectations held by others for one's job performance, concerning how to go about meeting those expectations, and concerning the consequences of one's job behavior. As Kahn notes, "efficient goal-directed behavior is based on predictability of future events" (Kahn et al., 1964). To this might be added the observation that instrumental behavior depends on achieving some degree of clarity on what goals (long-, medium-, and short-range) are relevant and on what behavior is essential in moving toward those goals. A person with a high degree of role ambiguity simply has no plans to guide behavior. Role ambiguity is apt to be an increasing problem in organizations as changes in the economy shift the bulk of the labor force away from production jobs into the service sector and professional, staff, and administrative jobs—many of which are newly created and are characterized by fuzzy job descriptions that leave the individual to operate in a context that is relatively devoid of stimulus cues for behavior. Furthermore, the pace of change and the demands for constant readjustment in today's large organizations often render old plans for behavior obsolete.

As is true for other sources of stress in organizations, individuals seem to differ vastly in the extent to which they find role ambiguity stressful. Some people, regardless of intelligence or competence, seem to demand a high degree of structure in their lives, while others are very tolerant of—even thrive on—ambiguity. Individual differences in the personality dimension of *neuroticism* (see Chapter 8) also seems to be an important factor in susceptibility to stress induced by role ambiguity: persons high on the scale of neuroticism, or emotionality, seem to experience more strain in unstructured job environments.

In addition to individual differences that determine the degree of stress caused by role ambiguity, there are factors in the job environment that make ambiguity more or less aversive. One of these seems to be the general level of *pressure* induced by organizational demands. When the stakes or consequences associated with instrumental role performance are very great, ambiguity is most aversive. When the job climate is rendered more protective and supportive, ambiguity seems to be more tolerable, and sometimes even preferable to highly structured roles. This should not be surprising, since greater amounts of freedom, autonomy, and discretion in one's job must inevitably mean some increase in role ambiguity as well. Perhaps the least ambiguous organizational roles are those associated with assembly line work or clerical office work, yet surely these are generally not preferred to creative or managerial jobs.

Thus, where role ambiguity is unavoidable—due to the very nature of the job or task—the administrator can ameliorate the resultant stress either by trying to provide a more supportive climate or by giving special attention and guidance to those persons thought to be high in emotionality and low in tolerance for ambiguity.

An extensive program of research by Thomas H. Holmes and his colleagues at the University of Washington School of Medicine has documented the *rate of life change* as a stress-generative factor which is related to the onset of disease or illness in numerous forms. Using psychological scaling techniques, they have found a remarkable agreement in the adjustment demands made by various types of change among people of different ages and cultures. Table 9–1 shows the relative impact of different life changes, with the universally agreed-upon

Table 9–1
Scaling of life-change units for various experiences

Life event	Scale value
Death of spouse	100
Divorce	73
Marital separation	65
Jail term	63
Death of a close family member	63
Major personal injury or illness	53
Marriage	50
Fired from work	47
Marital reconciliation	45
Retirement	45
Major change in health of family member	44
Pregnancy	40
Sex difficulties	39
Gain of a new family member	39
Business readjustment	39
Change in financial state	38
Death of a close friend	37
Change to a different line of work	36
Change in number of arguments with spouse	35
Mortgage over $10,000	31
Foreclosure of mortgage or loan	30
Change in responsibilities at work	29
Son or daughter leaving home	29
Trouble with in-laws	29
Outstanding personal achievement	28
Wife begins or stops work	26
Begin or end school	26
Change in living conditions	25
Revision of personal habits	24
Trouble with boss	23
Change in work hours or conditions	20
Change in residence	20
Change in schools	20
Change in recreation	19
Change in church activities	19
Change in social activities	18
Mortgage or loan less than $10,000	17
Change in sleeping habits	16
Change in number of family get-togethers	15
Change in eating habits	15
Vacation	13
Christmas	12
Minor violations of the law	11

Source: From L. O. Ruch and T. H. Holmes, "Scaling of Life Change: Comparison of Direct and Indirect Methods," *Journal of Psychosomatic Research,* 1971, *15,* 224.

most stressful change—death of a spouse—arbitrarily given 100 points, and others given a proportionate weight. Note that although some of the events listed are normally thought of as desirable—gain of a new family member, change of job, outstanding personal achievement, new work responsibilities—they generate stress nonetheless due to the accommodative demands made on the organism. Holmes has found that the accumulation of more than 200 units of change in a single year results in a better than 50 percent chance that the individual will sustain serious illness in the following year. The connection between life change and illness seems to involve the endocrine system, which provides the surplus of energy (in the form of hormones) needed to cope with new situations. When the rate of change approaches a certain level, the endocrine system is overloaded and cannot perform its normal function of defending against certain viruses, which are always present in the body but cause disease only when the body's defense system wears down.

Meyer Friedman and Ray Rosenman (1974) have evidence that personality determines to a considerable degree the amount and intensity of the stress that an individual experiences. They found that a trait labeled by them as Type A tended to predict the occurrence of premature coronary artery disease, even when they controlled for the effects of family medical history, smoking, blood serum cholesterol, high blood pressure, and other risk factors. The Type A manifests a behavioral syndrome that reflects a sense of urgency and constant competitive striving. The Type A habitually races against the clock, tries to do several different things at once (like driving and dictating memos, or watching TV and working on a speech), shows intense irritation at any kind of delay (such as having to creep behind a slow driver or wait for an elevator), and generally tries to stretch his or her abilities to the limit, even in social or leisure activities. Ironically, the extreme Type A's do not seem to experience stress in a subjective sense, or at least they seldom voice feelings of anxiety, and they are seldom afflicted by minor illnesses, such as colds (they don't have the time!). Even more surprising, despite their hard-driving and competitive nature, they seldom make it to the top rungs of corporations. They make good salespersons and middle managers, but the Type B—who is more reflective, more patient, and unhurried in manner and work—is more likely to be the president of the company.

Friedman and Rosenman believe that urban Western culture encourages the Type A syndrome because of its obsession with the clock and its tendency to evaluate people's accomplishments by quantitative (as opposed to qualitative) criteria. Thus, the extreme Type A, if he exercises at all, tries to play 36 holes of golf in an afternoon or takes a stopwatch with him as he jogs. To the extent that he reflects upon the previous day or month, it is in terms of miles traveled, pages written, books read, number of customers seen, and so on. While Friedman and Rosenman offer no quick and easy way to modify this behavior, they suggest that Type A's concentrate on doing one thing at a time, occasionally take time out to do something totally escapist (like walking through a park and trying to notice the order in which different flowers blossom), and set aside more time to accomplish a task than it will actually take. If the Type A does not modify his behavior, he runs a serious risk of incurring artery disease before age 60. The additional cost, of course, is running through life without experiencing the joys of very simple things.

CONCLUSION

To repeat, stress is endemic to life itself, and in moderation stress adds to the drama of life and the meaningfulness of existence. What is "moderate" is defined not only by objective conditions in the organizational milieu, but also in the subjective world of the individual— his physiological makeup, his previous history of development, his capacity and repertoire for dealing with the situation. The administrator's task is to know his people, to detect symptoms of stress that signal the onset of the "exhaustion" stage and to intervene when such symptoms are in evidence, and to anticipate how his own actions and decisions will contribute to stress. It should not be overlooked, of course, that any administrator has to deal with his own stress; it would be as unwise for the administrator to spare everyone else stress at the cost of overstressing himself as it would be unfair to force others to bear all the stress. Here, as in so many other facets of organizational life, equity and moderation are the only viable policies.

SUMMARY

Stress is defined by a set of circumstances in which an individual cannot respond instrumentally or can do so only at appreciable physical or psychological costs. The response to stress includes three phases: the alarm reaction, resistance, and exhaustion or collapse. Psychologists have found it useful to classify stress as frustration, anxiety, or conflict. Frustration may take a number of forms; at mild-to-moderate levels, it may have positive effects on psychological growth, development, and functioning, but chronic frustration may evoke aggressive behavior or depression. Anxiety also tends to have a positive motivational effect on behavior, particularly if the individual's repertoire of coping techniques is adequate, but severe anxiety typically leads to escapist methods of coping with the internal sensations of anxiety rather than with the cause of the anxiety.

Organizational factors implicated in the genesis of stress include the restriction of natural variance in human behavior, the hierarchical

Figure 9–2
Sources, forms, and consequences of psychological stress in organizations

Organizational stressors	Forms of psychological stress	Behavioral effects
Partial inclusion	Frustration	Increased arousal, effort
		Perceptual change
Hierarchy		Creative responses
		Aggression (direct, displaced, or siphoned through organizational
Competition		channels)
		Depression
Role conflict		
Role ambiguity		
Role overload	Anxiety	Arousal
		Communication of fears
Change		Group affiliations
		Escapism
Type A		Alcoholism, drugs
behavior syndrome		Illness

nature of organizations, and competition for scarce rewards. These sources of stress, while pervasive, typically do not cause serious problems. Role conflict, role overload, and role ambiguity lead to more acute, chronic, and debilitating stressfulness. Change, in the most generalized sense, has been shown to take its toll on the organism. Finally, some people generate their own stress, particularly if their behavior is characterized by the Type A syndrome.

Since the administrator cannot eliminate stress, stress management is the preferred goal. The administrator should try to keep stress within the "resistance" stage, promote positive methods of coping with it, and strive for equity in the shouldering of stressful burdens.

CONCEPTS TO REMEMBER

stress	displaced aggression
general adaptation syndrome	intropunitive aggression
alarm reaction	anxiety
resistance	partial inclusion
exhaustion	Peter Principle
frustration	role conflict
frustration tolerance	role ambiguity
depression	role set
aggression	role overload
Type A behavior	

QUESTIONS FOR DISCUSSION

1. Why do some individuals apparently have a greater capacity for tolerating stress?

2. Some companies recruit more college graduates into their training program than they can possibly use as managers, on the premise that competition among them will produce a few "stars." What are the pros and cons for this policy?

3. What types of jobs are most vulnerable to the development of role overload? What types of persons?

4. What factors might result in frustration being *perceived* as arbitrary, even though there is in fact a good rationale for the events that cause the frustration?

5. Should aggression in organizations be suppressed or extinguished? Explain.

6. What are likely to be the most prevalent forms of stress for executive managers? female factory workers? older factory workers? scientists and other professionals in industry?

7. What role does the work group play in regulating stress?

8. Over the course of this century—from 1900 to the present—what developments have tended to reduce stress? to increase it?

REFERENCES

Allport, F. H. *Institutional behavior.* Chapel Hill: University of North Carolina Press, 1933.

Allport, G. W., & Postman, T. *The psychology of rumor.* New York: Holt, 1947.

Cantril, H. Perception and interpersonal relations. *American Journal of Psychiatry,* 1957, *114*(2), 27–29.

Cherrington, D. J. Satisfaction in competitive conditions. *Organizational Behavior and Human Performance,* 1973, *10,* 47–71.

Costello, T. W., & Zalkind, S. S. (Eds.). *Psychology in administration.* Englewood Cliffs, N.J.: Prentice-Hall, 1963.

Friedman, M., & Rosenman, R. H. *Type A behavior and your heart.* New York: Knopf, 1974.

Hampton, D. R., Summer, C. E., & Webber, L. A. (Eds.). *Organizational behavior and the practice of management.* Glenview, Ill.: Scott, Foresman, 1968.

Harrell, W. A., & Moss, I. D. Two fixed-ratio schedules and their impact on aggression in humans. *Psychological Reports,* 1974, *34,* 785–786.

Henry, W. E. The business executive: The psychodynamics of a social role. *American Journal of Sociology,* 1949, *54,* 296–291.

Kahn, R. L., Wolfe, D. M., Quinn, R. P., Snoek, J. D., & Rosenthal, R. A. *Organizational stress.* New York: Wiley, 1964.

Lawson, R.   *Frustration.* New York: Macmillan, 1965.

Levinson, H.   The psychologist in industry. *Harvard Business Review,* 1959, *37,* 93–99.

Peter, L. F.   *The Peter principle.* New York: William Morrow, 1969.

Roethlisberger, F. J., & Dickson, W. J.   *Management and the worker.* New York: Wiley Science Editions, 1964.

Ruch, L. O., & Holmes, T. H.   Scaling of life change: Comparison of direct and indirect methods. *Journal of Psychosomatic Research,* 1971, *15,* 221–227.

Seligman, M. E. P.   Fall into helplessness. *Psychology Today,* June 1973, pp. 43–48.

Selye, H.   *The stress of life.* New York: McGraw-Hill, 1956.

Spielberger, C. D. (Ed.).   *Anxiety and behavior.* New York: Academic Press, 1966.

Strauss, G.   The personality vs. organization theory. In L. R. Sayles (Ed.), *Individualism and big business.* New York: McGraw-Hill, 1963.

Toffler, A.   *Future shock.* New York: Random House, 1970.

10

Job satisfaction

Why is job satisfaction important?

What is the extent of job satisfaction in the labor force?

What groups in the labor force express the most job satisfaction?

What are the sources of job satisfaction?

What types of work behavior are associated with levels of job satisfaction?

One criterion by which we evaluate an organization's functioning is, of course, *performance*. For a manufacturing firm, this criterion might take the form of labor productivity, share of the market, or return on investment; for a hospital, the quality and quantity of health care provided for patients; for local government, the efficiency with which socially mandated services are provided to the community. Whatever the actual measure or measures might be, we clearly evaluate the management of an organization, at least in part, on its track record in terms of quantifiable performance according to some goal or standard.

To an increasing extent, especially since the 1940s, organizations are also being evaluated on the basis of the need satisfactions of their participants. When participation takes the form of a full-time job, we refer to the *job satisfaction* of the organization's work force.

Why is job satisfaction a criterion of organizational functioning? It is *not* because greater satisfaction leads in any simple or direct way to superior performance. At various times in the last four decades a number of people have justified their concern for greater job satisfaction of organization members by arguing that such satisfaction easily translates into increased productivity. However, as we shall soon see, the results of a large number of studies suggest that this argument lacks support. This is not to say that job satisfaction has no desirable behavioral consequences, but rather to disabuse the reader of any simple notion that happier people are automatically more productive people.

Why, then, is job satisfaction so important? One reason stems quite simply from certain *value judgments*. People spend a sizable proportion of their waking lives in the work environment. From any minimally humanitarian point of view, we would want that portion of their lives to be more or less pleasant, agreeable, and fulfilling. Few people actually have the choice of working or not working; and of those who have to work for economic reasons, most have only a limited number of options as to where to work. Given such constraints, much of the population would find little cheer in their lives if the workplace offered no opportunity for satisfaction.

A second reason for attaching so much importance to job satisfaction is its relationship to *mental health*. In the realm of our subjective inner worlds, discontent about specific parts of our lives tends to have a "spillover" effect and to color our outlook even upon otherwise unrelated portions of our life space. Dissatisfaction with one's job seems to have an especially volatile spillover effect. People who feel bad about their work are apt to feel bad about many other things, including family life, leisure activities, even life itself. Psychiatrists tell us that most of their patients express negative feelings about their jobs. Admittedly, the direction of causation may sometimes run the opposite way;

unresolved personality problems or maladjustment may indeed be the cause of a person's inability to find satisfaction in work. Nevertheless, anyone who has ever had to live with a parent, spouse, sibling, or roommate who didn't like his or her job knows how tense relationships with that person can be. Both casual observation and scientific study seem to provide compelling evidence that job satisfaction is an important component of overall psychological adjustment and productive living.

Evidence also points to a relationship between job satisfaction and *physical health.* According to one study (Palmore, 1969) people who like their work are likely to live longer. Again, complicating factors preclude a hasty conclusion that job satisfaction, per se, is the causal factor, since people with greater job satisfaction also tend to have greater incomes and more education, and thus may coincidentally enjoy greater advantages and knowledge which promote longevity. Nonetheless, chronic dissatisfaction with work represents a form of stress, and stress does eventually take its toll on the organism. Emotional stress has been implicated as a contributing factor in the genesis of hypertension, coronary artery disease, digestive ailments, and even some types of cancer.

Value judgments, mental health, and physical health explain why the larger society holds organizations accountable for participants' satisfaction. From the organization's point of view, there are additional reasons for giving attention to the job satisfaction of its members. People who feel positively about their work life are more apt to voice *favorable sentiments about the organization to the community at large.* This represents a public relations function in the best sense: it facilitates recruitment of new members, fosters a pervasive residue of public goodwill toward the organization, and enhances the legitimacy of its purpose and operations in the minds of observers. In addition, people who like their jobs are *easier to "live with" inside the organization* as well as outside it. A chronically upset person—whether it be boss, co-worker, or subordinate—makes organizational life more vexatious for those who have to interact with him or her. Finally, as we shall note in more detail later, higher job satisfaction tends to *reduce absenteeism and turnover.* These are not abstractions—they are calculable costs; and in some industries they represent the most significant portion of variable labor costs. Even if managers ignored or remained unconvinced of the merits of other arguments for monitoring the level of member satisfaction, absenteeism and turnover alone would compel them to treat job satisfaction as an important variable.

WHAT IS JOB SATISFACTION?

Essentially, job satisfaction is a person's attitude toward the job. Like any other attitude, then, it represents a complex assemblage of cognitions (beliefs or knowledge), emotions (feelings, sentiments, or evaluations), and behavioral tendencies. A person with a high level of job satisfaction holds very positive attitudes about the workplace, and conversely, a person dissatisfied with the job embraces negative attitudes toward the job environment.

Thus, like other attitudes, job satisfaction is an unseen, unobserved variable. How, then, do we measure it? How do we indirectly observe it? Probably the simplest, most straightforward method is to ask an individual: On the whole, are you satisfied or dissatisfied with your job? A number of surveys of job attitudes in the work force have used just this technique, and for certain purposes it may suffice. For other purposes, it may be too crude a measure. A person with moderately negative job attitudes may feel too inhibited to make a direct, unqualified response of "Dissatisfied." Thus, among people responding "Satisfied," there is likely to exist a broad continuum ranging from passive dissatisfaction through indifference to strong and enthusiastic endorsement of their jobs. Analogous to this phenomenon were the findings of early sociological studies which asked people whether they regarded themselves as lower class, middle class, or upper class: almost everyone, from village pauper to resident millionaire, said "middle class." But when respondents were given more categories to choose from (for example, lower middle or upper middle), the answers spread out substantially.

To detect more subtle variations in the extent of job satisfaction, psychologists have developed a number of standardized *attitude scales* for measuring it. Different scales vary considerably in their length and format, but a typical job satisfaction instrument presents the respondent with a number of evaluative statements (some worded positively, some negatively) about various aspects of the job. The respondent is asked to indicate whether he strongly agrees, agrees, neither agrees nor disagrees, disagrees, or strongly disagrees with each statement. Each response is scored (for example, 5 for strongly agrees and 1 for strongly disagrees with positive statements, the opposite for negative items), and the scores on all items are summed for an overall estimate of job satisfaction. (See Figure 10–1 for representative items from such scales.)

Job attitude scales were originally developed for research purposes. Industrial psychologists were interested in such questions as: How closely does level of job satisfaction correlate with individual performance? How well can job attitudes be predicted by salary? What types of leadership styles result in greater job satisfaction? More refined measures than simple statements of "satisfaction" or "dissatisfaction," were needed in order to grapple with such questions. Increasingly, however, organization officials have been adopting job attitude scales for their own purposes, either directly or by way of consultants. By conducting periodic audits of job satisfaction, managers can spot trends

Figure 10–1
Representative items in job satisfaction measures

Indicate whether the various statements listed below describe something that is very good, good, fair, poor, or very poor about your job.

	VG	G	F	P	VP
Management's interest in welfare of employees.					
This company as a place to work.					
Fair treatment of employees by management.					
Credit given by my supervisor for doing a good job.					
The amount of money I am paid.					
Freedom to make decisions about my work.					
Interesting work to do.					
Chances of steady work.					

Adapted from Robert P. Bullock, *Social Factors Related to Job Satisfaction* (Columbus: Bureau of Business Research, Ohio State University, 1952).

in job attitudes which may not produce behavioral results until sometime later. Thus, they can take such actions as necessary to avert a rise in turnover rate or in labor grievances. Furthermore, they can isolate pockets of rife discontent in what might otherwise be an overall climate of positive feelings about management practices.

The reader may object to treating job satisfaction in such a global fashion. After all, might not one feel quite good about salary and fringe benefits, but be dissatisfied with one's boss? The answer is obviously yes. For this reason, most recently developed job attitude scales permit the scoring of subscales about different parts of the work environment. An overall job satisfaction score can be disassembled into scores indicating attitudes about pay, supervision, chances for promotion, co-workers, and the work itself (the intrinsic nature of the work activities performed). However, though people may be expected to hold opposing attitudes about separate job facets, we find, in fact, a rather high degree of consistency and intercorrelation in attitudes toward various aspects of the job. People who dislike their superiors show a better-than-chance probability of also complaining about working conditions, even about such objective physical referents as the quality of lighting or the adequacy of rest rooms. Individuals who are bored with what they do on the job are also likely to refrain from outright positive endorsement of the organization's salary structure. Roethlisberger and Dickson (1964) noted this covariation in job sentiments nearly 50 years ago in the massive interviewing phase of the celebrated Hawthorne studies; they attempted to account for the covariation by suggesting that the logic of sentiments is different from the logic of facts, especially in the sense that strong sentiments do not permit as fine a degree of perceptual discrimination. Whatever the reason, tightly compartmentalized attitudes toward components of the work environment appear to be the exception rather than the rule.

THE EXTENT OF JOB SATISFACTION IN THE LABOR FORCE

What percentage of the nation's workers are satisfied with their jobs? Which groups are more or less satisfied than other groups? Are people's attitudes toward their jobs becoming more or less favorable? A number of nationwide surveys of representative samples of the labor force have addressed themselves to these questions.

The longest running series of job satisfaction surveys is that conducted by George Gallup, probably the foremost name among professional pollsters. Gallup uses the simple, direct method of asking people whether they are, on the whole, satisfied or dissatisfied with their present jobs. As Table 10–1 indicates, from 1949 on up to the 1970s, only a small proportion of workers—20 percent at most, and usually much less—respond with "Dissatisfied." These figures come as quite a surprise to most people, especially students; contrary to many opinions, the vast majority of the nation's workers seem to feel at least moderately pleased with their jobs. They may have specific gripes about work (undoubtedly a favorite and traditional indoor sport of Americans), and they usually see plenty of room for improvement, but overall, they like their jobs. Furthermore, Gallup's findings are supplemented by other surveys of varying scope and representativeness (for a review of these, see Herzberg, Mausner, Peterson, & Capwell, 1955), and with

Table 10–1
Gallup polls of job satisfaction

	Satisfied	Dissatisfied	No opinion
1949	67%	20%	13%
1963	90	7	3
1965	87	9	4
1966	87	9	4
1969	88	6	6
1971	83	9	8

Source: George H. Gallup, *The Gallup Poll* (New York: Random House, 1972).

with almost uncanny consistency these studies show 70 to 85 percent of workers as saying that they are satisfied rather than dissatisfied with their jobs.

Some critics of these findings argue that Gallup's survey method, for reasons touched on earlier, yields an inflated measure of job satisfaction, and suggest that a less blunt way of phrasing the question would produce more realistic data. As it turns out, Gallup himself has used a variation in method. In his 1950 and 1955 surveys he asked:

1. If you were to begin all over again, would you go into the same line of work or not?

   Only 55 percent said yes, 35 percent said no, and 10 percent were undecided.

2. Do you think you would be happier in a different job?

   32 percent said yes.

3. Do you enjoy your work so much that you have a hard time putting it aside?

   Only 51 percent said yes, and 45 percent said no.

4. Generally speaking, which do you enjoy more—the hours when you are on your job, or the hours when you are not on your job?

   The 39 percent who answered "on the job" were outnumbered by the 48 percent who answered "not on the job."

There seems to be a basis, then, for arguing that forcing people to choose between saying that they are satisfied or that they are dissatisfied may overstate the positivity of job attitudes in the work force. Nevertheless, taking all the findings together—including the extremely conservative measure which asks people to compare life on the job with life off the job—it appears that job satisfaction is broadly distributed throughout the nation's labor pool.

Recent trends: Better or worse?

In the early 1970s, the changing nature of job satisfaction among employed workers became a matter of some controversy. The most vocal and publicized position—portrayed in books, magazine and newspaper articles, and television documentaries—purported to show that a crisis in job morale was developing, a crisis reflected not only in surveys of job attitudes but also in such behavioral indices as increased absenteeism, higher turnover, and declining economic growth and labor productivity. *Work in America* (1973), the report of a special task force to the Secretary of Health, Education, and Welfare, commented at length on the thesis of "job alienation," with particular reference to "blue-collar blues," "white-collar woes," the dissatisfaction of younger workers, and the prevalence of negative attitudes among women and minority workers. Sheppard and Herrick's *Where Have All the Robots Gone?* (1972), based largely on a study of approximately 1,500 workers by the Survey Research Center of the University of Michigan and supplemented by a less extensive study of male blue-collar workers, painted an equally gloomy picture of the typical worker's job attitudes. Judson Gooding's *The Job Revolution* (1972) conveyed the same message. These three books agreed that the course of job satisfaction was spiraling downward and shared a consensual judgment that the major cause of the decline was sterile work that offered too few people any opportunity for psychological growth and fulfillment in their jobs. The corrective approach, they urged, lay in a concerted program of job redesign in industry and business to render work more meaningful, interesting, and enriching.

Not all observers agreed that job attitudes had come to such a sorry state. Gallup's survey results, while showing a dip in the period 1963–71, suggested that the extent of job satisfaction had remained quite stable over the years since 1949, and if anything had risen between 1949 and 1971, especially for blacks. In fact, even in the Michigan study cited by Sheppard and Herrick, no more than 25 percent of any single subgroup of workers expressed negative attitudes toward work, and the overall figure for the entire sample was about 14 percent—remarkably close to the 13 percent which Herzberg et al. (1955) found as a median figure in their review of studies undertaken prior to 1955.

What about behavioral indices of job attitudes, such as turnover and absenteeism? A glance at Table 10–2 shows that the quit rate among employees surveyed by government agencies did undeniably increase steadily through the 1960s. One must, however, take into account the unemployment level throughout this period to place the trend in quit rate in proper perspective. People are more apt to quit their jobs—even jobs they would otherwise be satisfied with—when they have good prospects of finding better jobs. As the unemployment figures in Table 10–2 attest, the job market became increasingly favorable for workers as the nation's economy enjoyed the longest period of sustained growth since World War II. The expansionist fiscal policies of the Kennedy-Johnson administrations, compounded by the strain upon the economy of increasing U.S. involvement in Vietnam, led generally to a shortage of workers. As the economy cooled off and entered a severe recession in 1974–75, quits became less frequent. It should be pointed out, however, that after correcting for the effect of unemployment level on turnover, there remains a slight trend toward a higher quit rate; that is, for a *given* level of unemployment, turnover seems to have been slightly greater since 1963 than it was

Table 10–2
Turnover and unemployment, 1960–1975

	Average monthly quit rate (per 100 workers)	Unemployment (percent)
1960	1.3	5.6
1961	1.2	6.7
1962	1.4	5.6
1963	1.4	5.7
1964	1.5	5.2
1965	1.9	4.5
1966	2.5	3.8
1967	2.3	3.8
1968	2.5	3.6
1969	2.7	3.5
1970	2.1	4.9
1971	1.8	5.9
1972	2.2	5.6
1973	2.7	4.9
1974	2.3	5.6
1975	1.4	8.5

Source: U.S. Bureau of the Census, *Statistical Abstract of the United States,* 1963, 1970, and 1974.

before that time. Nevertheless, the lion's share of the increased turnover between 1961 and 1970 can be viewed as largely due to the tight labor market.

National absenteeism figures are harder to come by. It is well known, though, that absenteeism in certain sectors of the economy, such as the auto industry, doubled between 1960 and 1970. Again, much of this increase stemmed from labor market conditions. When help is scarce, employers are less apt to discipline workers for excess absences (for fear that they will quit) or to discharge workers; in either case, the employers would have to compete for replacements in a diminished pool, and employees are probably aware of this. Furthermore, when plants are short of the help necessary to fill production orders, they reach out for more and more marginal employees, accepting the risk that such individuals will have less than desirable attendance habits. Finally, with tight labor markets forcing up basic wage rates and leading to substantial overtime earnings, people can more easily afford lost earnings from occasionally playing hooky in order to go fishing, take in a ball game, or catch up on sleep.

Productivity trends are also affected by labor market conditions, as economic analyses of the business cycle have repeatedly shown: man-hour productivity is lowest when companies have recruited the greatest number of marginal workers.

There are a number of reasons, to be delineated later in this chapter, for thinking that there has been a *slight* trend—holding other factors constant—toward decreased job satisfaction. However, neither attitude surveys nor objective behavioral measures offer convincing evidence that any drastic change has occurred over the last decade or so. The vast majority of American workers still seem to be satisfied with their jobs.

Which groups are most satisfied?

While both historical and current analyses testify to a reasonably high level of job satisfaction in the labor force as a whole, clear-cut patterns of variation exist *within* the labor force. Among the demographic classifications showing differences between groups are those pertaining to age, length of tenure, occupational level, race, and sex.

Herzberg et al.'s review in 1955 showed a rather consistent trend in job attitudes according to age and length of service (see Figure 10–2). When people begin work (typically in their late teens or their early 20s), they appear to do so with a considerable degree of enthusiasm. This enthusiasm soon wanes, however, giving way to a steady decline in job morale which reaches its lowest depths in the early

Figure 10–2
Age and job satisfaction

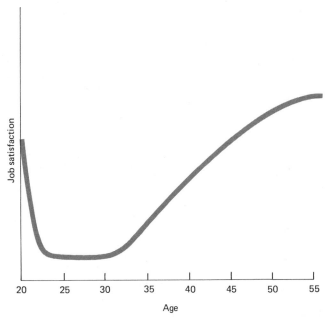

Source: F. Herzberg, B. Mausner, R. Peterson, and D. Capwell, *Job Attitudes: Review of Research and Opinion* (Pittsburgh: Psychological Service of Pittsburgh, 1955).

30s. Attitudes then become increasingly positive, at least well into the 50s. The trend after that is less certain, since different studies have drawn opposite conclusions. Some suggest that the level of job satisfaction continues to climb or at least that it holds steady; others point to another decline—possibly due to concern about health, approaching retirement, or the end of the road as far as further promotion is concerned. In any case, the point seems well established that workers in the middle 20s to early 30s are the least satisfied group. Sheppard and Herrick's data confirm that this is still the case; their study showed that among workers aged 20–29, 24 percent expressed negative attitudes toward work, as opposed to 13 percent in the 30–44 age bracket and 11 percent in the 45–54 range.

Why is this the case? Herzberg and his associates suggested a number of plausible reasons. When you evaluate anything—be it a job, a meal, a car, or a movie—you do so by implicitly comparing the object to others like it that you have experienced.When a person takes his first full-time job, he has no prior job to compare it with. How, then, does he evaluate it? Probably by comparing it with the next closest thing, school. School life is characterized by much variety, a wide circle of acquaintances, frequent opportunities for achievement, changes in activities, and a number of significant events (getting a driver's license, the first date, making a varsity athletic team, graduation, and so on). Most jobs suffer by comparison with the colorful world of academic life (more colorful in retrospect, of course). Few jobs offer that kind of variety and change of pace.

Second, and perhaps related to the forgoing consideration, is the nature of the expectations that people bring to their first job. Some people tend to expect their job experiences to be similar to those portrayed in the success stories so often encountered in movies, novels, and biographical sketches. They expect not only good earnings, but also the kind of continual excitement and interest that might characterize, say, the fascination of a Nobel prize–winning chemist with his researches into the mysteries of matter. In short, people probably tend to begin work with unrealistic expectations about what they will be able to derive from it, and finding that reality falls far short of their expectations, they endure the first decade of work with gradually increasing disillusionment. After some point, expectations are apparently modified and adjusted downward, and the job is seen in a more positive perspective.

We should hasten to remind the reader that even among this most dissatisfied age group, a *majority* are satisfied. Even high expectations usually seem to temper and restrain job attitudes rather than promote outright disaffection with the job.

Professional and managerial workers report the highest level of job satisfaction. Unskilled manual workers in the heavy industries, such as the automotive and steel industries, report the greatest extent of dissatisfaction. In between those two extremes are clerical and sales workers and skilled blue-collar operatives.

Blacks and other minorities are less likely to be satisfied with their work than are whites, probably because the former are overrepresented in marginal occupational categories and in unskilled blue-collar jobs. However, whereas Gallup found that in 1949 nearly half of the black workers surveyed expressed job dissatisfaction, in 1971 only about a fourth of the black workers surveyed voiced negative work attitudes.

Sex differences in job satisfaction show less consistency. Published studies up until the mid-1950s showed no clear-cut differences between males and females. Sheppard and Herrick's findings in 1972 showed females to be less satisfied than males, the difference reaching its maximum extent among workers under 30. It would appear that women, especially young women, are less likely to be satisfied with *just any* form of employment; they are, quite understandably, more sensitive about working under job conditions that are inferior to those prevailing among males with the same set of qualifications as their own. Despite some years of affirmative action programs, there is abundant evidence that equality of treatment between the sexes with respect to job opportunities has not been fully achieved.

CAUSES OF JOB SATISFACTION

One analytic approach to the sources of job satisfaction is to look at the groups that seem to have the most of it—professionals and managers—and to see what they have that other workers don't have, or don't have in as great measure.

First, the most satisfied groups typically earn higher salaries than do other occupational groups. In recent years, there may have been a tendency to underestimate the role of income in determining job attitudes. This is not to say that money is the only source, or even the most important source, of job satisfaction. Many people would probably agree that insufficient pay or perceived inequitable underpay is a more decisive determinant of dissatisfaction than sufficient or fair pay is of satisfaction. Nevertheless, as Saul Gellerman (1963) has noted, money is a "complex symbol"; it represents far more to individuals than the material goods and services it can command. Income level is inextricably associated with social status, independence, life-style, and the worthwhileness of what one is doing. Certainly *relative* pay—one's pay as compared to significant reference groups—seems to count for something in the calculus of job satisfaction.

Second, professionals and managers—we might also add proprietors—typically enjoy much more *autonomy* in their work than do other groups. They set their own hours, their own pace, and most of the time they are free from close supervision. They unilaterally make a large number of decisions about how they do their work; their time span of discretion is measured in months or years as opposed to hours for many workers.

Third, and perhaps most important, the professional derives a greater measure of *intrinsic rewards* from work. His or her work is varied and often stimulating. It offers a challenge to prove one's mettle. It allows or requires the use of the skills and knowledge one is most proud of. It affords opportunity for continual self-development, learning, and growth. Study after study shows that professionals and managers report greater satisfaction of their needs for achievement and self-actualization than do other occupational groups.

Another method of ascertaining the major causes of job satisfaction is to ask people to rank-order various aspects of work in terms of their importance. Herzberg et al. (1955) averaged the findings of 16 such studies, involving a total of over 11,000 employees. The first-ranked factor was security; the second was the "interest from intrinsic aspects of the job"; the third was opportunity for advancement; and the fourth was considerate and appreciative supervision. Wages ranked seventh.

Almost two decades later, Sheppard and Herrick found some changes in the ranking of job dimensions. "Interesting work" was ranked first; second, third, and fourth, respectively, were enough equipment, information, and authority "to get the job done." "Good pay" ranked fifth. Job security, so important in the 1940s and early 1950s, had dropped to seventh. However, there seemed to be some threads of continuity. Workers continued to place a high value on the inherent interest afforded by the job; they remained sensitive to the leadership styles of supervision, especially with regard to consideration displayed, but also with regard to structuring the work environment in a manner conducive to good work;[1] and economic benefits were still accorded substantial importance. Job security apparently matters a lot when you don't have it (the experience of many workers in the 1930s), but not when you've got it (as does more and more of the labor force).

It is important not to overlook the role of the work group in determining job satisfaction. The Hawthorne researchers in the 1920s and 1930s (Roethlisberger & Dickson, 1964) found that people working on isolated jobs were more apt to express irritation, dissatisfaction, or feelings of depression on the job. A later study based on interviews with automobile industry workers (Walker & Guest, 1952) found that isolated workers disliked their jobs; other workers mentioned pay and the people they worked with as the two best features of the job. Sea-

---

[1] An extended discussion of the effects of leadership styles on job attitudes is deferred until Chapter 17.

shore (1954) noted that cohesive industrial work groups were less likely to be adversely affected by pressure for production and to express anxiety about their jobs than were noncohesive work groups. The opportunity for frequent and pleasurable informal interaction with co-workers appears to atone for considerable shortcomings in other features of jobs, such as uncomfortable working conditions or tedious work. Interviews with those rare specimens who win enough money in lotteries or football pools to retire, yet soon return even to unskilled jobs, find that a frequently cited reason for going back to work is simply to be back with friends at the job.

The weights of the above-mentioned job attributes in contributing to job satisfaction or dissatisfaction vary considerably from one individual to another. For example, autonomy and the intrinsic interest of the work itself matter more to younger workers and highly educated employees than to their opposites; on the other hand, job security and pay take on increased importance for workers over age 40 (Herzberg et al., 1955). Some laboratory studies indicate that variety in the job means more to extraverts than to introverts. Similarly, the needs for achievement or for close social relationships on the job are parameters of variation among the working population.

Finally, individual *expectations* of what the job should offer must be reckoned with as a crucial variable in the makeup of job attitudes. Regardless of what the job offers—the level of pay, autonomy, interest, challenge, or social gratification—if the individual expects more, he or she is less likely to be satisfied. If the general level of job satisfaction in the labor force has declined in recent years, this is almost certainly *not* due to any worsening of job conditions or characteristics. Jobs today pay more, carry more collateral benefits, are performed under better physical conditions, are freer from arbitrary or capricious intervention by employers and bosses, and probably even offer more intrinsic appeal (given the dwindling percentage of jobs in unskilled categories, such as "assemblers") than did jobs a quarter of a century ago. However, it appears that expectations have risen at a faster rate than have such improvements.

THE CHANGING COMPOSITION OF THE WORK FORCE

As Table 10–3 shows, the portion of the work force in this country between ages 20 and 34 has been steadily increasing since 1965. This change reflects the recent entry into the labor pool of the large numbers of people born in the baby boom of the late 1940s and early 1950s. Furthermore, this part of the labor force will continue to grow at a faster rate than other age groups until well into the 1980s. When one couples this phenomenon with the reliable observation that historically this same age category has exhibited the lowest extent of job

Table 10–3
The changing age distribution of the labor force

	Age group			
	20–24	*25–34*	*Total, 20–34*	*35–44*
1960	10.6%	20.9%	31.5%	23.1%
1965	12.1	19.4	31.5	22.3
1970	14.3	20.6	34.9	19.5
1971	14.6	20.9	35.5	19.1
1972	14.8	21.7	36.5	18.7
1973	15.0	22.7	37.7	18.4

Source: U.S. Bureau of the Census, *Statistical Abstract of the United States,* 1974.

satisfaction, one can easily draw the inference that, for the next decade or so, the labor force *as a whole* will probably express less positive job attitudes than was the case up to about 1965.

This inference is strengthened by some additional considerations. The young adults of the present era and the years immediately ahead will probably be even harder to satisfy than were similar age groups in the past because they have been given reasons to expect more. They have come of age in an era of unprecedented affluence; they have acquired more formal education; and they have witnessed, and been influenced by, political and social changes that have severely challenged the legitimacy of authority in the American institutional framework. Conditioned to affluence, they will tend to take the material benefits of jobs for granted. Having invested more time in higher education, they want work which allows them to use their technical and analytic skills. Less awed by authority, they will demand more participation in the formulation of organizational goals, policies, and practices. All of these considerations add up to a formidable challenge to organizations drawing these people into their ranks if participant job satisfaction is indeed a criterion by which such organizations are willing to be judged.

CONSEQUENCES OF JOB SATISFACTION

Turnover

Empirical studies have pretty well established that the satisfied worker is less likely than his dissatisfied counterpart to quit the job over a given period of time. The actual strength of the relationship between satisfaction and turnover varies considerably from one organization to another and from one time period to another. Even dissatisfied employees try to hold on to their jobs when labor mobility is low or downturns in the economy make alternative work hard to find. Conversely, even individuals who feel very positively about their present jobs can be tempted by prospects of better pay, career advancement, or other opportunities existing elsewhere. As we have already seen, the level of unemployment determines much of the variance in turnover in the labor force. On the whole, however, the satisfied tend to stay and the dissatisfied to leave. Given the fact that an ever larger fraction of the work force is accounted for by young adults—who not only experience the lowest rate of job satisfaction but also typically enjoy the greatest mobility—many organizations are likely to find turnover accelerating in the years ahead unless they match job realities with the job expectations of this group.

Absenteeism

The decision not to show up for work on a given day represents a miniature, tentative, and temporary decision to quit. Thus, since turnover is inversely related to level of job satisfaction, so is absenteeism. However, just as the relationship between quit rate and job attitudes varies as a function of other complicating variables, so too the prediction of absence rate from job satisfaction must also take other factors into account. The relationship may be quite negligible when total absences for all reasons are computed. However, total absence figures are heavily weighted by long illnesses, which tend to produce large numbers of consecutive days absent. Job attitudes predict much better the *frequency* of absence—especially unexcused absence due to minor ailments—than they predict total days absent. Furthermore, the relationship between job satisfaction and absenteeism varies by sex and occupational group. Metzner and Mann (1953) found the relationship to be essentially nil for white-collar women; for men, the relationship was stronger for lower job classifications or ranks.

In some industries turnover and absenteeism account for a substantial share of total labor costs. The cost of recruiting and training new workers depends on a number of factors, including the conditions of the labor market and the length of time required to master job operations, but the figure would be in the hundreds of dollars even for most blue-collar jobs; it would be considerably higher for jobs using complex, highly specialized technology. In 1970, General Motors found that on Mondays or Fridays as much as 10 percent of production workers would be missing from work with no explanation; to avoid resultant unmanageable disruptions in the assembly line process, two extra workers would have to be retained for every ten full-time jobs (Gooding, 1972). To the extent that increased job satisfaction would reduce such costs, job attitudes translate into dollars and cents.

Productivity?

Does increased job satisfaction lead to higher productivity? Does job dissatisfaction result in restriction of output? These haunting questions have nagged at managers and industrial psychologists alike for nearly half a century.

Popular opinion apparently views job attitudes as having a direct effect on performance. As recently as 1971, Gannon and Noon found in a survey of personnel officers that 61 percent believed happier workers to be more productive workers. Somehow it seems natural that more positive feelings about work would lead to greater output and higher quality. Unfortunately, four decades of research into this issue give little basis for drawing such a conclusion.

An exhaustive review of studies concerning the relationship between job satisfaction and job performance is beyond the scope of this chapter; the interested reader may consult a number of excellent reviews elsewhere (Herzberg et al., 1955; Brayfield & Crockett, 1955; Vroom, 1964). For illustrative purposes, however, let us cite the experiences of researchers at the Survey Research Center of the University of Michigan. In 1950, they began a large-scale investigation into the types of supervision that result in individual satisfaction and productivity. Their guiding assumption was that morale acted as an *intervening variable* between supervision and performance. That is, certain supervisory styles would affect job attitudes, and these, in turn, would affect performance. In their first study, which dealt with female clerical workers in an insurance company, the researchers succeeded in identifying certain supervisory styles which were reliably associated with higher than average productivity (although they could not determine from their data whether supervisory style caused subordinate performance, or vice versa). To their surprise, however, the productive groups showed no greater job satisfaction than did the less productive groups. Further studies of 300 railroad laborers and 6,000 workers at a tractor factory yielded the same findings. In none of these studies did satisfaction significantly predict performance; in fact, no single subcomponent of satisfaction—satisfaction with the job itself, with the company, with supervision, or with pay and promotion opportunities—accounted for any reliable share of the variance in productivity (Kahn, 1960).

Vroom's (1964) review of 20 studies disclosed only the barest of evidence supporting a direct link between job attitudes and performance. While the relationship was almost always positive, the median correlation between satisfaction and productivity was .14—meaning that job satisfaction, on the average, accounts for about 2 percent of the differences among the performance levels of individuals. Thus, while job attitudes bear a discriminable relationship with such behavior as turnover and absenteeism, the evidence suggests that a similarly strong relationship with performance is lacking.

How do we explain the lack of this relationship? Deficiencies in measures of performance might constitute one explanation. Many jobs do not lend themselves to objective, concrete performance measures, and subjective ratings by superiors or peers have to serve as surrogate measures. Such rating scales often exhibit unreliability and low levels of agreement among different raters. In fact, Vroom (1964) found that, for those studies using objective performance criteria, a slightly higher relationship between performance and satisfaction emerged. Nevertheless, the actual correlation was still very low.

A second explanation could be that, in many instances, individual performance level simply cannot vary to any great extent. When the worker is paced by an assembly line or other technological constraints, he or she can hardly work faster or harder than the total flow of work. Similarly, a secretary can do no more work than is given to him or her, and in jobs which require coordination among several people, the fastest worker is apt to be limited by the pace of the slowest. In short, many work situations are pegged to a certain minimally acceptable performance level, with the consequence that administrators place no premium upon, or even discourage, a disruptingly higher level of performance by a few individuals.

More generally, however, the cumulative impact of empirical studies has forced organizational theorists and researchers to revise their thinking about the nature of the linkage between satisfaction and performance. That *some* linkage does exist is argued by the consistently positive, albeit very low, correlations between the two variables. The consensus of evidence and opinion on just how the two are connected is represented by Lawler and Porter's (1967) theoretical scheme (see Figure 10–3). In their model, satisfaction comes from rewards. Rewards, in turn, break down into two types: *extrinsic rewards*, such as salary increases and other reinforcements controlled by the organization; and *intrinsic rewards*, the gratifications that inhere in having done a job well or in having used one's abilities to solve a problem or meet some challenge. Rewards may or may not flow from performance in any predictable fashion, but intrinsic rewards are likely to be more closely connected to performance than are extrinsic rewards. The latter may accrue to employees in an across-the-board fashion; even if organization officials attempt to reward merit, they may find it difficult to measure performance in a reliable manner; and for many blue-collar jobs (as well as an increasing percentage of white-collar jobs), extrinsic benefits are determined by the union or by the government, leaving little flexibility in the reward system for recognizing the star performers. Finally, such determinants of job satisfaction as peer-group relations may be totally irrelevant to production.

Thus, we can see why there are many cases in which we ought not to expect much correlation between job satisfaction and performance. If a job holds little potential for intrinsic rewards, and if extrinsic

Figure 10–3
Conceptions of the satisfaction-performance link

A. A popular but discredited view

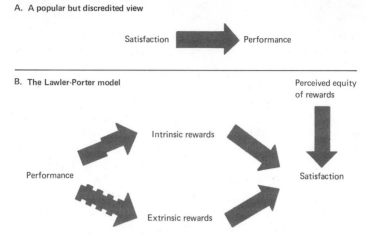

B. The Lawler-Porter model

Source: Adapted from E. E. Lawler III and L. W. Porter, "The Effect of Performance on Job Satisfaction," *Industrial Relations,* 1967, *7,* 20–28.

rewards bear little relationship to individual performance level, the resultant connection between performance and satisfaction is weak and tenuous. In any case, whatever connection does exist is due not to the causal effect of satisfaction on performance but rather to the fidelity with which rewards follow performance.

Should an organization strive for a high positive relationship between satisfaction and performance? On the one hand, the answer is yes, since satisfied people tend to stay. If the performance-satisfaction connection is strong, the ones who stay will be the more productive employees, and turnover will be more likely to occur among the less productive people. How, then, can organization officials make the connection stronger? The Lawler-Porter model indicates two methods: (1) correct the reward system so that top performers receive proportionately higher extrinsic rewards; and/or (2) modify the task so that it becomes capable of yielding intrinsic rewards for performance. The latter method amounts to a program of job enrichment, which will receive further discussion in the following chapter.

On the other hand, we must remember that not all organizations have "performance problems." Some companies would be satisfied with routine, minimally acceptable individual performance if they could just count on having a sufficient number of people show up for work at the start of each shift. For such companies, a frontal assault on job attitude problems would clearly make more sense than would efforts to manipulate satisfactions through an indirect and discriminative strategy centered on the reward system.

The important point is that we have learned now that working on the satisfaction end of the seesaw exerts little leverage on productivity. Administrators have to decide whether their primary problem is a performance deficit or excessive labor costs due to absenteeism and turnover. The two problems call for totally different managerial responses.

SUMMARY

Job satisfaction of participants is one criterion by which we evaluate organizations. The importance attached to job satisfaction rests on humanistic values, the effects of job satisfaction on mental and physical health, establishing and maintaining the legitimacy of an organization's existence and purpose, and lubricating social interaction within organizations. Job satisfaction, whether in toto or with specific aspects of the organization, is measured by specially constructed, standardized attitude scales. Surveys have repeatedly shown that between 80 and 90 percent of the labor force express satisfaction with their jobs. Although this may reflect in part a passive resignation to less than ideal job environments, there is little evidence to suggest (as some critics argue) that any sizable proportion of the labor force is "alienated." Job satisfaction tends to be highest among workers over age 35 and among professional and managerial workers. Income, autonomy, intrinsic psychological rewards from work, and social rewards from group membership appear to be the most important determinants of job attitudes in the contemporary work force. Initial expectations of the satisfactions that will be derived from the job are also important; younger employees with college degrees are most likely to have job expectations that will not be realized in job experiences. Employees with higher satisfaction exhibit lower levels of turnover and absenteeism, but not necessarily higher productivity. The contingency of rewards—both intrinsic and extrinsic—on performance determines whether job attitudes and productivity are closely related.

CONCEPTS TO REMEMBER

job alienation thesis   Lawler-Porter model of satis-
job expectations   faction and performance

QUESTIONS FOR DISCUSSION

1. What could be done by employers to prevent the "trough" in job satisfaction that seems to characterize younger workers? What could be done by schools and colleges?
2. Around 1985, the nation's work force as a whole will become in-

creasingly older. How will this affect job attitudes in the labor force?

3. Why does the layperson intuitively believe that "satisfaction causes productivity"? What are the assumptions and the logic underlying this belief?

4. If member job satisfaction is a criterion for evaluating organizations, should the satisfaction of subordinates also be a criterion for evaluating supervisors and managers? Defend your position.

5. Is it fair to stockholders for profit-seeking organizations to take steps to increase member job satisfaction *at the expense* of performance or profitability? Why or why not?

6. Historical statistics and economic projections indicate an accelerating trend toward an increase in the proportion of the work force in the *service sector* and a decreasing proportion in manufacturing. How is this trend likely to affect job attitudes in the work force?

REFERENCES

Brayfield, A. H., & Crockett, W. H. Employee attitudes and employee performance. *Psychological Bulletin*, 1955, *52*, 396–424.

Bullock, R. P. *Social factors related to job satisfaction*. Columbus: Bureau of Business Research, Ohio State University, 1952.

Gallup, G. H. The Gallup poll. New York: Random House, 1972.

Gannon, M. J., & Noon, J. P. Management's critical deficiency. *Business Horizons*, 1971, *14*, 49–56.

Gellerman, S. W. *Motivation and productivity*. New York: American Management Association, 1963.

Gooding, J. *The job revolution*. New York: Walker, 1972.

Herzberg, F., Mausner, B., Peterson, R., & Capwell, D. *Job attitudes: Review of research and opinion* (Pittsburgh: Psychological Service of Pittsburgh, 1955).

Kahn, R. L. Productivity and job satisfaction. *Personnel Psychology*, 1960, *13*, 275–287.

Lawler, E. E., III, & Porter, L. W. The effect of performance on job satisfaction. *Industrial Relations*, 1967, *7*, 20–28.

Metzner, H., & Mann, F. Employee attitudes and absences. *Personnel Psychology*, 1953, *6*, 467–485.

Palmore, E. Predicting longevity: A follow-up controlling for age. *Gerontology*, Winter 1969.

Roethlisberger, F. J., & Dickson, W. J. *Management and the worker.* (New York: Wiley Science Editions, 1964).

Seashore, S. *Group cohesiveness in the industrial work group*. Ann Arbor: University of Michigan, Institute for Social Research, Survey Research Center, 1954.

Sheppard, H. L., & Herrick, N. Q. *Where have all the robots gone?* New York: Free Press, 1972.

Statistical abstract of the United States. Washington, D.C.: U.S. Bureau of the Census, 1963, 84th ed.; 1970, 91st ed.; 1974, 95th ed.

Vroom, V. H. *Work and motivation.* New York: Wiley, 1964.

Walker, C. R., & Guest, R. H. *The man on the assembly line.* Cambridge, Mass.: Harvard University Press, 1952.

Work in America. Report of a Special Task Force to the Secretary of Health, Education, and Welfare. Cambridge, Mass.: MIT Press, 1973.

11

Worker motivation programs I

Increasing productivity and the quality of work life with positive reinforcement

Why has there been an increased demand for programs to improve the quality of work life?

What programs are currently being undertaken to improve the quality of work life?

How can the principles of positive reinforcement be applied to organization environments?

What evidence is there that positive reinforcement can be effectively and systematically applied to organizations?

What role does compensation play in applying reinforcement principles?

Chapters 11 and 12 present information about how theories of organizational behavior are applied in organizational settings in order to increase job satisfaction and productivity. Chapter 11 presents information about applied reinforcement programs. Chapter 12 discusses the application of task design programs, organizational development programs, and four-day workweek programs of motivation, and then concludes the material presented in both chapters.

INTRODUCTION

In the past few years, management, unions, and government agencies have joined workers in demanding that changes be made in the work environment in order to improve the quality of work life and to create an atmosphere which would lead to increased productivity. Levitan and Johnston (1973a) say that workers are able to demand more today because of a rise in income which has loosened the economic bonds of the workplace. Workers are now able to trade marginal boosts in income for more leisure. The work force today is better educated than ever before. The ratio of illiterates has declined from 1 in 5 in 1870 to 1 in 100 today, and the number of college degrees granted yearly has risen from 10,000 to 1,000,000. By 1973 the average manual worker had a 12th-grade education, and this high level of formal education is being supplemented by newspapers, radio, and television, which keep workers informed about the changes that are taking place around them.

In 1972, 21 percent of the work force was under 24 years of age. This age group was concentrated in the lowest-paid and lowest-skilled jobs even though the group was characterized by the highest level of education (Levitan & Johnston, 1973a). Because of changes in the educational and cultural backgrounds of the younger members of the work force, experts warn that unless something is done to improve the quality of work, a crisis of discontent may ensue. The evidence of discontent is abundant—high rates of absenteeism, high turnover rates, strikes, poor worker attitudes, and industrial sabotage (see, for example, Levitan & Johnston, 1973b, 1973c).

In order to examine the current status of worker discontent, the U.S. Secretary of Health, Education, and Welfare commissioned the Survey Research Center at the University of Michigan to examine the attitudes of workers toward their jobs and toward the organizations

Note: Some of the material presented in Chapters 11 and 12 was adapted from W. C. Hamner, "Applied Worker Motivation Programs," in W. C. Hamner and F. L. Schmidt (Eds.), *Contemporary Problems of Personnel* (Chicago: St. Clair Press, 1974). By permission of the publisher.

for which they worked. The results indicated that a significant number of American workers are dissatisfied with the quality of their working lives.[1] Dull, repetitive, seemingly meaningless tasks, offering little challenge or autonomy, are causing discontent among workers at all occupational levels. This discontent has resulted in a restricting of output, poor-quality work, and refusal of overtime work. It has contributed to high absenteeism and high turnover rates and to militant demands for higher wages, more fringe benefits, and greater participation in decision making (*Work in America*, 1973).

Long before the Survey Research Center's report was completed, management began to examine ways to improve the work environment in order to reverse the trends of higher absenteeism and higher turnover caused by worker discontent. Management's philosophy seems to be shifting away from the belief that an increase in the rights and benefits of workers leads to a decrease in the rights and benefits of management, and shifting toward the belief that investment in a program which will benefit the worker will also benefit management. Stephen H. Fuller, vice president of personnel and organizational development at General Motors has said, "We do not view this [worker motivation program] as an either/or situation. Our challenge is *not* people versus profit, it is people *and* profit" (Fuller, 1973). Two years earlier, John F. Donnelly, president of Donnelly Mirrors, Inc., had expressed the same point of view: "We continued to invest heavily in consulting services and training in the behavioral sciences because these investments seemed to pay off more consistently than investments in equipment. In fact, we began to see that the more effectively we used behavioral science to engage our people, the more wisely we made our capital investments" (Donnelly, 1971, p. 10).

In their attempts to improve the quality of the working experience, workers often find the union as much of an obstacle as management. When the auto workers at General Motors' Vega plant in Lordstown, Ohio, struck for an improvement in the quality of their work life, the international leaders of the United Automobile Workers insisted on bargaining for more pay and shorter working hours (Drucker, 1973). However, there are many indications that unions are becoming interested in "people programs" which will improve the quality of the work environment and increase productivity. The new union attitude favoring increased productivity resulted primarily from the pressure of the energy crisis and foreign competition, rather than from demands of workers, management, or governmental agencies. Unions, like management, appear to accept the premise that increased productivity is compatible with improvement in the quality of the worker's organi-

---

[1] As we explained in Chapter 10, many researchers dispute these findings, claiming that dissatisfaction may not be decreasing once the rate of unemployment is taken into consideration.

zational involvement and is in the best interest of unions, workers, and management. I. W. Abel, former president of the United Steel Workers of America, summarized the changing attitude of unions toward productivity and the quality of work life when he stated:

> I call upon every American to enlist in the crucial battle to improve our lagging productivity. Nothing less is at stake than our jobs, the price we pay, the very quality of our lives. . . . Things have been so good for so long that we've become wasteful and inefficient. So wasteful that, incredibly enough, many firms nowadays actually expect to scrap 20% of what they produce. . . . How can we improve? In these ways:
>
> *By stepping up the efficiency of each worker.* Does this mean work speedings, job eliminations? Hardly. It does mean cutting down on excessive absenteeism, tardiness, turnover, and overtime. It does mean improving the morale of workers, more effective work incentive—and really listening to the man at the work bench. . . .
>
> *By improving our technology and really using the technology we already possess.* . . . the steel industry and the United Steel Workers of America have established joint advisory committees on productivity at each plant. This co-operative venture is a recognition that workers and employers share a common problem. (Abel, 1973)

In response to pressure from these various groups to make work more challenging and rewarding, many organizations have set up formal motivation programs. Although there are many titles for these programs, most of the innovative programs currently being tried can be classified into one of three categories. The *positive reinforcement* program works on the premise that behavior is determined by its consequences. The *task structure* or job enrichment program assumes that a worker will be motivated to increase his level of performance by a job which he finds intrinsically rewarding and challenging. The *climate* or organizational development program is based on the theory that the organizational climate and the attitudes of fellow employees can enhance or be detrimental to employee performance.

Each of these programs works on the premise that some form of organizational change can lead to an improvement in employee performance. A climate approach is designed to change the task structure and the reinforcing consequences as well as the attitudes of people; a positive reinforcement approach operates on the feedback system; and a task structure approach changes the task involvement of the worker. Although the three programs reviewed in Chapters 11 and 12 are not independent approaches, they work on different components of the job and involve different levels of intervention by the organization.

In Figures 11–1 and 11–2 we show the interrelationships among these three components of the job. From Figure 11–1 we see that an improvement of the *work climate* can result from a change in leader-

Figure 11–1
Examples of the three components of job performance and satisfaction

Examples	*Work environment or climate* →→→	*Task assignment* →→→	*Contingent consequences*
A	Positive leadership style	Job responsibility	Feedback—both positive and negative
B	Supportive climate	Enriched task	Money
C	Clear goals	Low role conflict	Promotions
D	Active career development	Low role ambiguity	New assignments
E	Team building	Training and development	More control and influence
F	Safety program	Tools and equipment	Performance appraisal
	↑	↑	↑
	"Do I like the organization where I work?"	"Do I enjoy my task assignment?"	"Am I properly rewarded and fairly treated"

ship style (see Chapter 17), a change in the support given the work force, and clearer specification of goals. The *task assignment* can be made more positive by clearly specifying the responsibilities of the task, by making the task more challenging, and by reducing the amount of conflict and ambiguity associated with the task. The *consequences* of the job can be improved by making such rewards as money, praise, and promotions contingent on job performance (see Chapter 3).

We see in Figure 11–2 that if the answers to all three questions posed in Figure 11–1 are positive, then effort and satisfaction are highest. If one answer is negative, then effort and satisfaction are lower, and if two or three answers are negative, then effort and satisfaction are lower still. Given the fact that the perception of these three components of the job affects work effort and work satisfaction, managers can determine which, if any, applied motivation program would be most likely to increase these outcome variables. For example, if the work climate were viewed negatively, then it might be best to implement an organizational development program; if the task assignment were viewed negatively, then a job enrichment program might be implemented; and if the consequences of the task were viewed negatively, then a positive reinforcement program might be used. Obviously, using a positive reinforcement program where only the task is viewed negatively (row 3 in Figure 11–2) would have no positive effect and might even prove detrimental to improving performance or satis-

Figure 11–2
The effect of workers' perceptions of the climate, task, and consequences on work effort and job satisfaction

	Valences			Predicted results	
	Work environment or climate	Task assignment	Reward consequences	Effort	Satisfaction
1	+	+	+	Highest	Highest
2	+	+	−	Moderate	Low for reward
3	+	−	+	Moderate	Low for task
4	−	+	+	Moderate	Low for climate
5	+	−	−	Low	Low for task and reward
6	−	+	−	Low	Low for climate and reward
7	−	−	+	Low	Low for climate and task
8	−	−	−	Lowest	Lowest
	↑	↑	↑	↑	↑
	Is the work environment viewed as positive or negative by the employees?	Is the task assignment viewed as positive or negative by the employees?	Are the rewards administered by management viewed as contingent?	What will be the effect on job effort or motivation?	What will be the effect on overall satisfaction?

faction. The same would be true for any applied program used under the wrong circumstances.

Each of these three kinds of worker motivation programs is a "proactive" program in the sense that it is designed not only to cure current "industrial ills" but also to anticipate and prevent future problems with worker discontent. A fourth approach currently being used by some organizations is a program designed to give workers more time away from the workplace and more variety in scheduling their hours of work. The *flexitime* and *four-day workweek* programs are reactive approaches to the problem of worker alienation. They are designed to allow the workers more time away from a negative work atmosphere rather than to change the work environment. However, flexitime is proactive in that it allows workers to control *when* they offer their services to the organization.

These four approaches will be examined in Chapters 11 and 12 in relation to their theoretical assumptions and their effectiveness in organizational settings. Since each program has its own group of followers, it is only natural that criticisms of each program have been generated. These criticisms will be presented, along with recommendations for the future use of motivation programs.

POSITIVE REINFORCEMENT PROGRAMS

Theoretical background

As mentioned in Chapter 3, the principles of positive reinforcement are based on the premise that people perform in the way that they find most rewarding to them, a premise which implies that management can improve the worker's performance by providing the proper rewards. The theoretical underpinnings of positive reinforcement programs are the learning principles described by Thorndike (1911) and Skinner (1953).[2] As noted in Chapters 3 and 4, Thorndike's Law of Effect simply states that behavior which appears to lead to a positive consequence tends to be repeated, whereas behavior which appears to lead to a neutral or a negative consequence tends not to be repeated. Skinner and his followers contend that when workers enter the workplace they have developed a sense of right versus wrong and have been thoroughly conditioned by their parents and by society. Therefore, they argue that the only tool needed for worker motivation is the presence or absence of positive reinforcement. In other words, managers do not, as a general rule, need to use avoidance learning in order to control behavior. Drucker (1973) says, "B. F. Skinner's rigorous research on learning theory leaves little room to doubt that rewards, or positive reinforcements, are the efficient way to learn" (p. 92). Skinner best summarizes the simplicity of a positive reinforcement program when he says: "Supervision by positive reinforcement changes the whole atmosphere of the workspace and produces better results. A constantly critical position on the part of the supervisor encourages bad morale, absenteeism and job changing. . . . With positive reinforcement you get at least the same amount of work, and the worker is more likely to show up every day and less likely to change jobs. In the long run, both the company and the worker are better off" (Skinner, 1973, p. 35). Sorcher and Goldstein (1972) agree with Skinner that one reason organizations fail to motivate workers is that workers are "turned off" rather than "turned on" by the reinforcement practices of organizations. Sorcher and Goldstein state that a good

---

[2] For a detailed explanation, see Chapter 3.

illustration of such maladaptive behavior is that of the manager who attempts to motivate an employee to improve his poor performance by threatening the employee to such an extent that the employee becomes less effective and more hostile toward the manager.

A positive reinforcement philosophy of management differs from traditional motivational theories (see Chapter 7), in two basic ways. First, as noted above, a positive reinforcement program calls for maximum use of positive reinforcement and minimum use of punishment. Punishment may tend to leave the individual feeling controlled and coerced and may lead to immaturity in the individual especially if it is used incorrectly (see Chapter 4). Second, a positive reinforcement program avoids psychological probing into the worker's attitudes as a possible cause of behavior. Instead, it focuses on the reward contingencies of the work situation which cause a worker to act the way he or she does.

A positive reinforcement program, therefore, is results oriented rather than process oriented. Geary A. Rummler, president of Praxis Corporation, a management consultant firm, claims that motivational theories which stress workers' psychological needs, such as the theories of Herzberg and Maslow, are impractical. "They can't be made operative. While they help to classify the problem, a positive reinforcement program leads to solutions" ("Power of Praise," 1973, p. 35). Sorcher and Goldstein (1972) agree, stating that a positive reinforcement procedure is quite different from the traditional approach to behavior change in that it does not rely on changing attitudes in the hope that behavior will fall in line with those changes. "Instead, this procedure is based on some of the fundamentals of social learning, i.e., imitation [behavioral rehearsal] and reinforcement, and is aimed directly at behavior change without relying on the diversionary tactics of attitude change" (p. 41).

Stages in program development

Positive reinforcement programs currently used in industry generally involve at least four steps. The *first step*, according to E. J. Feeney, a former vice president of Emery Air Freight Corporation, is to define the *behavioral* aspects of performance and do a performance audit.[3] This step may be most difficult, since some companies do not have a formal performance evaluation program, especially for nonmanagerial

---

[3] A performance audit is a procedure in which management determines the behavioral and job-related aspects of a department or a work unit, such as a 10 percent rate of absenteeism, a 15 percent scrap rate, a 90 percent of standard production rate. This procedure should be distinguished from a performance evaluation, in which a manager rates an individual on both behavioral and nonbehavioral aspects of his or her job over a specified period of time.

employees, and those which do have such a program often rate the employee on nonbehavioral or non-job-related measures (for example, · friendliness and overall attitude). But once the behavioral aspects of the job are defined, and managers see how poorly some of these are being performed, it becomes simpler to convince managers that improvement is needed and to persuade them to cooperate with a reinforcement program. Feeney reports, "Most managers genuinely think that operations in their bailiwick are doing well; a performance audit that proves they're not comes as a real and unpleasant surprise" ("Emery Air Freight," 1973, p. 42).

The performance audit not only helps the manager accept the program, but also helps the employees identify themselves as meaningful contributors to the objectives of the organization. Frost (1973) says:

> If the employees are helped to identify "what day it is"—the competitive bid made for the job, the cost of the materials, the cost of the machine, its coolants, and maintenance, the cost of set-up and down time . . . the employees can perceive the relevance of their contribution and the rationale of management's administration. Everyone in the organization becomes important and an interdependent part. Everyone in the organization comes to play a small part or a big part, but an essential part. Everyone becomes a resource that is available and called upon to perform effectively to achieve the organization's objectives. The personal and professional goals for dignity, recognition and significance become compatible with the organization's need to be fiscally sound and competitive. (p. 4)

Thus, defined levels of performance which are specifically determined and clearly stated help both the manager and the employee establish a baseline against which to measure their future performance. Rummler ("Power of Praise," 1973) says that a person should get all the available data about his or her performance, not selective information. Ideally, the data should come from the system, for example, a computer, so that they appear objective, neutral, and unemotional. In this manner, both the employee and the manager are better able to accept the program as one that will be of mutual benefit.

The *second step* in developing a working positive reinforcement program is to develop and set specific and reasonable goals for each worker. Sorcher and Goldstein (1972) suggest that the failure to specify concrete, behavioral goals is a major reason why many programs do not work. They state, "Goals must be defined in measurable terms— they should be expressed in behavioral terms such as employee turnover or schedules met rather than only in terms of 'better identification with the company' or 'increased job satisfaction' " (p. 36). The goals set, therefore, should be in the same terms as those which the performance audit defines as being specifically related to the task at hand. The goals should be reasonable and set somewhere between "where you are" (as defined in the performance audit) and some ideal point.

Although work goals can be set by the manager, it is important that they be accepted by the employees. An even better approach would be to allow the employees to work with management in the setting of the goals. By using a participative management technique to enlist the ideas of those performing the job, you gain not only the acceptance of goals, but also ways and means of obtaining new goals.

Luthans and White (1971) see the popular management system Management by Objectives (MBO)[4] as providing an excellent means for meeting the first two stages of a positive reinforcement program. They state, "Manpower managers can utilize behavior modification techniques[5] to generate direction and self-control among all levels of personnel. . . . Management by objectives provides an opportunity for all personnel to contribute to job goals and encourages the setting of checkpoints to measure progress" (p. 45). MBO goal setting alone, however, is ineffective without feedback and positive reinforcement.

The *third step* in a positive reinforcement program is to allow the employee to keep a record of his or her own work. This process of self-feedback maintains a continuous schedule of reinforcement (see Chapter 3) for the worker and allows the worker to gain intrinsic reinforcement from the task itself. Where employees can total their own results, they can see whether or not they are meeting their goals and whether or not they are improving upon their previous level of performance (as measured in the performance audit stage). In other words, the worker has two ways of being successful—either by beating his previous record or by beating both his previous record and his established goal. E. D. Grady, division traffic manager for Michigan Bell, says that the manager should set up the work environment so that people have a chance to succeed. One way to do this, he says, is to "shorten the success interval." Grady states, "If you're looking for success, keep shortening the interval of measurement so you can get a greater chance of success which you can latch on to for positive reinforcements" ("Power of Praise," 1973, p. 34). For example, rather than set goals in monthly or quarterly terms, set them in weekly or daily terms. This doesn't reduce the level of the goal, but it may reduce the perceived difficulty of the goal.

The *fourth step* is the most important step in a positive reinforcement program. It is the step that separates such a program from all other motivation methods. The supervisor looks at the self-feedback report of the employee and/or other indications of performance (for

---

[4] See S. J. Carroll and H. L. Tosi, *Management by Objectives: Application and Research* (New York: Macmillan, 1973).

[5] Reinforcement techniques. See A. Bandura, *Principles of Behavior Modification* (New York: Holt, Rinehart and Winston, 1969).

example, sales records) and then praises the positive aspects of the employee's performance (as determined by the performance audit and the goals set). This extrinsic reinforcement should strengthen the desired performance, while the withholding of praise for performance which falls below the goals set should give the employee incentive to improve such performance. Since the worker already knows his or her deficiencies, there is no reason for the supervisor to criticize the worker. In other words, negative feedback is self-induced, whereas positive feedback comes from both internal and external sources.

As noted previously, this approach to feedback follows the teachings of B. F. Skinner, who believes that positive reinforcement leads to a greater feeling of self-control and that avoiding negative reinforcement keeps the individual from feeling controlled or coerced. Skinner says, "You can get the same effect if the supervisor simply discovers things being done right and says something like 'good, I see you're doing it the way that works best' " ("Conversation with B. F. Skinner," 1973). Sorcher and Goldstein (1972) believe that punishment fails because of the higher educational level and social status of employees. Drucker (1973) says, "The stick fails because fear is altogether incompatible with the reliable production of knowledge. It produces efforts and anxieties, but it generally inhibits learning" (p. 92). Rummler says that when a manager has to go into the negative aspect of a worker's performance, he should do it in a positive manner: "What can I do to help?" If a manager accuses the employee, the latter will have a dozen excuses.

Although the feedback initially used in step four of the positive reinforcement program is praise, it is important to note that other forms of reinforcements can have the same effect. M. W. Warren, director of organization and management development at the Questor Corporation, says that the five "reinforcers" Questor has found to be most effective are (1) money, but only when it is a consequence of specific performance and when its relation to that performance is known; (2) praise or recognition; (3) freedom to choose one's own activity; (4) opportunity to see oneself become better, more important, or more useful; and (5) power to influence both co-workers and management. Warren (1972) states, "By building these reinforcers into programs at various facilities, Questor is getting results" (p. 29). The need for using more than praise is also discussed by Skinner.

> It does not cost the company anything to use praise rather than blame, but if the company then makes a great deal more money that way, the worker may seem to be getting gypped. However, the welfare of the worker depends on the welfare of the company, and if the company is smart enough to distribute some of the fruits of positive reinforcement in the form of higher wages and better fringe benefits, everybody gains from the supervisor's use of positive reinforcements. (Skinner, 1973, p. 35)

RESULTS OF POSITIVE REINFORCEMENT PROGRAMS[6]

Early results of positive reinforcement programs in organizations, 1969–1973

Companies that claimed to be implementing and using positive reinforcement programs such as the one described above included Emery Air Freight, Michigan Bell Telephone, Questor Corporation, Cole National Company in Cleveland, Ford Motor Company, American Can, Upjohn, United Air Lines, Warner-Lambert, Addressograph-Multigraph, Allis-Chalmers, Bethlehem Steel, Chase Manhattan Bank, IBM, IT&T, Procter and Gamble, PPG Industries, Standard Oil of Ohio, Westinghouse, and Wheeling-Pittsburgh Steel Corporation (see *Business Week,* December 18, 1971 and December 2, 1972). Because such programs are relatively new in industrial settings (most have begun since 1968), few statements of their relative effectiveness have been reported. In the Winter 1973 issue of *Organizational Dynamics,* it was stated, "There's little objective evidence available, and what evidence there is abounds in caveats—the technique will work under the proper circumstances, the parameters of which are usually not easily apparent" (p. 49).

In the area of employee training, Northern Systems Company, General Electric Company, and Emery Air Freight claim that positive reinforcement has improved the speed and efficiency of their training program. In its programmed learning program, the Northern Systems Company structures the feedback system in such a way that the trainee receives positive feedback only when he demonstrates correct performance at the tool station. The absence of feedback is experienced by the trainee when he fails to perform correctly. Therefore, through positive reinforcements, he quickly perceives that correct behaviors enable him to satisfy his needs, and that incorrect behaviors do not. Emery has designed a similar program for sales trainees. *Business Week* reported the success of the program by saying:

> It is a carefully engineered, step-by-step program, with frequent feedback questions and answers to let the salesman know how he is doing. The course contrasts with movies and lectures in which, Feeney says, the salesman is unable to gauge what he has learned. The aim is to get the customer on each sales call to take some kind of action indicating that he will use Emery services. Significantly, in 1968, the first full year after the new course was launched, sales jumped from $62.4 million to $79.8 million, a gain of 27.8 percent compared with an 11.3 percent rise the year before.

---

[6] Material in this section was adapted from W. C. Hamner and E. P. Hamner, "Behavior Modification and the Bottom Line," *Organizational Dynamics,* Spring 1976, pp. 11–15.

Since 1969, Emery has instituted a positive reinforcement program for all of its employees. It credits the program with direct savings to the company of over $3 million in the first three years and indirectly with pushing 1973 sales over the $160 million mark. While Emery Air Freight is the biggest success story for a positive reinforcement program to date, other companies also claim improvements as a result of initiating similar programs. At Michigan Bell's Detroit office, 2,000 employees participated in a positive reinforcement program in 1973. Michigan Bell credits the program with reducing absenteeism from 11 percent to 6.5 percent in one group, from 7.5 percent to 4.5 percent in another group, and from 3.3 percent to 2.6 percent for all employees. In addition, the program has resulted in the correct completion of reports on time 90 percent of the time as compared with 20 percent of the time before the program's implementation. The Wheeling-Pittsburgh Steel Corporation credits its feedback program with saving $200,000 a month in scrap costs.

In an attempt to reduce the number of employees who constantly violated plant rules, General Motors implemented a plan in one plant that gave employees opportunities to improve or clear their records by going through varying periods of time without committing further shop violations. They credit this positive reinforcement plan with reducing the number of punitive actions for shop-rule infractions by two thirds from 1969 to 1972 and the number of production-standard grievances by 70 percent during the same period.

Although there was a great deal of interest in applying behavior modification in industrial settings after the successes of Emery Air Freight and other companies which followed suit were made known in 1971, the critics of this approach to worker motivation predicted that it would be short-lived. Any success would owe more to a "Hawthorne effect" (the positive consequences of paying special attention to employees) than to any real long-term increase in productivity and/or worker satisfaction. The critics pointed out—quite legitimately, we might add—that most of the claims were testimonial in nature and that the period between 1969 and 1973 was too short to accumulate enough data to determine the true successes of positive reinforcement in improving morale and productivity. With this in mind, Hamner and Hamner (1976) surveyed ten organizations, all of which used a behavior modification approach, to see whether the "fad" created by Emery Air Freight had died or had persisted and extended its gains.

Specifically, the researchers were interested in knowing: (1) how many employees were covered; (2) the kinds of employees covered; (3) the specific goals (stages 1 and 2); (4) the frequency of self-feedback (stage 3); (5) the kinds of reinforcers being used (stage 4); and (6) the results of the program. A summary of the companies surveyed and the information gained is shown in Figure 11–3.

Current results of positive reinforcement programs in organizations

The ten organizations surveyed included Emery Air Freight, Michigan Bell—Operator Services, Michigan Bell—Maintenance Services, Connecticut General Life Insurance Company, General Electric, Standard Oil of Ohio, Weyerhaeuser, the city of Detroit, B. F. Goodrich Chemical Company, and ACDC Electronics. In the interviews with each of the managers, the researchers tried to determine both the successes and the failures they attributed to the use of behavior modification or positive reinforcement techniques. They were also interested in whether the managers saw positive reinforcement as a fad or as a legitimate management technique for improving the productivity and quality of work life among employees.

Emery Air Freight.   Figure 11–3 shows that Emery Air Freight was still using positive reinforcement as a motivational tool in 1976. John C. Emery commented: "Positive reinforcement, always linked to feedback systems, plays a central role in performance improvement at Emery Air Freight. *All* managers and supervisors are being trained via self-instructional, programmed instruction texts—one on reinforcement and one on feedback. No formal off-the-job training is needed. Once he has studied the texts, the supervisor is encouraged immediately to apply the learning to the performance area for which he is responsible."

Paul F. Hammond, Emery's manager of systems performance, said that quantifiable success had been attained in a considerable number of company areas over the last six or seven years (1976). Apart from Emery's well-publicized container savings success (which had achieved $600,000 in gross savings in 1970 and over $2,000,000 in 1975), several other success stories were noted by Emery and Hammond.

1. Standards for customer service on the telephone had been set up, and service was running 60 to 70 percent of standard. A program very heavily involved with feed-back and reinforcement was introduced a few years ago and increased performance to 90 percent of objectives within three months—a level that has been maintained ever since.

2. Several offices have installed a program in which specified planned reinforcements are provided when targeted levels of shipment volume are requested by Emery customers. All offices have increased revenue substantially; one office doubled the number of export shipments handled, and another averages an additional $60,000 of revenue per month.

3. A program of measuring dimensions of certain lightweight shipments to rate them by volume rather than weight uses reinforcement and feedback extensively. All measures have increased dramatically since the program's inception five years ago, not the least of which

Figure 11–3
Results of positive reinforcement and similar behavior modification programs in organizations in 1976

Organization and person surveyed	Length of program	Number of employees covered/total employees	Type of employees	Specific goals	Frequency of feedback	Reinforcers used	Results
Emery Air Freight John C. Emery, Jr., President Paul F. Hammond, Manager—Systems Performance	1969–76	500/2,800	Entire work force	(a) Increase productivity (b) Improve quality of service	Immediate to monthly, depending on task	Previously only praise and recognition; others now being introduced	Cost savings can be directly attributed to program
Michigan Bell— Operator Services E. D. Grady, General Manager— Operator Services	1972–76	2,000/5,500	Employees at all levels in operator services	(a) Decrease turnover and absenteeism (b) Increase productivity (c) Improve union-management relations	(a) Lower level— weekly and daily (b) Higher level— monthly and quarterly	(a) Praise and recognition (b) Opportunity to see oneself become better	(a) Attendance performance has improved by 50% (b) Productivity and efficiency have continued to be above standard in areas where positive reinforcement (PR) is used
Michigan Bell— Maintenance Services Donald E. Burwell, Division Superintendent, Maintenance and Services Dr. W. Clay Hamner, Consultant	1974–76	220/5,500	Maintenance workers, mechanics, and first- and second-level supervisors	Improve (a) Productivity (b) Quality (c) Safety (d) Customer-employee relations	Daily, weekly, and quarterly	(a) Self-feedback (b) Supervisory feedback	(a) Cost efficiency increase (b) Safety improved (c) Service improved (d) No change in absenteeism (e) Satisfaction with superior & co-workers improved (f) Satisfaction with pay decreased
Connecticut General Life Insurance Company Donald J. Illig, Director of Personnel Administration	1941–76	3,000/13,500	Clerical employees and first-line supervisors	(a) Decrease absenteeism (b) Decrease lateness	Immediate	(a) Self-feedback (b) System feedback (c) Earned time off	(a) Chronic absenteeism and lateness have been drastically reduced (b) Some divisions refuse to use PR because it is "outdated"

Organization / Person	Year(s)	Number	Population	Objectives	Timing	Reinforcers	Results
General Electric* Melvin Sorcher, Ph.D., formerly director of Personnel Research, now Director of Management Development, Richardson-Merrell, Inc.	1973–76	1,000	Employees at all levels	(a) Meet EEO objectives (b) Decrease absenteeism and turnover (c) Improve training (d) Increase productivity	Immediate—uses modeling and role playing as training tools to teach interpersonal exchanges and behavior requirements	Social reinforcers (praise, rewards, and constructive feedback)	(a) Cost savings can be directly attributed to the program (b) Productivity has increased (c) Worked extremely well in training minority groups and raising their self-esteem (d) Direct labor cost decreased
Standard Oil of Ohio T. E. Standing, Ph.D., Manager of Psychological Services	1974	28	Supervisors	Increase supervisor competence	Weekly over five-week (25-hour) training period	Feedback	(a) Improved supervisory ability to give feedback judiciously (b) Discontinued because of lack of overall success
Weyerhaeuser Company Gary P. Latham, Ph.D., Manager of Human Resource Research	1974–76	500/40,000	Clerical, production (tree planters), and middle-level management and scientists	(a) To teach managers to minimize criticism and to maximize praise (b) To teach managers to make rewards contingent on specified performance (c) To use optimal schedule to increase productivity	Immediate—daily and quarterly	(a) Pay (b) Praise and recognition	(a) Using money, obtained a 33% increase in productivity with one group of workers, an 18% increase with a second group and an 8% decrease with a third group (b) Currently experimenting with goal setting and praise and/or money at various levels in organization (c) With a lottery-type bonus, the cultural and religious values of workers must be taken into account

Figure 11–3 (continued)

Organization and person surveyed	Length of program	Number of employees covered/total employees	Type of employees	Specific goals	Frequency of feedback	Reinforcers used	Results
City of Detroit garbage collectors†	1973–75	1,122/1,930	Garbage collectors	(a) Reduction in paid man-hour per ton (b) Reduction on overtime (c) 90% of routes completed by standard (d) Effectiveness (quality)	Daily and quarterly, based on formula negotiated by city and sanitation union	Bonus (profit sharing and praise	(a) Citizen complaints declined significantly (b) City saved $1,654,000 first year after bonus paid (c) Worker bonus = $307,000 first year or $350 annually per man (d) Union somewhat dissatisfied with productivity measure and is pushing for more bonus to employee (e) 1975 results not yet available
B. F. Goodrich Chemical Company Donald J. Barnicki, Production Manager	1972–76	100/420	Manufacturing employees at all levels	(a) Better meeting of schedules (b) Increase productivity	Weekly	Praise and recognition; freedom to choose one's own activity	Production has increased over 300%
ACDC Electronics Division of Emerson Electronics Edward J. Feeney, Consultant	1974–76	350/350	All levels	(a) 96% attendance (b) 90% engineering specifications met (c) Daily production objectives met 95% of time (d) Cost reduced by 10%	Daily and weekly feedback from foreman to company president	Positive feedback	(a) Profit up 25% over forecast (b) $550,000 cost reduction on $10 million sales (c) Return of 1,900% on investment, including consultant fees (d) Turnaround time on repairs went from 30 to 10 days (e) Attendance now 98.2% (from 93.5%)

* Similar programs are now being implemented at Richardson-Merrell under the direction of Dr. Sorcher and at AT&T under the direction of Douglas W. Bray, Ph.D., director of management selection and development, along with several smaller organizations. See A. P. Goldstein and Melvin Sorcher, *Changing Supervisor Behavior* Pergamon Press, 1974).
† From *Improving Municipal Productivity: The Detroit Refuse Incentive Plan,* The National Commission on Productivity, April 1974.
Source: From W. C. Hamner and E. P. Hamner, "Behavior Modification on the Bottom Line," *Organizational Dynamics,* Spring 1976, pp. 12–14.

has been an increase in revenue from $400,000 per year to well over $2,000,000 per year.

Although this information indicates that positive reinforcement has been more than a fad at Emery Air Freight, Emery pointed out that a major flaw in the program had to be overcome. He said, "Inasmuch as praise is the most readily available no-cost reinforcer, it tends to be the reinforcer used most frequently. However, the result has been to *dull* its effect as a reinforcer through its sheer repetition, even to risk making praise an *irritant* to the receiver." To counter this potential difficulty, Emery managers and supervisors have been taught and encouraged to expand their reinforcers beyond praise. Among the recommended reinforcers have been formal recognition, such as a public letter or a letter home, being given a more enjoyable task after completing a less enjoyable one, invitations to business luncheons or meetings, delegating responsibility and decision making, and tying such requests as special time off or any other deviations from normal procedure to performance. Thus it seems that Skinner's 1973 prediction about the need for using more than praise after the reinforcement program has been around for a while has been vindicated at Emery Air Freight.

Michigan Bell—Operator Services. The Operator Services Division was still actively using positive reinforcement feedback as a motivational tool in 1976. E. D. Grady, general manager for operator services said,

> We have found through experience that when standards and feedback are not provided, workers generally feel their performance is at about the 95 percent level. When the performance is then compared with clearly defined standards, it is usually found to meet only the 50th percentile in performance. It has been our experience, over the past ten years, that when standards are set and feedback provided in a positive manner, performance will reach very high levels—perhaps in the upper 90th percentile in a very short period of time. . . . We have also found that when positive reinforcement is discontinued, performance returns to levels that existed prior to the establishment of feedback.

Grady said that while he was not able to put a specific dollar appraisal on the cost savings from using a positive reinforcement program, the savings were continuing to increase and the program was being expanded.

In one recent experiment, Michigan Bell found that when goal setting and positive reinforcement were used in a low-productivity inner-city operator group, service promptness (time to answer call) went from 94 percent to 99 percent of standard, average work time per call (time taken to give information) decreased from 60 units of work time to 43 units of work time, the percentage of work time completed within ideal limits went from 50 percent to 93 percent of ideal time (standard was 80 percent of ideal), and the percentage of time operators made proper use of references went from 80 percent to 94 percent. This led to an overall productivity index score for these operators that was significantly higher than that found in the control group, in which positive reinforcement was not being used, even though the control group of operators had previously (six months earlier) been one of the highest producing units.

Michigan Bell—maintenance services. Donald E. Burwell, division superintendent of maintenance and services at Michigan Bell, established a goal-setting and positive reinforcement program in early 1974. He said, "After assignment to my present area of responsibility in January, I found that my new department of 220 employees (maintenance, mechanics, and janitorial services), including managers, possessed generally good morale. However, I soon became aware that 1973 performances were generally lower than the 1973 objectives. In some cases objectives were either ambiguous or nonexistent."

With the help of a consultant, Burwell overcame the problem by establishing a four-step positive reinforcement program similar to the one described earlier in this chapter. As a result, the 1974 year-end results showed significant improvements over the 1973 base-year averages in all areas, including safety (from 75.6 to 89.0), service (from 76.4 to 83.0), cost performance/hour (from 27.9 to 21.2, indexed), attendance (from 4.7 to 4.0), worker satisfaction and cooperation (from 3.01 to 3.51 on a scale of 5), and worker satisfaction with the supervisors (from 2.88 to 3.70, also on a scale of five). The figures for 1975 reflected continuing success.

Although Burwell was extremely pleased with the results of this program in 1976, he adds a word of caution to other managers thinking of implementing such a program: "I would advise against accepting any one method, including positive reinforcement, as a panacea for all the negative performance trends that confront managers. On the other hand, positive reinforcement has aided substantially in performance improvement for marketing, production, and service operators. Nevertheless, the manager needs to know when the positive effects of the reinforcement program have begun to plateau and what steps he should consider taking to maintain his positive performance trends."

Connecticut General Life Insurance Company. The director of personnel administration at Connecticut General Life Insurance Company, Donald D. Illig, stated in 1976 that Connecticut General had been using positive reinforcement in the form of an attendance bonus system for 25 years with over 3,200 clerical employees. Employees receive one extra day off for each ten weeks of perfect attendance. The results have been outstanding. Chronic absenteeism and lateness have been drastically reduced, and the employees are very happy with the system. Illig noted, however, "Our property and casualty company, with less than half the number of clerical employees countrywide, has not had an attendance-bonus system . . . and wants no part of it. At the crux of the problem is an anti-Skinnerian feeling, which looks at positive reinforcement—and thus an attendance-bonus system—as being overly manipulative and old-fashioned in light of current theories of motivation."

General Electric. A unique program of behavior modification has been introduced quite successfully at General Electric as well as several other organizations by Melvin Sorcher, formerly the director of personnel research at GE. GE's behavior modification program involves the use of positive reinforcement and feedback in training employees. Although the first program centered primarily on teaching male supervisors how to interact and communicate with minority and female employees and on teaching minority and female employees how to become successful by improving their self-images, subsequent programs focused on the relationship between supervisors and employees in general. By using a reinforcement technique known as behavior modeling, Sorcher goes beyond the traditional positive reinforcement (PR) program. The employee is shown a videotape of a model (someone with his or her own characteristics—that is, male or female, black or white, subordinate or superior) who is performing in a correct or desired manner. Then, through the process of role playing, the employee is encouraged to act in the successful or desired manner shown on the film (that is, he is asked to model the behavior). Positive reinforcement is given when the goal of successful display of this behavior is made in the role-playing session.

Sorcher notes that this method has been successfully used with over 1,000 GE supervisors. As a result, productivity has increased, the self-esteem of hard-core employees has increased, and EEO objectives are being met. Sorcher says,

> The positive results have been the gratifying changes or improvements that have occurred, especially improvements that increase over time as opposed to the usual erosion of effort after most training programs have passed their peak. . . . On the negative side, some people and organizations are calling their training "behavior modeling" when it does not fit the criteria originally defined for such a program. For example, some programs not only neglect self-esteem as a component, but show little evidence of how to shape new behaviors. . . . Regarding the more general area of behavior modification and positive reinforcement, there is still a need for better research. There's not a lot taking place at present, which is unfortunate because on the surface these processes seem to have a lot of validity.

Standard Oil of Ohio. T. E. Standing, manager of psychological services at SOHIO, tried a training program similar to the one used by Sorcher at General Electric. After 28 supervisors had completed five weeks of training, Standing disbanded the program even though there were some short-term successes. He said,

> My feelings at this point are that reinforcement cannot be taught at a conceptual level in a brief period of time. (Of course, the same comments can no doubt be made about Theory Y, MBO, and TA.) I see two alternatives: (1) identify common problem situations, structure an appropriate reinforcement response for the supervisor, and teach the response through the behavioral model; or (2) alter reinforcement contingencies affecting defined behaviors through direct alternatives in procedural and/or informational systems without going through the supervisor directly.

Weyerhaeuser Company. Whereas Emery Air Freight has the longest history with applied reinforcement theory, Weyerhaeuser probably has the most experience with controlled experiments using goal setting and PR techniques. The Human Resource Research Center at Weyerhaeuser in 1976, under the direction of G. P. Latham, was actively seeking ways to improve the productivity of all levels of employees using the goal-setting, PR feedback technique.

According to Latham,

> The purpose of our positive reinforcement program is threefold: (1) To teach managers to embrace the philosophy that "the glass is half full rather than half empty." In other words, our objective is to teach managers to minimize criticism (which is often self-defeating since it can fixate the employee's attention on ineffective job behavior and thus reinforce it) and to maximize praise and hence fixate both their and the employee's attention on effective job behavior. (2) To teach managers that praise by itself may increase job satisfaction, but that it will have little or no effect on productivity unless it is made contingent upon specified job behaviors. Telling an employee that he is doing a good job in no way conveys to him what he is doing correctly. Such blanket praise can inadvertently reinforce the very things that the employee is doing in a mediocre way. (3) To teach managers to determine the optimum schedule for administering a reinforcer—be it praise, a smile, or money in the employee's pocket. (Hamner and Hamner, 1976)

Weyerhaeuser has found that by using money as a reinforcer (that is, as a bonus over and above the worker's hourly rate), it obtained a 33 percent increase in productivity with one group of workers, an 18 percent increase in productivity with a second group of workers, and an 8 percent decrease in productivity with a third group of workers. Latham says, "These findings point out the need to measure and document the effectiveness of any human resource program. The results obtained in one industrial setting cannot necessarily be expected in another setting."

Latham notes that because of its current success (1976) with PR, Weyerhaeuser is currently applying reinforcement principles with tree planters in the rural South as well as with engineers and scientists at its corporate headquarters. In the latter case, Weyerhaeuser is comparing different forms of goal setting (assigned, participative, and a generalized goal of "do your best") with three different forms of reinforcement (praise or private recognition from a supervisor, public recognition in the form of a citation for excellence, and a monetary reward). Latham adds, "The purpose of the program is to motivate scientists to attain excellence. Excellence is defined in terms of the frequency with which an individual displays specific behaviors that have been identified by the engineers/scientists themselves as making the difference between success and failure in fulfilling the requirements of their job."

City of Detroit garbage collectors. In December 1972, the city of Detroit instituted a unique productivity bonus system for sanitation workers engaged in refuse collection. The plan, which provided for sharing the savings for productivity improvement efforts, was designed to save money for the city while rewarding workers for increased efficiency. The city's Labor Relations Bureau negotiated the productivity contract with the two unions concerned with refuse collection: the American Federation of State, County, and Municipal Employees (AFSCME), representing sanitation laborers (loaders), and the Teamsters Union, representing drivers. The two agreements took effect on July 1, 1973.

The bonus system was based on savings gained in productivity (reductions in paid man-hours per ton of refuse collected, reduction in the total hours of overtime, percentage of routes completed on schedule, and effectiveness or cleanliness). A bonus pool was established and the sanitation laborers share 50–50 in the pool with the city— each worker's portion being determined by the number of hours worked under the productivity bonus pool, exclusive of overtime.

By any measure, this program was a success. Citizen complaints decreased dramatically. During 1974, the city saved $1,654,000 after the bonus of $307,000 ($350 per man) was paid. The bonus system was still in effect in 1976, but the unions were disputing with the city the question of what constitutes a fair day's work. Both unions involved had expressed doubts about the accuracy of the data used to compute the productivity index or, to be more precise, how the data were gathered and the index and bonus computed. Given this expected prenegotiation tactic by the unions, the city and the customers both agreed that the plan had worked.

B. F. Goodrich Chemical Company. In 1972, a production section of the B. F. Goodrich Chemical plant in Avon Lake, Ohio was failing, as measured by standard accounting procedures. At that time, Donald J. Barnicki, the production manager, introduced a positive reinforcement program that included goal setting and feedback about scheduling, targets, costs, and problem areas. This program gave the information directly to the foreman on a once-a-week basis. In addition, daily meetings were held to discuss problems and describe how each group was doing. For the first time the foremen and their employees were told about costs that were incurred by their group. Charts were published that showed area achievements in terms of sales, cost, and productivity as compared with targets. Films were made that showed top management what the employees were doing, and these films were shown to the workers so that they would know what management was being told.

According to Barnicki, this program of positive reinforcement turned the plant around. "Our productivity has increased 300 percent over the past five years. Costs are down. We had our best start-up time in 1976 and passed our daily production level from last year the second day after we returned from the holidays."

ACDC Electronics. Edward J. Feeney, of Emery Air Freight fame, now heads a consulting firm that works with such firms as General Electric, Xerox, Braniff Airways, and General Atomic in the area of positive reinforcement programs. One of Feeney's current clients is the ACDC Electronics Company (a division of Emerson Electronics). After establishing a program that incorporated the four-step approach outlined earlier in this article, the ACDC Company experienced a profit increase of 25 percent over the forecast; a $550,000 cost reduction on $10 million in sales; a return of 1,900 percent on investment, including consultant fees; a reduction in turnaround time on repairs from 30 days to 10 days; and a significant increase in attendance.

According to Ken Kilpatrick, ACDC president, "The results were as dramatic as those that Feeney had described. We found that our output increased 30–40 percent almost immediately, and it has stayed at that high level for well over a year." The results were not accomplished, however, without initial problems, according to Feeney. "With some managers there were problems of inertia, disbelief, lack of time to implement, lack of interest, difficulty in defining output for hard-to-measure areas, setting standards, measuring past performance, estimating economic payoffs, and failure to apply all feedback or reinforcement principles." Nevertheless, after positive results began to surface and initial problems were overcome, the ACDC management became enthusiastic about the program.

CRITICISMS OF POSITIVE REINFORCEMENT PROGRAMS

Although critics of Skinner's theory are abundant, few have criticized the application of a positive reinforcement approach to industry. Whyte (1972) said that though he accepted the use of a positive reinforcement approach by management, he was not satisfied with the applications of this approach to the work force because these had generally been developed on an individual feedback basis, whereas many work situations depend on group cooperation. A second major criticism made by Whyte was that "at its simplest level, the problem of the prediction and control of behavior involves creating conditions in which the behavior that positively reinforces one person also positively reinforces the other person [in the same group or organization]" (p. 98). In other words, what one worker finds rewarding, another may not. The design of the rewards is crucial, according to Whyte.

Drucker (1973) is afraid that positive reinforcers may be misused by management to the detriment of the economy. "The carrot of material rewards has not, like the stick of fear, lost its potency. On the contrary, it has become so potent that it threatens to destroy the earth's finite resources if it does not first destroy more economies through the inflation that reflects rising expectations" (p. 89). Skinner (1973) agrees that reinforcers can be misused. He says that what must be accomplished is an effective training program for the managers, which he thinks is currently lacking. "In the not-too-distant future, however, a new breed of industrial manager may be able to apply the principles of operant conditioning effectively" (Skinner, 1973, p. 40).

MONEY AS A MOTIVATOR—A SPECIAL TYPE OF POSITIVE REINFORCER

Before we examine (in Chapter 12) the motivation programs designed to improve the task structure, we need to examine the potential use of money as a positive reinforcer. Merit pay or "pay for performance" is widely accepted by managers and researchers as one of the most important tools of motivation.

Despite the soundness of the Law of Effect, on which merit pay is based, academic researchers have criticized the merit system as being detrimental to motivation rather than enhancing motivation, as it is intended to. After reviewing research on pay systems in General Electric and other companies, Herb Meyer (1975) concluded that merit pay does not work with elegant simplicity. In practice, managers typically seemed inclined to make relatively small discriminations in salary treatment among individuals in the same job, regardless of perceived differences in performance. As a matter of fact, Meyer notes, when discriminations are made, they are likely to be based on factors other than performance, such as length of service, future potential, or perceived need for "catch-up" (in situations where one employee's pay seems low in relation to that of others in the group).

Michael Beer, former director of organizational development at Corning Glass, explains why the implementation of the merit system has lost its effectiveness. He states that pay systems evolve over time and that administrative considerations and tradition often override the more important considerations of behavioral outcomes in determining the shape of the system and its administration. Both Meyer and Beer seem to be saying that it is not the merit pay theory but its implementation that is defective. Let us look at the shortcomings that may cause low motivation to result from a merit pay program.

1. Pay is not perceived as being related to job perform-ance.   Edward E. Lawler III (1971), a leading researcher on pay and performance, has noted that a major reason why managers are unhappy with their wage system is that they do not perceive the relationship between how hard they work (their productivity) and how much they earn. In a survey of 600 middle- and lower-level managers, Lawler found virtually no relationship between their pay and their rated performance. Of the managers studied, those who were most highly motivated to perform their jobs effectively were characterized by two attitudes: (*a*) they said that their pay was important to them; and (*b*) they felt that good job performance would lead to higher pay for them.

2. Performance ratings are seen as biased.   Although many managers working under a merit program believe that the program is a good one, they are dissatisfied with the evaluation of their performance given them by their immediate superior. A merit plan is based on the assumption that managers can make objective (valid) distinctions between good and poor performance. Unfortunately, most evaluations of performance are subjective in nature and consist of a "summary score" from a general, and sometimes dated, performance evaluation form. The supervisor's key role in determining pay creates a problem, in that it reminds the employee very clearly that he is dependent on the supervisor for rewards. Therefore, the merit plan should, whenever possible, be based on objective measures (for example, group sales, cost reduction per unit, goal obtainment) rather than subjective measures (for example, cooperation, attitude, future potential).

3. Rewards are not viewed as rewards.   A third problem in administering a merit increase concerns management's ability to communicate accurately to the employee the information that it is trying to communicate through the pay raise. There is no doubt that the pay raise is more than money. It tells the employee such things as "I'm loved a lot," "I'm only average," "I'm not appreciated around here," or "I'd better get busy." Often management believes that it is communicating a positive message to the employee when the message being received by the employee is actually negative. This may have a detrimental effect on future potential. Therefore, the relationship between performing certain desired behaviors and attainment of the pay incentive must be explicitly specified.

The reward message may not be seen as a reward for these reasons: (*a*) conflicting reward schedules may be operating; (*b*) inequity among employees is perceived to exist; and (*c*) the merit increase is a threat to the self-esteem of the employee. All three of these problems center on the fact that pay increases are generally kept secret, thus causing employees to draw erroneous conclusions, or else there is little or no communication in the form of coaching and counseling by the supervisors following the performance appraisal. Instead, the employee is "expected to know" what the supervisor thinks about his or her performance. As Beer and Gery (1972) have stated, the more frequent the formal and informal reviews of performance and the more the employee is told about the reasons for an increase, the greater will be his preference for a merit increase and the lower his preference for a seniority system.

Conflicting reward schedules come about because of a defect in the merit plan itself. Thus, individual rewards (for example, the best manager will get a free trip to Hawaii) may be set up in such a way that cooperation with other managers is discouraged, or a cost reduction program may be introduced at the expense of production, causing one department (say, sales) to suffer while another department (say, manufacturing) benefits in the short run. As Kenneth F. Foster, former manager of composition at Xerox, has noted, pay plans must be changing constantly because of general business conditions, shifts in management philosophy, competitive pressures, participant feedback, and modifications in the structure and objectives of the organization. Nevertheless, these changes should be designed in such a way that the negative side effect of reduced cooperation does not result. For this reason, many companies use a company-wide merit plan (for example, the Scanlon Plan), in which there is a financial incentive to everyone in the organization based on the performance of the total organization.

Inequity in pay can come about for one of two reasons. First, the employee perceives a merit increase to be unfair relative to his own past year's performance. That is, he is dissatisfied with the performance evaluation, or else he feels that the performance evaluation is fair, but believes that his supervisor failed to reward him in a manner consistent with his rating. A much more common problem is that, while the employee may agree with the dollar amount of his pay increase, he perceives that others who are performing at levels below his own are receiving as large an increase or else those who are performing at the same level as his own are receiving larger increases. For example, an employee who was rated as above average receives an 8 percent pay increase. He perceives this to be low because he believes that the average increase was 9 percent, when in fact it was 6½ percent. In order to avoid the feelings of inequity, which will contribute to dissatisfaction with pay and possible lower job performance, Lawler recommends as a minimum requirement that managers tell their employees how the salary raises were derived (for example, 50 percent based on cost of living and 50 percent based on merit) and tell them the range and mean of the raises given in the organization to people at their job level. He therefore advocates the abandonment of secrecy policies—"there is no reason why organizations cannot make salaries public information."

Herb Meyer argues that the problem with merit pay plans may be more than a problem of equity. Drawing on his previous research, he concluded that 90 percent of the managers at General Electric rated themselves as above average. Meyer concludes that the inconsistency between the information of the merit raise and the manager's own evaluation of his performance will be a threat to the manager's *self-esteem,* and the manager may cope with this threat by denying the importance of hard work or disparaging the source of the merit raise. Meyer (1975) concludes:

> The fact that almost everyone thinks he is an above average performer probably causes most of our problems with merit pay plans. Since the salary increases most people get do not reflect superior performance (as determined by interpersonal comparisons, or as defined in the guide book for the pay plan), the effects of the actual pay increases on motivation are likely to be more negative than positive. The majority of the people feel discriminated against because, obviously, management does not recognize their true worth.

4. Managers of merit increases are more concerned about employees' satisfaction with pay than about employees' job performance. Most studies which survey managers' satisfaction with their pay have shown high levels of dissatisfaction. In 1961, Porter found that 80 percent of the managers surveyed from companies throughout the United States reported dissatisfaction with their pay. These same findings have been reported in surveys at General Electric, a large insurance firm, and a cross section of managers from many companies. Too often dissatisfaction with pay is assumed to mean dissatisfaction with the amount of pay. However, research suggests that a change to a merit system, with no increase in the amount paid out by the company, will increase employee satisfaction with pay if the reasons for the increases are explained.

Managers need to be concerned with two questions. First, *Is the merit raise based on performance?* Numerous studies show that pay is not closely related to performance in many organizations claiming to have merit ranges. Typically these studies show that pay is much more closely related to job level and seniority than to performance. In fact, Belcher reports that low, zero, and even negative relationships between pay and supervisory ratings of performance occur even among managers, where the relationship would be expected to be high.

Second, *Who is doing the complaining?* Donald Finn, compensation manager at J. C. Penney, says that managers are often "hung up" about the satisfaction of employees with their pay recommendations.

He states, "So who is complaining and why? If low producers are low earners, the pay plan is working—but there will be complaints. If a company wants an incentive plan in which rewards are commensurate with risk, it must be willing to accept a relatively broad range of earnings and corresponding degrees of manager satisfaction." ("Case of Big Mac's Pay Plans, 1974") Beer agrees with Finn when he says:

> A merit system can probably be utilized effectively by management in motivating employees. This concept has been in disfavor lately, but our findings indicate that more might be done with money in motivating people, particularly those who are work and achievement oriented in the first place.
>
> While a merit system would seem to be less need satisfying to the security-oriented individual and, therefore, potentially less motivating, there is probably a net gain in installing a merit system. Those who are high in achievement-oriented needs will be stimulated by such a system to greater heights of performance, while those high in security-oriented needs will become more dissatisfied and it is hoped, will leave. (Beer & Gery, 1972, p. 326)

5. Trust and openness about merit increases are low.

A merit system will not be accepted and may not have the intended motivational effects if managers do not actively administer a performance appraisal system, practice good human relations, explain the reasons for the increases, and ensure that employees are not forgotten when eligibility dates come and go. The organization must provide an open climate with respect to pay as well as an environment in which work and effort are valued.

The Xerox Corporation in a recent report on a compensation planning model (Xerox Corporate Planning Model, 1974) has recognized the problem of trust and openness and has stated that "if pay and satisfaction are to be high, pay rates must vary according to job demands in such a way that each perceived increment in a job demand factor will lead to increased pay" (p. 4). This same document notes that organizations expect extremely high trust levels on the part of their employees, in that:

1. Only 72 percent of 184 employing organizations had a written statement of the firm's basic compensation policies with regard to such matters as the payment of competitive salaries, the timing of wage and salary increases, and how raises were determined.
2. Only 51 percent of these same organizations communicated their general compensation policies directly to all employees, whereas 21 percent communicated the policies only to managers.
3. On the other hand, 69 percent of the firms did *not* provide their employees with wage and salary schedules or progression plans that applied to their own categories, indicating a low trust level toward employees.

4. Over 50 percent of the firms did *not* tell their employees where this information was available.

5. In only 48 percent of the firms did managers have access to salary schedules applying to their own level in the organization, and in only 18 percent of the companies did managers have knowledge of the salaries of other managers at their own level or at higher levels.

6. *Some organizations view money as the primary motivator, ignoring the importance of the job itself.* Skinner (1973) recommends that the organization design feedback and incentive systems in such a way that the dual objectives of getting things done and making work enjoyable are met. He says:

> It is important to remember that an incentive system isn't the only factor to take into account. How pleasant work conditions are, how easy or awkward a job is, how good or bad tools are—many things of that sort make an enormous difference in what a worker will do for what he receives. One problem of the production-line worker is that he seldom sees any of the ultimate consequences of his work. He puts on left front wheels day in and day out and he may never see the finished car. (p. 39)

Skinner also suggests that people be involved in the design of the contingencies of reinforcements (in this case merit pay plans) under which they live. In this way the rewards come from the behavior of the worker in the environment and not from the supervisor. Both Kenneth Foster of Xerox and Joe W. Rogers, chairman of the board of Waffle House, agree. Foster, commenting on the McDonald pay plan, said, "McDonald's management is to be commended for recognizing a number of important incentive reward axioms. Foremost, the reward system must be meaningful to the recipients. They must also see it as equitable and its financial outcomes and rewards as within their power to control." Rogers agreed, saying, "In the restaurant industry, a bonus system must be self-monitoring and deal only with the facts. All areas of judgment by a friendly or unfriendly superior should be absent in a bonus system. . . . let people participate in the design of the new pay. Credibility with the participants is much more critical." ("Case of Big Mac's Pay Plans," 1974)

B. F. Skinner warns managers that too much dependence on force and a poorly designed monetary reward system may actually reduce performance, whereas designing the task so that it is automatically reinforcing can have positive effects on performance. Skinner (1973) says:

> The behavior of an employee is important to the employer, who gains when the employee works industriously and carefully. How is he to be induced to do so? The standard answer was once physical force: men worked

to avoid punishment or death. The by-products were troublesome however, and economics is perhaps the first field in which an explicit change was made to positive reinforcement. Most men now work, as we say, "for money."

Money is not a natural reinforcer; it must be conditioned as such. Delayed reinforcement, as in a weekly wage, raises a special problem. No one works on Monday morning because he is reinforced by a paycheck on Friday afternoon. The employee who is paid by the week works during the week to avoid losing the standard of living which depends on a weekly system. Rate of work is determined by the supervisor and special aversive contingencies maintain quality. The pattern is therefore still aversive. It has often been pointed out that the attitude of the production-line worker toward his work differs conspicuously from that of the craftsman, who is envied by workers and industrial managers alike. One explanation is that the craftsman is reinforced by more than monetary consequences, but another important difference is that when a craftsman spends a week completing a given set object, each of the parts produced during the week is likely to be automatically reinforcing because of its place in the completed object. (p. 40)

Source: Reprinted by permission of Chicago Tribune-New York News Syndicate.

SUMMARY

In this chapter we have begun to examine how managers apply knowledge gained from theory and research to the work setting. We outlined what we believed to be the components of work which a manager controls. These are (1) the work environment, (2) the task assignment, and (3) the consequences or rewards resulting from task performance. This chapter focused primarily on the last component— the reinforcement outcome. The chapter reviewed how various organizations are using the principles of reinforcement to implement goal-setting and feedback programs in order to increase productivity and satisfaction. The chapter also examined in detail money as a motivator of performance.

Chapter 12 will continue our discussion of the worker motivation programs found in organizational settings today. The chapter will discuss job design and organizational development programs. The summary section of Chapter 12 will attempt to integrate the information we have about current and prospective attempts by managers to use organizational behavior theories in order to improve productivity and the quality of work life.

CONCEPTS TO REMEMBER

work climate	positive reinforcement
task structure	proactive programs
reactive programs	

QUESTION FOR DISCUSSION*

You have to make salary recommendations for six managers whom you supervise. They have just completed their annual appraisal period and are now to be considered for their annual raise. Your company has set aside 10 percent of departmental salary costs for merit increases. Your total current annual salary cost is $119,600, which means that you have $11,960 for salary increases. There are no formal company restrictions on how you may distribute the 10 percent merit increase. Please indicate the size of the raise that you would like to give each manager by writing the percentage amount of the raise next to the manager's name. All managers have the same job classification, and the salary recommendations are secret.

EMPLOYEE PROFILE SHEET

% _____ John Smith, age 30, three children, current annual salary $19,000, MBA, Harvard. John is married to the chairman of the board's daughter and has been with the company five years, the last three as manager. He has one of the easiest groups to supervise, doesn't impress you as being very bright, but is a hard worker. You rated him as "slightly above average" (68 percent) on his last performance

---

* Adapted from an unpublished exercise by E. E. Lawler III, 1973.

rating. You checked your view with others you respect, and they too felt that he was not as effective as other managers who work for you, but they reminded you of his potential influence in your group.

% _____ Larry Foster, age 27, single, current annual salary $16,300, BA degree, University of Maine. Larry has been with the company for four years, the last three as manager. He has a difficult group to supervise, is bright, often works overtime, and has "turned around the group" he supervises. You rated him as "an excellent manager with a good future" (89 percent) on his last performance rating.

% _____ Tim Hall, age 44, four children, two in college, current annual salary $26,100 (three years of college, no degree). Tim has been with the company for the past 18 years and has been in his current position for the past 8 years. He is unhappy that you were named boss because he was hoping to get the job. He is well liked by all the other managers and by his employees. He rarely works on weekends, and he seems to be easygoing with his employees. However, his group had the second highest performance of the groups you manage. You rated him as outstanding (85 percent) on his last performance appraisal.

% _____ Ellen Panza, age 30, married, two children, current salary, $20,000, BA, City University of New York. Ellen has been with the company for two years, and worked as an executive secretary for the first year, before being promoted to manager. You feel that she was given the job because she is a woman, and frankly you resent it. In addition, you feel that her salary is too high compared to the salaries of others in the company. However, you must admit that she has performed in an outstanding manner, since her group went from last to first place in performance this year. Her score on the rating sheet was 90 percent.

% _____ Otto Lechman, age 36, married (wife works for company as assistant personnel director), no children, current salary $19,000, MBA, University of Michigan. Otto has been with the company for nine years, the past six as manager. He is aggressive, hot-tempered, and though at one time you thought he was your best employee, during the past two years you have found him to be a disappointment. You rated him as "slightly below average" (59 percent) on his last performance rating. You believe that one of the reasons Otto's performance has fallen off is that he has found out about John Smith's and Ellen Panza salaries.

% _____ David L. Green III, age 29, single, current salary $19,000, BA, Wayne State University. David has been with the company for six years and became the first black manager in your company five years ago. He has been very instrumental in recruiting other blacks into the company and is often called on by the president to represent the company at civic and social events. You have found David's work to be marginal at best, and though you assigned him to manage the best group five years ago, the group is now the lowest performing. You rated David as being "below average" (43 percent) and would like to get rid of him, but you don't know how you would replace him.

Your company has a secret pay policy. What information do you plan to share with your employees? What was your decision rule for administering the pay increases?

REFERENCES

Abel, I. W.   Advertisement. *Sports Illustrated,* October 22, 1973.

Beer, M. & Gery, G. L.   Individuals and organizational correlates of pay system preferences. In H. L. Tosi, R. House, & M. Dunnette (Eds.), *Management Motivation and Compensation.* East Lansing, Mich.: Michigan State University Press, 1972, pp. 325–349.

Carroll, S. J., & Tosi, H. L.   *Management by objectives.* New York: Macmillan, 1973.

Case of Big Mac's pay plans, by Sasser, W. E. & Pettway, S. H.   *Harvard Business Review,* July–August 1974, pp. 118–127. Copyright © 1974 by the President and Fellows of Harvard College; all rights reserved.

Donnelly, J. F.   Increasing productivity by involving people in their total jobs. *Personnel Administration,* September–October 1971, pp. 8–13.

Drucker, P. F.   Beyond the stick and carrot: Hysteria over the work ethic. *Psychology Today,* November 1973, pp. 87; 89–93.

Emery, J. C.   How to double your sales and profits every 5 years. Speech before the Sales Executive Club of New York, 1973.

At Emery Air Freight: Positive reinforcement boosts performance. *Organizational Dynamics,* 1973, *1,* 41–50.

Frost, C. F.   A change agent's view of the Scanlon Plan. Paper presented at the meeting of the American Psychological Association, Montreal, August 1973.

Fuller, S. H.   Employee development. Speech before the National Alliance of Businessmen, Detroit, September 24, 1973.

Gamboa, V. U., & Pedalino, E.   Behavior modification and absenteeism: Intervention in one industrial setting. Working paper, University of Michigan, 1973.

Hamner, W. C.   Reinforcement theory and contingency management. In H. L. Tosi & W. C. Hamner (Eds.), *Organizational behavior and management: A contingency approach.* Chicago: St. Clair Press, 1974.

Hamner, W. C., & Hamner, E. P.   Behavior modification on the bottom line. *Organizational Dynamics,* American Management Association, Spring 1976, pp. 2–21.

Hamner, W. C. Worker Motivation programs. In W. C. Hamner & F. L. Schmidt (Eds.), *Contemporary Problems in Personnel.* Chicago: St. Clair Press, 1974.

Lawler, E. E., III. *Pay and organizational effectiveness.* New York: McGraw-Hill, 1971.

Levitan, S. A., & Johnston, W. B. Job redesign, enrichment—Exploring the limitations. *Monthly Labor Review,* July 1973, pp. 35–41. (a)

Levitan, S. A., & Johnston, W. B. Changes in work: More evolution than revolution. *Manpower,* September 1973, pp. 3–7. (b)

Levitan, S. A., & Johnston, W. B. *Work is here to stay, alas.* Olympus, 1973. (c)

Luthans, F., & White, D. O. Behavior modification: Application to manpower management. *Personnel Administrator,* July–August 1971, pp. 41–47.

Meyer, H. H. The pay for performance dilemma. *Organizational Dynamics,* Spring 1975, pp. 1–18.

New tool: Reinforcement for good work. *Business Week,* December 18, 1971, p. 76.

Nord, W. R. Beyond the teaching machine: The neglected area of operant conditioning in the theory and practice of management. *Organizational Behavior and Human Performance,* ©1969, I, 375–401.

Porter, L. W. Perceived need satisfactions. *Journal of Applied Psychology,* 1961, *45,* 27–31.

The power of praise. *International Management,* October 1973, pp. 32–35.

Rogers, C. R. *Counseling and psychotherapy.* Boston: Houghton Mifflin, 1942.

Skinner, B. F. *Science and human behavior.* New York: Macmillan, 1953.

Skinner, B. F. *Contingencies of reinforcement: A theoretical analysis.* New York: Appleton-Century-Crofts, © 1969. Reprinted by permission of Prentice-Hall, Inc., Englewood Cliffs, New Jersey.

Skinner, B. F. "Conversation with B. F. Skinner."*Organizational Dynamics,* Winter 1973, 31–40.

Sorcher, M. & Goldstein, A. P. A behavioral modeling approach in training. *Personnel Administration,* March–April 1972, pp. 35–41.

Thorndike, F. L. *Animal intelligence.* New York: Macmillan, 1911.

Warren, M. W. Performance management: A substitute for supervision. *Management Review,* Octover 1972, pp. 28–42.

Where Skinner's theories work. *Business Week,* December 2, 1972, pp. 64–65.

Whyte, W. F. Skinnerian theory in organizations. *Psychology Today,* April 1972, pp. 67–68; 96; 100.

Work in America. Report of a Special Task Force to the Secretary of Health, Education, and Welfare. Cambridge, Mass.: MIT Press, 1973.

Xerox Corporate Planning Model, The Xerox Corporation, Rochester, N.Y., 1974, pp. 1–53.

Worker motivation programs II

Increasing productivity and the quality of work life with job enrichment, organizational development, and flexitime programs

What are the theoretical bases for the application of job enrichment, organizational development, and flexitime programs?

How are these programs designed and implemented?

What evidence do we have for the success of these programs?

What do the critics of these programs have to say?

In this chapter we will continue our discussion of worker motivation programs. We have already discussed, in Chapter 11, the components of motivation which the manager controls (that is, the work environment, the task assignment, and the reinforcing consequences). Chapter 11 also presented information on how organizational leaders have designed reward programs in such a way that the rewards have positive effects on performance. This chapter will discuss motivation programs which change task assignments and the work climate in ways that lead to positive effects. We will begin by examining how task structures affect worker output and satisfaction.

TASK STRUCTURE OR JOB ENRICHMENT PROGRAM

Theoretical background

As noted in Chapter 11, both research and practical experience have indicated that jobs should include opportunities for personal achievement, responsibility, recognition, growth, and advancement in order to provide high levels of employee performance. In other words, work should provide employees with positive satisfaction which is derived from using their individual talents and skills.

One method by which this objective is being achieved in organizations is through *job enrichment.* Job enrichment is a concerted attempt to stem and even reverse long-standing trends toward job simplification and specialization among industrial engineering programs. In simple terms, job enrichment involves the redefinition or restructuring of jobs so that employees have greater planning and control responsibilities in the execution of their overall assignment. Job enrichment should be distinguished from *job enlargement,* in which workers are given a larger number of different things to do, without any greater planning and control responsibilities.

The theoretical principles on which job enrichment is based are not nearly as clear and straightforward as those which underlie positive reinforcement, which has previously been described. Skinner and his followers see job enrichment as a method of making the task reinforcing, and they therefore describe the enriched job as leading to higher levels of performance because it leads to a positive reward state, and the absence of enrichment as leading to a negative or neutral reward state (see "Conversation with B. F. Skinner," 1973; Nord, 1969). Job enrichment, as it is currently practiced in industry, is a direct outgrowth of Herzberg's two-factor theory of motivation (see Chapter 7). It is therefore based on the assumption that in order to motivate personnel, the job itself must provide opportunities for achievement, recognition,

271

responsibility, advancement, and growth. The program entails "enrich-ing" the job so that these factors are included.

Scott (1966) offers a third theoretical explanation of why an enriched task design increases the motivation level of the worker. Scott's activa-tion level theory is based on physiology. Briefly, this theory holds that cues received from the environment travel to the appropriate cortical projection region of the brain for information purposes and are also diffused over a wide area of the cortex in order to arouse or activate the organism.[1] According to Scott, the greater the variety and the amount of stimulation in an enriched task, the higher the state of arousal or activation, and the more motivated the worker. However, in short, routine, repetitive tasks, after a period of time the "sameness" of the cue received leads to a decrease in arousal level and therefore to a decrease in motivation and performance.

Lawler (1969) offers still a fourth theoretical explanation of why a task of increased complexity will lead to higher performance levels. The theory of motivation that best describes "why" job enrichment increases commitment and involvement on the part of the employee is an "internal state" theory called "expectancy theory." This theory, the details of which were presented in Chapter 7, says basically that an enriched task is *perceived* by the worker as leading to an intrinsic reward. Lawler (1969) says: "Thus, it appears that the answer to the *why* question can be found in the ability of job design factors to influ-ence employees' perceptions of the probability that good performance will be intrinsically rewarding. Certain job designs apparently encour-age the perception that it will, while others do not. Because of this, job design factors can determine how motivating a job will be" (p. 429).

Regardless of their theoretical position, most behavioral scientists believe that extreme divisions of labor and the resulting job simplifica-tion and specialization lead almost inevitably to monotony, job dissatis-faction, and decreased performance.

Even though there is disagreement as to *why* job enrichment works, the programs being put forth by the various "reformers" can be re-duced to a few common elements (Levitan & Johnston, 1973a). These elements are as follows: individuals should be given maximum freedom to control their work and develop their skills; jobs should be designed to give each person a series of varied, challenging, and meaningful tasks which are developed in terms of the end product; the status differentials which have separated supervisors and employees should be replaced by a team concept, with an emphasis on shared goals.

---

[1] This theory was explained in more detail in Chapter 8.

Stages in program development

The leading advocate of job enrichment in the United States today is probably Robert Ford, personnel director of work organizations and environmental research at AT&T. From 1965 to 1968 AT&T conducted 19 formal field experiments in job enrichment, and since then it has expanded the program to many additional areas of the Bell system. On the basis of AT&T's success with its job enrichment program, Ford (1973) sees the job enrichment strategy as involving three stages. The *first* stage is designed to improve work through systematic changes in the modules of work. During this stage each worker is given a whole, natural unit of work and is assigned specific or specialized tasks which enable him or her to become an expert in this expanded work module. Ford says that in defining modules that give each employer a natural area of responsibility, AT&T tries to accumulate modules (units) of work until one of the following three entities has been created for the worker: (1) a customer outside the organization; (2) a client within the organization; or (3) a manufacturing task in which an individual can produce a complete product or large portions of a complete product.

In order to improve morale and upgrade performance, AT&T has recently begun to "nest" jobs together during this stage. This method goes beyond enriching *individual* jobs by putting together people whose work modules complement one another. Job nesting is therefore the opposite of job pooling (for example, a secretarial pool), in which workers who perform a similar task are located together.

The *second* stage enriches the work through systematic changes in the control of the work module. During this stage, as an employee gains experience, the supervisor turns over responsibility to the employee until the employee is handling the work completely. The ultimate goal is to let the worker have complete control over the job. This increases the accountability and control of individuals over their own work, and indeed, makes each employee a manager of his or her task. Eugene Cafiero, group vice president at Chrysler, sees this as a crucial stage in getting the most out of a job enrichment program. In a recent speech Cafiero discussed the results of Chrysler's experience in enriching workers' jobs. He said: "A man doing a job all day long knows more about that job than anyone else; he knows how to improve it better than anyone else. We want to give our people a chance to speak up. We feel that this program is working through more satisfied employees. We at Chrysler Corporation are trying to avoid the impersonal feelings that are often associated with large corporations" ("Workers Get a Voice," 1971, p. 1).

The *third* and final stage is perhaps the most important to the success of the job enrichment program. During this stage the job is enriched through systematic changes in feedback signaling whether something has been accomplished. During this stage periodic reports are made directly available to the worker rather than to the supervisor. Like the positive reinforcement program, this stage allows the worker to monitor the quality and quantity of his or her own work in order to make the corrections necessary. Ford (1973) says, "Definition of the module and control of it are futile unless the results of the employee's effort are discernible. Moreover, knowledge of the results should go directly to where it will nurture motivation—that is, to the employee. People have a great capacity for midflight correction when they know where they stand" (p. 99).

Unlike a positive reinforcement program, job enrichment requires a big change in managerial style. It calls for increasing modules, moving controls downward, and designing effective feedback ideas. A positive reinforcement program, on the other hand, is not intended to change managerial style, but to increase the manager's ability to give varied kinds of feedback as it relates to worker performance (Sorcher & Goldstein, 1972). Therefore, the job enrichment program involves not only changing the feedback received by the worker and the worker's task involvement, but also changing the traditional relationship of the supervisor with his subordinates.

Results of job enrichment programs

Literally scores of companies are involved to some extent in job enrichment programs. These include Texas Instruments; Corning Glass Works; IBM; AT&T; Procter and Gamble; Bankers Trust; Merrill, Lynch, Pierce, Fenner and Smith; Donnelly Corporation; Imperial Chemical Industries, Ltd.; Maytag; Motorola; Gaines Food Company; and Buick.

Like the evidence for the effectiveness of positive reinforcement programs, the evidence for the effectiveness of job enrichment programs is sketchy, lacks empirical rigor, is probably reported only by companies which have experienced success, and is often qualitative in nature (Hulin, 1971). As Levitan and Johnston (1973a) warn: "These experiments with job redesign are all 'success stories.' Indeed, most of the literature on work reform is the product of advocates reporting positive results. But there are major gaps in the case for job reform. Companies which find authoritarian controls and unchanged job rewards to be as successful as ever are not included in the surveys. Companies whose enrichment and participation plans turn sour rarely trumpet the news" (p. 36). Nevertheless, many companies are reporting success, and as a result other companies are eagerly spending millions of dollars each year on efforts to duplicate that success.

In 1966, Reif and Schoderbek found that 41 of the 210 companies they surveyed had used job enrichment. <u>The most popular reasons for undertaking job enrichment were cost reduction, increased profits, and greater job satisfaction</u>. As far back as 1950, Walker reported that a job enrichment program at IBM had been a success (reported in Reif and Schoderbek, 1966). More recently, Ford (1969) reported that after the installation of job enrichment in the Shareholder Relations Department at AT&T there had been a 27 percent reduction in the termination rate and an estimated cost savings of $558,000 over a 12-month period. In 12 districts of AT&T which tried job enrichment with service representatives, <u>resignations and dismissals dropped by 14 percent,</u> which could mean an annual savings of $10 million in operating costs (Janson, 1970). In Imperial Chemical Industries, Ltd., <u>salesperson productivity increased by 19 percent a year after the introduction of job enrichment</u>, whereas in a similar group which lacked job enrichment, sales dropped by 5 percent a year (Janson, 1970).

Motorola found that <u>implementing a job enrichment program</u> among bench (individual) assembly workers <u>required 25 percent more workers and more training time</u>. The company reported, however, that the <u>higher wage costs were offset by greater productivity, less need for inspection, a higher-quality product, and lower work costs</u> ("Motorola," 1971). The Maytag Company found that greater flexibility in terms of production scheduling was a major advantage of job enrichment over assembly line production. The company reported that it could add or subtract work stations or shifts without affecting the production of other workers (Stewart, 1967).

Buick Motor Division has been involved in a substantial job enrichment program in its product engineering area since 1971. Prior to the introduction of this program, skilled hourly mechanics would work on cars in Buick's engineering fleet and perform assignments based on a work ticket that had been completed by engineering personnel. Now, mechanics not only complete the work tickets themselves, but are also encouraged to perform any repair they consider necessary and to inspect their work upon finishing it. Buick credits this program with increasing productivity by 13 percent, reducing petty grievances to near zero, and significantly reducing the number of rework cases (Schotters, 1973b).

Texas Instruments gave full responsibility for janitorial services to the workers involved. The employees met to decide how the work would be divided and to set up schedules and establish standards. As a result of this job enrichment effort, the number of workers needed declined from 120 to 71, cleanliness improved, and turnover was reduced from 100 percent to 10 percent quarterly (Herrick, 1971). In 1971, the Gaines Food plant in Topeka, Kansas, attempted to enrich all jobs by organizing workers into teams whose members were paid according to their skill level and not according to their position in the hierarchy (supervisor versus worker). Gaines eliminated such status symbols as assigned parking spaces and separate eating facilities, and all decision making, including goal setting, was made a team process. The company reported that its program had resulted in a 91 percent reduction in absenteeism compared to the industry average, 40 fewer employees than predicted, and the best safety record in the General Foods Corporation ("How Industry Is Dealing with People Problems," 1973). As a result of the success of the Gaines Food project, similar efforts are being made by the Mead Corporation, Procter and Gamble, and the Scott Paper Company. Scott Paper is building a small plant in Dover, Delaware, which it plans to operate under the new module approach in an attempt to combat production line boredom ("A New Way to Work," 1973).

Bankers Trust and Merrill, Lynch, Pierce, Fenner and Smith adopted a job enrichment program in which work modules were set up by customer or function. In both cases, significant money savings were realized in terms of increased productivity and reduced supervisory time (Rickleffs, 1972). Xerox initiated a similar job enrichment program for its technical representatives. Machine servicers were given more authority to decide expenses, schedule work, order inventories, interview and train new personnel, and determine work loads. Xerox credits this program with increased performance levels (Jacobs, 1972).

Other companies which have reported success with job enrichment programs include: Monsanto, Weyerhaeuser, Exxon, Polaroid, and Ampex Tape in the United States; Volvo and Kockums Shipyards in Sweden; Daimler-Benz and Volkswagen in West Germany; Renault in France; and Olivetti and Fiat in Italy ("How Industry Is Dealing with People Problems," 1973). Regardless of the criticisms leveled against job enrichment, many companies appear to regard it as a success and it cannot be dismissed as a passing fad. The president of Donnelly Mirror said, "If you need proof that involving people in their total job pays off, ask what you got in return for your last labor contract. If you are less than satisfied with the bargain, ask yourself how much it would be worth to get the support of your people in effecting just the cost reductions that your engineers already know about" (Donnelly, 1971, p. 12).

Criticisms of job enrichment programs

Criticisms of job enrichment programs have come from academicians, managers, workers, union representatives, and industrial engineers. Academicians criticize the success studies as incomplete and poorly designed, and generally hold the studies to have little empirical validity. Hulin (1971) wrote, "It is unfortunate that most of these studies provide indirect evidence, at best. . . . Many of these studies have been poorly controlled, and most of the authors have attempted to generalize from severely limited data."

Many groups criticize the job enrichment advocates for pushing job enrichment as a social cure for worker discontent, even when their organizations may lose profits as a result of such programs. Recognizing the costs involved in meaningful job reform, some reformers have argued that job enrichment should control the design of production processes, even if productivity is reduced thereby. These reformers suggest that "social efficiency" be given priority over considerations of purely economic efficiency. Many supporters of job enrichment criticize this stand as impractical and unnecessary. Levitan and Johnston (1973a) say, "If changes in technology and hardware to improve the quality of work are to be made, they must also promise higher profits" (p. 38). Drucker (1973) agrees: "The manager who pretends that the personal needs of the worker—for affection, for example—come before the objective needs of the task is indeed a liar or a poor manager. The rare worker who believes him is a fool" (p. 92).

Along these same lines, it should be noted that some jobs cannot be enriched beyond a certain point. All the redesign in the world cannot make certain dull tasks exciting. According to Levitan and Johnston (1973a), "The basic limit to work redesign is that society requires that certain tasks be done. . . . The prospects for humanizing work are limited by the realities of the work to be done—realities which are beyond the power of planners to control" (p. 5).

Perhaps the most damaging criticism leveled against job enrichment is that many workers do not feel alienated from their jobs and do not desire more responsibility or involvement at their workplace. Levitan and Johnston (1973a) ask, "Is the quality of work life the main standard by which they judge the quality of their lives? It appears that for most workers the quality of work is less important than the standard of living" (p. 40). According to the Bureau of Labor Statistics, the predominant issue in collective bargaining is still wages. In 1971, three out of every four days lost in strikes were the result of wage or benefit disputes.

Attempts to enrich jobs are often frustrated by union constraints in the form of restrictive job descriptions, tenure requirements, craft jurisdictions, and general mistrust. Some critics argue that labor unions tend to oppose job enrichment because they thrive on conflict with management. Leonard Woodcock, president of the United Automobile Workers, says, "Those who contend that boredom and monotony are the big problems among assembly workers are writing a lot of nonsense" (reported in Baxter, 1973, p. 35).

Little and Warr (1971) say that workers on a piece rate oppose job enrichment as an attempt to cut the rate and lower their earnings.

Conart and Kilbridge (1965) reported that in one company, about one third of the workers who had an opportunity to move to enriched jobs expressed a preference for their present job because they felt that the existing incentive system maximized their earnings.

According to Reif and Luthans (1972), many groups of workers are not alienated, other groups actually enjoy looking outside the organization for their intrinsic rewards, and still other groups may have a high need for structure. Job enrichment may have a negative effect on all of these groups.

Mitchell Fein's research for the American Institute of Industrial Engineers claims that a check into many of the job enrichment case histories and studies of workers done over the past ten years indicates that job enrichment does not work—primarily because workers do not want it (Baxter, 1973).

Despite these criticisms, the evidence still shows that job enrichment works for some groups of people. However, the criticisms do show the need to consider individual differences among workers when a company is deciding on a motivation program of job enrichment. Hulin and Blood (1968) emphasize this point when they say: "Specifically, the argument for larger jobs as a means of motivating workers, decreasing boredom and dissatisfaction, and increasing attendance and productivity is valid only when applied to certain segments of the work force— white-collar and supervisory workers and non-alienated blue-collar workers" (p. 50).

ORGANIZATIONAL CLIMATE AND DEVELOPMENT PROGRAMS

Theoretical background

Many writers praise positive reinforcement programs and job enrichment or task structure programs as being steps in the right direction in the fight against worker discontent. However, some of these same writers claim that such programs are not enough. Neither positive reinforcement nor job enrichment programs do much to change the hierarchical structure of the organization and neither type of program examines the attitudinal problems of the worker in interpersonal transactions. Lawler (1973b) suggests that what workers want most, as reflected in over 100 studies in the past 20 years, is to become the masters of their immediate environment and to feel that they and their work are important. Although advocates of positive reinforcement and job enrichment programs would argue that the high self-esteem of workers is a purpose of their respective programs, others contend that workers cannot have high self-esteem unless the climate in which they work is a healthy one. The term *climate,* as used by these writers, can be defined as a set of properties of the work environment that is assumed to be a major force in influencing the behavior of the employees on the job. These properties include the size, structure, leadership pat- CLIMATE terns, interpersonal relationships, systems complexity, goal direction, and communication patterns of the organization. Therefore, an improvement in the organizational climate would involve more than changing the task structure (job enrichment) or the reinforcing consequences (positive reinforcement), but might also involve changes in the structure of interpersonal relationships.

Proponents of an improved climate contend that "the traditional hierarchical system of organizations breeds a climate of fear and mistrust, which reduces management effectiveness. Programs in team building, sensitivity training, encounter groups . . . are advocated to unfreeze the climate" ("How Industry Is Dealing with People Problems," 1973, p. 80). Often, the task of building a climate which encourages achievement in an organization is one of changing the concern of management from an insistence on power compliance ("Here is what needs to be done, and here is how to do it") to an approach that offers warmth and support to each individual, communicating organizational goals and standards, but not attempting to control the means of reaching those goals and standards.

The climate that characterizes the work situation helps determine the kinds of worker motivation that are actually aroused. Climates tend to mediate between the task requirements of the organization and the needs of the individual. "The capacity to influence the organizational climate is perhaps the most powerful leverage point in the entire management system. Because climates can affect the motivation of organizational members, changes in certain climate properties could have immediate and profound effects on the motivated performance of all employees" (Litwin & Stringer, 1973, p. 539).

A healthy organizational climate, according to Schein (1970, p. 126), is one that:

1. Takes in and communicates information reliably and validly.
2. Has the internal flexibility and creativity necessary to make the changes which are demanded by the information obtained.
3. Includes integration and commitment to the goals of the organization, from which comes the willingness to change.
4. Provides internal support and freedom from threat, since being threatened undermines good communication, reduces flexibility, and stimulates self-protection rather than concern for the total system.

In recent years the term *organizational development*, or "OD," as it is commonly called, has become the recognized classification for the motivation program used to help an organization reach the healthy climate described by Schein. Blake and Mouton (1967) say that "organizational development deliberately shifts the emphasis away from the organization's structure, from technical skill, from wherewithal and results *per se,* as it diagnoses the organization's ills. Focusing on organization purposes, the human interaction process, and organization culture [climate], it accepts these as the areas in which problems are preventing the fullest possible integration within the organization" (p. 11). French (1969) adds, "Organization Development refers to a long range effort to improve an organization's problem solving capabilities and its ability to cope with changes in its external environment with the help of external or internal behavioral scientist consultants (change agents)" (p. 387).

A successful OD program requires the intervention of skillful change agents. The change agents' purpose is to effect planned change in the total personnel system, both in the present and in the future. The term *OD,* therefore, implies a strategy of normative re-education intended to affect systems of beliefs, values, and attitudes within the organization so that the organization can adapt better to the accelerated rate of change in technology, in the industrial environment, and in the society as a whole. Later stages in the OD process may include formal organizational restructuring, which is frequently initiated, facilitated, and reinforced by the normative and behavioral changes.

Organizational development is based more on history and less on theory than are positive reinforcement and job enrichment. The overall OD approach is an extension of the use of laboratory or sensitivity training methods. Sensitivity or laboratory (T-group) training evolved primarily from the field theory and group dynamics concepts of Lewin (1944, 1951, 1952). In addition, Rogers' (1942) client-centered therapy had a great impact on the change agent's behavior in sensitivity sessions. Rogers emphasized the permissive and supportive, but at the same time nondirective, role of the counselor. In Rogers' therapy, the counselor does not set the goals or the direction of change, but instead provides a method by which the client can set these for himself.

Based on the work of Lewin and Rogers, sensitivity training attempts to make the individual within the group more aware of himself and of his impact on others. The objective of a sensitivity training session is to provide an environment which produces a learning experience for the group. The role of the trainer or change agent is to facilitate the learning process by encouraging the group to set its own directions and goals. Laboratory training as an organized method of bringing about attitudinal and behavioral change within groups began in 1947 at the National Training Laboratory in Bethel, Maine, under the direction of Lewin, Benne, Bradford, and Lippitt. Since the beginning at Bethel, sensitivity training has become *one* of the widely used techniques in formal OD programs.

In 1957, McGregor at Union Carbide and Shepard and Blake at

Esso began to apply laboratory training systematically to the problems facing these organizations. On the basis of his experience in ongoing organizations, McGregor (1960) wrote his exposition of participative theory "Y" approaches to management to replace authoritarian theory "X" approaches. McGregor's development of theory "Y" and Likert's (1961) development of Interaction Influence Theory, both of which call for "supportive relationships" by leaders in industry, have contributed a great deal to the usefulness of laboratory training in organizations. Other theorists who have contributed to the introduction of organizational development as we know it today include Argyris (1962), Bennis (1966), Beckhard (1969), Burke (1971), Blake and Mouton (1967), and Greiner (1967).

Stages in program development

Because OD is an evolving field, it is difficult to describe a "typical" OD program. Strauss (1973) says that "as an evolving field, OD presents a moving target, making it difficult to define or criticize" (p. 2). The general similarities in most approaches to OD have led Strauss (1973) and French (1969) to describe various stages in a "typical" OD program. The reader is reminded, however, that the actual OD program in any given organization may vary from the "typical" program described below.

The *first* stage of the OD program is a diagnostic stage of planned organizational change. This stage involves gathering data about the state of operations in the organization and the state of interpersonal attitudes and behavior. In this stage, sessions of a T-group type may be held in order to develop problem-solving skills, examine interpersonal relations, and examine basic attitudes. These sessions are generally designed to foster team-building or group problem-solving abilities. During this stage the change agent, who has usually interviewed each participant prior to the first session, frequently provides *feedback* to the group in terms of the items or themes which have emerged. One purpose of this stage is to improve the way people work together. The stage involves changing basic attitudes of both supervisors and subordinates and opening up communications channels to allow all employees a larger voice in how they do their jobs.

Many advocates of OD recommend that the first team session be held by the president of the firm and his or her staff, and that later sessions be held with groups throughout the organization. It is generally felt that without top management support an OD program is probably doomed to failure. William Crockett, vice president of Saga Foods, recalls his fears about this first stage: "Do you really want him [the change agent] to dredge into the depths of all our feelings about one another and about you? Isn't it being disloyal for us to tell him our

problems and our feelings? Does it serve any purpose for these problems to be brought in the open and exposed?" (Crockett, 1970, p.
295). The fears expressed by Crockett are not uncommon. Schein (1969)
and others use the term *unfreezing* to describe this stage because
people have a way of becoming "frozen" in their attitudes and in
their relations with other people and are often unaware that they
are seen as obstacles to the solution of operational problems.

The *second* stage of the OD program is an *action* stage of planned
organizational change. After group and intergroup relationships have
been identified and trust and communication have been established
within the organization, the work groups begin to establish ways to
deal with on-the-job structural and human relations programs. This
stage is equivalent to the participative stage of positive reinforcement
and job enrichment programs. The work team may suggest actual
changes in structure and in the monitoring of the task, interdepartmen-
tal communication procedures, or other changes that it deems necessary to solve the problems it identified in the first stage. This second
stage may involve all of the steps comprised in positive reinforcement
and job enrichment programs, including team performance appraisal,
goal setting, task redesign, and self-monitoring. Of course, the team,
group, or department works within the boundaries set up by the organization and must be able to show that its suggested changes will lead
to improvements for both the organization and the individuals
involved.

The *third* and final stage is an extension of the first two stages in
the sense that the teams continue to search for *new problems* and to
offer *new solutions* as such problems arise in the organization. The
third stage is a *proactive* stage, whose purpose is to maintain the healthy
climate established in the first two stages by a continual monitoring
of the system and by continually examining the working relationship
of the teams to the system.

Unlike the positive reinforcement program and the job enrichment
program, the OD program examines attitudes as well as behavior, is
an organization-wide program as well as a department or team program, and is a broad-based program which continues to examine the
organizational climate, the task structure, *and* the reinforcement consequences. Strauss (1973) notes that for OD to have a lasting effect,
the participants must (1) move from confrontation to behavior, (2)
move from training groups to work problems, (3) move from intent
to implementation (including structual change), (4) move from sporadic
action to routinization, and (5) broaden and make permanent the entire
OD effort. The essence of OD, therefore, is the concept of helping
the organization to gain insight into its own processes, to develop its
own diagnostic and coping resources, and to improve its internal rela-

tionships with the help of an outside and/or inside consultant who
acts as a catalyst (Schein, 1970).

Results of OD programs

OD has become a big business. In 1969–70, one firm which special-
izes in OD consulting, Scientific Methods, Inc., numbered among its
clients 45 of the top 100 U.S. corporations, conducted courses on every
continent, and projected profits of $1.1 million (Strauss, 1973). Exam-
ples of companies using OD as a motivation plan include TRW, Polaroid, Union Carbide, Royal Dutch/Shell Group, J. Lynons and Company,
Esso, Weyerhaeuser, U.S. Steel, Corning Glass, Clark Equipment, and
General Motors.

Even though many companies are reportedly using OD programs,
research on the effectiveness of OD efforts is as yet sparse, partly because of the great difficulty in defining criteria for organizational effectiveness (Schein, 1970). Strauss (1973) adds, "In the end, OD is likely
to be evaluated in terms of gut reactions rather than dispassionate
research. After all, OD deals with emotions [attitudes], and it engenders
emotional reactions. For some, it is almost a religion" (p. 42).

Although most of the evidence on the effectiveness of OD is testimonial in nature, there is some evidence that OD has led to greater
worker satisfaction and to higher company profits. Schein (1970) credits
a team-building program in group dynamics and interpersonal relations
for management trainees as resulting in the rejection of a union by
the workers in a large oil refinery. Kaiser Steel credits a team effort
by workers with increasing a plant's productivity by 32 percent and
thereby keeping the plant open after its closing had been scheduled
due to low productivity and financial losses.

Texas Instruments has initiated an OD program which it calls a
People and Asset Effectiveness Program. Mark Shepard, president of
Texas Instruments, said, "We've found that if you get people involved,
they'll set tougher goals for themselves than you would dare do, and
have fun doing it" ("How Texas Instruments Turns Its People On,"
1973, p. 88). After a three-year period, Texas Instruments found that
this program had increased the return on assets per employee from
5.6 percent to 10.1 percent. When asked to what he credited the success of the program, Frederick Ochsner, vice president of personnel
at Texas Instruments, said, "It is a whole bunch of things acting syner-
gistically. It's the attitudes, team improvement programs, the campus
involvement, the open-door management policy, the non-structural
pecking order. It's the unified goal-approach—with everybody looking
at his own piece of that goal. . . . The key is flexibility. Two things
people want in life. They want to achieve and they want to be loved.

And if you provide an atmosphere where these things can occur with a minimum amount of structure in the work flow, you are going to get what you want" ("How Texas Instruments Turns Its People On," 1973, pp. 88, 90).

Saga Foods began an OD program in 1971 and today employs six full-time change agents. Saga stresses team building and has developed an overlapping team approach to management. In 1972, Saga held 225 team-building sessions. Although the costs of the benefits obtained from Saga's OD program are not measurable, W. P. Laughlin, Saga's board chairman, claims that the program's profitability is borne out by increased productivity. Saga claims that as a result of its OD program, the turnover rate among its 23,000 employees has been reduced to 19 percent annually, as compared to 34 percent for the entire food industry.

Donnelly Mirror Company has the longest history of success with an OD program. In the early 1950s Donnelly instituted democratic reforms which sought to humanize assembly line production. Using the Scanlon plan, a type of OD program, Donnelly has been able to show that its "humanistic" approach works. The president of Donnelly says, "We are not talking about a gimmick that someone can install by himself. The company has to change its relationship to its people. The company has to lead, it has to create the climate of trust. This is hard, demanding work that needs the leadership and support of the top people in the company" (Donnelly, 1971, p. 13). Although the Scanlon plan is similar to most other OD programs in that it follows the three stages of a "typical" OD program, it is unique in that the employees share directly in increased profits in the form of a monthly bonus. All employees receive salaries, and the employees collectively set the rates at which they are paid. In return, the employees have the responsibility for implementing productivity increases to support pay raises.

As a result of its unique OD program, Donnelly's productivity gains have resulted in an average salary bonus of 12 percent of wages since the changes were instituted. Wages have risen steadily, while unit productivity costs have fallen, enabling the company to decrease prices, expand sales, and increase profits. Under the program, scrap losses dropped 75 percent and goods returned due to poor workmanship dropped 90 percent (Gooding, 1970).

Although Donnelly Mirror has one of the longest histories with an OD program, the largest OD program is currently being conducted in the General Motors Corporation. Stephen H. Fuller, GM vice president of personnel and development, reports that formal OD functions are now operating in 20 major GM organizations. More than 125 OD change agents are working full time in 55 GM plants in the United States, Canada, and overseas (Fuller, 1973). General Motors' OD program uses an eclectic approach in which each plant program is designed differently, according to the particular needs of the plant. F. J. Schotters, GM director of personnel development, describes the OD program at GM as "a long range, planned program to improve the effectiveness of the *total* organization—whether it be a work group, department, plant or staff. It can involve many types of activities, such as greater involvement and participation by employees with respect to their own jobs and in the particular areas in which they work, better communications, team building and changes in job content, supervisory relationships and organizational structure" (Schotters, 1972d).

A survey conducted by the Institute for Social Research of the University of Michigan "clearly demonstrated to G.M. that the way employees see (and react to) the management climate and organizational structure has a direct, measurable effect on both employee behavior and work performance" (Schotters, 1972b). Landen and Carlson (1973) said, "The survey findings clearly indicated sources of motivational potential needing improvement at each of the plant sites. The long-range program designed to bring about needed changes in the organization is now entering its third year [since 1969]. Results to date have been very encouraging."

One of the reasons that GM felt it had to institute some type of motivational program was a dramatic rise in absenteeism and turnover rates. In 1972 Schotters reported, "Conservative estimates indicated that the current annual cost of absenteeism—considering only fringe benefits—is about $50 million. The cost of turnover involves another estimated $29 million. Thus, these are areas of major concern for every operation in G.M.—not only because of the costs involved but also because these trends indicate a serious deterioration of employee attitudes toward their work" (Schotters, 1972a). To combat the high absenteeism rate, one Oldsmobile engine plant put several foremen and their hourly workers through a group problem-solving (team-building) program. As a result of the program, several suggestions by the group for reducing absenteeism and turnover were accepted by the plant's management. Management credits this program with reducing total absenteeism in the plant by 6 percent during the first five months of 1971 while absenteeism in Oldsmobile's other operations went up by 11 percent. Turnover in the engine plant was down by 38 percent, while turnover in Oldsmobile's other operations was down by only 14 percent. Because of the success of this program, it was decided to extend the project throughout the Oldsmobile Division (Schotters, 1972a).

A full-fledged OD program was begun in 1971 in the Chassis Department of the General Motors Assembly Division (GMAD) at Arlington, Texas. With the help of two change agents, 104 hourly employees and 4 foremen were involved in a program designed to improve communications and attitudes. General Motors reports that this program resulted in a 50 percent decrease in grievances filed per month, improved housekeeping, and a greater willingness of foremen to make decisions on problems as they arose without relying on higher supervision. As a result of the program's success, similar projects were inaugurated at GMAD (Schotters, 1972c).

Space does not allow us to give all the results of the OD program in the 55 GM plants. Landen and Carlson (1973) summarized the status of the OD programs in GM as follows: "One vital point can be concluded from these and a variety of other programs now underway in the corporation: we are probably only beginning to touch the surface of a deep reservoir of untapped human potential among *all* G.M. employees. . . . employee motivation is increasingly regarded as a core issue in the future of General Motors."

Criticisms of OD programs

Of the current motivational programs currently in use by industry, OD is probably the most controversial. Strauss (1973) says:

> For my taste, OD has been plagued by too much evangelical hucksterism. Though considerable thought has been given to professional ethics, there are as yet no generally accepted codes of behavior. OD techniques have been subjected to some scientific research, but it is a bit premature to conclude that OD is truly a scientific method or the "science-based" approach. And it is downright misleading to suggest that OD's utility has been proven scientifically valid. . . . OD is a fad, and American companies are suckers for gimmicks. (p. 14)

Much of the criticism leveled against OD programs centers on the "unfreezing" stage, during which attitudes and interpersonal relationships are examined. Whyte (1972) writes, "Executives say, 'What we must do is change people's attitudes': as politely as I can I tell them to forget attitudes. The problem is to change the conditions to which people are responding. If he does that, people will behave differently, and he will find that attitudes—if they still interest him—will adjust themselves to the new situation" (p. 67). Sorcher and Goldstein (1972) report that "difficulties encountered by those who try to change behavior by first changing attitudes are well known [see Chapter 6]. Moreover, there is no certainty that attitude change will lead to behavior change on the part of managers or supervisors, since other attitudes may intrude and prevent behavior change" (p. 36).

Such criticisms of the attitude change process center on three issues. First, many psychologists believe that attitudes do not cause behavior, but rather that behavioral experiences lead to the formation of attitudes. Second, many critics feel that changing attitudes in a group setting may do more harm than good because the rewards of the organization will not reinforce the changed attitudes. Third, many writers contend that many change agents and consultants are poorly trained, and that having such people conduct team-building sessions may do more harm than good.

Maslow described his experiences in trying to apply theory Y management for Non-Linear Systems of Del-Mar, California, and concluded that "the demands of theory Y were far higher than I had recognized and many involve 'inhumanity' to the weak, the vulnerable and the damaged who are unable to take on responsibility and self-discipline" (quoted in Drucker, 1973, p. 87). Not only are some employees unable to cope with the OD process, but many managers are not willing to accept a different style of management. Andrew Kay, president of Non-Linear Systems, Inc., said that OD programs work fine during good times and periods of economic gains. In fact, from 1960–65 production rose 30 percent and customer complaints dropped 70 percent under the OD program set up by Maslow. But when the aerospace industry fell apart in 1970, Kay said he had lost touch with his company and the company was not ready to respond to the changing environment. Vice President Coombe agreed. "So much emphasis was put on the results of sensitivity sessions—and the long run planning was not carried on in a businesslike manner" ("Where Being Nice to Workers Didn't Work," 1972, p. 68). Kay claimed that he got back on solid financial grounds by returning to a more autocratic leadership style.

Hampton, Summer, and Webber (1973) summarize the stage of development of OD by saying that until the advent of OD nobody made participative management and structural job enlargement operational. They also warn:

> But OD has its limitations; analysis, clarity, reality, openness, and facing up to the truth may be an alternative to closed-system stereotypical thinking, but there is no guarantee that it will work in all organizations. The viewpoint which the modern manager must take, therefore, is that this method of management has both powerful benefits and powerful limitations. The key is to try to understand when and under what circumstances such a technique will succeed. (p. 870)

FLEXITIME—ESCAPE OR MOTIVATION?

An alternative means of coping with worker discontent has recently been introduced in many firms throughout the world. This program, called *flexitime,* is designed to allow the employee more latitude and freedom in setting up his or her work schedule. This motivation plan originated in West Germany in the late 1960s. The program allows workers, either as individuals or teams, to establish their own starting times, within limits set by the company (for example, between 7:30 and 9:30 A.M.). The employee must complete 8 hours of work before leaving. In some companies, the employees can build up time during the week by reducing their lunch hours and breaks and can use the time either to leave early on Friday afternoon (for example, at 3:00 P.M.) or else to leave earlier in the day (for example, at the end of 7½ *work* hours if the lunch hour is reduced by 30 minutes). The extent of flexibility is related to the degree of interdependence among jobs.

A program similar to flexitime is the four-day week. Under this program, each employee has to work 40 hours a week, but has a three-day weekend rather than the traditional two.

As noted earlier, positive reinforcement, job enrichment, and organization development programs are *proactive* because they seek to examine the causes of worker discontent and to solve the problems by making the workplace more stimulating and exciting. The flexitime and four-day week programs have been criticized by some as being *reactive* programs which ignore the real problems of worker discontent. These critics claim that rather than facing up to the fact that high turnover and absenteeism are symptoms of basic problems, such as boring tasks or an unhealthy climate, flexitime concedes to workers' discontent by giving them more time away from the workplace. Herzberg (1968) says, "This represents a marvelous way of motivating people to work— getting them off the job! We have reduced (formally and informally) the time spent on a job over the last 50 or 60 years until we are finally on the way to the '6½-day weekend.' . . . The fact is that motivated people seek more hours of work, not fewer" (p. 67). Ford (1973), though not as critical as Herzberg, agrees: "The growing pressure for a four-day workweek is not necessarily evidence that people do not care about their work: they may be rejecting their work in the form that confronts them" (p. 96).

Counterarguments against the critics could be made by saying that the flexitime and four-day week programs are really considering the "total man" by allowing him the freedom to schedule, within reason, his work time to better meet his personal and family needs. Kahn (1973) says that allowing people freedom in choosing the hours they work and allowing them freedom to bid for the task they wish to perform are natural ways to recognize their individuality. It should also be noted that as currently designed, the programs do not call for a reduction in hours, but only for their rearrangement. However, the critics feel that this may only be a first step in an effort by unions to reduce the number of hours and even the number of years an employee would have to work before being allowed to retire from the organization.

Regardless of these arguments, many companies are finding a flexitime program beneficial. Moles (1973) reported that 5,000 companies and 2.5 million workers worldwide were currently on the flexitime plan. In the United States, 100,000 workers are currently on this plan in such companies as Sun Oil, National Bank, the city government of Baltimore, the city government of Washington, D.C., Hewlett-Packard, Samsonite, Nestle's, and Scott Paper Company. Werther (1973) reviewed these programs and reported that the companies which used them found that <u>tardiness decreased, absenteeism due to medical appointments or family commitments was reduced,</u> and <u>better use of parking facilities, cafeterias, and locker rooms was possible.</u> Werther also noted, however, that more time had to be spent on scheduling and that flexitime wouldn't work on shift and assembly line operations because of the interdependence of the workers. Sandoz-Wander of East Hanover, New Jersey, implemented a flexitime program for a six-month trial period. After the trial period, 88 percent of the supervisory personnel voted to adopt the system permanently, citing better worker morale and increased productivity as the reasons (Cray, 1973). The flexitime program adopted by Hewlett-Packard of Palo Alto, California, did not increase productivity, but it did lead to a significant reduction in absenteeism and turnover ("How Industry Is Dealing with People Problems," 1973).

Although the evidence on flexitime (like the evidence on all the programs described in Chapters 11 and 12) still lacks empirical validity,[2] it appears that flexible working hours may become the way of the future for many workers. The United Auto Workers, for example, is fast making the 32-hour workweek a reality. Before the program can claim to be a successful method of reducing worker discontent, much more objective research is needed.

SUMMARY: MOTIVATION PROGRAMS IN THE FUTURE

The four programs described in Chapters 11 and 12 (positive reinforcement—money and feedback; task design; organizational development; and flexitime) represent the most current programs designed to reduce worker discontent and increase productivity. Many writers believe that we have only begun to "scratch the surface" and call for more innovative steps.

Porter (1973) sees the way of the future as more effective positive reinforcement programs. He states:

> Whatever new systems are adopted by organizations, there is sure to be one prominent feature of the work environment in [the year] 2001: work and fun will be combined on the job. . . . The merger of work and enjoyment will not, however, occur at the expense of organizational performance; through the effective restructuring of the reward environment, high levels of organizational performance can become the means for direct, personal

---

[2] See Riva Poor, *4 Days, 40 Hours: Reporting a Revolution in Work and Leisure,* rev. ed. (Cambridge, Mass.: Bursk and Poor, 1973), for the latest information on changing work hours in the United States and abroad.

gratification. Employees of progressive organizations of the future will be eager to perform. (p. 131)

Porter believes that in the future the following types of rewards will be used in addition to pay in order to gain commitment to the organization and/or as compensation for superior performance: (1) opportunity to schedule one's own working hours, (2) a redistribution of job duties, (3) opportunity to create new jobs, (4) opportunity to participate in bonus drawings, (5) opportunity to work in any area of the organization for a limited period of time, (6) on-the-job nonwork activities, (7) participation in new organizational ventures, (8) accrual of time off for sabbatical or educational leave, and (9) participation in intercompany exchanges of employees (p. 127).

Rewards

Lawler (1973a) views the programs being implemented in industry today as a step in the right direction in the fight to humanize work. He fears however, that most of these programs will fail unless the worker's individuality is considered in the design of motivational programs. Lawler states:

> When I look at the psychological research on people, I see convincing evidence that individuals differ significantly in their needs, skills and abilities. This is not to say that individuals aren't similar in many ways, for they are; but to be human is to be unique. To be humanized, an organization must recognize the uniqueness and sovereignty of each human being. In practical terms, this means that organizations and jobs must be designed in ways that are responsive to the differences which exist among people. Approaches to organization design and management which recommend standardized jobs, authoritarian management, and piece-rate incentive plans for all don't do this, and neither do approaches which recommend enriched jobs, democratic management and MBO plans for all. Therefore, neither of these approaches has produced or is likely to produce a humanized organization (1973, p. 2).

Lawler contends that the place to start in individualizing the work available to people is the selection and placement process. During the job interview, the applicant should be given information about the environment which exists and about the available jobs for which he is qualified. The interview should include more of a counseling atmosphere in order to allow the applicant to make self-selection decisions. Weitz (1965) and Wanous (1975) report evidence showing that job applicants make better choices if they are given valid information about the job. In building a selection model, the personnel manager should consider such items as motivation, reactions to different leadership styles, and preferred organizational climate, and should use such data to place employees where they will have the greatest chance of success.

Texas Instruments is currently experimenting with this approach of placing people in the department and under the leadership style most appropriate to their personality makeup. Charles L. Hughes, director of personnel and organization development at Texas Instruments, says, "Companies must develop existentially managed organizations that truly accept and respect people with differing values" ("How Texas Instruments Turns Its People On," 1973). As a first step, Hughes classified 600 employees into six work-personality categories according to the way they perceived the world: (1) tribalistic—workers who respond to strong leadership and who are happy and dedicated when shown genuine care and concern; (2) existential—employees willing to do a job only if it is meaningful; (3) egocentric—entrepreneurial workers; (4) conformist—traditional workers; (5) manipulative—achievement-oriented workers; and (6) sociocentric—socially oriented employees. Hughes hopes that this research will influence Texas Instruments' selection and placement procedures, producing a more flexible organization. In the future, for example, Hughes would like to see an existential worker given an existential supervisor.

In order to overcome the deficiencies of the current motivation program and make the workplace more adaptive to individuality, and thereby to increase the productivity of the labor force, Jackson Grayson, former dean of the Graduate School of Business at Southern Methodist University, recommends the creation of an American Productivity Institute. Grayson says:

> The current exploding attention to human factors in the work place is a relatively new Western phenomenon. I believe it will have as profound an impact on our ways of performing and regarding work and increasing productivity as the phenomenon of capital investment did during the Industrial Revolution. So far, though, it has emerged more extensively abroad than in the U.S. It manifests itself in the groups called Quality Control Circles in Japan, and at Olivetti in Italy, Norsk-Hydro in Norway, ICI in Britain, and in the U.S. in companies such as AT&T, Procter and Gamble, Corning Glass, and Texas Instruments ("How to Make Productivity Grow Faster," 1973, p. 16).

Through this private institute, Grayson hopes that sociologists, psychologists, labor relations experts, industrial relations officers, union leaders, plant managers, and others could be brought together to share ideas on ways to solve worker discontent and make the future of worker motivational programs more successful and rewarding for all.

It appears that the organization of the future will truly be a more enjoyable and exciting place. What is needed now is more sharing of information and ideas by advocates of various programs and by organizations themselves. In this way, methods of increasing productivity and decreasing worker discontent can be speeded up and we can move into the 21st century with a renewed pride in our jobs and in the quality of our work life.

CONCEPTS TO REMEMBER

job enrichment   sensitivity training
activation theory   unfreezing
organization climate   flexitime
organizational development   individualizing work

QUESTIONS FOR DISCUSSION

1. What does "activation theory" have to do with job design? Can jobs be designed so that employees are "overactivated" and their performance is lower than that of less activated employees?

2. What implications do each of the four motivation programs discussed in Chapters 11 and 12 have for personnel selection and placement?

3. In the October 24, 1976, issue of the *New York Times*, in an article entitled "Ways to Improve Job Conditions" (outlined by a corporate psychologist), it was noted, "We have smarter people doing dumber things. Those 'things' can be more readily identified as idiot work. . . . Those jobs do not challenge and motivate people to perform at the levels they are capable of achieving." Several suggestions for overcoming this problem were made by the corporate psychologist. One suggestion was to develop job procedures that give people a complete unit of work to do, make them responsible for the quality of the product or service performed, and provide them with as much autonomy in their jobs as possible. Another psychologist suggested that workers should be able to participate in the operation of the plant and in the distribution of a monthly bonus. It seems that each psychologist is suggesting a different approach to solving the same problem. Is it possible that both approaches are valid for this situation? Why or why not? Also, does a motivation program work because the manager implementing the program is concerned and progressive or because the program itself is innovative and progressive? In other words, how do you separate out the charisma and style of the leader from the effect of the program?

4. In the very near future, Ford Motor Company, along with most other manufacturing organizations, will be on a 32-hour, four-day workweek. In a recent article in the *Boston Herald American*, it was noted, "Management in most industries regards the renewed drive for an abbreviated work week as a cancerous growth in the vitals of the American economy, a trend that will slow down industrial productivity and give workers more pay for less work—the very thing that brought Britain to virtual bankruptcy, forced her out of the world marketplace, gave her the highest rate of inflation

in Europe, and reduced the standard of living for all her citizens. British workers have a productivity rate of only 52 percent of that for comparable American workers." As you can imagine, union economists and others refute this argument. What are the advantages and disadvantages to the total economy and to specific organizations of a shorter workweek in 1980? How do you think a shorter workweek will change work? Does productivity in terms of manufactured goods require longer workweeks? What will be the advantages and the disadvantages of a shorter workweek for the individual employee?

5. It seems that Burger King and McDonald's use worker motivation programs successfully. Since the product is the same, why have these two organizations chosen different methods of structuring the environment and the task? Visit both of these establishments, and compare and contrast the work environment and the task environment as well as the behavior modification attempted through advertising to the general public. From the point of view of a child and of an adult, evaluate the effectiveness of each establishment. From the point of view of an owner and of an employee, make the same evaluation. Perhaps you will have to refer to financial data on these corporations for the owner comparison. Given the nature of the job, how is it that both of these companies seem to have a highly motivated work force?

REFERENCES

Abel, I. W.   Advertisement. *Sports Illustrated*, October 22, 1973, p. 17.

Argyris, C.   *Personality and organization.* New York: Harper, 1957.

Argyris, C.   *Interpersonal competence and organizational effectiveness.* Homewood, Ill.: Dorsey Press, 1962.

Baxter, J. D.   Whatever happened to job enrichment? *Iron Age,* November 8, 1973, pp. 35–36.

Beckhard, R.   *Organizational development: Strategies and models.* Reading, Mass.: Addison-Wesley, 1969.

Bem, D. J.   *An experimental analysis of beliefs and attitudes.* Unpublished doctoral dissertation, University of Michigan, 1964.

Bennis, W. G.   *Changing organizations.* New York: McGraw-Hill, 1966.

Bennis, W. G.   *Organizational development: Its nature, origins, and prospects.* Reading, Mass.: Addison-Wesley, 1969.

Blake, R. R., & Mouton, J. S.   Grid organization development. *Personnel Administration,* January–February 1967, 18–24.

Bradford, L. P., Gibb, J. R. & Benne, K. D.   *T-group theory and laboratory method.* New York: Wiley, 1964.

Burke, W. W.   Management and organizational development: What is the target of the change? *Personnel Administration,* 1971, *34,* 44–56.

Campbell, J. P., & Dunnette, M. D.   Effectiveness of T-group exercises in managerial training and development. *Psychological Bulletin*, 1968, *70*, 73–104.

Carroll, S. J. & Tosi, H. L.   *Management by objectives.* New York: Macmillan, 1973.

Case of Big Mac's pay plans. *Harvard Business Review*, July–August 1974, pp. 118–127.

Conart, E. H. & Kilbridge, M.   An interdisciplinary analysis of job enrichment. *Industrial and Labor Relations Review*, April 1965, pp. 377–395.

Conversation with B. F. Skinner. *Organization Dynamics.* Winter 1973, pp. 31–40. (a)

Cray, D. W.   Coming to work whenever you want. *New York Times*, February 4, 1973, p. 1.

Crockett, W. J.   Team building—One approach to organizational development. *Journal of Applied Behavioral Science*, 1970, *6*, 291–306.

Donnelly, J. F.   Increasing productivity by involving people in their total jobs. *Personnel Administration*, September–October 1971, pp. 8–13.

Drucker, P. F.   Beyond the stick and carrot: Hysteria over the work ethic, *Psychology Today*, November 1973, pp. 87; 89–93.

Emery, J. C.   How to double your sales and profits every 5 years. Speech before the Sales Executive Club of New York, 1973.

At Emery Air Freight: Positive reinforcement boosts performance, *Organizational Dynamics*, Winter 1973, pp. 41–50. (b)

Ford, R.   *Motivation through the work itself.* New York: American Management Association, 1969.

Ford, R.   Job enrichment lessons at AT&T. *Harvard Business Review*, *73*, 1973, 96–106.

Forehand, G. A.   On the interactions of persons and organizations. In R. Tagiuri & G. H. Litwin (Eds.), *Organizational climate.* Cambridge, Mass.: Harvard University, Division of Research, 1968.

French, W.   Organizational development objectives: Assumptions and strategies. *California Management Review*, 1969, *12*, 23–34.

Frost, C. F.   A change agent's view of the Scanlon Plan. Paper presented at the meeting of the American Psychological Association, Montreal, August 1973.

Fuller, S. H.   Employee development. Speech before the National Alliance of Businessmen, Detroit, September 24, 1973.

Gamboa, V. U., & Pedalino, E.   Behavior modification and absenteeism: Intervention in one industrial setting. Working paper, University of Michigan, 1973.

Gibson, J. L., Ivancevich, J. M., & Donnelly, J. H.   *Organizations: Structures, processes, and behavior.* Dallas: Business Publications, 1973.

Gooding, J.   It pays to wake up the blue-collar worker. *Fortune*, September 1970, 21–26.

Greiner, L. E.   Patterns of organization change. *Harvard Business Review*, 1967, *45*, 119–130.

Hamner, W. C. Reinforcement theory and contingency management. In H. L. Tosi and W. C. Hamner (Eds.), *Organizational behavior and management: A contingency approach.* Chicago: St. Clair Press, 1974.

Hamner, W. C., & Hamner, E. P. Behavior modification on the bottom line. *Organizational Dynamics,* Spring 1976, pp. 2–21.

Hampton, D. R., Summer, C. E., & Webber, R. A. *Organizational behavior and the practice of management.* Glenview, Ill.: Scott, Foresman, 1973.

Herrick, N. Q. The other side of the coin. Paper delivered at the 20th Anniversary Invitational Seminar of the Profit Sharing Research Foundation, Evanston, Ill., November 17, 1971.

Herzberg, F. One more time: How do you motivate employees? *Harvard Business Review,* 1968, *46,* 53–62.

House, R. J. T-group education and leadership effectiveness: A review of the empirical literature and a critical evaluation. *Personnel Psychology,* 1967, *20,* 1–32.

How industry is dealing with people problems on the line. *American Machinist,* November 12, 1973, pp. 79–91.

How Texas Instruments turns its people on. *Business Week,* September 29, 1973, pp. 88; 90.

How to make productivity grow faster. *Business Week,* July 14, 1973, pp. 15–16.

Hulin, C. L. Individual differences and job enrichment—The case against general treatments. In J. Maher (Ed.), *New perspectives in job enrichment.* Berkeley: Van Nostrand Reinhold, 1971.

Hulin, C. L., & Blood, M. R. Job enlargement, individual differences, and worker responses. *Psychological Bulletin,* January 1968, pp. 41–55.

The "humanistic" way of managing people. *Business Week,* July 22, 1972, pp. 48–49.

Hunt, J. G., & Hill, J. W. The new look in motivation theory in organizational research. *Human Organizations,* Summer 1969, pp. 100–109.

Jacobs, C. D. Job enrichment at Xerox Corporation. Paper presented at the International Conference on the Quality of Work Life, September 24–29, 1972, Arden House, New York.

Janson, R. Job enrichment: Challenge of the 70's. *Training and Development Journal,* June 1970, pp. 7–9.

Kahn, R. L. The work module—A tonic for lunchpail lassitude. *Psychology Today,* 1973, *6,* 35–39; 94–95.

Kolb, D. A., Rubin, I. M., & McIntyre, J. M. *Organizational psychology: An experimental approach.* Englewood Cliffs, N.J.: Prentice-Hall, 1971.

Korman, A. K. *Industrial and organizational psychology.* Englewood Cliffs, N.J.: Prentice-Hall, 1971.

Kornhauser, A. W. *Mental health of the industrial worker: A Detroit study.* New York: Wiley, 1965.

Landen, D. L., & Carlson, H. C. Employee motivation: A vast domain of unrealized human and business potential. Chapter to be included in A. J. Marrow, (Ed.), *American Management Association,* 1973, 48–59.

Lawler, E. E.   Job design and employee motivation. *Personnel Psychology,* 1969, *22,* 426–435.

Lawler, E. E.   *Pay and organizational effectiveness.* New York: McGraw-Hill, 1971.

Lawler, E. E.   Individualizing organizations: A needed emphasis in organizational psychology. Paper presented at the American Psychological Association Convention, Montreal, August 1973. (a)

Lawler, E. E.   What do employees *really* want? Paper presented at the American Psychological Association Convention, Montreal, August 1973. (b)

Leavitt, H. J.   Applied organizational change in industry. In J. G. March (Ed.), *Handbook of organizations.* Chicago: Rand McNally, 1965.

Levitan, S. A., & Johnston, W. B.   Job redesign, enrichment—Exploring the limitations. *Monthly Labor Review,* July 1973, pp. 35–41. (a)

Levitan, S. A., & Johnston, W. B.   Changes in work: More evolution than revolution. *Manpower,* September 1973, pp. 3–7. (b)

Levitan, S. A., & Johnston, W. B.   *Work is here to stay, alas.* Olympus, 1973. (c)

Lewin, K.   Constructs in psychology and psychological ecology. *University of Iowa Studies in Child Welfare,* 1944, *20,* 1–29.

Lewin, K.   *Field theory in social science.* New York: Harper, 1951.

Lewin, K.   Group decision and social change. In G. E. Swanson, T. M. Newcomb, & E. L. Hartley (Eds.), *Readings in social psychology.* New York: Holt, 1952.

Likert, R.   *New patterns of management.* New York: McGraw-Hill, 1961.

Little, A., & Warr, P.   Who's afraid of job enrichment? *Personnel Management,* February 1971, pp. 34–37.

Litwin, G. H., & Stringer, R. A.   Motivation and organizational climate. In Hampton, Summer, & Webber, *Organizational behavior and the practice of management.*

Luthans, F.   *Organizational behavior.* New York: McGraw-Hill, 1973.

Luthans, F., & White, D. O.   Behavior modification: Application to manpower management. *Personnel Administrator,* July–August 1971, pp. 41–47.

McGregor, D.   *The human side of enterprise.* New York: McGraw-Hill, 1960.

Meyer, H. H.   The pay for performance dilemma. *Organizational Dynamics,* Spring 1975, pp. 1–18.

Moles, L.   Workers decide own hours. *State Journal,* Lansing, Mich., September 23, 1973, p. 10.

Motorola creates a more demanding job. *Business Week,* September 4, 1971, p. 32.

Myers, M. S.   Overcoming union opposition to job enrichment. *Harvard Business Review,* May 1971, 68–74.

New tool: Reinforcement for good work. *Business Week,* December 18, 1971, pp. 68–69.

A new way to work. *Detroit Free Press,* October 29, 1973, Section B, pp. 10–11.

Nord, W. R. Beyond the teaching machine: The neglected area of operant conditioning in the theory and practice of management. *Organizational Behavior and Human Performance*, 1969, *5*, 375–401.

Porter, L. W. Perceived need satisfactions. *Journal of Applied Psychology.* 1961, *45*, 27–31.

Porter, L. W. Turning work into nonwork: The rewarding environment. In M. D. Dunnette (Ed.), *Work and nonwork in the year 2001.* Copyright © 1973 by Wadsworth Publishing Company, Inc. Reprinted by permission of the publisher, Brooks/Cole Publishing Company, Monterey, California.

The power of praise. *International Management,* October 1973, pp. 32–35.

Reif, W. E., & Luthans, F. Does job enrichment really pay off? *California Management Review,* Fall 1972, pp. 34–35.

Reif, W. E., & Schoderbek, P. Job enlargement: Antidote to apathy. *Management of Personnel Quarterly,* Spring 1966, pp. 16–23.

Rickleffs, R. The quality of work. *Wall Street Journal,* August 21, 1972, p. 1.

Rogers, C. R. *Counseling and psychotheraphy.* Boston: Houghton Mifflin, 1942.

Schein, E. H. *Process consultation: Its role in organizational development.* Reading, Mass.: Addison-Wesley, 1969.

Schein, E. H. *Organizational psychology* (2d ed.). Englewood Cliffs, N.J.: Prentice-Hall, 1970.

Schotters, F. J. Oldsmobile action program on absenteeism and turnover. *G.M. Personnel Development Bulletin,* No. 2, Feb. 3, 1972. (a)

Schotters, F. J. New tool to measure organizational effectiveness. *G.M. Personnel Development Bulletin,* No. 5, May 1, 1972. (b)

Schotters, F. J. Organizational development at GMAD-Arlington. *G.M. Personnel Development Bulletin,* No. 6, May 17, 1972. (c)

Schotters, F. J. What is 'organizational development'? Does it work? *G.M. Personnel Development Bulletin,* No. 9, August 17, 1972. (d)

Schotters, F. J. GMAD Fremont's absenteeism and discipline programs. *G.M. Personnel Development Bulletin,* No. 18, April 2, 1973. (a)

Schotters, F. J. Job enrichment at Buick Products Engineering. *G.M. Personnel Development Bulletin,* No. 22, June 4, 1973. (b)

Scott, W. E. Activation theory and task design. *Organizational Behavior and Human Performance,* 1966, *1*, 3–30.

Skinner, B. F. *Science and human behavior.* New York: Macmillan, 1953.

Skinner, B. F. *Contingencies of reinforcement.* New York: Appleton-Century-Crofts, 1971.

Sorcher, M., & Goldstein, A. P. A behavioral modeling approach in training. *Personnel Administration,* March–April 1972, pp. 35–41.

Stewart, P. A. *Job enrichment: In the shop, in the management function.* Center for Labor and Management, Iowa City: University of Iowa, 1967.

Strauss, G. Organizational development: Credits and debits. *Organizational Dynamics,* Winter 1973, pp. 2–18.

Thorndike, F. L. *Animal intelligence.* New York: Macmillan, 1911.

Wanous, J. P.   Effect of a realistic job preview on job acceptance, job survival, and job attitudes. *Journal of Applied Psychology*, 1975, *60*, 29–31.

Warren, M. W.   Performance management: A substitute for supervision. *Management Review*, October 1972, pp. 28–42.

Weitz, J.   Job expectancy and survival. *Journal of Applied Psychology*, 1965, *41*, 245–247.

Werther, W. B.   The good news and bad news of flexible hours. *Administrative Management*, November 1973, pp. 78–79; 96.

Where being nice to workers didn't work. *Business Week*, September 2, 1972, p. 81.

Where Skinner's theories work. *Business Week*, December 2, 1972, pp. 64–65.

Whyte, W. F.   Skinnerian theory in organizations. *Psychology Today*, April 1972, pp. 67–68; 96; 98; 100.

Winn, A.   The laboratory approach to organizational development. Paper read at the Annual Conference, British Psychological Society, Oxford, September 1968.

Workers get a voice in Chrysler operations. *Detroit Free Press*, July 25, 1971, p. 10.

Work in America. Report of a Special Task Force to the Secretary of Health, Education, and Welfare. Cambridge, Mass.: MIT Press, 1973.

13

Introduction to group behavior

Why and how do individuals become integrated into psychological groups?

What are the antecedents and the consequences of group cohesiveness?

How do groups differ in structure, and what are the effects of such differences?

In the previous chapters, a great deal of attention has been given to the individual within the organization. As you may recall, we often referred to the importance of the co-worker's and the supervisor's influence on the individual's performance or satisfaction level. That is, we know that the other people with whom a person interacts can greatly affect how that person thinks, feels, and acts. In this chapter we will examine individual-group relationships in organizations in order to better understand the importance of the group's impact on the individual's contribution to the organization.

GROUP MEMBERSHIP

Under the assumption that people join groups voluntarily, we need to ask, Why do people join groups? Of course, there are some task activities (for example, assembly line production) that can only be accomplished by groups. However, we often form groups when the task does not dictate group performance (for example, a study group or a travel group). A number of social and organizational psychologists have proposed theories of *interpersonal attraction* to explain the attractiveness or lack of attractiveness of others with whom we interact.

Thibaut and Kelley (1959) proposed the *exchange theory of attraction.* This theory explains group interaction in terms of the rewards and costs incurred by the participants in the interaction. A reward is any satisfaction or need reduction gained from the relationship. Costs include the punishments resulting from the relationship, such as fatigue, boredom, anxiety and fear of embarrassment. Homans (1961) notes that "a man in an exchange relation with another will expect that . . . the net rewards, or profits, of each man be proportional to his investments—the greater the investment, the greater the profit" (p. 75).

According to this theory, there are two standards against which each party to the exchange evaluates his or her reward-cost outcomes. The *comparison level* is an average value derived from a person's past experiences and from the person's knowledge of comparable relationships. For example, a worker who has received praise for a given level of performance from the previous supervisor expects similar treatment from the new supervisor. The second standard which is used to evaluate a relationship is the *comparison level of alternatives,* based on the costs and rewards available in alternative relationships. In the above example, a worker who was nearing retirement and had no acceptable employment opportunities would accept the new supervisor, even if the supervisor were a tyrant compared to the last supervisor. Clearly, this theory assumes that the individual establishes and maintains an interpersonal relationship because of the comparative rewards that accrue from it.

Newcomb (1961) proposed a similar theory of attractiveness. Drawing on the aphorism "Birds of a feather flock together," Newcomb predicts that people with similar *attitudes* become attracted to one another. He postulates a "strain toward symmetry" in interpersonal relationships; individuals who have similar attitudes toward important issues are attracted to one another. This is illustrated by two studies conducted by Newcomb. In the first of these (1943), the effects of three years' attendence at Bennington College (a liberal arts college) were studied. The students whose values became more liberal, in accordance with the dominant campus climate, identified with others who were liberal. The students who did not depart from their initial conservative attitudes identified more closely with their predominantly conservative families.

Newcomb's later study (1961) examined the "acquaintance process" in a group of 17 students at the University of Michigan. These 17 students, who were initially strangers to one another, shared common living quarters for several months. Newcomb found that perceived similarity of attitudes was the most significant determinant of interpersonal attraction.

Winch (1958) argues that attraction is explained by the *principle of complementarity* rather than by the principle of similarity. Under this theory, the adage "Opposites attract" refers to the fact that people with complementary needs and/or abilities are attracted to one another. This theory is really in harmony with the exchange theory offered by Newcomb. That is to say, social psychologists predict that people who have similar attitudes, complementary needs, and complementary abilities are more likely to find one another mutually rewarding than are people who do not possess these characteristics. Thus, when people join groups voluntarily, it is predicted that they find the characteristics of the people in the group rewarding.

Festinger's (1954) *social comparison* theory argues that membership in a group is necessary because we all have a drive for self-evaluation, which is the need "to know that one's opinions are correct and to know precisely what one is and is not capable of doing" (p. 217). The individual in the group "tests" himself against other members—a check which allows him to determine whether or not his opinions, ideas, and judgments correspond to social reality.

WHAT IS A GROUP?

From the above discussion on group membership, it may seem that all interaction with other people represents group behavior. However, it is useful to delimit somewhat our conception of a psychological group. When you ride on a bus, go to the movies, buy groceries, and so forth, you are probably not engaging in *psychological* group behavior as we conceive it. As Schein (1970) says, *"A psychological group is any number of people who (1) interact with one another, (2) are psychologically aware of one another, and (3) perceive themselves to be a group."* (p. 69) We would add a fourth criterion: *(4) A psychological group works toward a common goal.* The key words in the above definition are *interaction, awareness,* and *goal accomplishment.*

Collective action can involve as few as two people. As Steiner (1972) notes, in some respects everyone on earth is dependent upon everyone else, though such interdependencies often go unrecognized. Within a society, for example, people rely upon one another for military security, protection from disease, and economic stability. However, awareness of such mutual relationships is likely to be intense only when wars, epidemics, or depressions are a possibility. On other occasions, the behavior of members of groups may be so effectively guided by norms and role systems that people scarcely realize that they are participating in a nationwide network of cooperative activity. Examples of nationwide groups of which we are probably aware include political groups, church memberships, business organizations, and social fraternities. Such awareness forces us to recognize the need to find a collective solution (for example, electing a particular person president) to the group's problems. We are probably more aware and more active in smaller units, such as families, work groups, and friendship cliques, in which people generally employ face-to-face communication to coordinate their individual efforts. We refer to the larger groups as *secondary* groups and to the smaller groups or subgroups as *primary* groups.

In the work organization there are two types of primary groups with which most of us will identify. First, there are *formal* groups—that is, the groups to which a member is assigned as a part of his or her work role. Second, there are *informal* groups—that is, friendship groups, which develop on the basis of mutual attraction; or task groups, which develop in order to reach a mutually set goal. It is important that a manager understand the psychology of the behavior in both types of groups, since both types have the power to affect whether or not organizational goals are accomplished.

The importance of the impact of informal groups on work behavior can be seen in Roy's (1961) descriptive studies of the culture and interaction patterns of work groups. In one of his studies, "Banana Time," Roy describes a small group of men engaged in exceedingly simple manual work operating a punch press. The entire task could be learned in about 15 minutes. While working in this small group, he noticed that several of the men had formed an informal group in order to reduce the boredom of the task. The men engaged in bantering and "kidding," which Roy described as follows:

> What I saw at first, before I began to observe, was occasional flurries of horseplay so simple and unvarying in pattern and so childish in quality

that they made no strong bid for attention. For example, Ike would regularly switch off the power at Sammy's machine whenever Sammy made a trip to the lavatory or the drinking fountain. Sammy invariably fell victim to the plot by making an attempt to operate his clicking hammer after returning to the shop. And, as the simple pattern went, this blind stumbling into the trap was always followed by indignation and reproach from Sammy, smirking satisfaction from Ike, and mild paternal scolding from George. My interest in this procedure was at first confined to wondering when Ike would weary of his tedious joke or when Sammy would learn to check his power switch before trying the hammer.

But, as I began to pay closer attention, as I began to develop familiarity with the communication system, the disconnected became connected, the nonsense made sense, the obscure became clear, and the silly actually funny. And as the content of the interaction took on more and more meaning, the interaction began to reveal structure. (p. 161)

Group formation does not stop with the affiliation of members. Instead, groups develop over a moderately long period of time and probably never reach a completely stable structure. Tuckman (1965) identified four stages of group development. In the realm of group structure, the first stage is that of *testing and dependence* ("*forming*"). The term *testing* refers to an attempt by group members to discover from the reactions of other group members what interpersonal behaviors are acceptable in the group. Coincident with testing in the interpersonal realm is the establishment of dependence relationships with supervisors, other group members, and group rules and regulations. In other words, this is a period of establishing the "ground rules" both for task requirements (How much am I expected to do? Which rules are not enforced?) and for interpersonal relationships (Who has the "real" power? What are the informal norms?).

The second stage in the development of group structure is labeled *intergroup conflict* ("*storming*"). Group members become hostile toward one another and/or toward the leader as a means of expressing their individuality and of resisting the formation of a group structure. During this stage, goals set by the leader may be ignored and resistance to task requirements is common.

The third stage described by Tuckman is a stage in which in-group feelings and cohesiveness develop, new standards evolve, and new roles are adopted. In the task realm, intimate, personal opinions are expressed. This stage is commonly referred to as the "*norming*" stage of group development.

Finally, the group attains the fourth and final stage, in which interpersonal structure becomes the tool of task activities. Roles become flexible and functional, and group energy is channeled into the task. Structural issues have been resolved, and structure can now become supportive of task performance. This stage is labeled the "*performing*" stage of group development. The sequence of group development can be seen in Figure 13–1.

According to this model of group development, then, groups can be in any one of these four stages of development at any time. The farther away from the performing stage, however, the longer it takes to become an effective work unit. Those of you who follow professional sports can see your favorite teams go through these four phases each season. First, new players are selected and old favorites are cut or traded. Then personality power plays and position power plays (for example, starting position versus reserve position) occur. Then with each new season a fresh testing of the rules (for example, the rules governing dress, outside interests, and curfews) generally takes place. It is hoped that these first three stages will end prior to the start of the official season. If not, we generally find that the collective performance of the group is lower than expected. For example, Kent Benson, a member of the 1976 Indiana University basketball team, which won

Figure 13–1
Stages of group development

the NCAA championship, was quoted as saying: "This team is neat because other teams can't concentrate on one individual star. They've got to respect all of us. As long as you play your potential, and everyone else plays to his potential, there's no way they're going to stop the whole team by stopping one guy" ("Bob Knight," 1976, p. 26).

PROPERTIES OF GROUPS

Regardless of the performance effectiveness of previous groups, each group generally has a unique "personality." This is due in part to the uniqueness of each member of the group, but it is also due in part to the structure of the group on a number of dimensions. When individuals join together for the first time and interact with one another, differences will develop among the members of the new group. Some persons exert more influence than others. Some have more prestige, some more influence, and some more knowledge. *Group structure* can be defined as the relatively stable pattern of relationships among members within a group. There are numerous dimensions of group structure along which the group becomes differentiated. Among the known dimensions of group structure, perhaps the most significant ones for group functioning are size, cohesiveness, communication, norms and goals, role assignments, and the power of the group leader.

Size

The number of individuals in a group can determine the activity levels of individuals within the group. As you can imagine, the larger the number of people in a group, the less intimate the relationships would be. The sheer volume of interactions would tend to make any concerted effort more difficult. The group leader is much more crucial in larger groups than in smaller groups.

The appropriate size of a group depends to a great extent on the group's situation and purpose. Sargent and Williams (reported in Kolasa, 1969) found that a fact-finding group is probably most effective when it is composed of about 14 members. An executive or action-taking group functions best at a size of approximately seven members. According to Kolasa (1969), the validity of these figures is reinforced by information from many legislative bodies which indicates that the number of members in these two types of groups hovers close to the figures given.

Berelson and Steiner (1964) conclude that even-numbered groups show more disagreement than do odd-numbered groups because in even-numbered groups subgroups of equal size can be pitted against each other. Berelson and Steiner also conclude that the "perfect" group size is five because if subgroups develop in a group of five, a minority group of two is large enough to permit participation and individual development in support of a position, and a majority of three is strong enough to prevail, yet is not completely overwhelming.

Thelen (1949) proposed that groups achieve maximum *productivity* when they contain only as many members as are needed to supply the necessary task and interaction skills. Steiner (1972) has drawn a series of charts depicting relationships among group size and the potential and actual productivity of individual group members. These charts are shown in Figure 13–2.

The curves in Figure 13–2 show how group size might affect productivity. Although the curves are not intended to depict universal trends, they do indicate relationships that are postulated to prevail in many situations. As group size increases, potential productivity rises at a decelerating rate, whereas process losses (actual productivity versus potential productivity) increase at an accelerating rate. Given the relationships described in Figure 13–2b, actual productivity equals potential productivity minus process losses, and in the present example it reaches its maximum when the group contains four or five members.

Figure 13–2
Illustrative curves depicting relationships among group size and potential productivity, process losses, total actual productivity, and mean actual productivity per member.

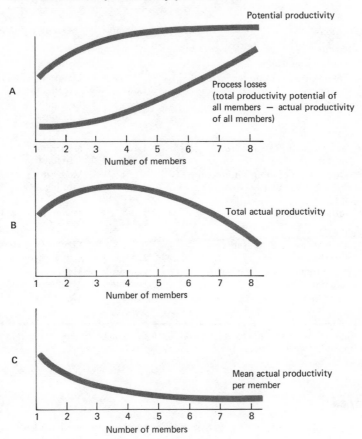

Source: From I. D. Steiner, *Group Processes and Productivity* (New York: Academic Press, 1972), p. 96.

Average productivity per member is greatest when an individual works alone on the task, and it declines as more people are added (13–2c). The most desirable group size depends upon whether one wishes to maximize total productivity or productivity per member.

Hellriegel and Slocum (1976) summarize the effects of size on group behavior, as shown in Figure 13–3. Again we see that as the size of the group increases, the "personality" and the performance of the group shift.

Figure 13–3
Some possible effects of size on groups

	Group size		
Dimensions	*2–7 members*	*8–12 members*	*13–16 members*
Leadership			
1. Demand on leader	Low	Moderate	High
2. Differences between leaders and members	Low	Low to moderate	Moderate to high
3. Direction of leader	Low	Low to moderate	Moderate to high
Members			
4. Tolerance of direction from leader	Low to high	Moderate to high	high
5. Domination of group interaction by a few members	Low	Moderate to high	High
6. Inhibition in participation by ordinary members	Low	Moderate	High
Group processes			
7. Formalization of rules and procedures	Low	Low to moderate	Moderate to high
8. Time required for reading decisions	Low to moderate	Moderate	Moderate to high
9. Tendency for subgroup to form	Low	Moderate to high	High

Source: From D. Hellriegel and J. W. Slocum, *Organizational Behavior: Contingency Views* (St. Paul: West Publishing, 1976), p. 166.

Cohesiveness

The cohesiveness of a group refers to the degree to which its members are attracted to the group, are motivated to remain in the group, and mutually influence one another. According to Shaw (1971), members of highly cohesive groups are more energetic in group activities, are less likely to be absent from group meetings, and are happy when the group succeeds and sad when it fails, whereas members of less cohesive groups are less concerned about the group's activities.

There is substantial evidence that both the quality and the quantity of group interactions are related to the cohesiveness of the group. Lott and Lott (1961) studied groups of from six to ten friends from college student organizations representing religious, academic, athletic, and social activities, and compared their behavior to the behavior of groups of strangers who were taking classes together. As one would expect, the more cohesive groups had greater amounts of communication when they met to discuss a preassigned topic than did the "stranger" groups who were assigned the same topic, even though the opportunity for interaction was the same in both types of groups.

Studies have also shown that members of highly cohesive groups are more likely to conform to group pressures than are members of low-cohesive groups. Festinger, Schacter, and Back (1950), for example, found that members of cohesive groups in university housing units held uniform opinions and usually acted in conformity with group standards. They also found that pressures toward uniformity increased with increasing group cohesiveness.

Whether or not high cohesiveness affects productivity in a positive way depends to a great extent on the *goals* of the group. High cohesiveness in a work group may actually be associated with low productivity if the goals of the group are contrary to organizational and/or managerial goals. Roy (reported in Whyte, Dalton, Roy, Sayles, Collins, Miller, Strauss, Fuerstenberg, & Bavelas, 1955) described the pressures against deviance from the point of view of a person who had been the object of such group pressures. Roy's job was paid on a piece-rate basis; the more he produced, the more he would earn. He reported:

> From my first to my last day at the plant I was subject to warnings and predictions concerning price cuts. Pressure was the heaviest from Joe Mucha, . . . who shared my job repertoire and kept a close eye on my production. On November 14, the day after my first attained quota, Joe Mucha advised: "Don't let it go over $1.25 an hour, or the time-study man will be right here! And they don't waste time, either! They watch the records like a hawk! I got ahead, so I took it easy for a couple of hours."
>
> Joe told me that he had made $10.01 yesterday and warned me not to go over $1.25 an hour. . . .
>
> Jack Starkey spoke to me after Joe left. "What's the matter? Are you trying to upset the applecart?" Jack explained in a friendly manner that $10.50 was too much to turn in, even on an old job. "The turret-lathe men can turn in $1.35," said Jack, "but their rate is 90 cents, and our rate is 85 cents."
>
> Jack warned me that the Methods Department could lower their prices on any job, old or new, by changing the fixture slightly or changing the size of the drill. According to Jack, a couple of operators . . . got to competing with each other to see how much they could turn out. They got up to $1.65 an hour, and the price was cut in half. And from then on, they had to run that job themselves, as none of the other operators would accept the job.
>
> According to Jack, it would be all right for us to turn in $1.28 or $1.29 an hour, when it figured out that way, but it could not be all right to turn in $1.30 per hour.
>
> Well, now I know the maximum is—$1.29 an hour.

Seashore (1954) also found that cohesiveness affected group performance. In a study of 228 small work groups in a plant manufacturing heavy machinery, he found that:

1. Productivity among workers was more uniform in highly cohesive groups than in groups with lower cohesion, suggesting that cohesion had a conformity effect (that is, reduced *within-group* variance).
2. Productivity differences among work groups were greater in high-cohesion groups than in low-cohesion groups (maximizing between-group variance).
3. High cohesiveness was associated with either high or low productivity, depending upon the degree to which members felt that management was supportive or threatening to them.

The cohesiveness of the group has an impact not only on the group's performance level but also on the group's level of satisfaction. Members of cohesive groups are generally better satisfied with the group than are members of noncohesive groups. Seashore found that workers in cohesive groups felt less tension and anxiety and were better able to cope with the pressures of work.

Communication patterns

From the previous discussion, it is obvious that size and cohesiveness affect the possible communication patterns or "networks" that take place in groups. A *communication network* is defined as the flow of verbal and nonverbal messages exchanged between two or more group members. The volume, capacity, and distribution of communication networks all affect group functioning, especially in solving problems, distributing information, and organizing for work. Groups differ in the degree to which members are free to communicate with one another. For example, in a company it is necessary for a management trainee to go through proper channels in order to communicate with the company president.

In 1948, Bavelas suggested a procedure by which the complex structures found in large and rather formal organizations might be reduced to manageable size and studied in a simulated (laboratory) setting. Each of five persons could be given one fifth of the information needed to solve a problem, and the freedom of those individuals to communicate with one another could be restricted to rules permitting messages to flow along only specified channels. Figure 13–4 shows several possible communication networks, each providing a different combination of open channels of communication. For example, in the *circle*, adjacent persons can talk directly with one another, but persons who are not adjacent to each other can establish contact only by having their messages relayed by one or more intermediaries.

Several interesting findings have been made in studies using these communication networks (see Leavitt, 1951; Guetzkow, 1960). In general, a person who occupies a centralized position (for example, person A in the *wheel*) is better satisfied with his or her position than are persons who occupy peripheral positions with limited communication

Figure 13–4
Five-person communication networks

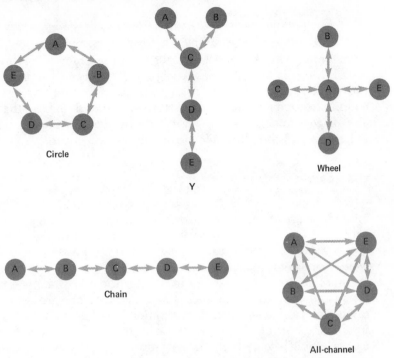

Circle

Y

Wheel

Chain

All-channel

Note: Arrows depict direction messages flow. Lines denote target and sender of message.

facilities. Overall group satisfaction is greater in decentralized net-works (for example, the *all-channel*) than in centralized networks (for example, the *chain*). The study by Leavitt (1951) showed that central-ized networks were most efficient for solving simple problems. The circle network was least efficient in terms of time required for solution, number of errors, and number of messages, whereas the "Y," the wheel, and the chain were most efficient by these criteria.

Although these results may seem to lack "real-world" importance, many uses have been made of them. Sommer (1967), for example, has studied the restrictions which the environment can place on group interaction. He found that different seating patterns in groups were associated with different types of group atmosphere. In studies with students, different sections of the same class were experimentally scheduled for rooms with quite different physical layouts. It was found that students participated more in the discussions if a circular layout of chairs was used. They participated least in a setting with a series of parallel benches. These results combined with those from other studies lead us to conclude that the wheel and the "Y" are better for simple tasks and that the "all-channel" network is better for complex decision-making tasks.

These findings have enormous practical implications. They show that decisions customarily made by architects and interior designers have a marked effect on the social structures which emerge. Herman Miller, Inc., maker of expensive high-quality office furniture, has used these findings in designing office layouts. After studying the existing communication flow in an office, Herman Miller designs both furniture and office layouts in such a way that the flow of communication is enhanced and the efficiency of the office is improved.

Norms and goals

It is difficult to separate a group's activities from its goals, and most individuals are attracted to a group both because they enjoy the group's activities and because they value its goals or purposes. The role of group goals in the foundation stage of group development has been well established. Sherif and Sherif (1953), for example, investigated group relations and found that even after the experiments established intergroup hostility and tension, the members of the groups attempted to reestablish harmony and integration. In the initial stages of this study, members of a boys' summer camp were formed into five groups on the basis of selected activities. For approximately five days, situations were arranged in which it seemed that one group interfered with or frustrated another group. For example, following an athletic victory by the Bulldogs (Camp 1) over the Red Devils (Camp 2), both groups were invited to attend a party in the mess hall with the stated purpose of reducing intergroup conflict. However, it was arranged to have the Red Devils get to the mess hall first. There they found that half of the refreshments were battered and broken, whereas the other half were in good condition. The Red Devils were told to serve themselves and to leave the Bulldogs their share. Without comment, they chose the good half and carried it to their table. The reaction of the Bulldogs to this treatment was predictable. They called the Red Devils "pigs" and "bums," and generally lambasted them. When the intergroup conflict created by procedures of this sort had been firmly established, Sherif and Sherif attempted to reduce the conflict and to rearrange group boundaries by introducing common "supraordinate" goals. The most effective of these was a campwide softball game in which a team of best players from both groups was elected by the boys from the entire camp to compete with a team from a neighboring camp. Although the supraordinate goal approach did not completely eliminate the hostilities produced by the earlier manipulations, there was a significant reduction in the amount of hostility and tension and some realignment of group boundaries.

Thus we see that in the early stages of group development, conflict between groups leads to increased intragroup cohesiveness. One element of this cohesiveness is the "common enemy" phenomenon. However, Sherif and Sherif demonstrated that a common group goal can produce new group memberships and reduce hostilities.

Whereas group goals are the specification of desired objectives to be reached by a group, *group norms* are "shared ways of looking at the world," that is, the attitudes, values, and rules for member behavior. These norms result in agreed-upon standards of members and group behavior that are anticipated and expected by the members of the group. Once a standard or norm is established, there is pressure to adhere to the standard and a reluctance to violate it. McGrath (1964) says that group norms include: (*a*) a frame of reference for viewing relevant objects; (*b*) prescribed "right" attitudes or behavior toward those objects; (*c*) affective feelings about the rightness of these attitudes and about tolerance of norm violations; and (*d*) positive and negative sanctions by which proper behavior is rewarded and improper behavior is punished.

Festinger (1950) states that two factors are responsible for the emergence of group norms. First, groups provide individuals with a frame of reference for understanding their world which they might lack alone. Second, some degree of uniformity of action is necessary if the group is to survive and move toward its goal. Control and coordination of norms regulating the conduct of members promote the continuity and success of the group.

Hackman (1976) specifies five major characteristics of group norms, which have been disclosed by studies in organizational settings.

1. *Norms are structural characteristics of groups which summarize and simplify group influence processes.* Thus, norms represent a means of "shortcutting" the need to use specific stimuli (for example, the presence of a manager) on a continuous basis to control the behavior of individual group members. In this way, group norms obviate the need for power plays. Norms become an impersonal means for resolving differences.

2. *Norms apply only to behavior—not to private thoughts and feelings.* Although the origin of norms may be emotionally or attitudinally based, organizations can really only control behavioral compliance. *Private acceptance* of norms by individuals is an unnecessary requirement and can be detrimental to the survival of the group if it is imposed too rigidly.

3. *Norms are generally developed only for behaviors which are viewed as important by most group members.* Norms generally develop

only for continuously required behavioral patterns which otherwise would have to be controlled by direct and continuous social influence.

4. *Norms usually develop gradually, but the process can be short-cutted if members so desire.* If, for some reason, group members decide that a particular norm is now desired, they may simply agree to institute such a norm suddenly by declaring that "from now on" the norm exists.

5. *Not all norms apply to everyone.* High-status members often have more "freedom" to deviate from the letter of a norm than do other people. This is why more employees with more seniority and more rank seemingly have more freedom to break rules, whereas other employees are forced to follow the "letter of the law."

Role assignment

The role or work structure is the pattern of members' tasks and responsibilities in the group and the way in which groups divide up labor requirements. Each position in the group structure has an associated role which consists of the desired behaviors of the position's occupant. These expected behaviors are generally agreed upon, not only by the occupants, but also by other members of the group and often by members of other groups as well.

A study by Torrance (1954) gives some evidence of the consequence of the role configuration on the influence of different members in the group. Torrance studied 62 permanent and 32 temporary aircrews, consisting of a pilot, a navigator, and a gunner. The roles of these positions are clearly different. The pilot is in charge of flying the plane, the navigator has to see that it reaches its destination, and the gunner has to protect it. Other differences also separate these role holders. The pilot has the highest status and the gunner the lowest status. This study revealed that the amount of influence on the group's decision was generally correlated with the role held, the pilot having the greatest influence and the gunner the least.

Several things may cause a person in a given role to perform at a level less than that desired by the role occupant. For example, a new person in an organizational role may need to acquire knowledge about many relevant norms before he or she can perform in the role. For this new person, the behaviors that are appropriate in the role may be undetermined and ambiguous. The new person may discover that his belief about how he should perform his role is incompatible with other members' expectations. His boss may demand that he perform the role in one manner, his co-workers may prefer a second method, and he may prefer a third. Thus we see that *role ambiguity* and *role conflict* may cause confusion and be detrimental to role performance (see Chapter 9 for more detail).

In addition, a person occupies many different roles in many different groups. Under unusual circumstances, a person who holds two different positions in two different groups may be called upon to enact both roles simultaneously.[1] When this happens, the individual will probably resolve the conflict in the direction of greatest group attraction. Again, *role conflict* can affect our performance.

Another complicating factor in role performance is *role overload.* Overload is typically encountered when various members of a group impose legitimate and compatible demands upon a role occupant. The role occupant, however, finds that he or she cannot complete all of the tasks urged by various people within the specified time limits. The role occupant must then decide which pressures to comply with and which to fend off. Either way, the role occupant may "lose" in the exchange, for reasons not under his or her control. For example, in many organizations two or more managers of equal status often share the services of one secretary. The secretary may have no ambiguity about the job and feel no conflict with his or her other roles, yet on many occasions may feel the pressure of role overload. The secretary may be expected to complete more work in a day than he or she is able to because more than one manager comes up with a rush job on the same day. As we note in Chapter 9, one of the greatest sources of frustration in organizations arises from role overload. Control tower operators, elementary school teachers, and students, have often complained about work overloads.

Power of the group leader

One property that differentiates groups from one another is the power of the leader. We will have much to say about this in Chapter 17, so only a brief discussion will be presented at this time.

Etzioni (1961) discusses the difference between the *position power* and the *personal power* of the group leader. Power is the ability to induce or influence behavior, and that power can come from the organizational office or role (position power) and/or from personal influence. The best situation for a leader is to have both personal and position power. Personal power can come from friendship and expertise, whereas position power usually implies formal authority to reward and punish group members. A group leader who possessed both types of power base would naturally be better able to meet the needs of the group members, and thus under such a leader a more cohesive group atmosphere should prevail.

---

[1] For example, a graduate student who serves as an instructor may attend a social gathering at which some of his undergraduate students and some of his professors are present. In those circumstances, he might find it awkward to behave either like a student or like a professor.

SOCIALIZATION OF THE NEW GROUP MEMBER

In our discussion on the properties of groups, we referred to the need of groups to establish and abide by norms in order to maintain the high degree of group cohesion needed to accomplish group goals. Mann (1969) says that through the process of socialization the individual becomes a member of a group, endowed with the social attitudes and role behaviors appropriate to his particular group and his place in it. The individual adjusts to the group by learning behavior which meets with group approval. Socialization occurs throughout life, especially at transitional phases, such as entering school, taking a job, and getting married. Mann states:

> The aim of socialization is to induce the individual to conform willingly to the ways of society and the groups to which he belongs. On the surface it may appear that socialization and conformity are synonymous, that a person must be slavishly conventional in his behaviors and attitudes if he is to be an accepted member of the social group. This is true to some extent in childhood, but in adulthood, after the person learns what the social group expects of him, greater variation in behavior is not only permissible, but desirable. The rigid conformist is not regarded as an ideal product of socialization because he is unable to adjust to changing circumstances. (p. 6)

Schein (1970) agrees. He says that the organizational group and the individual mutually attempt to influence each other in the early stages of interaction (when the socialization process occurs) for the purpose of establishing a workable "psychological contract." The process of socialization is a method by which a group establishes psychological contracts with its new members. Schein states:

> For example, *organizational socialization* is one such concept [by which people establish psychological contracts], referring to the fact that organizations have goals, norms, values, preferred ways of doing things which are usually taught systematically, though not necessarily overtly, to all new members. Some of the norms can be thought of as *pivotal*, in the sense that adherence to them is a requirement of continued membership in the organization. For a manager it is required that he believe in the validity of the free enterprise system; for a professor, that he accept the canons of research and scholarship. Other organizational norms are *peripheral* in the sense that it is desirable for members to possess them but not essential. For example, for a manager it may be desirable from the point of view of the organization that he be a man, have certain political views, wear the right kind of clothes. . . . In thinking about the adjustments of the individual to the organization, we can identify three types of possible adjustments, based on which sets of norms are adhered to. Acceptance of *neither* pivotal nor peripheral norms can be thought of as *"active rebellion"* and is likely to lead to voluntary or involuntary loss of membership. Acceptance of *both* pivotal and peripheral norms can be thought of as *"conformity"*

and is likely to lead to the loyal but uncreative "organization man" or "bureaucrat." Acceptance of pivotal norms but rejection of peripheral norms can be thought of as *"creative individualism."* (p. 79)

From the point of view of the organization, it is desirable to create conditions which make it possible for members to be creative individualists rather than conformists or rebels. Leavitt (1972) says that groups try to form methods in order to get rebels (deviants) to comply. He states that group members think, "Let's reason with him; if that doesn't work, let's try to tease him by emotional seduction; and if even that doesn't work, let's beat him over the head until he has to give up. Failing this, we'll excommunicate him, we'll amputate him from the group; we'll disown him" (pp. 224–225).

SUMMARY

In this chapter we have explored with you the fact that "behavior does not occur in a vacuum." We still maintain our individuality by deciding which groups we will join and which group norms we will conform to. But the fact remains that our needs and goals force us to seek out other people in order to survive and prosper. The ways in which a group varies on such dimensions as size, cohesiveness, communication flow, norms, goals, role assignments, and leadership will determine, in part, the "personality" of the group and our enjoyment in being associated with the group. A certain amount of conformity is necessary in order for collective action to be channeled toward mutual goal attainment. In the next chapter we will explore how the presence of other people enhances or impairs our performance and satisfaction as individuals.

CONCEPTS TO REMEMBER

comparison level	circle
comparison level of alternatives	wheel
principle of complementarity	Y
psychological group	chain
primary groups	all-channel
secondary groups	supraordinate goal
forming	group norms
storming	pivotal norms
norming	peripheral norms
performing	creative individualism
group structure	conformity
cohesiveness	active rebellion

QUESTIONS FOR DISCUSSION

1. Why do people join groups?
2. What disadvantages are there in joining a group?
3. Do groups really have "personalities"? Why or why not?
4. "Without deviation among group members, creativity dies." Comment.
5. "Socialization of new members is crucial for organizational survival." Do you agree?

REFERENCES

Bavelas, A. A mathematical model for group structure. *Applied Anthropology*, 1948, *7*, 16–30.

Berelson, B, & Steiner, G. *Human behavior.* New York: Harcourt, Brace and World, 1964.

Bob Knight, the volatile coach of basketball's superteam. *Chicago Tribune Magazine*, January 11, 1976, pp. 11 and 26.

Etzioni, A. *A comparative analysis of complex organizations on power involvement and their correlates.* New York: Free Press, 1961.

Festinger, L. Informal social communication. *Psychological Review*, 1950, *57*, 271–282.

Festinger, L. A theory of social comparison processes. *Human Relations*, 1954, *7*, 114–140.

Festinger, L., Schacter, S. & Back, K. *Social pressures in informal groups.* New York: Harper and Row, 1950.

Gross, E. Primary functions of the small group. *American Journal of Sociology*, 1954, *60*, 24–30.

Guetzkow, H. Differentiation of roles in task-oriented groups. In D. Cartwright & A. Zander (Eds.), *Group dynamics: research and theory.* Evanston, Ill.: Row, Peterson, 1960.

Hackman, J. R. Group influence on individuals. In M. P. Dunnette, *Handbook of industrial and organizational psychology.* Chicago: Rand McNally, 1976.

Hellriegel, D., & Slocum, J. W. *Organizational behavior: Contingency views.* St. Paul: West Publishing, 1976.

Homans, G. C. *Social behavior: Its elementary forms.* New York: Harcourt, Brace, 1961.

Kolasa, B. J. *Introduction to behavioral science for business.* New York: John Wiley & Sons, Inc., 1969.

Leavitt, H. J. Some effects of certain communication patterns on group performance. *Journal of Abnormal and Social Psychology*, 1951, *46*, 38–50.

Leavitt, H. J. *Managerial psychology* (3d ed.). Chicago: University of Chicago Press, 1972.

Lott, A. J., & Lott, B. E.   Group cohesiveness, communication level, and conformity. *Journal of Abnormal and Social Psychology,* 1961, *62,* 408–412.

Mann, L.   *Social psychology.* New York: John Wiley & Sons, Inc., 1969.

Marquis, P. G., Guetzkow, H., & Heynes, R. W.   A social psychological study of the decision-making conference. In H. Guetzkow (Ed.), *Groups, leadership, and men.* Pittsburgh: Carnegie Press, 1951.

McGrath, J. E.   *Social psychology: A brief introduction.* New York: Holt, Rinehart and Winston, 1964.

Newcomb, T.   *Personality and social change: Attitude formation in a student community.* New York: Holt, Rinehart and Winston, 1943.

Newcomb, T.   *The acquaintance process.* New York: Holt, Rinehart and Winston, 1961.

Roy, D.   Efficiency and 'the fix': Informal intergroup relations in a piecework machine shop. In S. M. Lipset and N. J. Smelser (Eds.), *The progress of a decade.* Englewood Cliffs, N.J.: Prentice-Hall, 1961.

Schein, E.   *Organizational psychology* (2d ed.). © 1970. Reprinted by permission of Prentice-Hall, Inc., Englewood Cliffs, New Jersey.

Seashore, S. E.   *Group cohesiveness in the industrial work group.* Ann Arbor: University of Michigan Press, 1954.

Shaw, M. E.   *Group dynamics.* New York: McGraw-Hill, 1971.

Sherif, M., & Sherif, C. W.   *Groups in harmony and tension.* New York: Harper and Row. 1953.

Smith, P. B.   *Groups within organizations.* New York: Harper and Row, 1973.

Sommer, R.   Small group ecology. *Psychological Bulletin,* 1967, *67,* 145–152.

Sommer, R.   Personal space: The behavioral basis of design. Englewood Cliffs, N.J.: Prentice-Hall, 1969.

Steiner, I. D.   *Group processes and productivity.* New York: Academic Press, 1972.

Thelen, H. A.   Group dynamics in instruction: Principles of least group size. *School Review,* 1949, *57,* 139–148.

Thibaut, J. W., & Kelley, H. H.   *The social psychology of groups.* New York: Wiley, 1959.

Torrance, E. P.   Some consequences of power differences on decision making in permanent and temporary three-man groups. *State College of Washington Research Studies,* 1954, *22,* 130–140.

Tuckman, B. W.   Developmental sequence in small groups. *Psychological Bulletin,* 1965, *63,* 384–399.

Van Zelst, R. H.   Validation of a sociometric regrouping procedure. *Journal of Abnormal and Social Psychology,* 1952, *47,* 299–301.

Whyte, W. F., Dalton, M., Roy, D., Sayles, L., Collins, O., Miller, F., Strauss, G., Fuerstenberg, F., & Bavelas, A.   *Money and motivation: An analysis of incentives in industry.* New York: Harper, 1955.

Winch, R. F.   Mate-selection: A study of complementary needs. New York: Harper and Row, 1958.

14

Effective work groups

How does the presence of others affect individual performance?

How do the problem solving and the decision making of groups differ from the problem solving and the decision making of individuals?

How does group structure affect group performance?

In the last chapter we examined how the various properties of a group can determine, in part, the personality of the group. We also found that the properties of groups can affect the performance of their individual members.

The study of the importance of group properties for individual performance was begun in the United States in the late 1920s. A series of studies which first gave an indication of which properties of groups affect performance and satisfaction were conducted at the Hawthorne works of the Western Electric Company (Roethlisberger & Dickson, 1939). In the first study, conducted in the Relay Assembly Test room of the plant, various changes were made in the working conditions of a group of five women. It was discovered that, regardless of the change introduced (increased lighting, decreased lighting, break time allocation, hours of work), productivity increased. This was true even after the 14th change, which eliminated all the benefits previously introduced and restored the status quo. The investigators concluded that the changes in productivity were due to the fact that at each stage the experimenters had sought the women's advice as to which changes to introduce, and that the women had been allowed to coalesce as a group. Thus, by expressing interest in the women, the experimenters had modified the situation in an unintended manner.

In a second study, conducted in the Bank Wiring room of the Hawthorne plant, a group of 14 men wired telephone banks for nine months, while under constant observation. No changes were deliberately introduced. The level of work of the group was maintained at a very steady, less than maximum rate. Roethlisberger and Dickson concluded that this low level of performance was held stationary by a variety of social influences within the work group. The norm of 6,600 connections per day, though unstated, was understood by all. Members of the group who exceeded or failed to reach the group norms were ostracized by the other group members. When group norms support high productivity (as in the Relay Assembly Test room), productivity is generally higher than when the group norms discourage high productivity (as in the Bank Wiring room).

After the Hawthorne studies were published, behavioral scientists became very interested in how the group environment affected an individual's performance and satisfaction in a work setting. Managers and behavioral scientists have discovered two important phenomena related to the group's impact on the individual. First, there are apparently *psychological effects* of participating in group activities. Second, the *structure* of the group affects the level of output of individual members. We will discuss both of these phenomena in detail before returning to a more general discussion about the ways groups influence work effectiveness.

THE PSYCHOLOGICAL EFFECTS OF PARTICIPATION IN GROUPS: BEHAVIOR IN THE PRESENCE OF OTHERS

In Chapter 13 we noted that people are concerned with what others think and do in response to their own behavior. Even in front of a total stranger we often try to convey a positive (correct?) impression. We know from our own experience that people pay attention to other people and react to what they say or do. Several theories have been introduced to explain why and how the presence of other people affects our behavioral patterns.

Social facilitation

One of the first studies in psychology (Triplett, 1897) investigated the manner in which an individual's performance is enhanced by the presence of others. Social facilitation deals with how an individual's task performance is affected by working in the presence of other individuals, but independently of them. Allport (1924) called this a coacting group situation and predicted that the presence of others has an energizing effect on the individual, causing him or her to work with greater intensity but to lose accuracy. Thus the conclusion was that the presence of other people increases one's motivation but reduces the quality of one's performance. How could this be?

Zanjonc (1965), a psychologist at the University of Michigan, found the solution to this seemingly inconsistent statement. He postulated social facilitation theory as we know it today. *The presence of other people, either in a setting in which they act together or in front of an audience, impairs the learning of new responses but facilitates the performance of those previously learned.* This is true because the presence of other people has drive-producing properties which raise our awareness, arousal, or activation level. In a well-learned task this energizing effect enhances performances (for example, a new actor in a play), but in a poorly learned task the individual is "overenergized." That is, the new task (learning one's lines) has drive-producing properties, as does the presence of other people. Thus one tends to be "overaroused," and performance quality is therefore impaired. This is illustrated in Figure 14–1.

As illustrated in Figure 14–1, a person's level of performance (*y*-axis) increases as external forces are presented. For example, if one is driving on a long trip and starts to get sleepy (fatigued), then the task has lost drive-arousal properties and fatigue is detrimental to performance. But if one turns on the radio or talks on the Citizen's Band radio, then the interaction with other people raises one's arousal level and highly productive performance (cue-attentive behavior) returns. In heavy traffic, driving in a new city, or driving for the first time, one

Figure 14–1
The effect of one's level of arousal on performance

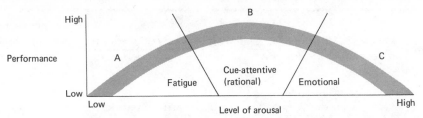

is already highly aroused. The presence of several passengers or the noise of a radio may introduce additional arousal that causes a person to be nervous (emotional), and performance efficiency is reduced.

Based on social facilitation theory, Zanjonc (1965) concludes that practical advice for students can be offered. "These results would lead us to discourage study groups and other togetherness aids in learning, while they would simultaneously lead us to encourage taking exams in large groups and preferably in the presence of large audiences. This latter advice applies only when the student has learned the material rather well. An audience during exams will otherwise have disastrous effects" (p. 27).

Social comparison

The theory of social comparison (Festinger, 1954) postulates that we each have a drive to evaluate our opinions, abilities, and performance appropriateness. If we have a choice, we prefer to compare our responses against an objective standard (for example, in a footrace, a four-minute mile). Often, however, objective standards are not available, and under such circumstances we compare our responses to those of other people who are similar to ourselves. This theory, then, would predict that we are always comparing ourselves to others in our peer group to "see where we stand." The theory has great importance for performance feedback and reward administration.

As discussed in Chapter 7, Adams (1961) uses social comparison theory to explain how individuals compare their work efforts and work rewards to the work efforts and work rewards of an other. If this ratio, as depicted in Figure 14–2, is unequal, then dissatisfaction is likely to result.

We see from Figure 14–2 that perceived inequity (14–2b and 14–2c) can have a detrimental effect on performance and on the satisfaction of individual members in a group and thus on group productivity and morale. Obviously, the most problematic form of inequity for managers is some form of perceived underpayment or relative deprivation among some of his or her group members. Unfortunately, this type

Figure 14–2
Equity relationship and satisfaction

(a) $\dfrac{\text{Work rewards of person A}}{\text{Work input of person A}} = \dfrac{\text{Work rewards of person B}}{\text{Work input of person B}} =$ A is satisfied with the treatment he is receiving from supervisor

(b) $\dfrac{\text{Work rewards of person A}}{\text{Work input of person A}} > \dfrac{\text{Work rewards of person B}}{\text{Work input of person B}} =$ A is overpaid and will either increase inputs or rationalize overpayment

(c) $\dfrac{\text{Work rewards of person A}}{\text{Work input of person A}} < \dfrac{\text{Work rewards of person B}}{\text{Work input of person B}} =$ A feels deprived and will leave, reduce inputs, change comparison, sabotage the work of B

---

of inequity is also most prevalent. As Brickman and Campbell (1971) have noted, it may be virtually impossible to remove the perception of deprivation for all members of a given group. Yet, it may be possible to manage the consequences of perceived deprivation more effectively.

Some practical recommendations can be made from equity theory. First, it would seem that the entire process of performance evaluation must be made an explicit, public process, perhaps even with provision for some form of adjudication or appeal. At the very least, it would seem essential that managers make explicit exactly what inputs are valued for members of his or her group. Similarly, outcomes (rewards) within work groups should be overtly tied to work inputs. Lawler (1971), for instance, reports that employees tend to overestimate the pay others receive.

Panic behavior in groups

It has often been found that the collective actions of a group in a crisis situation can determine whether or not people survive. The combination of responses as well as the individual response can determine whether or not people will suffer. Mann (1969) states that a classic example of a social situation in which almost everyone suffers when there is a breakdown in cooperation is the panic behavior of a theater audience during a fire. Under the threat of a common danger the crowd disintegrates into a mass of violent, competitive people. The essence of panic is competition for a scarce resource.

Mintz (1951) predicted that breakdown in cooperative behavior is an important cause of panic behavior. He says, "At a theater fire, if everyone leaves in an orderly manner, everybody is safe and an individual waiting for his turn is not sacrificing his interest. But if the cooperative pattern of behavior is disturbed, the usual advice, 'Keep your head, don't push, wait for your turn and you will be safe,' ceases to be valid. If the exits are blocked the person following this advice is likely to be burned to death" (p. 151). Thus disaster can occur if a few people fail to cooperate. Brown (1965) sees such uncooperative behavior as coming from those with the most to lose and the least to gain. He states that in a bad fire the rush of uncooperative, panicky behavior is initiated by those members of the group farthest from the exits who know that they are lost if they cooperate and take their turn. Only desperate competition provides some chance of escape.

Although it is unlikely that the average group leader will need to concern himself with group panic behavior, there are certain group leaders who need to be made aware of this phenomenon, since their jobs have built-in situations in which panic behavior could erupt. Examples include airline flight attendants, bus drivers, platoon leaders, ship captains, and bank managers. One way in which such leaders attempt to avert panic behavior is through socializing the members of the group (each time you fly, the flight attendant "prepares" you for the possibility of an emergency landing). Cooperation by means of conformity is generally the mode of panic management used by group leaders.

Decision making in groups

In Chapter 13 we noted that one property of groups is the amount of cohesiveness in them. We then went on to say that cohesiveness is attained through socialization but that unless conformity attempts were confined to pivotal norms, rigidity and low creativity might result. Although conformity can help us survive some crisis situations, it can cause us to fail in others.

Recent work by Janis (1972) suggests that in some circumstances high cohesiveness can be actively dysfunctional for the effectiveness of the group as a whole. Janis suggests that as a group becomes exclusively close-knit and develops a clubby feeling of "we-ness," it will become susceptible to a pattern of behavior that he calls "groupthink." Among the several symptoms of groupthink are a marked decrease in the openness of the group members to unsettling information and an unwillingness to examine such information when it is brought to the attention of the group. Although groupthink may result in goodwill or *esprit de corps*, it may render the group ineffective. Janis has shown that groupthink may have contributed substantially to a number of historic "fiascos" planned and executed by groups of government officials (for example, the Bay of Pigs invasion and Britain's do-nothing policy toward Hitler prior to World War II). Thus, before the Bay of Pigs invasion, President John F. Kennedy assembled his cabinet and members of his White House staff to plan a strategy for dealing with Cuba. White House adviser Schlesinger noted:

> Had one senior advisor opposed the adventure [the invasion of Cuba], I believe Kennedy would have canceled it. No one spoke against it. . . . Our meetings took place in a curious atmosphere of assumed consensus. . . .
>
> In the months after the Bay of Pigs I bitterly reproached myself for having kept so silent during those crucial discussions in the Cabinet Room, though my feelings of guilt were tempered by the knowledge that a course of objection would have accomplished little save *to gain me a name as a nuisance.* I can only explain my failure to do no more than raise a few timid questions by reporting that one's impulse to blow the whistle on this nonsense was simply undone by the *circumstances of the discussion.* (Quoted in Janis, 1972, pp. 39–40)

We see from the above discussion that conformity can have an effect on the quality of a decision made in a group. However, this need not be the case. Generally, we think of groups as rendering better decisions than individuals. For example, after reviewing the results of group and individual decisions, Davis (1969) concluded: "If we were to summarize the comparison of group to individual products, the gross conclusion would be that on most criteria, groups are generally superior to individuals but that the existence and degree of superiority depend upon a number of situational and task factors. . . . If the emphasis is on achieving a correct or good or early answer, then a group has a higher probability of achieving this aim (other things being equal) than does the single individual" (p. 43).

Not only do groups make different decisions than do average individuals, but often that decision is riskier. Take this case for example:

> John Case has been accepted as a premed student at two prestigious schools and one second-rate university. He knows that if he attends one of the prestigious schools, he would have a greater chance of getting into its medical school, but that his chances of failing would be greater. If he attends the second-rate university he will have a greater chance of getting high grades, but will probably only be a viable candidate for the second-rate university's medical school, since no one has ever been accepted at any other medical school from its premed program. Acceptance at the second-rate med school is almost assured if John maintains a "C" average. All three medical schools accept only their own premed students. John wants to attend one of these three medical programs, since they are all located near the home of his ailing mother.
>
> Imagine that you are advising John. Listed below are several probabilities of odds that the first project (attending a prestigious premed school) will lead to successful acceptance into its medical school.

Please check the lowest probability of success which you would consider acceptable to make it worthwhile for John to attend a prestigious school.

The choices of success are:

_____ 0 in 10	_____ 6 in 10
_____ 1 in 10	_____ 7 in 10
_____ 2 in 10	_____ 8 in 10
_____ 3 in 10	_____ 9 in 10
_____ 4 in 10	_____ 10 in 10
_____ 5 in 10	

It is usually found that groups come up with much riskier opinions than does the average individual. This is because, in an open environment, groups are able to share information. Second, risk taking is rewarded in our society. Third, if a project adopted by a group fails, less blame accrues to any one individual.

In summarizing the decision-making ability of groups, Maier (1973) points out that groups have certain assets as well as certain liabilities which affect the quality of the decisions reached. The assets of groups include *greater amounts of knowledge,* a *greater number of approaches,* and a *better comprehension* and a *better chance of acceptance* of the solution. The liabilities of groups include a tendency to demand *conformity* and the risk that one or two individuals will *dominate* them. If the assets are utilized and the liabilities avoided, groups are better decision-making units than individuals.

Two approaches to group decision making have recently been proposed as alternatives to the conventional *interacting* or discussion group. These two approaches, known as the *nominal group technique* (Van de Van and Delbecq, 1974) and the *delphi technique* (Dalkey, 1969), were designed to avoid the liabilities of groups and to utilize the assets of groups for effective problem solving.

The *nominal group technique* is a meeting in which a structured format is utilized for decision making among individuals seated around a table. This structured format proceeds as follows: (*a*) Individual members first silently and independently generate their ideas on a problem or a task in writing. (*b*) This period of silent writing is followed by a recorded round-robin procedure in which each group member (one at a time, in turn, around the table) presents one of his or her ideas to the group without discussion. The ideas are summarized and written on a blackboard or a sheet of paper on the wall. (*c*) After all the individuals have presented their ideas, the recorded ideas are discussed for the purposes of clarification and evaluation. (*d*) The meeting concludes with a silent, independent vote on priorities through a rank ordering procedure or a rating procedure, depending upon the group's decision rule. The "group decision" is the pooled outcome of individual votes.

Unlike the interacting or nominal group technique processes, partic-

Table 14–1

Comparison of qualitative differences between three decision processes based upon evaluations of leaders and group participants

Dimension	Interacting groups	Nominal groups	Delphi technique
Overall methodology	Unstructured face-to-face group meeting High flexibility High variability in behavior of groups	Structured face-to-face group meeting Low flexibility Low variability in behavior of groups	Structured series of questionnaires and feedback reports Low-variability respondent behavior
Role orientation of groups	Socioemotional Group maintenance focus	Balanced focus on social maintenance and task role	Task-instrumental focus
Relative quantity of ideas	Low; focused "rut" effect,	Higher; independent writing and hitchhiking round robin	High; isolated writing of ideas
Search behavior	Reactive search Short problem focus Task-avoidance tendency New social knowledge	Proactive search Extended problem focus High task centeredness New social and task knowledge	Proactive search Controlled problem focus High task centeredness New task knowledge
Normative behavior	Conformity pressures inherent in face-to-face discussions	Tolerance for non-conformity through independent search and choice activity	Freedom not to conform through isolated anonymity
Equality of participation	Member dominance in search, evaluation, and choice phases	Member equality in search and choice phases	Respondent equality in pooling of independent judgments
Method of problem solving	Person-centered Smoothing over and withdrawal	Problem-centered Confrontation and problem-solving	Problem-centered Majority rule of pooled independent judgments
Closure decision process	High lack of closure Low felt accomplishment	Low lack of closure High felt accomplishment	Low lack of closure Medium felt accomplishment
Resources utilized	Low administrative time and cost High participant time and cost	Medium administrative time, cost, preparation High participant time and cost	High administrative time, cost, preparation
Time to obtain group ideas	1½ hours	1½ hours	Five calendar months

Source: From A. H. Van de Van and A. L. Delbecq, *Academy of Management Journal*, 1974, *17*, 618.

ipants in the *delphi technique* are physically dispersed and do not meet face-to-face for group decision making. The delphi technique provides for the systematic solicitation and collation of judgments on a particular topic through a set of carefully designed sequential questionnaires interspersed with summarized information and feedback of opinions derived from earlier responses.

Although considerable variance exists in administering the delphi process, the basic approach is as follows: Only two iterations of questionnaires and feedback reports are used. First, a questionnaire designed to obtain information on a topic or problem is distributed by mail to a group of respondents who are anonymous to one another. The respondents independently generate their ideas in answering the questionnaire, which is then returned. The responses are then summarized into a feedback report and sent back to the respondent group along with a second questionnaire which is designed to probe more deeply into the ideas generated in response to the first questionnaire. After receiving the feedback report, the respondents independently evaluate it and answer the second set of questions. Typically, respondents are requested to vote independently on priority ideas included in the feedback report and to return their second replies, again by mail. Generally, a final summary and feedback report is then developed and mailed to the respondent group. The effects of the three approaches to group problem solving and decision making is shown in Table 14–1.

THE IMPACT OF GROUP STRUCTURE ON INDIVIDUAL PERFORMANCE AND SATISFACTION

As we reported earlier in this chapter, not only does behavior in the presence of others have a psychological effect on task performance, but the *structure* of the group also tends to influence the satisfaction and performance of individual members. We now need to examine how several structural properties of groups can affect these variables. We have already discussed in Chapter 13, for example, how group size and communication patterns can affect productivity and satisfaction. Let us now look at other structural variables.

Unorganized versus organized group structures

In 1941, French compared the behavior of individuals in unorganized and organized groups. The unorganized groups were college undergraduates assembled for the purpose of solving problems. The organized groups were college athletic teams and community clubs. The groups were given problems to solve, some requiring intellectual ability and others requiring motor coordination. The problem in most cases were difficult or insolvable, even though they looked easy initially.

One of the insolvable problems required group members to fill in rows and columns of numbers that would add across and down to a certain sum. One of the difficult problems required each member of a group to take one handle of a large cone-shaped apparatus and then, in unison with the other members, to roll a small ball up a path from the base to the top. French was interested in determining how the differently structured groups would respond to the frustration these tasks generated.

As one might expect, once the previously unorganized groups failed to meet with initial success, they lost interest in the problems fairly rapidly and either worked in subgroups or talked about unrelated matters. The organized groups had the greatest number of disruptions, however. They appeared more deeply frustrated, directed more aggression toward one another, and felt freer to express their feelings. Apparently, their common interest in doing well as a team kept them focused on the problem. French argued that the members of the organized groups were motivated not only by the demands of the experiment, but also by a group-shared desire to do well as a team.

Lambert and Lambert (1973) interpreted these and similar studies as showing both the advantages and the disadvantages of group organization. The mutual attraction of group members substains motivation to succeed and keeps members functioning as a team. These characteristics can be of great advantage in many circumstances. But groups that are too well organized might suffer from a lack of flexibility in adjusting to frustration or danger. For example, in another part of French's experiments (1944), he put organized and unorganized groups to work on various tasks in separate rooms of an old building. After a short time, smoke began to fill the rooms, fire engine bells rang, and the rooms appeared to be on fire. When the students tried to get out, they found the doors locked. The organized groups were less effective at resolving this crisis dilemma, and fear and panic appeared to spread more rapidly among the organized groups.

Homogeneity-heterogeneity of group membership

Most people would agree that for many group activities, a variety of skills and knowledge is required. Therefore, the more heterogeneous a group, the more likely it is that the necessary abilities and information will be available and the more effective the group is likely to be. Triandis, Hall, and Ewen (1965) conducted experiments to investigate the relationship between the heterogeneity of group members and creativity. In one experiment, subjects were given 18 opinion questionnaires concerning such issues as war, socialized medicine, and immortality. Groups were then formed on the basis of responses to these scales, in such a way that they were either high, medium, or low on cognitive similarity. Experienced heterogeneous groups performed better than experienced homogeneous groups. Other studies (for example, Hoffman & Maier, 1961) have substantiated these findings.

Shaw (1971) summarizes our knowledge about the composition of groups along the homogeneity-heterogeneity dimension. He says that when a group is heterogeneous in terms of personality, opinions, abilities, skills, and perspectives, the probability is increased that the group as a whole will possess the characteristics necessary for efficient group performance. These findings about the advantages of a heterogeneous group have a direct relevance for managers. In the selection process, particular attention should be paid to the ability of the new member to complement the existing talents of the group. Unfortunately, as you will recall from our earlier discussion of perception (Chapter 5), we often tend to rate people who are like ourselves higher than we rate those who are unlike us. This tendency may be detrimental to the overall success of the group.

Democratic and autocratic groups

A classic study of the effects of variations in group structure was conducted by Lewin, Lippitt, and White (1939). They attempted to create different social climates for groups of 11-year-old boys by varying how adult supervisors performed their role. The democratic supervisor called the boys together and asked them how they would like to spend their time and how they would like to allocate the resources available to them in the group's clubhouse. The leader of this group sought to be accepted as a member of the group. He worked, played, and went along with agreed-upon plans like any other member. On the other hand, the authoritarian supervisor called his group together and described what each member should do and how he should do it. He supervised the boys closely and gave them instructions at each step.

Apathy, lack of motivation, "scapegoating" of other group members, and dependence on the supervisor became the major characteristics of the autocratic groups. The communication in the authoritarian groups tended to be limited to club activities. The democratically structured groups, however, were freer in their communication, demonstrated affection for their leader, and were highly motivated.

This finding is not universal, however. Meade (1971) replicated the Lewin et al. study in India and found that among Hindu boys, morale and the quality and quantity of work completed were all superior under the autocratic leader. Lambert and Lambert (1973) suggest that the combination of these findings shows that young people brought up in a comparatively authoritarian society are more accustomed to and more comfortable with an authoritarian work-group atmosphere.

Nevertheless, in the United States democratic leadership in organizations is expected in certain situations. For example, almost every organization has temporary or permanent committees established which follow a democratic procedure (for example, *Robert's Rules of Order*). Tillman (1960) surveyed 1,200 *Harvard Business Review* subscribers and found that 949 of the organizations with more than 10,000 employees had formal committees. In another study, Kriesberg (1950) found that executives spend an average of ten hours per week in formal committee conferences. Thus we can see that democratically structured group activities are built into much of the activity of specific groups in organizations. We will have more to say about this phenomenon when we discuss the leadership responsibility of managers (Chapter 17.)

Competitively and cooperatively structured groups

Deutsch (1949) created cooperative and competitive classroom atmospheres by varying the information students received about the class makeup and the grading system. The competitive classes were told that students would be ranked from the best to the worst in terms of skill in analysis and discussion, and that each student's final grade would be based on the average of his or her daily ratings. The cooperative classes were told that the major part of individual course grades would depend on the quality of discussion shown by the group as a whole. The results showed that the cooperative groups developed into psychological groups, whereas the competitive groups did not. The cooperative groups were rated as superior on ideas generated, communication among their members, interpretation of ideas, friendliness, and satisfaction of the members with the group performance.

On the basis of these and other findings, many management theorists believe that competition among groups is healthy but that competition within groups is not. However, because each of us is brought up differently and because competition plays a major part in our development, we find that learning to work together is sometimes difficult. One purpose of the socialization process, as you recall from our discussion in Chapter 13, is to develop group cohesiveness and cooperation. In a recent interview with Gay Gray, one of the first 20 women to drop out of West Point, it was pointed out that the hardest thing to accept was the emphasis on group unity in the socialization of new cadets. She said:

> I think every girl that was there had been brought up independently. That was the hardest thing to do—to learn how to work as a unit. Everyone was just used to doing their part of the job, and all of a sudden we had to do it all together. One of our squad's biggest problems was getting ready for anything on time. We were never ready on time. We had some guys— they were perfectionists or something—and they wouldn't leave their rooms and be ready on time, and the whole squad would get in trouble. . . .

The women didn't really need each other. We needed the squad, the total unit. Everyone seemed capable of handling their own load except for just a few, and I hear it's not just the women who couldn't handle the load. . . .

It was the initiation period [that upset me]. It was necessary because you had to learn to react, to be able to function under stress. I realize that. That's why I went through it this summer. I didn't do too well. I cried a lot. . . . The haircut really got to me at first. I think it got to a lot of girls at first. I think you have to be able to—like they said, don't let them get that little part inside of you. Just let them have everything they want, give them all they can take except that little part that is you. I guess I felt threatened. I felt like either I was going to have to give my whole self to stay there or leave before they got that part of me. ("The Corps Demands All," *National Observer*, 1976, pp. 1, 18)

Whereas most organizations do not demand total cooperation, or attempt to get it through coercion, cooperation within groups is often structured into the task and the compensation system. Many firms, such as Donnelly Mirror, Herman Miller, and Kaiser Aluminum, base their salary increases on group and organization-wide performance. Under this method, known as the Scanlon plan, a representative committee within the organization participates in determining how much of the quarterly profit or the profit from some other period to allocate to a bonus pool. Each individual's percentage of the bonus pool is based on his salary as a percentage of all the salaries paid by the company. For example, if an employee earned $10,000 a year and all the salaries paid by the company totaled $1,000,000, the employee would receive 1 percent of the bonus pool. Under this system, cooperation is encouraged and competition is discouraged.

Source: (c) King Features Syndicate Inc. 1976.

Task structure

As discussed in Chapter 12, task assignments can have positive or negative motivational impacts on individuals. Research has shown that task assignments have the same impacts on groups. Moderately difficult group tasks are more stimulating and produce better-quality perform-

ance than do easier group tasks (Hackman, 1968). Changing the task
structure to make it easier, and at the same time changing the interaction patterns of the individual members to make them less dependent
on one another, has been shown to reduce morale. For example, Trist,
Higgins, Pollock, and Murray (1963) investigated changes in group
structures in the coal-mining industry. The coal-mining industry developed a more mechanized system of coal extraction which reduced
overall cost, even though the labor cost per individual continually increased. In a study of the Durham coal mine, Trist et al. described
the replacement of the 'room-and-pillar' method of coal extraction
by the 'longwall advance' method of coal extraction. In the room-and-
pillar system, a small group of men worked autonomously, sharing
all the requisite tasks among themselves and bargaining for the piece
rate directly. The newly introduced system of longwall advance divided
the component tasks into a number of specified roles. The coal-mining
process became a three-phase cycle, whereby each successive shift
was given different tasks to perform.

The small-group system was, in effect, replaced by a factory production line system. The work team became a unit of 30 to 40 men,
but these men were not all in the mine or pit at the same time. Although
the changes increased productivity per man, they drastically reduced
the morale of the workers. A great deal of conflict developed among
the shifts. The preceding shift was invariably accused of leaving work
for the next shift.

Changes were made in the work-group assignments in order to reduce the negative effects created by the new task structure. The rigid
system of fixed roles was abandoned, and a rule of "composite" working
was introduced. Under composite working, each miner worked on
whatever needed to be done next and the *team* took responsibility
for the task as a whole. Morale was thus restored, and fighting among
the teams was drastically reduced.

Participation in group decision making

Participation in group decision making has been shown to be an
effective way to increase the productivity and morale of work groups.
Participation increases the accuracy of the information workers have
about work practices and the group contingencies associated with those
practices. In 1971, Hackman and Lawler found that groups of workers
who participated in the design of a new pay plan aimed at reducing
absenteeism responded more quickly and more positively to the new
pay plan than did other groups which had the same pay plan imposed
on them by the company. One of the reasons the Scanlon plan has
been successful is that it too is based on the principle of participation
(see, for example, Frost, Wakeley, & Ruh, 1974).

The Hackman and Lawler (1969) study also pointed out a second advantage of participation. Participation was found to increase the degree to which members feel that they "own" their work practices (remember the coal-mining study?) and therefore, to increase the likelihood that the group will develop a norm of support for those practices. Such norms provide a striking contrast to the "restrictive" output norm which often emerges when control is perceived to be exclusively and unilaterally under the control of management.

Hackman (1976) says that participative techniques can facilitate group effectiveness under three conditions:

1. The participation is relevant to the work itself. Participation in planning the company picnic, for example, will probably have little effect on work productivity.

2. The objective task and environmental contingencies in the work setting are actually supportive of more effective performance. If participation causes the group members to discover that hard work leads only to more hard work, then productivity may decrease after participation.

3. The task structure and task activities are such that increased effort or a better work strategy can lead to higher work effectiveness. If the worker has little control over the amount of work which arrives at his or her station (for example, the assembly line phenomenon), then participation is not likely to change output significantly. (This issue is discussed further in our treatment of the "participation controversy" in Chapter 16.)

Integration of the group with other groups in the organization

In organizations, competition for scarce resources often causes conflict among groups. Likert (1961) has proposed a method for reducing such conflict by ensuring that groups are integrated into the organization (a larger group). Likert argues that the overlapping group memberships of a large organization constitute the major channel of influence within the organization. A group leader's role, in Likert's view, is to act as a "linking pin" among the various groups to which he or she belongs. The manager will have high power (as the supervisor) in some of these groups, will be a peer in other groups, and will be a subordinate in still other groups. These relationships are shown in Figure 14–3.

The goal of the linking pin agent is to ensure that the demands of the various groups are communicated and decided upon. The ease or difficulty of doing this will depend in part on the nature of the task and the norms of the groups with which the leader interacts.

As Smith (1973) argues, unacceptable pressure from above may easily produce a hierarchical system of integrated coalitions rather than Li-

Figure 14–3
Likert's linking pin model of an organization

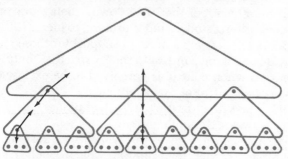

The arrows indicate the linking pin function.
Source: Taken from R. Likert, *New Patterns of Management*
(New York: McGraw-Hill, 1961), p. 369.

kert's model of linking pins extending both vertically and horizontally throughout the organization. Lawrence and Lorsch (1967) paid considerable attention to the process of organizational integration in the plastics industry. They found that integrative procedures in more successful firms differed greatly from those used by less successful firms. The plastics firms had a considerable need of integration since their structures were strongly differentiated in response to their varied and changing environments. In addition to using the integrating procedures found in most organizations, such as hierarchy to resolve disputes and standardized reporting procedures, the firms also had one or more cross-functional liaison teams act as a separate department whose prime function was to achieve integration among the different groups in the organization.

The more successful firms were found to differ from the less successful ones in six ways. First, the integrating department contained individuals from the departments whose efforts it sought to integrate. In the less successful organizations, the integrating department tended to be more similar to one or another of those departments and was therefore seen as partisan in disputes. Second, the integrator's power was seen as being based on technical expertise rather than on the integrator's position in the organization. Third, the integrator groups in the more successful firms felt that their own rewards were contingent on achieving integration, whereas such groups in the less successful firms did not. Fourth, the managers in the more successful firms felt that they had more influence in general than did the managers in the less successful firms. Fifth, in the more successful firms there was a close match between the levels at which information was available and the levels at which relevant disputes were involved. Finally, in the more successful firms there was a greater tendency for conflicts to be resolved through constructive confrontation of differences, rather than through smoothing things over.

THE WAYS GROUPS INFLUENCE WORK EFFECTIVENESS: A SUMMARY STATEMENT

In the Hawthorne research, the formation of a tight-knit group in the Relay Assembly Test room seemed to be effective for the steady increase in production. Increased cohesiveness, however, does not necessarily result in increased productivity, and can in fact be detrimental to productivity.

In this chapter we presented information which shows that both the psychological and the structural properties of groups affect performance and satisfaction. Although each of us is vaguely aware of the powerful influence of groups, normally we do not realize how much we behave in accordance with group norms and expectations. Our definition of appropriate behavior, our definition of satisfaction, and even our definition of "self" is closely tied to the "significant others" with whom we interact. We have learned here that our need for approval often causes us to overconform and that if conformity among group members is too great, creativity can be stifled and the survival of the group may actually be threatened.

In pursuing our investigation of groups, we gave a great deal of attention to the various ways in which groups can be structured along certain dimensions, and how such structuring, as well as the "personality" of the group, can enhance or hurt performance. Very subtle changes in the structure of groups can have a great impact on group interactions, group morale, and total organizational success. The integration of groups into the total organization was also discussed.

Each of you can probably identify with the group as a phenomenon. Understanding group behavior is a prerequisite for successful management. Managers are judged by the success of the groups they supervise. Since many organizations are large, it is impossible for top management to work with and respond to each member of the organization. The major unit in most organizations is therefore the group. One of the biggest problems faced by group managers is that of conflict within and among groups. The next chapter will examine in detail the management of group conflict.

CONCEPTS TO REMEMBER

Hawthorne studies
social facilitation
social comparison
groupthink
linking pin role of leader

assets and liabilities
  of group problem solving
nominal group technique
delphi group technique

QUESTIONS FOR DISCUSSION

1. "One way that managers can increase their power or level of influence is to turn over part of their decision-making functions to groups of subordinates." Comment.

2. In 1976, Sears, Roebuck and Company instituted the "Office of the President." Three executives share the responsibilities of the chief executive officer, What advantages and disadvantages do you think this system will have? Find out how successful this change has been for Sears.

3. A favorite stalling tactic of managers faced with an unpopular decision is to involve groups in the process. When do you think this tactic would be most effective?

4. When would an autocratic leader be more effective than a democratic leader?

5. How does the structure of a group affect the "personality" of the group?

REFERENCES

Adams, J. S. Wages in a clerical task. Unpublished study, General Electric Company, New York, 1961.

Allport, F. H. *Social psychology.* Boston: Houghton Mifflin, 1924.

Brickman, P., & Campbell, D. T. Hedonic relativism and planning the good society. In M. H. Appley (Ed.), *Adaptation-level theory: A symposium.* New York: Academic Press, 1971.

Brown, R. *Social psychology.* New York: Free Press, 1965.

The corps demands all of you. *National Observer,* September 25, 1976, pp. 1, 18.

Dalkey, N. C. *The Delphi method: An experimental study of group opinions.* Santa Monica, Calif.: Rand Corp., 1969.

Davis, J. *Group performance.* Reading, Mass.: Addison-Wesley, 1969.

Deutsch, M. A theory of cooperation and competition. *Human Relations,* 1949, *2,* 129–152.

Festinger, L. A theory of social comparison processes. *Human Relations,* 1954, *7,* 114–140.

French, J. R. P. The disruption and cohesion of groups. *Journal of Abnormal and Social Psychology,* 1941, *36,* 361–377.

French, J. R. P. Organized and unorganized groups under fear and frustration. *University of Iowa Studies in Child Welfare,* 1944, *20,* 229–308.

Frost, C. F., Wakeley, J. H., & Ruh, R. A. *The Scanlon Plan for organizational development.* East Lansing: Michigan State University Press, 1974.

Hackman, J. R. Effects of task characteristics on group products. *Journal of Experimental Social Psychology,* 1968, *4,* 162–187.

Hackman, J. R. Group influence on individuals. In M. D. Dunnette (Ed.),

Handbook of industrial and organizational psychology. Chicago: Rand McNally, 1976.

Hackman, J. R., & Lawler, E. E.   Employee reactions to job characteristics. *Journal of Applied Psychology Monographs,* 1971, *55,* 259–286.

Hoffman, L. R., & Maier, N. R. F.   Quality and acceptance of problem solutions by members of homogeneous and heterogeneous groups. *Journal of Abnormal and Social Psychology,* 1961, *62,* 401–407.

Janis, I. L.   *Victims of groupthink.* Boston: Houghton Mifflin, 1972.

Kriesberg, M.   Executives evaluate administrative conferences. *Advanced Management,* 1950, *15,* 15–17.

Lambert, W. W., & Lambert, W. E.   *Social psychology* (2d ed.). Englewood Cliffs, N.J.: Prentice-Hall, 1973.

Lawler, E. E.   *Pay and organizational effectiveness: A psychological view.* New York: McGraw-Hill, 1971.

Lawrence, P. R., & Lorsh, J. W.   Organizations and environment: Managing differentiation and integration. Cambridge, Mass.: Division of Research, Graduate School of Business, Harvard University, 1967.

Lewin, K., Lippitt, R., & White, R. K.   Patterns of aggressive behavior in experimentally created "social climates." *Journal of Social Psychology,* 1939, *10,* 271–299.

Likert, R.   *New patterns of management.* New York: McGraw-Hill, 1961.

Maier, N. R. F.   *Psychology in industrial organizations* (4th ed.). Boston: Houghton Mifflin, 1973.

Mann, L.   *Social psychology,* New York: Wiley, 1969.

Meade, R. D.   An experimental study of leadership in India. In W. W. Lambert & R. Weisbrod (Eds.), *Comparative perspectives on social psychology.* Boston: Little, Brown, 1971.

Mintz, A.   Non-adaptive group behavior. *Journal of Abnormal and Social Psychology,* 1951, *46,* 150–159.

Roethlisberger, F. J., & Dickson, W. J.   *Management and the worker.* Cambridge, Mass.: Harvard University Press, 1939.

Shaw, M. E.   *Group dynamics.* New York: McGraw-Hill, 1971.

Smith, P. B.   *Groups within organizations.* New York: Harper and Row, 1973.

Tillman, R.   Problems in review: Committee on trial. *Harvard Business Review* 1960, *47,* 162–172.

Triandis, H. C., Hall, E. R., & Ewen, R. B.   Member heterogeneity and dyadic creativity. *Human Relations,* 1965, *18,* 33–55.

Triplett, N.   The dynamogenic factors in pacemaking and competition. *American Journal of Psychology,* 1897, *9,* 507–533.

Trist, E. L., Higgins, G., Pollock, H. E., & Murray, H. A.   *Organizational choice.* London: Tavistock, 1963.

Van de Van, A. H., & Delbecq, A. L.   The effectiveness of Nominal and Delphi techniques in interacting group decision making processes. *Academy of Management Journal,* 1974, *17,* 605–621.

Zanjonc, R. B.   Social facilitation. *Science,* 1965, *149,* 269–274.

Managing conflict within and between groups

What are the sources of conflict within and between groups?

What are the functions and dysfunctions of conflict?

What are the various strategies for resolving conflict?

Paraphrasing Mark Twain, Webber (1975) noted that "life is just one damned conflict after another. Conflict and stress are common when complex entities such as individuals and small groups are brought together in formal organizations" (p. 583).

Conflict refers to all types of antagonistic interaction. It can be overt or subtle. The position taken here is that conflict found in organizations is inevitable in most instances, often legitimate, and very often desirable. Conflict does not necessarily indicate organizational breakdown or management failure, as was implied by previously accepted principles of industrial and organizational psychology. As Pondy (1972) suggests: "Conflict, like pain, is a signal that the organization is in trouble or on the verge of trouble. An organization or other social system which suppresses conflict, which prohibits the expression of dissent, is depriving itself of the feedback loop necessary for self-regulation and stability" (p. 49).

Janis (1972) is perhaps the strongest proponent of the need for dissension and conflict in organizations and groups. As noted in Chapter 14, Janis labels the repression of dissension in groups as "groupthink" and argues that "the U.S. road to disaster—in Vietnam, the Bay of Pigs, Korea, and Pearl Harbor—is paved with Groupthink—the desperate drive for consensus at any cost that suppresses dissent among the mighty corridors of power" (p. 43).

This chapter will examine: (1) the causes or *antecedents of conflict,* (2) the *functional* and *dysfunctional conflict* found in most organizations, and (3) the *strategies* managers can use to manage conflict.

ANTECEDENTS OF CONFLICT

What causes conflict? Why do we have conflict? Is all conflict "bad" to the extent that it causes someone to lose or fail? We will attempt to examine these and other questions in this section on the antecedents of conflict. The antecedents of conflict can vary according to the *situation* in which conflict arises and according to the *type* of conflict which presents itself.

THE CONFLICT SITUATION

Boulding (1964) has provided a framework for a composite view of the antecedents and resolution of the total conflict situation. He suggests that the conflict process has four components. The *parties* involved are the first component. According to Boulding, conflict must involve at least two parties—individuals, groups, or organizations.

Boulding identifies the second component of conflict as the *"field of conflict."* This he defines as "the whole set of relevant possible states of the social system. (Any state of the social system which either

341

of the parties to a conflict considers relevant is, of course, a relevant state)" (p. 138). Boulding seems to be referring to all of the possible alternative positions toward which the conflict could move.

The third component of the conflict situation, according to Boulding, is the *dynamics* of the situation. This refers to the fact that each party in a conflict situation will adjust his or her position to one that he or she feels is congruent with the position of the opponent. In other words, the strategies used by each party to a conflict will be determined in part by the responses of the other party or parties to earlier attempts at conflict resolution. For example, *U.S. News & World Report* (1975, p. 3) stated that John Connally failed to adjust to the position of others when negotiating conflict resolution and therefore was seen as "not playing by the rules" (the implication being that conflict resolution is a dynamic and interdependent process). The report stated: "A Belgian banker's private size-up of U.S. Treasury Secretary John B. Connally as a bargainer on international monetary problems: 'He does not seem to realize that to succeed in these matters you must be extremely frank and that there must be concessions from both sides. Negotiation needs a spirit of compromise. I haven't seen much sign of that.' "

The fourth component in the Boulding model is the *"management, control, or resolution of conflict."* These terms used by Boulding suggest that conflicts are not discrete situations with a clear beginning and end. Conflict obviously emerges out of a preexisting situation, and it doesn't usually end with a settlement, even though the intensity of the conflict may shift, as one would expect in a dynamic situation. Boulding notes that the organization's main goal should be to prevent conflict from becoming "pathological" and thus destructive of the parties involved and the larger system.

TYPES OF CONFLICT

In general three types of conflict are found in work settings. These are: (1) within-group conflict; (2) conflict between groups in a particular organization; and (3) conflict between organizations.

Within-group conflict

One type of conflict found in virtually every organization is conflict between two or more people within the same group or department. Such within-group conflict generally falls into one of three categories: (1) *role conflict,* (2) *issue conflict,* or (3) *interaction conflict.*

As discussed in Chapters 9 and 13, *role conflict* is conflict which results when the expectations associated with two or more positions that a person occupies are incompatible with one another (interrole conflict), or when the various expectations associated with a single position that a person occupies are mutually incompatible. Regardless of the source of role conflict, when role conflict occurs with enough intensity to preclude adequate role performance by the person experiencing the conflict, he or she seeks to resolve it.

For the most part, external role pressures are exerted by other members in adjacent positions in the organizational structure, that is, by superiors and subordinates in the authority structure; by those who have a functionally dependent relationship in the work-flow structure, requiring some coordination of activities; or by close friends or respected "significant others" in the informal structure.

A common type of role conflict found in an organization is labeled "authority conflict" by Adams and Romney (1959). In this type of role conflict, external role pressures are exerted by superiors in two or more authority sequences in such a way that they specify to the same subordinate responses that are either contradictory or cannot be performed simultaneously. Adams and Romney give the example of two bosses making simultaneous typing requests of a secretary late in the workday. Because of time limitations, the secretary can comply with only one of the requests. Thus, he or she can (1) type boss A's letter, (2) type boss B's letter, or (3) do neither.

Research studying the impact of role conflict (for example, that faced by the secretary) on work outcomes has shown that high levels of role conflict are related to low levels of job satisfaction, low confidence in the organization, a high degree of job-related tension, and a high propensity to leave the organization.

One of the reasons role conflict has such a detrimental effect on work outcomes is that role behavior is constantly being *evaluated* and *sanctioned* (Biddle & Thomas, 1966). Evaluating involves the making of "positive" or "negative" judgments about a particular role behavior, and sanctioning is a procedure engaged in either to maintain positively evaluated role behaviors or to change negatively evaluated ones.

Issue conflict, a second type of conflict experienced within most work groups, generally results from disagreement between two or more members of the work group concerning the solution to a particular problem. Often individuals in groups are aware of different definitions of a problem or have different pieces of information relevant to the problem. Issue conflict can involve disagreements about the *facts* in a case, the *goal* to be accomplished by a group, the *methods* for accomplishing a goal, or the *personal values* associated with the various methods that might be used to reach a goal or solve a problem.

For example, a marketing research group which has a large amount of autonomy in a company may see as its overall goal the development of new product concepts and improvement of the image of existing products. If the group is comprised of highly talented and well-educated people, in discussing the introduction of product X to the market or the improvement of product Y's image in the marketplace, the group's members will probably differ strongly about the facts in the case. If, for example, only 28 percent of the consumers prefer the company's product Y over its competitor's product Y, does this mean that product Y is in trouble? Not necessarily. Suppose that this company's product Y sells for four times the price of its competitor's product Y and that 90 percent of all people in the $20,000 and above income bracket prefer the more expensive product. Two members of the marketing research group could each be using the same information and disagree as to the facts of the case. Similar comparisons could be made about *methods, values,* and *goals.* When people who bring diverse backgrounds and talents into a group are asked to express their opinions, then disagreement is a natural and healthy by-product.

Whether disagreement is the same as conflict depends to a large extent on the perceptions of the parties involved. Thus, a key to whether the situational parameters discussed above actually develop into *interaction conflict,* a third type of group conflict, may be one of attribution in which both sides perceive themselves to be in conflict. Research on attribution has found that an individual often perceives his or her own behavior as being motivated by situational and external causes, whereas observers of the same behavior tend to perceive the individual's actions as the result of personal motivations. Thus, when two parties in a work group achieve success by coordinating their work activities, the tendency might be for each party to view the success as an individual accomplishment, but if the actions lead to failure, each party might attribute the failure to the other person's sabotage while seeing his own inability to succeed as due to the exigencies of the situation. The result may be the common situation in which each party blames the other for the conflict that ensues, while absolving himself of any responsibility. In such instances, though the cause of the conflict may soon be forgotten, the dislike engendered by the conflict may carry over to future interactions.

Between-group conflict

A "law of intergroup conflict," which maintains that all groups or organizations are in partial conflict with one another, has been suggested by Downs (1968). Kahn (1964) has identified three intergroup bases of conflict. The first, which he labels *functional conflict,* is induced by various subsystems within an organization. This form of conflict involves the fact that:

> Every subsystem of an organization with its distinctive functions develops its own norms and values and is characterized by its own dynamics. People in the maintenance subsystem have the problem of maintaining the role

system and preserving the character of the organization through selection of appropriate personnel, indoctrinating and training them, devising checks for ensuring standard role performance, and so on. These people face *inward* in the organization and are concerned with maintaining the *status quo*. People in the procurement and disposal subsystems, however, face *outward* on the world and develop a different psychological orientation. These differing orientations are one built-in source of conflict. Put in another way, the systems of maintenance, production, and adaptive development each develop their own distinctive norms and frames of reference which contain their own elements of potential conflict. (pp. 105–106)

Functional conflict seems to come about because of *task* or *goal incompatibility* and/or *boundary role* incompatibility. According to Schmidt and Kochan (1972), perception of goal incompatibility is a necessary precondition for intergroup conflict. They state, "This im-

Figure 15–1
The boundary-role person's dual membership

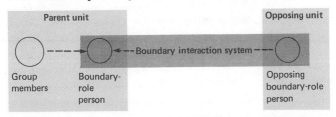

Source: Adapted from J. A. Wall and J. S. Adams. Some variables affecting a constituent's evaluation of and behavior toward a boundary role occupant, *Organizational Behavior and Human Performance*, 1974, *11*, p. 28.

plies that goal attainment by one unit is seen to prevent others from achieving their goals under the same circumstances or with equivalent outcomes. Thus for example, the units within the organization strive to attain their respective goals at each other's expense" (p. 361). Goal incompatibility motivates interdependent groups to engage in conflict, but for overt conflict to occur among the groups, they must have the ability to interfere with the attainment of one another's goals.

An unique type of task or goal incompatibility is associated with a *boundary* position. Kahn, Wolfe, Quinn, Snoek, and Rosenthal (1964) define a boundary position as one in which some members of a role set are located in two or more groups within the same organization or within more than one organization. An organization member who occupies such a position finds himself in a structurally unique situation. He is not only a member of his parent unit, and thereby subject to the expectations and influence attempts of its members, but he is also a member of a boundary interaction unit. Wall and Adams (1974) depict the conflict situation as shown in Figure 15–1.

As Figure 15–1 shows, a boundary role-member is the target of potentially conflicting demands, some received from his constituents and some received from individuals outside his organization. Recent work on boundary roles (Chapter 18 elaborates on the nature of boundary roles) has focused on the conflicting influence exerted on a boundary-role person by his own group and opposing groups. The parent group's evaluation of a boundary-role person and its behavior toward him have both been shown to exert a significant influence on the behavior of such a person. Wall and Adams (1974), for example, found that salespersons who were obedient to the parent group's wishes and/or effective in outside performance, avoided conflict and were rated higher on performance and other attributes than were salesmen who were disobedient and/or ineffective with the outside group.

The *second* basis of intergroup conflict identified by Kahn (1964) is *hierarchical conflict* which stems from interest-group struggles over the organizational rewards of status, prestige, and money. As March and Simon (1958) point out, when an organization's resources are relatively unlimited, the organization need not resolve the merits of subgroup claims. In these circumstances, such claims tend to be unchallenged even though substantial differentiation of goals occurs within the organization. However, when an organization's resources are restricted, the relations among its subgroups become more competitive. On the basis of this assumption, March and Simon predict that as resources are reduced (for example, during a business recession), intergroup conflict tends to increase.

An example of conflict over a loss of intergroup status was reported in the *Wall Street Journal.* The report states:

> Upheavals in the executive suite generally are so candied over with public relations that outsiders rarely catch even a glimpse of the bitter corporate infighting that preceded them. Most times the loser departs the scene showered with compliments for his "vital contribution" to the company and that's the end of that.
>
> Not so in the case of Consolidated Foods Corp., the billion-dollar Chicago merchandising conglomerate that unceremoniously dumped its chairman and chief executive officer, 53-year-old William Howlett, a month ago.
>
> "Everybody's just jubilant," Nathan R. Cummings, Consolidated's founder and largest stockholder, told a reporter at the time. "Can't you hear over the phone how everyone is laughing and talking?"
>
> The vote wasn't even close—15 directors to one, Mr. Howlett's own vote. And then the board speedily chose William A. Bazick, Jr., Consolidated president, as Mr. Howlett's successor. . . .
>
> Many of the top brass of Consolidated's complicated corporate structure must feel a bit uneasy at the moment. The company has 32 separate divisions, each with its own president, gathered in a semi-autonomous system reporting to six executive vice-presidents. Says one insider, "Bill Buzick probably won't do anything with unseemly haste, but you may see several

of the executive vice-presidents who are considered Howlett protégés get the axe." ("Ousted Chairman of Consolidated Foods," 1970, p. 1.)

The *third* basis of intergroup conflict arises from the fact that units in an organization have similar functions. Conflict in this instance can take the form of hostile rivalry or good-natured competition. Not all competition leads to conflict and hostility, however. Boulding (1962), for example, states:

> Competition in its broadest sense exists when any potential positions of two behavior units are mutually incompatible. This is a broader concept than conflict. . . . whereas all cases of conflict involve competition in the above sense, not all cases of competition involve conflict. . . .
>
> Conflict may be defined as a situation of competition in which the parties are *aware* of the incompatibility of potential future positions and in which each party wishes to occupy a position that is incompatible with the wishes of the other. (p. 4)

One important reason that competition between groups turns to conflict centers again on group norms and the perceptions held by members of a group toward "outsiders" in other groups. LeVine and Campbell (1972) labeled as *ethnocentrism* the natural progression from perceived competition among groups to perceived hostility. Ethnocentrism is an attitude or outlook in which values and norms derived from one's own cultural and group background are applied to other cultural or group contexts in which different values are operative. LeVine and Campbell note that symbols of one's own group or of the values shared by that group "become objects of attachment, pride and veneration; symbols of other groups or their values become objects of contempt and hatred" (p. 1). This would be especially true, for example, of groups with different ethnic or national backgrounds, or with conflicting value systems (for example, blue-collar groups versus white-collar groups versus management groups; Democratic senators versus Republican senators; the American delegation versus the Cuban delegation at the United Nations; female race car drivers versus male race car drivers at Indianapolis; or researchers and other professionals versus traditional managers in an organization).

Summer (1906) hypothesized that the syndrome of ethnocentrism is functionally related to group formation and intergroup competition, and that to some extent *all* groups show this syndrome. LeVine and Campbell (1972) specify several facets of the syndrome of ethnocentrism. These are described in Figure 15–2.

As can be readily seen from Figure 15–2, ethnocentrism can lead from group rivalries to intergroup hostilities. Sherif, Harvey, White, Hood, and Sherif (1961) state that the more important the goal competed for, the greater is the value that is being threatened, the *perceived* interference with goal attainment, and therefore, intergroup

Figure 15–2
Facets of the syndrome of ethnocentrism

Attitudes and behaviors toward in-group	*Attitudes and behaviors toward out-group*
See selves as virtuous and superior	See out-groups as contemptible, inferior, and perhaps immoral
See own standard of value as universal, intrinsically true; see own customs as original, centrally human	See out-groups as weak
	Maintain social distance from out-groups
See selves as strong	Approve hatred of out-groups
Impose sanction against violations of in-group norms	Sanction absence of cooperation with out-group members
Cooperative relations with in-group members	Sanction absence of obedience to out-group authorities
Obedience to in-group authority	Unwilling to join and/or fight for out-groups
Willing to remain in-group members (loyalty)	Use out-groups as bad examples in training
Willing to fight for in-group	Blame out-groups for in-group trouble
	Distrust and fear out-groups

Source: Adapted from R. A. LeVine and D. T. Campbell, *Ethnocentrism: Theories of Conflict, Ethnic Attitudes, and Group Behavior* (New York: Wiley, 1972), p. 12.

hostility. In addition, according to LeVine and Campbell (1972), threat to in-group goal attainment leads to increased in-group solidarity, increased awareness of in-group identity, increases in the tightness of group boundaries, reduction in defection from the in-group, increased punishment and rejection of defectors and deviants, and therefore, increased ethnocentrism.

LeVine and Campbell (1962) predict that "intergroup conflict and mutual ethnocentric hostility can only be removed by superordinate common goals or shared threats" (p. 11). The capacity of superordinate goals to remove well-developed intergroup hostility has been experimentally demonstrated by Sherif et al.(1961). (See Chapter 13 for more information about the Sherif et al. experiment.)

Whether or not hostility and conflict should be removed depends, of course, on whether or not these have dysfunctional or functional consequences for the organization. Conflict can lead to heightened morale within a subsystem, and it can lead to solutions which move toward integration rather than compromise. Before we examine the functional and dysfunctional consequences of conflict and strategies for resolving and managing dysfunctional conflict, we need first to examine the third type of conflict found in organizational settings, namely conflict which takes place between organizations.

Interorganizational conflict

It will not be necessary to devote a great deal of space to interorganizational conflict since, as March and Simon (1958) state: "Many of the phenomena of intergroup conflict within the organization are almost indistinguishable from the phenomena that we might consider under the present heading (interorganizational conflict). The distinction between internal and external relations for an organization is a cloudy one. However, there will generally be more pressure toward use of analytic techniques within the organization than in relations between organizations. Of course, this pressure will operate through broad social institutions and reference groups, but with substantially reduced effect" (p. 131).

This is not to say that it is not important to examine interorganizational conflict or that interorganizational conflict doesn't exist—only that the types of conflict found between groups also exist, on a much larger scale, between organizations. Interorganizational relations have been described as varying on a continuum from conflict to cooperation. Most interorganizational interactions take the form of bargaining and exchange relationships, and most relationships occur at the organization's boundaries (for example, sales, public relations, purchasing, lobbyists, and receptionists).

Government regulations in the United States encourage competition and discourage cooperation among competing firms. Competition tends to lead to conflict whenever the "rules" governing relations among organizations are violated. Such rules are generally of two types. First, there are rules which discourage cooperation, for example, antitrust laws, patent laws, and bribery laws. Second, there are rules which, to some extent, discourage competition, for example, the National Labor Relations Act and Title VII Civil Rights Act. Whenever a written or unwritten rule is violated, conflict takes place. For example, Polaroid recently sued Kodak for patent infringement; the major cereal manufacturers are being investigated for ostensible restraint of trade and price fixing; Gulf Oil and Lockheed have been charged with paying bribes to boundary-role agents from foreign organizations; and the Democrats charged the Republicans with unfair campaign practices in the 1972 presidential election.

Aldrich (1971) noted that the limited evidence that is available suggests that similarities in operating principles, priorities, and structures (for example, among the airlines) lead to cooperation among organizations, whereas dissimilarities in these respects plus competition for scarce resources contribute to conflict. Aldrich further notes the frequent but mistaken assumption that cooperation among organizations is by definition good.[1]

Stagner and Rosen (1965) identified five types of interorganizational conflict that the typical industrial organization faces. The varieties of industrial conflict situations faced by most organizations are shown in Figure 15–3. One of the most common and visible of these types of interorganizational conflict takes place between trade unions and employer organizations. Since the two parties have different goals, partial conflict is viewed as a legitimate characteristic of their relation-

Figure 15–3
Types of interorganizational conflicts

Parties to conflict	*Example of conflict*
Management-government	Antitrust action, EEO suits, NLRB investigations, OSHA inspections, political contributions, bribery
Intermanagement	Price competition between companies, disputes over patents and fulfillment of contracts
Interunion	Jurisdictional disputes (for example, the Teamsters and Cesar Chavez)
Union-government	Secondary boycotts, illegal strikes (public sector), discrimination, criminal activities
Union-management	Union and management debate over division of earnings between wages and profits

Source: Adapted from R. Stagner and H. Rosen, *Psychology of Union-Management Relations* (Belmont, Calif.: Brooks/Cole, 1965), p. 91.

ship with each other. Students of industrial relations have long held that there is an inherent conflict of interest between employees and their employing organizations and that this conflict is institutionalized and legitimated in the collective bargaining process. Kochan (1975) points out, quite correctly, that the conflict is only partial. "Since the parties are tied together in a continuous interdependent relation, they must accommodate their conflicting interests by establishing a structural relation that can endure over time" (p. 435).

Even though the rules governing interorganizational conflict are set, in part, by the federal and state governments, the bases of interorganizational conflict are essentially the same as the bases of intergroup conflict. These bases include (1) *functional conflicts* (noncomparable

---

[1] For the interested reader, Assael (1969) discusses in greater detail the constructive role of cooperation and conflict in the automobile industry.

tasks and goals and boundary-role conflict); (2) conflicts over *status, prestige,* and *money;* and (3) *hostile rivalry.* LeVine and Campbell's (1972) description of group ethnocentrism would be directly relevant for describing interorganizational conflict, especially among multinational firms and multinational governments. In comparing intergovernmental conflict with union-management conflict, "labor leader George Meany recently said, after noting the deterioration of détente between the U.S. and Russia, 'if relations between management and labor ever reached such a low level in my negotiations I would go on strike,'" (*U.S. News & World Report,* May 3, 1976, p. 4).

FUNCTIONAL AND DYSFUNCTIONAL CONFLICT

We have constantly noted that conflict can further as well as impede goal attainment. It has long been recognized that conflict is not inherently destructive. On the contrary, conflict has many positive functions. It prevents stagnation; it stimulates interest and curiosity; it is the medium through which problems can be aired and solutions reached; it is at the root of personal and social change. Conflict can help individuals to test their capacities, to learn and grow. It helps groups and individuals to establish identities and self-images. Coser (1956) stated:

> In loosely-structured groups and open societies, conflict, which aims at a resolution of tension between antagonists, is likely to have stabilizing and integrative functions for the relationship. By permitting immediate and direct expression of rival claims, such social systems are able to readjust their structures by eliminating the sources of dissatisfaction. The multiple conflicts which they experience may serve to eliminate the causes for dissociation and to re-establish unity. These systems avail themselves, through the toleration and institutionalization of conflict, of an important stabilizing mechanism. (p. 154)

Nevertheless, the management of conflict is important because conflict which is left unresolved tends to lead to dysfunctional conflict. At the individual and group level, people should be encouraged to express differences of opinion on issues and to discuss the role conflicts which they perceive. If this is not done, conflict may tend to be internalized (intrapersonal conflict) or else to be transformed into personality conflict. At the intergroup and organizational level, conflict should be channeled in such a way that competition and conflict are changed from a "win-lose" situation to a "win-win" situation. For example, a union wage demand negotiated in such a way that increases in wages and salaries are tied to increases in plant productivity and/or profit rather than to increases in the cost of living might be more beneficial to both labor and management.

Deutsch (1969) suggests that an unpressured and unthreatening environment facilitates the restructuring of a problem or conflict, and by so doing, makes it more amenable to solution. The ability to reformulate a problem and to develop solutions depends upon the availability of cognitive resources. As Deutsch notes:

> Ideas *are* important for the creative resolution of conflict and any factor which broadens the range of ideas and alternatives cognitively available to the participants in a conflict will be useful. . . . The availability of ideas is also dependent upon social conditions such as the opportunity to communicate with and be exposed to other people who may have relevant and unfamiliar ideas (i.e., experts, impartial outsiders, people with similar or analogous situations), a social atmosphere which values innovation and originality and which encourages the exchange of ideas, and a social tradition which fosters the optimistic view that, with effort and time, constructive solutions can be discovered or invented to problems which seem initially intractable. (p. 43)

It is argued, therefore, that the internal conflict which is found in most organizations is not per se "bad," but that the repression of conflict or the channeling of conflict into hostility and personality fights may be detrimental to the survival of persons, groups, or organizations. Most of the conflict found within organizations is *unregulated* by law, the control of such conflict being left to management.

Nevertheless, some intraorganizational conflict situations and most interorganizational conflict situations are regulated by law because of their destructive potential to the parties involved and to third parties which are subject to the solutions reached. Conflict is limited and controlled by institutional forms (for example, collective bargaining and the judicial system), social roles (mediators, conciliators, referees, judges, police), social norms (justice, equity, nonviolence), rules for conducting negotiations, and specific procedures (public versus private sessions) (Deutsch, 1969).

Thus, it seems that conflict is viewed as a natural interaction process among people and institutions. It is legally recognized as a valid and useful process of decision making. Managers are constantly called upon to make decisions or to solve problems which have arisen from conflicts between individuals, groups, or departments within organizations. In such situations the manager's first step is to accept the fact that conflict does exist and to be aware that it may offer many side benefits to the organization (new ideas, adapting to changes in the external environment). The manager's second step is to be open to conflict and to establish rules that allow conflict to surface but do not lead to hostility or destructive behaviors. Finally, since managers often negotiate conflicts, the manager must understand the underlying dynamics of conflict and must be aware of available strategies for resolving conflict which will enable him or her to reach the solution most beneficial to all concerned.

STRATEGIES OF CONFLICT RESOLUTION

In the previous two sections covering the antecedents of conflict and the dysfunctional and functional consequences of conflict, we have discussed in some detail the *parties* involved in conflict and, to some extent, the *field* of conflict. These, you will recall, are two of the four components of conflict suggested by Boulding (1964). Now that we have elaborated on these antecedents of conflict, we need to look at ways in which conflict can be resolved. Boulding, as previously noted, sees the process of conflict resolution as involving two components —the *type* of strategy chosen and the *strength* of the strategy chosen.

Type of resolution strategy chosen

According to March and Simon (1958), an organization can use one of four major processes to resolve conflict: (1) problem solving, (2) persuasion, (3) politics, and (4) bargaining. In *problem solving*, it is assumed that objectives are shared and that the need is to identify a solution that satisfies the shared criteria. According to Maier (1970), problem solving involves two processes—the idea-getting process and the idea-evaluation process. Research has shown that problem-solving discussions are more productive if ideas are collected before they are appraised. Experimental results have also shown that the quality of a solution is upgraded if the leader of a problem-solving group explores the problem with the group before talking about solutions. Since the purpose of the problem-solving group is to examine the various alternatives and the various conflicting points of view, it is necessary to promote rather than stifle disagreement in the group's discussion. Research evidence has shown that heterogeneous groups are more innovative than homogeneous groups since individual differences tend to lead to disagreement and people from different groups are more likely to express their opinions more freely.

In the *persuasion* attempt, it is assumed that disagreement over subgoals (among individuals or groups) can be mediated by reference to common goals. Implicit in the use of persuasion, according to March and Simon (1958), is the belief that, at some level, objectives are shared and that disagreement over subgoals can be mediated by reference to common goals. Whether or not a persuasion attempt is successful depends in part on the characteristics of and the relationships among the communicator, the message transmitted, and the recipients of the message in the conflict resolution process.

A classic study examining the use of persuasion as a tool for inducing opinion change was conducted at Yale University by Hovland, Janis, and Kelley in 1953. They found that the communicator is more likely to induce change if his or her credibility is high. The way in which a persuasive communication is worded, organized, and presented is also an important determinant of its reception. For instance, if there are two sides to an issue, then a two-sided communication in which pros and cons are mentioned will be more effective than a one-sided communication that attempts to shield each party from opposing viewpoints.

Copley News Service recently discussed the terms used to describe the effectiveness of diplomats using persuasive techniques with their foreign counterparts:

> Diplomats use a standard jargon to describe high-level discussions between heads of state. As a quick guide to better understanding of diplomatic terms, we offer those definitions:
>
> "Useful"—No progress, but we learned where the other side stands, and that could be fruitful.
>
> "Fruitful"—This round was deadlocked, but the next could be productive.
>
> "Productive"—Still no agreement, but we are proceeding in an atmosphere that is frank and open.
>
> "Frank and open"—Complete and total disagreement, but something meaningful may come of it.
>
> "Meaningful"—Everybody enjoyed the tour of the museum. (Copley News Service, *Reader's Digest,* 1975, p. 82).

A recent article in the *Harvard Business Review* (Jan.–Feb., 1976) suggested that the leader of group meetings had an obligation to let conflict surface. In response to this article, presidents of two major firms wrote letters to the editors of the *Harvard Business Review* giving their views on conducting group meetings. The president of United Air Lines, Richard J. Ferris, spoke in favor of a problem-solving arena when he said:

> The role of the chairman is crucial to the success of a meeting, and I concur that "the meeting must be a contention of ideas, not people." At United we like to encourage our people to disagree but not to be disagreeable. . . . Structured meetings are definitely a necessity for managing meeting time. A balance must be struck, however, to prevent the inhibition of creativity and the flow of new ideas. ("Letters to the Editors," 1976, p. 172)

The president of Joseph E. Seagram and Sons, Inc., Jack Yogman, argued that persuasion prior to the meeting was a preferable arena for resolving conflict. He said:

> Occasionally there is a meeting in which no impasse should arise—for example, a board meeting of a major public company. One of the most successful chairmen I have ever met makes it a point to meet individually with every single board member before every board meeting at which a controversial issue is to be aired. Together, they iron out whatever problems might exist

so that the meeting itself can be free of acrimony and dissension. ("Letters to the Editors," 1976, p. 172)

Problem solving and persuasion are more likely to be used to resolve unregulated conflict. For example, an ad hoc business or a government committee would be more likely to use problem solving as a method of resolving differences among its members. Organizational development as a motivational tool (see Chapter 13) uses group involvement and group participation techniques to improve the work environment and resolve conflicts. Governor Carter used persuasion to gain support for his bid for the presidential nomination among uncommitted delegates to the 1976 Democratic National Convention. In regulated conflict, one is more likely to see the arena being specified as one for either a bargaining solution or a political solution. As we will soon show, both bargaining and politics can contain some techniques used in the problem-solving and persuasion arenas—but conflicts using these latter approaches are more readily identified as conflicts, and the rules to be followed are generally more rigidly structured and more formally stated.

In contrast to the persuasion and problem-solving arenas, in the *political* arena objectives and goals are not shared, and conflicts of interest are evident even though one or both parties to such a conflict can probably not succeed without the help or the resources of a third party. By identifying potential allies, each of the parties to a political conflict hopes to persuade the other party to concede or else face intervention by a third party. For example, U.S. Secretary of State Kissinger's 1976 visit to Rhodesia for the purpose of demonstrating U.S. support of majority rule in Rhodesia left Rhodesian Prime Minister Ian Smith with the choice of bargaining with the black nationalists or else facing the use of force by the black nationalists, who now had the apparent moral support of both the United States and Great Britain.

Examples of the use of political maneuvers in conflicts between organizational units are plentiful—fights between boards of directors and stockholders for influence over companies, government intervention in union-management disputes, joint bids by oil companies for exploration in a foreign country, and so forth. Political maneuvers are often a method used by a weaker power to get a stronger power to begin bargaining over a conflict of interest. The weaker party appeals to a third party in order to expand or change the field of force. The party appealed to can be either a neutral third party or a third party to the conflict. First, the party appealed to can be a *neutral* third party whose main interest is in seeing a compromise reached and in giving guidance to one or both parties to the conflict with that interest in mind. In many conflict of interest situations, third-party agents are licensed by federal, state, or local governments for the purpose of mediating conflict (for example, the judge in a civil suit, real estate agents, stockbrokers, and auctioneers). The term *neutral third party* therefore refers to any nonparticipant in a conflict outcome whose role is to facilitate the resolution of a conflict or to control a conflict between the primary disputants.

It is generally argued that the extent to which a neutral third party is successful in resolving conflict is often determined, in part, by the power granted the third party, that is, the amount of pressure the third party can bring to bear upon the parties to force closure. In a union-management impasse, for example, there are generally four types of power which can be granted to the neutral third party: (1) conciliation and mediation, (2) fact-finding, (3) voluntary arbitration, and (4) compulsory arbitration. *Conciliation and mediation* consists of those responses which a neutral third party makes with the intention of enabling the two primary disputants to overcome mutual distrust in order to bring about agreement or compromise. In addition, the neutral third party should attempt to help *both* disputants to "save face" so that further conflict is not used as the grounds to carry on old fights. The decision-making responsibility remains internalized within the bargaining dyad. *Fact-finding* involves the neutral third party in an investigative role in which the neutral third party is obligated to explore the issues causing the conflict and to report each disputant's position relative to a conflict settlement. Under *voluntary arbitration,* the disputants have reached an impasse on specific points. Under *compulsory arbitration,* the neutral third party is empowered to make the final determination by contractual arrangement or by judicial ruling if both disputants state that they cannot settle their disagreement.

In many cases, rather than appeal to a neutral third party, one or both parties to a conflict can *expand the conflict's field of force* by persuading other parties to enter the conflict. Thus, while party A's power is less than party B's power ($A < B$), $A + C$'s power is greater than B's power ($A + C > B$) and therefore, if A can persuade party C to join the fight, then A has a much better chance of winning. Party C's motive for joining the fight is that its rewards will also increase, if the coalition formed is successful.

The fourth conflict resolution strategy which could be chosen is *bargaining.* Where bargaining is used, disagreement over goals is taken as fixed, and an appeal to a neutral or biased third party is not considered feasible or desirable. The process of bargaining can be defined as the interaction that occurs when two or more persons attempt to agree on a mutually acceptable outcome in a situation in which their orders of preference for possible outcomes are negatively correlated. In this negotiation situation, a number of proposed settlements can be offered, such that both sides have the possibility of improving their outcomes if an agreement can be reached. Interpersonal and inter-group bargaining is a common method of resolving conflict (for example, purchasing by companies, real estate sales, car sales, union-management negotiations, and Paris peace talks).

SUMMARY

The focus of this chapter was (1) on the complexities of the participants in conflict within and between organizations (including their "functional" and "dysfunctional" effects, their conscious and unconscious behavior, and the motivations and calculations of their behavior) and (2) on the more rational, skillful, and conscious strategies used to resolve conflict situations.

Three types of conflict found in most work organizations were identified: (1) within-group conflict, (2) between-group conflict, and (3) interorganizational conflict. The types of *within-group* conflict discussed were role conflict, issue conflict, and interaction conflict. Three types of between-group conflict were then examined: *functional* conflict (task or goal incompatibility and/or boundary-role incompatibility), *hierarchical* conflict (fights over rewards of status, prestige, or money), and *hostile rivalry*. Five types of interorganizational conflict faced by most organizations today were then identified: *management-government* conflict, *intermanagement* conflict, *interunion* conflict, *union-government* conflict, and *union-management* conflict.

The chapter emphasized that conflict is not inherently destructive but, to the contrary, correctly managed conflict can further goal attainment. It can prevent stagnation, stimulate interest and curiosity, and be a forum for airing problems and examining solutions. It is generally the ignored and poorly managed conflict situation that has dysfunctional individual and organizational effects. One of the premises of this chapter has been that conflict is a natural evolutionary process associated with goal-directed behavior. When one party's goals are blocked or perceived to be blocked by another party, then conflict is bound to surface. The "aftermath" of conflict can be healthy or pathological, depending on the process by which the conflict is managed.

After examining the types of conflict found in organizations and presenting reasons why conflict is a predictable outcome of interactions among work units, we examined four arenas in which conflict could be resolved and the various strategies commonly used to resolve conflict. The four major processes to resolve conflict examined were: (1) *problem solving,* (2) *persuasion,* (3) *politics,* and (4) *bargaining.* In comparing and contrasting these processes, the appropriateness of each was evaluated and research evidence concerning each process was presented. It was noted that while problem solving and persuasion are more likely to be used to resolve unregulated conflict (for example, attitude incompatibility and goal inconsistency), politics and bargaining are more likely to be used in regulated conflict settings (for example, boundary-role conflict, union-management conflict, and legal disputes).

CONCEPTS TO REMEMBER

authority conflict	conciliation
functional conflict	mediation
boundary position	voluntary arbitration
hierarchical conflict	compulsory arbitration
ethnocentrism syndrome	

QUESTIONS FOR DISCUSSION

1. Distinguish between functional and dysfunctional behavior.
2. What is the difference between disagreement and conflict?
3. How does the "field of conflict" affect the solution reached?
4. Which type of between-group conflict (functional conflict, hierarchical conflict, or hostile rivalry) do you think is most detrimental to organizations?
5. How does *ethnocentrism* differ from *xenophobia?*
6. Distinguish between goal-directed and goal-blocked behavior. How does conflict affect these two types of behavior?

REFERENCES

Adams, J. S. & Romney, A. K.   A functional analysis of authority. *Psychological Review*, 1959, *66*, 234–251.

Aldrich, H.   Organizational boundaries and inter-organizational conflict. *Human Relations*, 1971, *24*, 279–293.

Assael, H.   Constructive role of inter-organizational conflict. *Administrative Science Quarterly*, 1969, *14*, 573–582.

Biddle, B. J., & Thomas, E. J. (Eds.).   *Role theory: Concepts and research.* New York: Wiley, 1966.

Boulding, K. E.   *Conflict and defense: A general theory.* New York: Harper and Row, 1962.

Boulding, K. E.   A pure theory of conflict applied to organizations. In R. L. Kahn and E. Boulding, *Power and conflict in organizations.* New York: Basic Books, 1964.

Copley News Service. *Reader's Digest,* October 1975, p. 82.

Coser, L.   *The functions of social conflict.* New York: Free Press, 1956.

Deutsch, M.   Conflicts: Productive and destructive. *Journal of Social Issues,* January 1969, pp. 7–41.

Downs, A. *Inside bureaucracy.* Boston: Little, Brown, 1968.

Hamner, W. C. A review of bargaining behavior. In D. L. Harnett and L. L. Cummings (Eds.), *Bargaining behavior and personality: An international study.* Bloomington: Indiana University Press, 1977, in press.

Hamner, W. C., & Yukl, G. The effectiveness of various concession-making strategies on bargaining outcomes. In D. Druckman (Ed.), *Negotiations: A social psychological perspective.* New York: Sage Publishing, 1977, in press.

Hovland, C. K., Janis, I., & Kelley, H. *Communication and persuasion.* New Haven: Yale University Press, 1953.

Janis, I. L. *Victims of Groupthink.* Boston: Houghton Mifflin, 1972.

Jay, A. How to run a meeting. *Harvard Business Review,* March–April 1976, pp. 43–57.

Kahn, R. L. Field studies of power in organizations. In R. L. Kahn and E. Boulding (Eds.), *Power and conflict in organizations.* New York: Basic Books, 1964.

Kahn, R. L., Wolfe, D. M., Quinn, R. P., Snoek, J. D., & Rosenthal, R. A. *Organizational stress: Studies in role conflict and ambiguity.* New York: Wiley, 1964.

Kochan, T. A. Determinants of power of boundary limits in an interorganizational bargaining unit. *Administrative Science Quarterly,* 1975, *20,* 434–452.

Letters to the editors. *Harvard Business Review,* May–June 1976, p. 172.

LeVine, R. A., & Campbell, D. T. *Ethnocentrism: Theories of conflict, ethnic attitudes, and group behavior.* New York: Wiley, 1972.

Maier, N. R. F. *Problem solving and creativity: In individuals and groups.* Belmont, Calif.: Brooks/Cole, 1970.

March, J. G., & Simon, H. A. *Organizations.* New York: Wiley, 1958.

"Ousted Chairman of Consolidated Foods Says He Was Victim of Founder's Vanity." *Wall Street Journal,* January 14, 1970, p. 1.

Pondy, L. R. Some cybernetic models of conflict in organizations. In M. R. Negandhi (Ed.), *Conflict and power in complex organizations: An institutional perspective.* Kent, Ohio: Comparative Administration Research Institute, Kent State University, 1972.

Schelling, T. C. *The strategy of conflict.* Cambridge, Mass.: Harvard University Press, 1960.

Schmidt, S. M., & Kochan, T. A. Conflict: Toward conceptual clarity. *Administrative Science Quarterly,* 1972, *17,* 359–370.

Sherif, M., Harvey, O. J., White, B. J., Hood, W. R., & Sherif, C. W. *Intergroup conflict and cooperation: The robber's cave experiment.* Norman: University of Oklahoma Press, 1961.

Stagner, R., & Rosen, H. *Psychology of union-management relations.* Belmont, Calif.: Brooks/Cole, 1965.

Sumner, W. G. *Folkways.* New York: Ginn, 1906.

Thibaut, J. W., & Kelley, H. H. *The social psychology of groups.* New York: Wiley, 1959.

U.S. News and World Report, January 7, 1975, p. 3.

U.S. News & World Report, May 3, 1976, p. 4.

Wall, J. A., & Adams, J. S.   Some variables affecting a constituent's evaluation of and behavior toward a boundary role occupant. *Organizational Behavior and Human Performance,* 1974, *11*, 390–408.

Webber, R. A.   *Management.* Homewood, Ill.: Irwin, 1975.

16

Social influence, power, and control in organizations

What are the common misconceptions about control and influence in organizations?

What is the social exchange context of reciprocal influence patterns?

What are the different bases for influence in organizations, and how do their dynamics vary from one another?

It is probably impossible for any group of two or more people to interact without having each member of the group influence, and be influenced by, the others. This is not to say that anyone necessarily aims at influencing, or that the cumulative effect of everyone's influence accomplishes any constructive ends. The point we wish to make is that a person's behavior is not merely a set of responses; the behavior plays a double role in that it also represents stimuli to which others respond. These may be discriminative stimuli (cues which signal the occasion for the responses of others) or reinforcing stimuli (cues which reinforce or punish the behavior of others).

Influence—the process by which one person affects or acts as a force upon the behavior of another person—is therefore not unique to formal organizations. Nor is *power,* which we define as the potential or the ability to influence. What sets organizations apart from informal interaction seems to be a higher degree of *control*—the regulation of influence toward specified, agreed-upon directions. If I see you coming down the street and, knowing that I owe you $25, I duck into an alley, you have influenced my behavior, but you have not controlled it. If you arrange to dine with me at an expensive restaurant and leave your wallet at home, thus forcing me to pick up the tab, you have controlled my behavior to your purposes. The exercise of control serves the function of limiting the natural, inherent variability of behavior among and within individuals. Control acts as the glue that holds organizations together, offsetting the centrifugal forces that would pull behavior "out of orbit."

MISCONCEPTIONS ABOUT CONTROL IN ORGANIZATION

Although everyone recognizes the fact of and the need for control in organizations, many people cling to oversimplified assumptions about the nature of control (and the related concepts "influence" and "power"). For example, many people seem to have the notion that power and control are palpable, monolithic substances that are concentrated in some physical location. Student activists in the late 1960s seemed to believe that they could capture control by seizing some office or quarantining some university official. That is, power and control were thought to be "located" or "hidden" somewhere. Even their more law-abiding comrades, who petitioned college presidents and deans, held the notion that control was personalized. Although the activists may have had a flair for the dramatic and certainly received their share of publicity, they did not find the control they were looking for, because control is necessarily diffused throughout an organization. This is not meant to imply that universities or any other organizations are inherently democratic, since democracy is defined by the distribution of formal authority, and formal authority is only one of the influence bases which contribute to control.

What about business corporations? Surely these efficient engines of enterprise must be tightly controlled by a handful of tough-minded titans at the top. Here again, however, we are misled by such symbols as organization charts, titles, and written descriptions of formal authority. Galbraith (1967) argues that control is broadly distributed throughout the middle layers of the business organization in what he calls the "technostructure," the phalanx of engineers, scientists, accountants, and other professionals whose combined efforts shape the activity of the firm. As Galbraith notes, "Thus decision in the modern business enterprise is the product not of individuals but of groups. The groups are numerous, as often informal as formal, and subject to constant change in composition. . . . Effective participation is not closely related to rank in the formal hierarchy of the organization. This takes an effort of mind to grasp (pp. 65–66).

The widely diffused nature of control in organizations has two consequences: (1) Organizations do not change or adapt easily or quickly. No one is more impressed with this fact than are university presidents and corporate chief executives, who are often amused at the amount of power attributed to them by casual observers. (2) On the other hand, organizations have a certain degree of protection against turbulence in the environment or the insanities of any one participant, however lofty his or her rank. Although we may sometimes moan, as frustrated participants, about the inertia and the hidebound resistance to change of the sprawling bureaucratic organization, we should also recognize that these characteristics afford us a measure of stability and predictability.

A second widespread misconception is the assumption that, for any organization, there is a fixed or constant amount of control. One consequence of this assumption is the belief that if some groups exert an increased degree of control, there must be a corresponding decrease in the amount of control exerted by other groups. Thus, if workers or staff gain more control, then managers sacrifice control. This erroneous belief has given rise to pointless controversies about the proper way to divide up the "influence pie."

However, the research conducted by Arnold Tannenbaum and his colleagues at the Survey Research Institute of the University of Michigan has shown that the *total amount of influence* in an organization can increase, and that what differentiates effective from ineffective plants, unions, and voluntary organizations is *not the distribution* of the influence pie, but the *total amount* of control exerted by all groups, officers and members alike. In fact, Tannenbaum's research demonstrated that the correlation between the control exerted by rank-and-file groups and the control exerted at the management levels is not inverse, as we are accustomed to thinking, but positive: when lower-ranking groups exert more influence, the management and administrative echelons also exert more influence.[1]

Finally, there is the mistaken idea that influence and control are one-way processes. Campbell, Dunnette, Lawler, and Weick (1970) have called attention to the implicit assumption in discussions of management style that the "initiating behavior" of managers is unidirectional: "That is, managers are viewed as persons who initiate actions for others and whose interactions end once these directives are issued. . . .

"The basic factor that is missing from these unilateral views is that persons who interact undoubtedly behave as if relationships were reciprocal rather than unilateral" (p. 422).

The manager's actions and words are indeed stimuli to which others respond. When an administrator makes a request, issues a directive, specifies a procedure, or clarifies a situation, subordinates typically respond in some manner. But that by no means ends the influence episode. The responses made by subordinates are also stimuli—stimuli which the manager cannot ignore. If the subordinates comply in good spirit, they strengthen the behavior of the manager; furthermore, they earn credits with the manager, credits that they may draw upon if they later seek favors, privileges, or special consideration. If regular compliance generates expected credits that are later "presented for payment," the manager is likely to feel an obligation to reciprocate. If subordinates show reluctance to comply, the manager is likely to amend his directive and/or to seek modification of procedures from his own superiors. The point, then, is that the manager can hardly hope to exert influence without displaying a willingness to be influenced.

An experiment conducted by Lowin and Craig (1968) provides further proof of the reciprocal flow of influence and control. Applicants for a temporary office manager's job were asked to supervise the work of a Job Corps typist named Charlie while the recruiter stepped out, supposedly to attend a short meeting. Actually, Charlie was a stooge who played a predesigned role. For some applicants, Charlie worked conscientiously and competently; for other applicants, he deliberately appeared to be incompetent, casual, and frivolous about his work responsibilities. Charlie's behavior had an overwhelming impact on the applicant's leadership style. The "good" Charlie received special breaks, was allowed to make his own decisions about handling the typing work, and elicited friendly social reactions from the prospective supervisor. The "loser" Charlie got no privileges, was ordered to follow

---

[1] The reader should note that the Tannenbaum studies were correlational in nature. Thus, the effectiveness of the organization may have led to greater total and mutual influence, rather than the other way around.

a rigid routine in his work, and got a cold shoulder when he tried to approach the applicant on a social basis.

David Mechanic (1962) has pointed out that lower-ranking participants in organizations often exert considerable influence by their control of access to information, persons, and resources. In addition, the members of the "lowerarchy," by making decisions which their superiors delegate because of lack of interest, often exert leverage over the implementation of organizational policies; in effect, lower-ranking participants then actually *make* policy, and have the power to sabotage the entire system if they perceive their rights to be in jeopardy.

THE SOCIAL EXCHANGE BASIS OF INFLUENCE

Influence and control in organizations occur in the context of a *social exchange* process. Gouldner (1960), Homans (1961), Blau (1964), and Adams (1965) have been the leading architects of theoretical frameworks of social exchange.

Gouldner (1960) proposed the *norm of reciprocity* as one which appears to apply in all cultures. According to this norm, when a person does something for you, you are obligated to return the favor in some way.

Homans (1961) contributed the concept of *distributive justice* as a rule governing social exchange. According to this rule, a person expects his *profits* or outcomes in the exchange relation with another person to be proportionate to the *investments* he makes. Such investments can take the form of time, effort, forgone opportunities, deprivations, and the value placed by the person on any special skills or expertise that he provides. When distributive justice fails of realization to a person's disadvantage, he is likely to demonstrate emotional behavior, take aggressive action calculated to restore justice, or if possible, withdraw from the relationship. In organizations withdrawal may take the form, not of physical withdrawal or resignation, but rather of an unwillingness to enter into informal exchanges not specifically required by the job definition. Such unwillingness can threaten the existence of an organization, since organizational survival hinges upon many informal, spontaneous social exchanges to meet exigencies (great or small) that can never be foreseen and provided for in organizational blueprints (Katz, 1964).

Blau (1964) developed the conceptual framework of social exchange theory. Blau defines social exchange as "voluntary actions of individuals that are motivated by the returns they are expected to bring and typically do in fact bring from others" (p. 91). Unlike the exchange of physical or economic goods and services, social exchange entails unspecified obligations—when one person does a good turn for another, "there is a general expectation of some future return [but] its exact nature is definitely *not* stipulated in advance" (p. 93). In other words, there always exists some ambiguity concerning the nature, value, and timing of the reciprocal obligations incurred in social exchange.

Antagonistic forces govern the timing of reciprocated favors. On the one hand, we generally feel uncomfortable about prolonged indebtedness to others. This may arise in part from guilt. In addition, indebtedness in social exchange narrows our flexibility and freedom. As long as we are indebted to a person, we are hard put to decline any reasonable service requested by that person, and the greater our indebtedness, the more difficult it is to refuse the request, regardless of the cost or inconvenience to us. Thus, we prefer to "even the account" as soon as possible, and to return favors sooner rather than later. However, Blau (1964) notes that "posthaste reciprocation of favors, which implies a refusal to stay indebted for a while and hence an insistence on a more businesslike relationship, is condemned as improper . . . social bonds are fortified by remaining obligated to others as well as by trusting them to discharge their obligations for considerable periods" (p. 99).

Due to their special abilities, resources, or knowledge, some persons are in a position to do frequent good turns for other persons who are hard pressed to find ways to suitably repay them. It's not unlike the familiar dilemma of "what kind of Christmas gift do you get for someone who has everything." Yet the obligation to repay is real and remains. Therefore, those who have received generous benefactions may be able to reciprocate only by a generalized "willingness to comply" or by according their benefactor superior status in the group. "Willingness to comply with another's demands is a generic social reward, since the power it gives him is a generalized means, parallel to money, which can be used to attain a variety of ends. The power to command compliance is equivalent to credit, which a man can draw on in the future to obtain various benefits at the disposal of those obligated to him. . . . Exchange processes, then, give rise to differentiation of power" (Blau, 1964, p. 22).

Adams (1965) added precision to social exchange concepts with his notion of equity. This notion resembles Homans' rule of distributive justice, except that it takes more factors into account, is more precise, and specifies various means of restoring equity to an inequitable relationship. Adams argues that whether or not we feel that we have been treated equitably (for example, whether we feel that we have been equitably compensated for our job efforts) does not depend solely on the absolute magnitude of our rewards or outcomes (such as wages, privileges, benefits, or status). We also take into account what we believe to be our relevant "inputs": effort, training, seniority, productivity, or deprivations. But there is yet another factor that we take into account, namely the outcomes and inputs of one or more "comparison persons," such as colleagues, co-workers, friends, or some imaginary person whom we see as "justly treated" as defined by a standard ratio of outcomes to inputs. As we have noted in previous chapters, we implicitly compare the outcomes to oneself divided by one's inputs versus the outcomes and inputs of the comparison person:

$$\frac{Os}{Is} \text{ versus } \frac{Ocp}{Icp}$$

If the ratios are judged to be equal, we feel equitably treated. If the first ratio is greater than the second, we experience inequitable overpayment. We may restore equity by reducing our outcomes, increasing our inputs (so that we feel justified in receiving the outcomes), or seeing that the comparison person receives greater outcomes or is required to furnish fewer inputs. Or we can simply rationalize by altering our perceptions of one of the numerators or denominators. For example, we may decide that our original appraisal of our inputs was too modest: we really gave up more, or worked harder, or contributed things of greater value than we had assumed earlier. Adams suggests that when inequity in the form of overreward is experienced, we may be more likely to change our perceptions of various factors than to alter the actual outcomes we receive, especially if the inequity is not great.

If we experience inequity in the form of underpayment, we feel anger and resentment, as Homans predicted, and we try to increase the outcomes we receive, to decrease our inputs (for example, by reducing our work efforts or by keeping our resources to ourselves), to get others to increase their inputs, or to reduce the outcomes of others. Again, we may change our perceptions (for example, upgrade the estimate we place on certain benefits), but we will probably be more reluctant to change our perceptions of inequitable underreward than of inequitable overreward. Finally, we may terminate the relationship.

Adams' equity theory has stimulated considerable research, most of which has been applied to the study of work performance under conditions of inequitable overpayment or underpayment of wages. Clearly, the concepts involved have a broader range of applicability in social exchange, and they fit well with Blau's treatment of power and influence in the exchange process. For example, if a superior gives special rewards or privileges to subordinates, he probably generates feelings of inequitable overreward. One way in which the subordinates can restore equity is by manifesting an increased willingness to comply with the superior's requests, including those which go beyond the contractual requirements of the job or the official job description. The reverse is also true. When subordinates go "beyond the call of duty," for example, by willingly enduring unusual deprivation or by helping the boss out in a pinch, they can place the boss in a condition of inequitable overpayment. The boss can then restore equity by granting special breaks, increasing his or her own efforts, or agreeing to a lower level of future inputs by workers.

The fact that reciprocity and equity in social exchange involve *unspecified, imprecise obligations* raises a number of issues. First of all, the parties in the social exchange relationship often differ in their subjective perceptions of the nature and the degree of the obligations incurred. Suppose that the boss gives his crew an unscheduled break. He might believe that this obligates the crew to work a few minutes' overtime without pay if the need should arise on that day or the next. The workers, however, might not see it that way. They might feel that the break only evened up the score because they had already been working up a head of steam. Or they might view the break as neutral in social exchange value, since past practice had made occasional unscheduled breaks something of a tradition—as Homans observes, "Precedents become rights"; or as Blau puts it, "Regular rewards create expectations that redefine the baseline in terms of which positive sanctions are distinguished from negative ones" (p. 117). In either case, the workers obviously feel no obligation to accede to the boss's request for overtime. Moreover, even if the workers do recognize the break as a social gift and are willing reciprocate in some fashion, they might regard uncompensated overtime work as disproportionate to their debt. So they refuse to comply with the boss's request. Now the boss regards himself as inequitably treated, responds in anger and resentment (for example, enforcing rules to the hilt), and the crew now regard *themselves* as inequitably put upon; they attempt to restore equity by dragging their feet through the next morning's work ("reducing inputs"). This vicious circle would end only when one party recognizes the differences in perceptions and, even though not necessarily conceding the legitimacy of the other party's views, stoically endures what it may regard as inequity simply in order to start the social exchange process anew on a more auspicious footing.

A study by Martin Patchen (1974) nicely illustrates the working of social exchange influence processes. Patchen, who was interested in identifying the relative importance of various factors in organizational decision making, conducted in-depth interviews in 11 firms with people who had been involved in 33 major purchase decisions. Despite the limited consensus among the various parties as to who had the most influence on the final decision, Patchen did find that the most frequently mentioned characteristics of those judged to be most influential concerned the *extent to which a person would be affected* by the decision. In other words, organizational officials tended to defer to the party who had to "live with the consequences." This proved to be more important in determining influence than did such characteristics as expertise, official responsibility for making the decision, authority, or the capacity to reward and punish.

Patchen (1974) poses the question, Why should being affected by, and thus having a stake in a decision, give one strong influence on the outcomes? The answer, he suggests, basically boils down to the norm of reciprocity. Those who defer to the wishes of the party most affected by a decision can expect that on other decisions the latter will similarly defer to the parties most affected; "those who are affected by a decision usually have resources (their cooperation at least) which are relevant to the needs of others." Thus influence works by a quid pro quo process of accommodation. Patchen cites a passage by Raymond Bauer (1968) which underscores the importance of reciprocity:

> In any ongoing institution, the ability to get important things done is dependent upon maintaining a reservoir of goodwill. The person who fights every issue as though it were vital exhausts his resources including, most especially, the patience and goodwill of those on whom he has to depend to get things done. Therefore, it should be considered neither surprising nor immoral that, when an issue is of low salience, the sensible individual may use it to build goodwill for the future, or pay off past obligations, by going along with some individual for whom the issue is of high salience. (Bauer, 1968, p. 17)

AUTHORITY, EXPERTISE, AND FRIENDSHIP AS BASES OF INFLUENCE

Authority

Katz and Kahn (1966) define authority as "simply legitimate power, power which is vested in a particular person or position, which is recognized as so vested, and which is accepted as appropriate not only by the wielder of power but by those over whom it is wielded and by the other members of the system" (p. 203). In other words, authority is the ability to influence specified others in accordance with the definition of certain organizational role relationships. Authority in contemporary formal organizations represents a highly rationalistic-legalistic basis of influence, in comparison to the influence bases of *traditional status* and *charismatic power* so dominant in pre-industrial revolution times or even today in some non-Western cultures (Weber, 1947). Authority inheres in the office occupied by an individual; all persons holding a given office possess the same degree of authority, though some, of course, may be more influential than others due to their ability to draw upon other bases of influence (such as expertise or friendships).

The social exchange character of influence by authority is represented by something like an "informal contract" entered into by the individual and the organization. The individual, in exchange for material benefits of the type Katz calls instrumental system rewards (accruing to all who hold membership) or the attainment of some valued goal (achievable only by organizational action), endorses the authority structure of the organization—implicitly agreeing to comply with any request by a superior which the authority structure legitimates. Failure to comply with such requests constitutes ground for disciplinary measures (since formal authority is typically bolstered by some degree of coercive power) or expulsion. Discipline and expulsion, however, represent exceptional cases, since deference to authority figures arises from a more generalized respect for legitimated authority which is inculcated by socializing influences in the larger cultural context.

Barnard (1938) believed that the range of authority—the extent of a subordinate's behavior to which authority applies—correlates with the "zone of indifference" in each person, within which orders are acceptable without conscious questioning. The zone of indifference refers to those orders for actions to whose content a person is relatively indifferent; "such an order lies within the range that in a general way was anticipated at the time of undertaking the connection with the organization." Furthermore, "the zone of indifference will be wider or narrower depending upon the degree to which the inducements exceed the burdens and sacrifices. . . . it follows that the range of orders that will be accepted will be very limited among those who are barely induced to contribute to the system." (p. 169)

What functions does authority serve? First of all, it constitutes a force toward the "reduction of human variability" (Katz & Kahn, 1966). The natural variability and alteration inherent in human action (among and within persons) must be constrained if organizations are to survive; individuals must operate reliably within the range of behaviors specified by their roles. Since organizational roles are usually imperfectly defined by such documents as formal job definitions—which can never completely anticipate all the contingencies created by a changing environment and unforeseen operational problems—authority is the means by which the roles of subordinates are "pieced out" by superiors in order to respond to task demands and to reduce behavioral variability.

Second, authority helps reduce the time lag between subordinates' inputs and ultimate outcomes. It would be awkward if subordinates had to be tangibly reinforced for every role-relevant response; furthermore, organizational participants must often endure prolonged periods of deprivations and impositions *en route* to the attainment of goals. Authority helps overcome the extinction in task behavior that would otherwise occur during such periods when rewards are not at hand or their future receipt is not highly salient.

Third, authority—since it is an organizational creation—outlives the specific individuals who use it. This guarantees that from the outset replacements will possess some minimum degree of power by which to influence subordinates. Lacking authority, they would require an inordinate amount of time to establish other bases of influence by means of informal social exchange processes.

Finally, authority gives the administrator "chips to bargain with" (Gouldner, 1954). The manager often has within his province the power to enforce a great many housekeeping rules (such as no smoking, no early breaks, no extended breaks, no early punch-out, and no gambling on the premises). If he chooses to enforce these rules to the letter, his subordinates may defer to his authority, but concede nothing beyond the absolute minimum. On the other hand, the boss may wink his eye if members of the crew match coins to see who buys the Cokes, smoke occasionally, or take a few minutes extra lunchtime during the world series, *in exchange for which* the crew may do some things (say, work extra hard to clear up a production bottleneck) which the boss could not demand by pure authority. Ironically, the boss may gain power by occasionally giving up some power—by not exercising his authority to the hilt. "By not using some of his power, he invests it in social obligations. . . . The advantages subordinates derive from his pattern of supervision obligate them to reciprocate by complying with his directives and requests" (Blau, 1964, p. 206).

Limitations of authority.   Authority would hardly suffice as the sole basis of influence in organizations. This is because of the limiting conditions under which authority is appropriate or feasible and because of certain side effects generated by its use.

Barnard (1938) noted that "if a person is unable to comply with an order, obviously it must be disobeyed, or better, disregarded." Since authority, like the law, must apply equally to all subordinates, it must therefore be geared toward the lowest common denominator among those to whom it applies. As Leavitt (1972) puts it, authority "is an important and efficient tool because it has the advantages of the shotgun over the rifle", but by the same token, "emphasis on the legalities of organizational control tends in practice to mean that the minimal acceptable standard for quantity and quality of performance becomes the maximal standard" (Katz & Kahn, 1966). Once a person has complied with the minimum standard, authority alone can hardly influence him to do more; used for such purposes, authority would become so subjective in varying demands from one person to another, that eventually the consensus which legitimates authority would break down.

The official authority inherent in an organizational position applies only to those subordinates who report directly to the occupant of that office. Most responsible organizational officials, however, must also exercise *lateral* (and occasionally, *upward*) influence. A production line supervisor depends upon people outside his or her unit for materials, maintenance, information, and various other services. The purchasing officer depends upon parties totally outside the organization—for example, vendors or suppliers. The sales or marketing manager must influence the people in the plant to schedule production; the financial manager needs the services of experts in the data processing department. All of these cases illustrate situations in which a manager must influence people who, by definition, are not under the "jurisdiction" of his authority. At these times, the manager simply has to operate with other bases of influence, such as friendship or exchanges of favors. The manager who becomes so accustomed to influencing subordinates by authority that he makes requests in lateral job contacts in an "authoritative tone" may find himself dealing with uncooperative colleagues. The latter will be only too quick to remind him, in words or in manner, that "I don't work for you" or "You're not my boss!"

The exclusive use of influence processes that strongly emphasize authority often generates unwelcome side effects. Most people have ambivalent feelings toward authority figures. On the one hand, they respect authority (provided, of course, that it is not abused to their disadvantage). On the other hand, they incline somewhat toward a generalized *avoidance* response to authority figures. Differences in authority imply such differences as superiority-inferiority, more valuable-less valuable, more mature-less mature; and people generally do not like to be confronted in such a way that they are on the shorter end of these dimensions. Furthermore, authority figures are associated with the threat of punishment, which means that people generally prefer not to be around such persons. Kids on the playground at recess time become uneasy when the principal is nearby, even though they are behaving themselves; drivers start to squirm when they see a police car close behind in the rearview mirror, even when they know that they haven't been committing any traffic violations. This generalized avoidance tendency works at cross-purposes with the superior's aims to coach, teach, and nurture. The point here is not that authority per se is undesirable, but rather that influence based solely on authority has costs associated with it.

Expertise

Physicians, attorneys, and tax accountants have no formal authority over their clients. Yet they often exert influence. They influence others who attribute a degree of *expert power* to them (French & Raven, 1959) and who need that expertise in order to solve a problem or get something done. Galbraith (1967) believes that, in today's large corporations, it is increasingly expert power which runs the operations.

What conditions must exist in order for me to influence another person by this means? First of all, someone else must realize his ignorance on a subject. This must represent a frank admission to himself that he does need someone's expertise. If he does not realize it, I may be able to put him into a situation that forces him to realize it. Hersey and Blanchard (1972) give an illustration. Before trying to change his freshman 6 foot 3 inch former high school center to a guard or forward, the college basketball coach lets him scrimmage against the 6–10 senior, who then forces the freshman to eat every one of those fancy jump shots he tries. Only when the freshman realizes the inadequacy of his offensive and defensive repertoire of skills and techniques can he be influenced by the special expertise of the coaches and the senior players. As Leavitt (1972) notes, Alcoholics Anonymous cannot influence the problem drinker until he recognizes that his problem is too big for him to solve by himself.

Second, the other person must recognize that I have the requisite information, expertise, or judgment. This condition may be fulfilled by my official credentials, the testimonials of others whom I've helped, or by my assertions about my knowledge. It is most likely to be guaranteed, however, by my demonstrated ability to solve certain kinds of problems. Furthermore, my credibility is apt to be preserved by my refraining from making prescriptions about things in which I have no expertise and by my open-mindedness on topics that aren't an exact science—showing that I know the limits to my knowledge.

Third, I must be careful not to punish—however unintentionally—the other person's admission of ignorance and request for help. Otherwise, he will not soon ask for help again, and I will be prevented from influencing him further. If a student asks in class, "What is a correlation?" and I respond with "Didn't you study the assignment?" or "Just where did you go to school?" I will extinguish his inquisitiveness. Along the same lines, the manager should reinforce (or in any case, not punish) admissions of ignorance.

Fourth, people find it easier to seek knowledge from others if they can also occasionally give knowledge to those same others. Repeated requests for information, no matter how genuine or urgent, do something to the status of requesters by making them feel obligated and in a sense inferior; such obligations are easier to bear if requesters can count on repaying the obligation by sharing some of their own expertise. A superior, therefore, should feel no hesitancy about seeking the expertise of subordinates, for that makes it easier for the subordinates to approach the superior with questions. Thus, expertise works best as a two-way street of influence. Unfortunately, some managers are afraid that they will lose respect if they admit ignorance; if they then try to bluff it, they probably *do* lose respect. Most of us, of course, are more inclined to respect a superior's true areas of expertise if he is mature enough to admit to his areas of deficiency.

Of course, a superior may draw upon his own expertise in the exercise of authority. On the basis of his engineering knowledge, he may order a subordinate to use certain procedures. But now the dynamics of the social exchange process are different. "Indeed, giving advice and issuing orders have opposite consequences; advising another creates obligations, while ordering him to do something uses them up, as it were, by enabling him to discharge his obligations through his compliance" (Blau, 1964, p. 131).

Ordering someone to do something in a specified manner is a credit to his account and a debit in yours; giving helpful, solicited advice to someone to help accomplish an end he's committed to is a credit for you, a debit for him.

Friendship

Some people influence others simply on the basis of a relationship of mutual liking. When two persons enjoy an association built over a period of time marked by mutually rewarding interactions, reciprocated esteem, and interpersonal attraction, they generally wish to continue and reinforce that association. Each of these persons wants to continue to be well thought of by the other. Therefore, when one of them makes a request of the other, the latter must either grant the request (if it is reasonable and can be granted without excessive cost) or else place a sudden strain on the relationship. To the degree that such a strain is an unpleasant consideration because it threatens to cut off the rewards from the association, he will comply with the request.

In this case, influence is based on the intrinsic gratifications of a relationship. Here, as Blau (1964) notes, "it is not so much a specific kind of social reward as the fusion of a variety of rewards in a given association that makes these fused rewards inseparable" from the individual who is their source (p. 38). The basis of the social exchange, then, is compliance in return for continuation or enhancement of a personal relationship.

Undoubtedly a substantial amount of influence in organizations rests on the compelling power of friendships. People who like one another can exert influence on matters that are instrumental, dysfunctional, or simply irrelevant to formal organization aims, all depending on the extent to which the goals of the parties exerting influence are consonant, dissonant, or neutral with respect to organizational goals. The impact of cohesive groups (Chapter 12) over their members attests to the force of friendship power; even aside from ongoing work groups, however, the influence of friendship power is felt. For example, a sales manager who gets along with the credit officer may finagle an extended credit line for important clients.

The recognized force of friendship power has led some observers to suggest that a manager should go easy on exercising authority and try instead to build personal relationships with subordinates. The assumption is that they will then carry out their roles conscientiously because they want to (that is, because they like the boss) rather than because they have to; and that they will be willing to do a number of things that they could not legitimately be ordered to do. This argument, however, should not overlook some subtle aspects of influence based on friendship.

First of all, friendship must be genuine if it is to endure. A facade built on contrived attempts at *ingratiation* (Jones, 1964) soon wears out and may even backfire. A superior who only wants to appear friendly in order to cash in on the relationship for ulterior motives will be put to the test when subordinates come back with personal requests of their own. If it begins to look as if the favors run on a one-way street, even the most obtuse underlings will get the message and see the relationship for what it is—a calculated manipulative tactic in the form of ingratiation. Of course, once someone acquires the reputation of being manipulative, others are likely to limit social exchange transactions with him to only formal interactions.

Although either authority or friendship can form a basis for influence, these certainly do not represent faucets that can be turned on and off alternately. Authority emphasizes status distinctions, and friendship emphasizes basic equality. Authority is impersonal, friendship quintessentially personal. Authority works best in the realm of facts; friendship unavoidably engages feelings and emotions. Authority and friendship are therefore irreconcilable insofar as a dominant mode of influence is concerned. This is not to say that a manager who makes full use of his authority cannot still be friends with subordinates, or that it is impossible to exercise authority over friends. The point, rather, is to recognize that authority and friendship are somewhat antagonistic in their effects and in the processes used to make influence attempts by their means. The administrator who prefers to exert influence on the basis of a friendly relationship must be prepared to de-emphasize the trappings and language of official authority. If he cannot or will not do that, he is perhaps better advised to use his authority and if desirous of a friendship association, to forgo the temptation of appealing to that relationship when trying to influence his charges on job-related matters.

INFLUENCE: CONCLUDING NOTES

This chapter does not in any sense represent an exhaustive treatment of influence. One could argue that this entire book, and indeed the bulk of the published literature of the social sciences, bears in one way or another on the subject. Certainly the shaping of behavior by reinforcement and punishment, attitude change, and group dynamics, to cite a few examples, carries immediate implications for power, influence, and control. It would seem that practically all behavior in organizations represents either attempts to influence or the results of influence attempts. (Much organizational behavior is, of course, influenced by impersonal mechanisms, such as technology, job design, and other physical components of the organizational ecology. Cartwright and Zander, 1967, discuss some nonobvious aspects of ecological control.)

The social exchange flavor of the discussion in this chapter underscores the bidirectionality of interpersonal influence. From his studies of influence patterns in effective plants, unions, and voluntary organizations, Tannenbaum (1962) concludes that the inevitable price of influencing is to leave oneself susceptible to influence. The image of the uncompromising, unswerving antagonist with nonnegotiable creed and incorruptible conscience may lend itself to the epic poem, but it is out of place in the mundane world of organizational realities.

SUMMARY

Organizational control is the regulation of power and influence toward specific ends. Misconceptions about the nature of control in organizations include the belief that it is localized, the assumption that the total amount of control is fixed, and the notion that control is a one-way process. Control in organizations works through a social exchange process, in which the norms of reciprocity, distributive justice, and equity govern participants' behavior; the operation of these norms is illustrated in Patchen's study of organizational decision making. Authority, expertise, and friendship represent three important bases of influence in organizations. The contradictory nature of the social exchange dynamics operative within these bases of influence has also been discussed.

CONCEPTS TO REMEMBER

technostructure	expert power
norm of reciprocity	equity
distributive justice	inequity
zone of indifference	ingratiation

QUESTIONS FOR DISCUSSION

1. How do you account for Tannenbaum's finding that when lower-ranking groups exerted more influence, management also exerted more (not less) influence?
2. Why do you suppose that the unilateral rather than the reciprocal view of management influence tends to characterize people's thinking?

3. What are the implications of the Lowin and Craig "Charlie" study for evaluating different styles of supervision?

4. What are the implications of the fact that equity is ultimately subjective? What other criteria of "fairness" or "justice" are there besides equity (as defined in Adams' theory)?

5. The fact that organizational decisions are often made through the type of reciprocity described by Patchen does not mean that such decisions are always optimal. What are the pros and cons of reaching decisions in such a manner?

6. Some observers believe that authority is becoming less and less viable as a basis for influencing people in organizations. In his book *Nice Guys Finish Last,* Leo Durocher has a chapter entitled "Whatever Happened to Sit Down, Shut up, and Listen?" What developments do you suppose account for this observation?

7. In some organizations there exists a traditional, though subtle, proscription against off-the-job, informal social interaction among people of different ranks. What considerations give rise to such a proscription? What are the pros and cons with respect to it?

8. To what extent are the uses of authority, expertise, and friendship mutually incompatible as bases of influence? How is it that some people seem to be able to make use of them simultaneously?

REFERENCES

Adams, J. S. Inequity in social exchange. In L. Berkowitz (Ed.), *Advances in experimental social psychology* (Vol. 2). New York: Academic Press, 1965.

Barnard, C. I. *The functions of the executive.* Cambridge, Mass.: Harvard University Press, 1938.

Bauer, R. The study of policy formation: An introduction. In R. Bauer & K. Gergen (Eds.), *The study of policy formation.* New York: Free Press, 1968.

Blau, P. *Exchange and power in social life.* New York: Wiley, 1964.

Campbell, J. P., Dunnette, M. D., Lawler, E. E., III, & Weick, K. E., Jr. *Managerial behavior, performance, and effectiveness.* New York: McGraw-Hill, 1970.

Cartwright, D., & Zander, A. Power and influence in groups: Introduction. In D. Cartwright & A. Zander (Eds.), *Group dynamics: Research and theory.* New York: Harper and Row, 1968.

French, J. R. P., Jr., & Raven, B. The bases of social power. In D. Cartwright, (Ed.), *Studies in social power.* Ann Arbor, Mich.: Institute for Social Research, 1959.

Galbraith, J. K. *The new industrial state.* Boston: Houghton Mifflin, 1967.

Gouldner, A. *Patterns of industrial bureaucracy.* Glencoe, Ill.: Free Press, 1954.

Gouldner, A.   The norm of reciprocity. *American Sociological Review,* 1960, *25,* 161–178.

Hersey, P., & Blanchard, K. H.   *Management of organizational behavior.* Englewood Cliffs, N.J.: Prentice-Hall, 1972.

Homans, G. C.   *Social behavior: Its elementary forms.* New York: Harcourt, Brace and World, 1961.

Jones, E. E.   *Ingratiation.* New York: Wiley, 1964.

Katz, D.   The motivational basis of organizational behavior. *Behavioral Science,* 1964, 131–146.

Katz, D., & Kahn, R. L.   *The social psychology of organizations.* New York: Wiley, 1966.

Leavitt, H.   *Managerial psychology,* 3d ed. Chicago: University of Chicago Press, 1972.

Lowin, A., & Craig, J. R.   The influence of level of performance on managerial style: An experimental object-lesson in the ambiguity of correlational data. *Organizational Behavior and Human Performance,* 1968, *3,* 440–458.

Mechanic, D.   Sources of power of lower participants in complex organizations. *Administrative Science Quarterly,* 1962, *7,* 349–364.

Patchen, M.   The locus and basis of influence on organizational decisions. *Organizational Behavior and Human Performance,* 1974, *11,* 195–221.

Tannenbaum, A. S.   Control in organizations: Individual adjustment and organizational performance. *Administrative Science Quarterly,* 1962, *7,* 236–257.

Weber, M.   *The theory of social and economic organization.* Glencoe, Ill.: Free Press, 1947.

Leadership

How important are personal attributes of the leader?

What are the dimensions of behavior along which leaders vary?

How does leader behavior affect subordinate satisfaction and performance?

How important is participative decision making in leadership?

How do situational factors determine what leader behavior styles are appropriate?

Is leader behavior a cause or an effect of subordinate performance?

Depending on how broadly one uses the word *leadership*, it can be argued that this entire book—not just this one chapter—is about leadership. If leadership is simply a shorthand term for the multifaceted process by which people's behavior is influenced, then conditioning, motivation, group dynamics, and recognition of personality differences, to mention only a few areas, are part and parcel of leadership. There is, moreover, an increasingly verbalized acknowledgment that leadership is best viewed in this broad sense, referring to the aggregate patterns of reciprocal influence by all members of a group or organization.

In practice, however, as well as in the tradition of most studies of the subject, leadership is viewed as a *role* and refers to either the attributes or the behavior of the person executing that role. The role need not be formal or official, since both laboratory and field studies have found that individuals carry out leadership functions not formally defined within their job description or responsibilities. In this sense, leadership, like gold, "is where you find it." For the most part, however, students of organizational behavior are interested in leadership primarily as it pertains to persons who are expected—by virtue of their official roles or their assigned responsibilities—to be leaders. In other words, we want to draw from leadership studies the implications for supervisors, managers, administrators, officers, and others who are organizationally responsible for the performance and behavior of subordinates, particularly to the extent that such performances and behavior affect progress toward the achievement of group or organizational objectives.

LEVELS AND FORMS OF LEADERSHIP

Even within this somewhat delimited context of looking at leadership as a formal role responsibility, we should recognize that the leadership function can take on a great many different shades, contours, and patterns. Leadership at the first level of supervision, for example, may involve primarily rule enforcement and communicating the technical knowledge needed for task completion (Katz & Kahn, 1966). At middle-management levels, leadership may require more sophistication and subtlety in dealing with people, modifying or adapting existing rules and the existing departmental or divisional structure, and unprogrammed decision making. At upper levels of an organization, leadership takes the form of long-range planning, dealing with parties outside the organization, and developing conceptual models for relating the organization's identity and missions to the broader societal matrix in which it exists. Alfred Sloan, who as chief executive officer brought General Motors to a position of dominance in its industry and the economy, attributed his success to the fact that very early in his career he had formulated a "concept of the industry" and a model of the kind of organization structure needed to combine flexibility and decentralized decision making with centralized control of resource allocation (Sloan, 1965).

Krech, Crutchfield, and Ballachey (1962) have developed a catalog of leadership functions, which probably vary in importance with the organizational level of leadership responsibility. Among these functions are the following: coordinating the activities of subordinates; acting as a father figure; formulating ideology; settling internal disputes; dispensing rewards; representing the group to outsiders; serving as the scapegoat for group failure; providing a model of behavior for group members to emulate; and negotiating for added resources or other inputs for group needs. The reader could probably make additions to this list.

The complexity and multidimensional character of leadership should keep us from jumping prematurely to prescriptions and generalizations from leadership research. Not all of the leadership functions have received equal emphasis from researchers. There has been, for example, a surprisingly narrow preoccupation (some would say obsession) with the tone or style of the leader's interpersonal relationships with subordinates; indeed, the great bulk of leadership studies have probably been directed at this single issue. It is undoubtedly an important issue, but it is far from being the only issue, and in many cases it may not be the crucial issue for leadership effectiveness, particularly at levels of institutional leadership in the upper echelons of the formal organization. In the years to come, we would hope that the study of leadership will become more balanced, with studies about how the leader copes with organizational dependence on outside agencies, derives a "concept of the industry," negotiates, and administers justice. These are not idle questions.

THE PARADIGM OF LEADERSHIP THEORY AND RESEARCH

Traditionally, leadership studies have taken as their *independent variable* (that is, the cause or antecedent) either an *attribute* of the leader (such as a skill or a personality trait), a *dimension of leader behavior* (such as the style of supervision or interaction with subordinates), or—more recently—some combination of leader attributes or behavior with a *situational variable,* such as the type of technology, the task, or the group characteristics salient in the situation.

Dependent variables (effects or results of the independent variables) have been *satisfaction* of subordinates and *performance* (productivity, effectiveness, efficiency, or adaptation to the environment) of the group or organization. Some theories have gone a bit farther and speculated about *intervening variables,* those that link or transmit the independ-

or might cause the person to be too openly critical of and impatient with the others.

The other dimension discriminating with fair reliability between leaders and subordinates does not easily lend itself to a one-word label, because it represents a core or commonality among various overlapping "traits" studied by a number of different people. If one were to choose a short label, it might be something like *energy* or *activity*. Initiative, persistence, ambition, and application are among the traits that connote this dimension and that were found to be associated with leadership.

Attributes which proved unreliable in predicting leadership status included emotional stability (11 studies found leaders to be more stable, 5 found them to be less stable, and 3 found no differences between leaders and others); and extraversion (5 studies indicated that leaders were more extraverted, 2 revealed them to be introverts, and 4 found no differences between leaders and others).

One important pattern of evidence unearthed by Stogdill—one which, more than any other, made his 1948 review a watershed in the transition of leadership studies to the pursuit of fresh questions— was his citation of 19 studies which found the profile of leadership traits to vary with the situation. Differences in group activities or tasks and group composition, in particular, seemed to require leaders with different types of attributes. As Stogdill concludes, "The total weight of evidence presented in this group of studies suggests that if there are general traits which characterize leaders, the patterns of such traits are likely to vary with the leadership requirements of different situations."

Stogdill's review raised, but did not answer, the question, Is leadership transferable? Does the person who emerges as leader in one situation have a better than even chance of rising to the fore in a different situation? Or is leadership specific to the immediate task and group characteristics? Carter (1953) and Gibb (1949) conclude that leadership is far from situation-specific; it seems, rather, to be general over some range of related tasks and some cluster of situational components. Just how broad the range and how dense the cluster (or, indeed, what task factors or situational dimensions are the crucial ones) are still open questions.

Two points deserve mention. First, most of the studies reviewed by Stogdill attempted to find correlates of leadership status, not correlates of leader effectiveness within the leadership role. In other words, the prevailing issue was whether or not certain attributes (such as intelligence) reliably predict who will be appointed, elected, or deferred to as leader. In effect, this may be equivalent to asking "What attributes do people seek in their leaders?" or "What attributes do people *believe* to be important for leadership?" People just might have a naive, stereotyped conception of what the effective leader is like, and thus they may screen out potential leaders who deviate markedly from this stereotype.

Second, as Krech, Crutchfield, and Ballachey (1962) suggest, "It is of interest to speculate that the personality traits which have been found to characterize leaders may, in part, *develop* in individuals as they act as leaders." People respond to the expectations of others concerning what is viewed as appropriate role behavior, and continued reinforcement of such behavior presumably affects personality.

Since 1950, the study of leadership has, for the most part, de-emphasized the importance of personal attributes. Fiedler's Contingency Model of Leadership Effectiveness, discussed later in this chapter, does include a type of personality factor, but not as one which is taken as a prediction of leadership status or leader effectiveness, regardless of the situation. The loss of interest in leader traits may stem from a fairly widespread belief that concepts and measures of personality in general have not demonstrated the precision or power needed to advance our understanding of behavior. Furthermore, reviews by Guion and Gottier (1965), Hedlund (1965), and Campbell, Dunnette, Lawler, and Weick (1970) found little evidence that personality measures could reliably predict effectiveness in the more specific leadership role of the manager.

LEADER BEHAVIOR

Since 1950, the study of leadership has turned to looking more closely at what the leader does, or how he acts, as opposed to the traits of the leader. Paving the way in this direction were the pioneering Ohio State Leadership studies, carried out at that institution in the late 1940s and early 1950s under the direction of Carroll Shartle, Ralph Stogdill, John Hemphill, Edwin A. Fleishman, A. W. Halpin, and B. J. Winer.

These studies identified two relatively independent dimensions of behavior along which leaders differ. One of these, *consideration,* involves the extent to which the leader establishes mutual trust, rapport, and communication between himself and his subordinates. A high consideration score indicates psychological closeness between leader and subordinate; a low consideration score indicates a more psychologically distant and impersonal posture on the part of the leader.

The second factor, *initiating structure,* pertains to leader acts of organizing, defining relationships, setting goals, emphasizing deadlines, giving directions—in short, concern for the task or getting the work done.

The two factors uncovered by the Ohio State studies resemble the two types of leaders Bales (1953) found to emerge in laboratory discus-

Source: (c) King Features Syndicate Inc. 1976.

sion groups: the task leader or specialist and the human relations specialist. However, where Bales concluded that these roles conflict somewhat and are usually split between two persons, the Ohio State studies suggested that the roles were independent (that is, not necessarily correlated or conflicting) dimensions of leader behavior. A leader could be high on both consideration and initiating structure, low on both, or high on one and low on the other. Leadership style, then, could be defined by the combination of relative standings on these two dimensions of behavior.

A comprehensive review of empirical studies investigating the relationships between consideration and initiating structure, on the one hand, and various criteria of leader effectiveness, on the other, would be inappropriate here. However, reviews by Korman (1966) and Fleishman (1973) provide some perspective on the cumulative evidence. Leader consideration appears to be a consistent, reliable predictor of subordinate satisfaction and the behavioral consequences of job satisfaction-dissatisfaction. In a study conducted in the factories of a farm equipment manufacturer, the rates of subordinate turnover and officially processed grievances accelerated as the consideration scores of the leader declined. Grievances and turnover changed very little as the level of initiating structure moved from low to moderate, but at very high degrees of initiating structure, grievances and turnover again accelerated markedly. While high consideration seemed to offset the otherwise negative effect of high initiating structure, the reverse was not true: low consideration, even when coupled with low initiating structure, led to behavioral indices of dissatisfaction and low morale.[1] However, while consideration generally correlates positively with subordinate job satisfaction, the magnitude of the relationship does vary from situation to situation according to the level of the job, the nature of the task, the characteristics of subordinates, and other parameters.

---

[1] These results are not necessarily generalizeable to nonindustrial or nonfactory settings.

Figure 17–1
Leader behavior and subordinate
responses

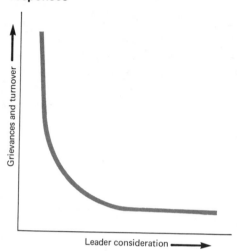

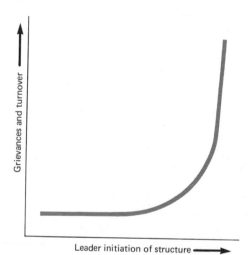

Source: From E. A. Fleishman, "Twenty Years of
Consideration and Structure," in E. A. Fleishman and
J. G. Hunt (Eds.), *Current Developments in the Study
of Leadership* (Carbondale: Southern Illinois University Press, 1973).

The relationships between these two dimensions of leader behavior
and subordinate performance or productivity cannot be summed up
so easily. In fact, Korman (1966) found no discernible pattern in predicting group performance from measures of leader consideration and
initiating structure. The extent to which these leader behaviors affect

Leader's initiating structure and subordinate response

Source: G. B. Trudeau, *The President Is a Lot Smarter Than You Think* (New York: Popular Library, 1973).

subordinate performance is either (*a*) negligible or (*b*) very much dependent on the situation (a statement which, in itself, tells us little). Korman issued a call for more explicit categorization of situations in order to determine when consideration or initiating structure, or both, become important determinants of group functioning.

Intuitively, one would regard the high consideration–high structure combination as the optimal blend of leader behavior. After all, both task effectiveness and human relations (or participant satisfaction) represent desirable end products of group activities; presumably, initiating structure facilitates task accomplishment and consideration promotes group maintenance and involvement by affecting participant attitudes.

These assumptions formed the basis of the *Managerial Grid*, a management development program that Robert Blake and Jane Mouton

(1968) have used in numerous large corporations. Blake and Mouton conceptualize "concern for production" and "concern for people" as two independent but essential factors for managerial effectiveness. Concern for each factor can be represented as varying from 1 (very low) to 9 (very high). A 9,1 manager places high emphasis on production and little on people; a 1,9 leader invests all of his emotional reserves in attention to the feelings and satisfactions of subordinates. A 5,5 leader compromises by placing moderate emphasis on both production and people. All three of these combinations apparently reflect an individual's assumption that concern for production and concern for people conflict with each other rather than being independent and potentially reconcilable. The Managerial Grid program uses diagnostic tools to help the manager realize his current blend of these concerns and then embarks on a training regimen to bring each manager to a 9,9 philosophy—maximal emphasis on both task and relationships, without making a trade-off between the two.

We would do well, however, to reexamine our instinctive beliefs that what the leader does is either necessary or sufficient to achieve high task effectiveness or high participant satisfaction. To take an extreme case, the 1,1 leader style (low concern for production and people) might well be associated with high group performance and satisfaction provided that the members of the group were "mature" (for example, experienced and competent, achievement oriented, deriving intrinsic

Figure 17–2
The Managerial Grid®

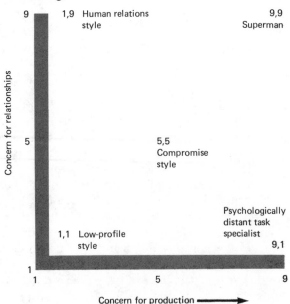

gratification from interesting jobs); indeed, Hersey and Blanchard's life cycle theory of leadership (1972) suggests that with such a group, the low-profile leadership style is the appropriate one. The point we wish to underscore here is that leader behavior is only one variable among many that determine subordinate behavior and attitudes. The evidence from empirical studies investigating initiating structure and consideration lend little support to the notion that the 9,9 blend represents the ultimate leadership style for which every manager should strive.

HOUSE'S PATH-GOAL THEORY

Taking note of the varying magnitudes of the relationships between leader behavior dimensions and group effectiveness criteria, Robert J. House has formulated a path-goal theory of leadership in order to identify the situations in which the leader's consideration or initiating structure become important determinants of performance or satisfaction. House's theory is derived from an expectancy model of motivation. The model posits five crucial components of subordinate motivation: (1) the intrinsic rewards of work-related activities; (2) the intrinsic rewards of task accomplishment or work achievement; (3) the extrinsic rewards which follow or depend upon level of work achievement; (4) the clarity of the "path" or "plan" by which work behavior culminates in achievement; and (5) the subjective probability that various extrinsic rewards do depend on achievement. All of these motivational components, House (1971) argues, depend in part on what the leader does; "the behavior of the leader is clearly relevant to all of the independent variables in this formulation" (p. 322). The leader, in part, determines what extrinsic rewards depend on achievement and the degree to which subordinates perceive this to be the case. He may, by his instructions, clarify the path or plan of work activities that lead to achievement. He may affect the intrinsic gratification derived by subordinates from work activities to the extent that he allows them choice or discretion in such activities, or by the manner in which his interpersonal relationships establish a climate which renders work activities more or less irritating.

House's theory predicts that the consideration displayed by the leader is most important when the work itself is uninteresting, tedious, or irksome: "If you've got a lousy job, you don't want a lousy boss also." When the work provides intrinsic satisfaction by its challenges, stimulation, or use of important skills, consideration declines in importance.

House also believes that initiating structure contributes most to group effectiveness and subordinate satisfaction when the task is unstructured, when subordinates experience a high degree of ambiguity about their work roles, or when stress or crisis suddenly endanger group existence. On the other hand, when the work is already highly structured, a high level of initiating structure by the leader becomes an unnecessary added irritant; subordinates perceive it as unwarranted close supervision.

Tests of House's theory have yielded mixed results. The most consistent evidence in his support is that which reaffirms the importance of leader consideration when the work itself provides no immediate reinforcement or, by itself, would only be aversive. However, most of the studies testing House's propositions have taken the form of cross-sectional surveys. These are weak tests of any theory and allow numerous extraneous or uncontrolled variables to contaminate the results. House's theory will undoubtedly be refined and modified in the future to take into account unpredicted findings from more precise tests. In any case, it represents a significant step forward from previous theorizing about leadership, one which defines explicitly the conditions under which dimensions of leader behavior have decisive impact on group performance and sentiments.

THE PARTICIPATION CONTROVERSY

Should leaders exercise influence in an autocratic or a democratic fashion? This emotionally charged issue continues to reverberate in the leadership literature as well as in informal discussions about managerial behavior. Unfortunately, the labels "autocratic" and "democratic" contain explosive value connotations which have made it difficult to investigate this issue in a detached, dispassionate mood. The labels suggest analogies with dictatorial versus democratic regimes, and such analogies are not necessarily appropriate when viewing leader behavior in the context of groups striving to achieve task goals. More recent discussion of this issue has employed the terms *participation* and *decision centralization* (Yukl, 1971), which carry less emotional cargo.

We can define the dimension of participation in leadership style in terms of such leader behavior as the following: the degree to which the leader unilaterally makes decisions (especially the important ones); the extent of consultation by the leader with subordinates; the amount of communication flowing between leader and subordinates in comparison to that which takes place in interaction among subordinates; and the degree of input by subordinates in setting goals. A highly participative leader consults frequently with subordinates concerning both the group's ultimate goals and preferred means for pursuing those goals, and he encourages subordinates to work out numerous problems among themselves. The directive, more nonparticipative leader makes decisions based on his own convictions and expertise, and he exercises greater surveillance over group members' activities. He leans toward the formal authority of his role as the dominant mode of influence, whereas his participative counterpart prefers collaborative, reciprocity-based influence modes. Of course, the directive-participative dimension is a continuum, and as Tannenbaum and Schmidt (1958) suggest, a variety of styles exist between the extremes.

A question that sometimes arises is whether participation = consideration and nonparticipation = initiating structure. Intuitively, we might expect a leader who emphasizes consideration to be participative and a leader high in initiating structure to be directive. Conceptually, however, these are separate issues. Remember that consideration and initiating structure emerged as independent (not polar opposite) dimensions of leader behavior, whereas the participation continuum represents a single dimension anchored by opposite styles. Furthermore, one could imagine a highly directive, nonparticipative manager who nevertheless exhibits considerable concern over the welfare and feelings of subordinates (the "benevolent autocrat"). Similarly, a manager might view his highly participative style as mandated solely by task considerations, not to be rationalized by any socioemotional results that might or might not coincidentally correlate with such a style.

The argument for directive leadership rests implicitly on a number of assumptions about human nature and about the manager's job: that most people have strong needs for security and for clarity in what is expected of them; that people hold more respect for the leader who acts decisively; that groups find it vexing to try to achieve consensus; and that the "buck stops" with the manager—he abdicates his role if he fails to take charge of group activities.

The case for participative leadership follows from two identifiably separate sets of premises, first noticed by Miles (1965). One rationale, which he dubs the "human relations" argument, says that if subordinates have the opportunity to contribute to the definition of group goals and strategies, they satisfy higher-order needs for self-esteem and achievement. This need satisfaction leaves them more pliable and amenable to organizational influence, more committed to resultant group goals, and more motivated to perform in a fashion that will achieve those goals. In other words, participation leads to greater satisfaction, which in turn leads to greater effort, efficiency, and effectiveness. Miles suggests that this is the rationale managers use when justifying the use of a participative style with subordinates, but that they often "fudge" by simply going through the ritual of participation in order to sell their own decisions by making them seem like group decisions.

The "human resources" rationale for participative management rests on the assumptions that knowledge and expertise are widely distributed throughout work groups and that decisions are best made by those closest to, or most conversant with, the particular problem addressed. Participation, then, because it represents decentralized decision making, leads to higher-quality and more informed decisions, which lead to better group performance, which may result in greater satisfaction (to the extent that rewards hinge on performance criteria). This, Miles conjectures, is the argument managers pursue for urging a participative style on the part of their bosses.

So much for the argument. What does the empirical research literature have to say? Again, space does not permit a detailed review of the evidence bearing on this question, but we will look briefly at some of the more celebrated studies that have investigated this issue.[2]

Beginning in the late 1930s, Lippitt and White (1958) carried out a series of experimental studies regarding the effects of adult supervisory styles on the behavior of groups of 11-year-old boys. The adults had been trained to supervise the recreational activities of these boys in either a democratic, an autocratic, or a laissez-faire fashion. When the leader was present, the groups under autocratic leaders spent more time at work than did the groups under democratic leaders, but the reverse was true when the leader left the room. No overall objective measures of productivity were reported, so the studies failed to provide an answer to the question of which leadership style leads to greater productivity. The investigators did find that the autocratic groups expressed more hostility to the leader and to each other, and that they seemed to exhibit less spontaneous interest in work activities than did the democratic groups. Moreover, the democratic groups experienced no dropouts, whereas the autocratic groups did.

McCurdy and Eber (1953) and Shaw (1955) compared laboratory groups working under autocratic or democratic leaders on problem-solving tasks. McCurdy and Eber found no differences in productivity, whereas Shaw found that autocratic groups took less time to solve problems and made fewer errors.

Coch and French (1948), in a classic field experiment, studied the effects of participation on worker resistance to changes in methods of production. The Harwood Company, where the study took place, had historically encountered stiff resistance by the work force whenever it had introduced more sophisticated work processes. Such resistance took the form of higher turnover, hostility toward management, grievances, and output restriction. Coch and French seized on the occasion of a work methods change to compare the subsequent behavior of groups allowed to participate in the change versus those not

---

[2] For a more comprehensive review, see P. Blumberg, *Industrial Democracy: The Sociology of Participation* (New York: Schocken Books, 1974), especially chapters 5 and 6; or S. M. Sales, "Supervisory Style and Productivity: Review and Theory," *Personnel Psychology*, 1966, *19*, 275–286.

allowed to participate. One group, the no-participation group, was simply called together and told about the changes that would be effected. A second group was allowed to elect representatives, who discussed with management and the engineering staff the best ways of implementing the change. Two other groups were given a "total participation" treatment—all members of those groups participated in planning the job modifications. In the no-participation group, 17 percent of the workers quit in the first 40 days after the change, and a number of those who stayed processed grievances about the new production standards. Furthermore, production dropped and stayed low long after the passage of the time needed to master the changes in work methods. No turnover occurred in either the representative-participation or the total participation groups, and productivity in both groups climbed to record highs after a temporary drop. The total participation group experienced the highest rates of productivity increases.

Two confounding variables in the Harwood experiment complicate the interpretations of the results. First, all three of the participation groups were given a demonstration of two pieces of material produced in the factory, one of which had cost twice as much to produce as the other. The workers were asked to identify the cheaper cloth, but could see no difference between them. This demonstration, which vividly illustrated the economic and competitive rationale for production methods changes, was not given to the nonparticipation group.

Second, the two total participation groups were smaller than the two other groups. Group size often correlates inversely with cohesiveness, satisfaction, and productivity per person, and affects the structure and interaction of the group (Thomas & Fink, 1963).

To what extent these confounding differences—by themselves and apart from differences in participation—might have accounted for subsequent differences in turnover and productivity is unknown. Given the very dramatic attitudinal and performance differences between the nonparticipation and participation groups one could argue plausibly that the demonstration and group size effects probably do not account for the full effects attributed to participation. A subsequent development at Harwood adds weight to this view. The workers who had originally been in the no-participation group and had stayed with the company were given the participation treatment on other assignments several months later. No additional turnover followed, and productivity among these workers showed the same recovery and increase that had characterized the earlier participation groups. Of course, it is possible that the most discontented workers had already left and that the remaining workers therefore constituted a rather select group.

Coch and French attempted a repeat of this study at a Norwegian shoe factory. In general, the participation groups expressed greater satisfaction with the company and displayed better morale on a number of indices. Unlike the Harwood study, however, the Norwegian experiment found no differences in productivity between participation and nonparticipation groups. The authors suggest that the Norwegians might not have regarded participation in managerial decisions as culturally legitimate (but if so, why were the participating groups more satisfied?). In addition, the procedures by which the investigators implemented worker participation in the Norwegian experiment varied somewhat from that used in the Harwood study.

Morse and Reimer (1956), in an 18-month study conducted in the offices of a large insurance company, varied the level of decision making for 500 clerical workers in four divisions. Decision making was made more centralized in two divisions and more decentralized in the other two. Both groups showed increases in productivity over the 1½-span, with the centralized (autocratic) divisions registering a slightly greater increase than the decentralized divisions. Morse and Reimer suggest that this difference in productivity increases was attributable to the fact that the centralized groups experienced greater turnover, leaving fewer girls to accomplish a roughly constant flow of work and therefore yielding higher production per individual employee. With regard to job attitudes, the centralized groups showed a *statistically* significant drop in job satisfaction and the decentralized groups a *statistically* significant increase. The actual changes, however, were quite small. On a five-point scale, the mean decrease for hierarchically controlled sections was −.13 (2.37 to 2.24) and the increase for the autonomous sections was +.14 (2.43 to 2.57).

Vroom (1960) investigated the extent to which differences in personality might determine people's responses to autocratic versus participative management. His study, which focused on supervisors in a delivery service company, found that supervisors who scored high in need for independence or low in authoritarianism preferred a participative boss. Those low in need for independence or high in authoritarianism were indifferent to the degree of participation they were allowed. Tosi (1970) found a positive relationship between participation and satisfaction, but—unlike Vroom—did not find need for independence or authoritarianism to affect this relationship.

Numerous other studies, varying in methodology and the types of populations used, have addressed the participation issue, but those cited above will suffice to illustrate the mixed nature of the empirical results accumulated. Generally speaking, we find that participative leadership is associated with greater satisfaction on the part of subordinates than is nonparticipative leadership; or, at worst, that participation does not lower satisfaction. We cannot summarize so easily the findings with respect to productivity. Some studies find participative groups to be more productive; some find nonparticipative groups to be more effective; and quite a few studies show no appreciable differences in productivity between autocratically versus democratically managed work groups.

One might conclude from the numerous technological, ability, and work-flow variables which determine level of productivity that leadership style has a greater effect on subordinate satisfaction than on subordinate productivity. To rest on this conclusion—of course, many of us would prefer not to—does *not* represent a denial of the importance of leadership. Subordinate satisfaction, after all, often does predict absenteeism, turnover, loyalty, spontaneous cooperation, and other desirable behaviors. Absenteeism and turnover represent potentially significant labor costs.

The other, more persevering, reaction to the mixed findings relating participation and productivity emerges as a search for *situational factors* which determine whether participative leadership affects productivity positively or negatively. The cohesiveness of the group, the nature of the task, the maturity of subordinates, time pressures, the vested interests of members in the outcome of the decision, and a host of other situational parameters could conceivably mediate the effects of leadership style on the performance of the group. No one so far has formulated a theory of leadership which takes account of all these variables, but Fred Fiedler has offered a model which tries to incorporate three pivotal components of the situation in order to predict the effects of leadership style on group performance.

FIEDLER'S CONTINGENCY MODEL OF LEADERSHIP EFFECTIVENESS

Fiedler's work on leadership actually began over 25 years ago with a study of psychotherapeutic relations. He found that psychotherapists with reputations of clinical effectiveness tended to see their clients as more similar to themselves than did therapists not regarded as effective. This suggested that a counselor or helping agent who sees similarity between himself and others tends to feel psychologically closer to them and to be more permissive and less judgmental. The analogy between a counselor and a group leader immediately suggested itself, since a leader's responsibilities include—but are not limited to—the nurturance, coaching, and developmental growth of subordinates.

In order to extend this inquiry to the study of leadership in applied settings, Fiedler developed an instrument which purports to measure the leader's "Esteem for Least Preferred Co-worker" (LPC). Fiedler asks the leader to think about the person he least prefers to work with, and to rate that person in terms of a number of adjectives that imply personal evaluation ("pleasant-unpleasant," "friendly-unfriendly," and so forth). The higher the LPC score, the more the leader can distinguish between the person as a worker (not wanted) and the person as an individual (who may have a number of good qualities, despite his deficiencies as a co-worker). The lower the LPC score, the more the leader rejects his least preferred co-worker out of hand—not only as a worker, but as a person. Fiedler assumed that the leader who scores high on the LPC measure tends to operate in a nondirective, relationships-oriented manner toward group members, whereas the leader with a low LPC score acts in a more controlling, task-oriented, even punitive manner.

Impressed by the results he had obtained in the psychotherapy study, Fiedler anticipated that high-LPC leaders would generally show greater group effectiveness than their low-LPC counterparts. However, his early leadership studies—carried out with high school basketball teams and student surveying parties—suggested just the opposite. Contrary to expectation, leader LPC score correlated negatively with group performance. These results cast doubt on the utility of viewing the leader as one who must play primarily the role of therapist, and raised the possibility that in task-oriented groups the leader must be able to reject poor performers. Presumably, a psychologically distant leader does this best.

Further studies with other types of work groups muddied the waters even more, for sometimes the low-LPC leaders proved more effective and at other times the high—LPC leaders were associated with better team performance. After a decade of seemingly inconsistent, erratic findings, Fiedler attempted to sort out the crucial situational factors that determined which leadership style would predict effectiveness. Fiedler (1964) identified three situational parameters which, in combination, helped account for the inconsistent findings: leader-group relations, task structure, and position power.

The *leader-group relations* parameter refers to the tone or climate of the personal relationships between the formal leader and his or her subordinates, especially key subordinates. The more positive and pleasant the tone of these relationships, the more the leader feels accepted by the group.

Task structure concerns the clarity or ambiguity of the task confronting the group. Tasks can vary from the highly programmed (such as assembling an appliance or planting pine seedlings) to the vague and amorphous (developing a policy for corporate social responsibility or formulating a program to decrease employee absenteeism). Task structure is defined by the degree to which the final decision can be verified as correct or incorrect, the ease with which procedures for accomplishing the task can be specified, the number of ways to approach the problem, and the number of viable solutions that are equally correct or good.

Position power is defined by the formal authority that inheres in the leader's organizational role and the leverage he or she has over the rewards and punishments meted out to group members.

Leader-member relations, task structure, and position power—in that order of importance—interact, according to Fiedler, to determine the ease or difficulty with which the leader can influence group members. Put another way, these factors make the situation more or less favorable for the leader, as shown in Figure 17–3. The extreme left combination—good leader-member relations, highly structured task, and high position power—represents a very favorable situation for the leader, one in which it should be easy to influence subordinates. The opposite extreme (relatively poor relationships with subordinates, unstructured task, low power) is a leader's nightmare.

Figure 17–3
Fiedler's analysis of situations in which the high- or the low-LPC leader is the more effective

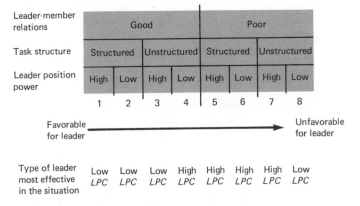

Fiedler found that psychologically distant (low-LPC) leaders were more effective—in terms of objective performance criteria—than psychologically close leaders when the situation was either very favorable or very unfavorable for the leader, whereas high-LPC leaders were more effective in situations of intermediate favorableness.

> In very favorable conditions, where the leader has power, informal backing, and a relatively well-structured task, the group is ready to be directed on how to go about its task. Under a very unfavorable condition, however, the group will fall apart unless the leader's active intervention and control can keep the members on the job. In moderately favorable conditions . . . a relationship-oriented, nondirective, permissive attitude may reduce member anxiety or intra-group conflict, and this enables the group to operate more effectively. (Fiedler, 1964, p. 165)

Fiedler has assumed that the LPC measure taps a dimension of the leader's personality which predisposes the leader toward a certain interpersonal style vis-à-vis subordinates. He therefore argues that leaders cannot easily change their behavioral styles, since in the mature adult personality does not change easily within reasonably short periods. Therefore, in order to maximize managerial or administrative leadership effectiveness, we must try to make the situation fit the leader's style—or as Fiedler puts it, "engineer the job to fit the manager." We can do this by altering the position power of the leader, changing the task structure, or improving the interpersonal climate between the leader and subordinates.

Fiedler's model, which at one time gave promise of making a major breakthrough in the use of the situational approach to leadership, has been the focus of considerable controversy in the past few years. Critics of the model contend that the LPC measure remains something of a mystery. Little evidence exists that it accurately reflects a person's predisposition toward any particular leadership style, either in terms of participativeness or of initiating structure and consideration levels. They charge that Fiedler used inappropriate statistical analysis to support his propositions and that laboratory studies designed to test the theory provide little or no support for the validity of the model. Fiedler's critics have also raised the question of whether Esteem for Least Preferred Co-worker can reasonably be regarded as independent of the three major situational dimensions proposed by Fiedler, especially relations between the leader and group members.

Fiedler readily concedes that the personality factor tapped by the LPC instrument needs clarificatioin. Recently, he suggested that it reflects a leader's behavioral inclinations only under stress. Low-LPC leaders may display a relationships-oriented style in a climate of security, but when threatened by the possibility of group failure on a task they change to a task orientation and maintain psychological distance toward subordinates. Fiedler dismisses the evidence from laboratory studies of ad hoc groups as irrelevant to his model, which he regards as an attempt to understand and predict leader effectiveness in ongoing organizations where there are important stakes in the outcomes of group efforts.

Although the status of Fiedler's model remains in doubt, his theory shares with other contemporary approaches a concern for task dimensions that moderate the effects of leader behavior on group effectiveness. While a considerable amount of effort has gone into the analysis of task characteristics, we still do not have consensus on what the most important aspects of the task are (aside, perhaps, from task ambiguity), nor do we have as reliable or valid measures of task dimensions as we would like. Indeed, a workable theory of task requirements as they affect behavior and a set of improved measurement tools appear to be the bottlenecks we must work through before we can add significantly to our knowledge of leadership.

THE VROOM-YETTON NORMATIVE MODEL

Vroom and Yetton (1973), like Fiedler, take a situational approach to the issue of participation. Unlike Fiedler, however, they envisage a continuum in which there are at least five possible levels of participation by subordinates in decision making. At one extreme, the leader makes the decision based on his or her information at the time. A second strategy would involve making the decision after collecting relevant information from subordinates. A third technique would be to discuss the problem on a one-on-one basis with individual subordinates, soliciting their individual thoughts but then unilaterally making the decision, regardless of whether the decision actually reflected subordinates' views. A fourth approach would be for the leader to share the problem with the *group as a whole,* but once again preserve the prerogative of rendering a final judgment. Finally, the leader might involve the group in the decision from beginning to end, acting as a broker for the exchange of information and as a representative of the group's consensual decision.

The desirability—indeed the *feasibility,* in Vroom and Yetton's model—of any one of the above strategies depends on certain characteristics of the decision problem. Particularly crucial attributes are the immediate availability of information to the leader versus the amount of additional information possessed by subordinates, the importance of group acceptance of the final solution, and the extent to which the group is willing to accept the leader's decision. The more important group acceptance is in determining the implementation of the decision, the greater the degree of input required of the group.

The Vroom-Yetton model is actually embodied in a decision tree with branch points representing sequential questions concerning the attributes of the decision problem, thus generating 14 types of problems. Vroom and Yetton specify which levels of participation are acceptable for each type of problem. (The interested reader may consult Vroom and Yetton, 1973, chapter 3, for a more detailed exposition of the logic of this model.)

Vroom and Yetton present evidence, based on how managers indicated they would deal with a number of hypothetical problems, which suggests that many managers intuitively practice what the model prescribes. At present, however, there is no evidence documenting the validity of the model for maximizing leadership effectiveness in decision making.

THE RECIPROCAL CAUSALITY QUESTION

Studies about leadership style or leader behavior have typically proceeded on the assumption that leader behavior affects subordinate behavior. Particularly in correlational field studies, any correlation between descriptions of leader behavior and indices of subordinate performance has been interpreted as measuring the causal impact of the leader's actions on group responses.

Lowin and Craig (1968), in a study referred to in the previous chapter, raised the question of whether correlations between leader style and subordinate behavior might not also be reflecting a reverse causal sequence: the effect of subordinate behavior on what the leader does. To answer this question, they conducted a study in which they had a stooge typist named Charlie deliberately play the role either of conscientious-competent worker or of unconscientious-incompetent subordinate. The subjects, who were actually applicants for a temporary supervisory job, were exposed to one of these two subordinate work styles enacted by Charlie. The results showed quite clearly that when Charlie performed competently, the supervisor displayed more consideration, initiated less structure, and allowed more participation by Charlie in decision making.

Greene (1975) conducted a study inquiring into the nature and degree of reciprocal causality between leader and subordinate behavior. His study took place in ongoing organizations, but his method of research represented somewhat of a departure from the usual field studies of leadership. He obtained measures of subordinate performance and satisfaction, along with descriptions of supervisors' leadership style (in terms of consideration and initiating structure) at three different points in time, each separated by one-month intervals. His analysis took the form of cross-lagged correlations. If, for example, leader consideration exerts a positive effect on subordinate performance, then we would expect to find a reasonably high positive correlation between leader consideration at time 1 and subordinate performance at time 2. On the other hand, if leader consideration is a *result of* (or response to) subordinate performance, then we would expect the correlation between subordinate performance at time 1 and leader consideration at time 2 to emerge as high and positive.

Greene did find, in support of previous thinking, that leader consideration directly affected subordinate job satisfaction. However, the bulk of his evidence suggested that the causal relationship between leader style and subordinate performance ran in the reverse direction. When subordinates' performance was unsatisfactory, supervisors responded by increasing the emphasis on task and structure; when subordinates' performance was satisfactory or better, supervisors reacted by decreasing the emphasis on structure and increasing the emphasis on consideration toward subordinates. In other words, whether knowingly or unconsciously, supervisors appeared to be using consideration as a contingent reinforcer for performance and initiating structure as a punisher for unacceptable quality of work.

Barrow (1976) conducted back-to-back laboratory studies, first manipulating the style of the leader to see its effects on subordinates' performance, then varying the performance level of subordinates to see how that affected leader behavior. His evidence indicated that the greater effect was that due to group productivity on leader style.

These studies do not rule out the possibility that leadership style affects subordinate performance, but they do argue convincingly against a simple, one-way flow of causation. They also suggest the desirability of looking at leader behavior as both a *dependent variable* and an independent variable. If subordinate performance represents one environmental factor influencing the tone of leader actions, then surely there are other factors. At present it is far from obvious what these other factors might be, because traditional theorizing about leadership has taught us to view leader behavior as cause rather than effect.

LEADERSHIP: CONCLUDING NOTE

Clearly, we are a long way from being able to offer leaders prescriptions about how to behave. The effect of several decades of leadership research has been largely to cast doubt on the meager fund of knowledge we thought we had acquired from naturalistic observation. House's Path-Goal theory offers promise for predicting when and how leader consideration and initiating structure will affect subordinate attitudes, but we have little to go on if we want to predict what the leader's behavior will do to productivity.

Again, as noted in the opening pages of this chapter, we may be looking in the wrong places for the causes of productivity. Technology and work methods surely account for much of the variance in worker productivity. To the extent that anything about the leader fits in here, it is the leader's intelligence, training, experience, or skills—not his or her interpersonal "style"—that come to the fore. Other determinants of productivity include, of course, the cognitive and/or motor skills of subordinates and perhaps their deeply ingrained work habits developed through previous histories of reinforcement. For example, Merrens and Garrett (1975) found that subjects who strongly endorsed the Protestant work ethic (presumably a residual of early reinforcement contingencies) spent more time and produced more on a boring, repetitive task than did subjects who tended to reject the Protestant work ethic. Finally, the larger organizational environment, as a complex system of many variables, exerts behavioral effects on both the leader and the group. Even such mundane and unglamorous factors as noise level, heat, humidity, lighting, and space can, in some cases, account for a considerable proportion of differences in productivity.

Perhaps we need to look more at the possible effects of leader behavior on criteria other than productivity—for example, its possible effects on *variability* in productivity (from one subordinate to another or from one time to another), on subordinates' informal modes of cooperation with or accommodation to organizational requests, or on the informal contributions which subordinates make to departments other than their own. Such criteria may not directly or immediately affect overall organizational effectiveness, but they nevertheless represent behavioral dimensions that are of concern to practically all organization members.

SUMMARY

The study of leadership has traditionally taken as its independent variables the attributes of the leader, dimensions of leader behavior, or leadership styles; dependent variables have included measures of performance and satisfaction. Stogdill found certain attributes to be somewhat consistently related to attainment of the leadership role, but little evidence that any single trait or cluster of traits predicted the effectiveness of persons in leadership positions. The Ohio State Leadership studies identified initiating structure and consideration as two dimensions of leader behavior. Empirical work has shown leader consideration to be consistently related to subordinate satisfaction and correlated subordinate behaviors, such as turnover and grievance processing. However, relationships between initiating structure and satisfaction, or between productivity and either consideration or initiating structure, have varied in size and direction from study to study. House's path-goal theory of leadership attempts to identify situational factors that would explain such variations. Participative styles of leadership generally produce greater subordinate satisfaction than do directive styles, but again the relationship with performance varies. Fiedler's Contingency Model of Leadership Effectiveness has demonstrated some explanatory power in resolving inconsistencies in the effects of participation on group performance; but the logic and research underlying Fiedler's theory have been subjects of considerable controversy. Recent evidence strongly suggests that leader behavior is itself determined by level of group performance—as much as or more than it determines group behavior. Further advances in our understanding of leadership effectiveness will probably hinge on a viable taxonomy of tasks and a suitable reconceptualization of causes and effects of the leader's behavior.

CONCEPTS TO REMEMBER

Ohio State Leadership studies
consideration
initiating structure
Managerial Grid®

human resources rationale for
   participation
Contingency Model of Leadership Effectiveness

path-goal theory of leadership
participation controversy
human relations rationale for
participation

Esteem for Least Preferred
Co-worker (LPC) scale
reciprocal causality

QUESTIONS FOR DISCUSSION

1. Why do you suppose that leaders tend to be taller than average? More articulate? More active or energetic?

2. How do you explain Fleishman's finding that leaders high in consideration could also generate high levels of initiating structure without increasing turnover and grievances? That leaders showing low consideratiion experienced higher turnover and grievances even when they were low in initiating structure?

3. Under what job conditions, or in what types of work environments, would a leader profile high in both consideration and initiating structure probably *not* be appropriate?

4. What are the risks inherent in holding a "human relations" rationale for participative supervision?

5. How do you account for the inconsistent findings regarding the effect of participative supervision on group productivity?

6. Does a leader have a single "behavioral profile" or "style" with each member of his or her group, or would his or her style be more likely to vary with the individual subordinate? Explain.

7. What background, motivational, or personality factors do you think would make a leader high LPC or low LPC?

8. Why have leadership theorists and researchers only recently addressed the "reciprocal causality question"?

9. Suppose that we are eventually forced to conclude from accumulated empirical research findings that differences in leader behavior or leader style have a negligible effect on group or unit productivity. Should we then discontinue the study of leadership? Why or why not?

REFERENCES

Bales, R. F. The equilibrium problem in small groups. In T. Parsons, R. F. Bales, & E. A. Shils, *Working papers in the theory of action.* Glencoe, Ill.: Free Press, 1953.

Barrow, J. C. Worker performance and task complexity as causal determinants of leader behavior style and flexibility. *Journal of Applied Psychology,* 1976, *61,* 433–440.

Blake, R. R., & Mouton, J. S. *Corporate excellence through grid organizational development.* Houston: Gulf Publishing, 1968.

Blumberg, P. *Industrial democracy: The sociology of participation.* New York: Schocken Books, 1974.

Campbell, J. P., Dunnette, M. D., Lawler, E. E., III, & Weick, K. E., Jr. *Managerial behavior, performance, and effectiveness.* New York: McGraw-Hill, 1970.

Carter, L. F. Leadership and small group behavior. In M. Sherif & M. O. Wilson, *Group relations at the crossroads.* New York: Harper, 1953.

Coch, L., & French, J. P. Overcoming resistance to change. *Human Relations,* 1948, *1,* 512–532.

Dubin, R. Supervision and productivity: Empirical findings and theoretical considerations. In R. Dubin, G. C. Homans, F. C. Mann, & D. C. Miller, *Leadership and productivity.* San Francisco: Chandler, 1965.

Fiedler, F. E. A contingency model of leadership effectiveness. In L. Berkowitz (Ed.), *Advances in experimental social psychology* (Vol. 1). New York: Academic Press, 1964.

Fleishman, E. A. Twenty years of consideration and structure. In E. A. Fleishman & J. G. Hunt (Eds.), *Current developments in the study of leadership.* Carbondale: Southern Illinois University Press, 1973.

French, J. P., Jr., Israel, J., & Äs, D. An experiment on participation in a Norwegian factory. *Human Relations,* 1960, *13,* 3–19.

Gibb, C. A. The emergence of leadership in small temporary groups of men. Unpublished doctoral dissertation, University of Illinois, 1949. Cited in C. A. Gibb, Leadership. In G. Lindzey (Ed.), *Handbook of social psychology* (Vol. 2). Reading, Mass.: Addison-Wesley, 1954.

Greene, C. N. The reciprocal nature of influence between leader and subordinate. *Journal of Applied Psychology,* 1975, *60,* 187–193.

Guion, R. M., & Gottier, R. F. Validity of personality measures in personnel selection. *Personnel Psychology,* 1965, *18,* 135–164.

Hedlund, D. E. A review of the MMPI in industry. *Psychological Reports,* 1965, *17,* 874–889.

Hersey, P., & Blanchard, K. H. *Management of organizational behavior* (2d ed.). Englewood Cliffs, N.J.: Prentice-Hall, 1972.

House, R. J. A path-goal theory of leader effectiveness. *Administrative Science Quarterly,* 1971, *16,* 321–338.

Katz, D., & Kahn, R. L. *The social psychology of organizations.* New York: Wiley, 1966.

Korman, A. K. "Consideration," "Initiating structure," and organizational criteria—A review. *Personnel Psychology,* 1966, *19,* 349–361.

Krech, D., Crutchfield, R. S., & Ballachey, E. L. *Individual in society.* New York: McGraw-Hill, 1962.

Lippitt, R., & White, R. K. An experimental study of leadership and group life. In E. E. Maccoby, T. M. Newcomb, & E. L. Hartley (Eds.), *Readings in social psychology* (3d ed.). New York: Holt, 1958.

Lowin, A., & Craig, J. R. The influence of level of performance on managerial style: An experimental object-lesson in the ambiguity of correlational data. *Organizational Behavior and Human Performance,* 1968, *3,* 440–458.

McCurdy, H. G., & Eber, H. W. Democratic versus authoritarian: A further investigation of group problem-solving. *Journal of Personality,* 1953, *22,* 258–269.

Merrens, M. R., & Garrett, J. B.   The Protestant ethic scale as a predictor of repetitive work performance. *Journal of Applied Psychology*, 1975, *60*, 125–127.

Miles, R. E.   Human relations or human resources? *Harvard Business Review*, July–August, 1965, 148–163.

Morse, N., & Reimer, E.   The experimental change of a major organizational variable. *Journal of Abnormal and Social Psychology*, 1956, *52*, 120–129.

Sales, S. M.   Supervisory style and productivity: Review and theory. *Personnel Psychology*, 1966, *19*, 275–286.

Shaw, M. E.   A comparison of two types of leadership in various communication nets. *Journal of Abnormal and Social Psychology*, 1955, *50*, 127–134.

Sloan, A. P., Jr.   *My years with General Motors.* New York: MacFadden Books, Doubleday, 1965.

Stogdill, R. M.   Personal factors associated with leadership: A survey of the literature. *Journal of Psychology*, 1948, *25*, 35–71.

Tannenbaum, R., & Schmidt, W. H.   How to choose a leadership pattern. *Harvard Business Review*, March–April 1958, pp. 95–102.

Thomas, E. J., & Fink, C. F.   Effects of group size. *Psychological Bulletin*, 1963, *60*, 371–384.

Tosi, H. A.   A reexamination of personality as a determinant of the effect of participation. *Personnel Psychology*, 1970, *23*, 91–99.

Vroom, V.   *Some personality determinants of the effects of participation.* Englewood Cliffs, N.J.: Prentice-Hall, 1960.

Vroom, V. H., & Yetton, P. W.   *Leadership and decision-making.* Pittsburgh, University of Pittsburgh Press, 1973.

Yukl, G.   Toward a behavioral theory of leadership. *Organizational Behavior and Human Performance*, 1971, *6*, 414–440.

18

Organization and the environment

How is an organization's functioning affected by its external environment?

What are the important dimensions of organization environments?

What functions do organization boundaries serve?

What are the distinctive qualities of organization boundary roles?

The focus of this book, as the title implies, has been on the *psychology* of organizational behavior. Thus, our units of analysis throughout have been the individual and the small group. This, however, represents only (roughly) half of the total field of organizational behavior. The other half—sometimes called "organizational theory"—is essentially *sociological* in its thrust. Whereas the psychology of organizational behavior dwells at the "micro" (as in microeconomics) level of analysis, the sociology of organizational behavior is decidedly more "macro" in flavor. The sociological perspective considers the organization as the unit of analysis, and deals with such topics as organization structure, relationships between organizations, and the interaction between the organization and its environment.

The purpose of the present chapter is to introduce the reader to this "other half" of organizational behavior and to provide some conceptual links between the psychology and the sociology of organizational behavior. Obviously, the chapter is intended to be illustrative rather than exhaustive in its treatment.

The distinction between psychological and sociological approaches to organizational behavior is more often blurred than precise. It is hoped that this chapter imparts a sense of the continuity between these fields.

Perhaps the most sweeping change in writings about organizations since the 1960s has been the increased attention given to the *environment* of the organization. The precise meaning of the term varies with the writer who uses it. However, implicit in practically all discussions of the topic is the definition given by Churchman (1968): the environment of an organization is composed of those variables that affect the performance of the organization, but over which the organization has little or no direct control.

The development of open systems theory and its application to organizations (Katz & Kahn, 1966) underscored the importance of effective interaction with the environment for organizational survival and functioning. The mass media have helped make "ecology" a household word, and its connotation has probably broadened to refer not only to the physical environment but also to broad classes of external constraints and forces. Finally, one can discern in the public utterances of management practitioners a heightened awareness of the complex interdependence among the elements of modern society.

Organizations depend on the environment for a steady flow of *inputs* of various kinds—raw materials, supplies, capital, energy, and personnel—to sustain their productive cycle. They reach out beyond their finite borders for *information* on a wide range of subjects: technological innovations, shifting economic winds, changing attitudes among the clients they serve, and opportunities for expansion. They dispose of their finished products—their outputs—to the environment; whether such products be physical goods, as is the case for some industries, or trained people, as is the case for universities, the products must find an appropriate new home. (As Katz and Kahn, 1966, note, business organizations direct considerable attention to this disposal function because of its immediate and direct feedback relationship to the acquisition of new inputs; nonbusiness organizations, such as universities, have until recently expended little energy on product disposal because of the delayed and indirect feedback effect on acquisition.) Finally, and perhaps most important, organizations depend on their environ-

Figure 18–1
Example of the organization set: A focal organization and its relationships with environmental organizations

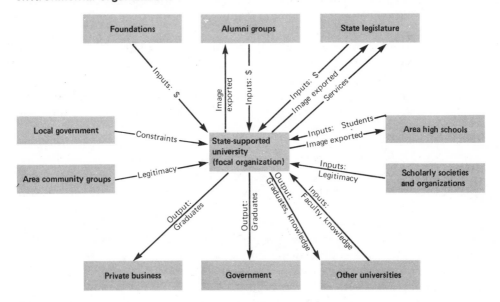

ment to accord *legitimacy* to their existence and functioning (Parsons, 1960). To the extent that an organization's activities are viewed as consonant with the expressed values and goals of the larger culture, the organization is granted autonomy, freedom from onerous constraints, and the likelihood of subsidies or other forms of help in hard times.

To an increasing extent, the environment of organizations in modern societies is composed of other organizations. Evan (1966) has offered the concept of *organization set* as a methodological tool for characterizing an organization's interaction and relationships with its environment. Figure 18–1 provides an example of a hypothetical organization set. The *focal organization* in this case is a state-supported university.

The university's survival and effectiveness depend upon inputs in the form of money from the state legislature, foundations, and alumni groups. The university's raw materials—educable pupils—come predominantly from state and area high schools. Its output—educated students—flows to corporations, government, and other schools (for graduate work or to join their faculties). The legitimacy of the university is a function of the perceptions of scholarly societies, alumni, community groups, and other organizations which include in their purposes the evaluation of the university's service to the public. The local municipal government, state government agencies, and similar groups exert some constraints on the university's activities.

Not all of these interorganizational relationships need to be formalized, nor are they all characterized by similar frequencies of interaction episodes. One could follow the example of Hall (1972) by using darker or thicker lines to represent more frequent interaction episodes, or use dotted lines to represent unofficial or ad hoc interaction patterns.

Evan developed the idea of organization set from Merton's (1957) concept of the *role set*. The role set is composed of the roles and role relationships that an individual has by virtue of occupying a particular focal role or office. The analogy is apt, for organizations experience stresses in their relationships with other organizations similar to those that an individual experiences in his relationships with other individuals. Just as a person may fall prey to role conflict due to the conflicting expectations of other persons, so an organization can find itself caught in the middle among the conflicting demands of its various publics. The state university in our example may be called upon by the legislature to adopt expense-saving measures which scholarly societies or other universities regard as inimical to quality teaching and the pursuit of new knowledge. Just as an individual may experience role overload, the state university may be pressed upon to do so many different things that it ends up doing none of them very well. One suspects furthermore that organizations use much the same coping mechanisms, whether functional or dysfunctional, that individuals employ for managing such stresses. These coping mechanisms include the following: formulating a policy by which some claims are given greater priority than others; tilting toward the agents who possess greater capacity to reward or harm; double-talk, by which verbal or symbolic but not substantive systemic concessions are made to some agents; outright repudiation of some expectations; and simple "muddling through," taking whatever steps are necessary when dealing with one public or one problem at a time. As a consequence, the operational goals of an organization seldom coincide with those expressed in its charter or publicly espoused by its leaders. The goals of day-to-day organizational functioning represent a continuous evolutionary process that is shaped in part by components of the organization's environment (Thompson & McEwen, 1958).

A further observation that Figure 18–1 implies, but that should be made explicit here, is that the nature of the relationships in the organization set exerts great influence on the goings-on *inside* the focal organization. The state university represents a good case in point. From the end of World War II until the mid-1960s, universities easily disposed of their outputs, flourished in a cultural climate which readily endorsed the value of higher education and research, and went about their business in a relatively autonomous fashion. (A deviation from this trend occurred in the early 1950s—the McCarthy era—when some states exacted loyalty oaths from faculty in publicly supported schools.) Beginning around the late 1960s, many universities began to face difficulty in placing their graduates; the value of higher education became a moot point in the views of many community groups; state legislatures and alumni tightened their grip on the money faucet; and both federal government and civil rights agencies demanded that universities demonstrate affirmative action in the treatment and hiring of women and minority groups. The placement problem has apparently increased the concern of university officials over ensuring adequate curriculum options for vocational training. The reappraisal of the unquestioned value of higher education has permeated the classrooms with an atmosphere that puts the burden of proof on the scholars ("Just why is this course or this material essential to our knowledge?"), and this defensive posture greatly complicates the design and implementation of curricula. The drying up of input dollars tends to stimulate competition among departments for student bodies, which could ideally be a healthy guard against complacency but could also lend itself to the subversion or compromise of traditional educational values. Accountability for affirmative action corrects old wrongs, but also makes more legalistic and formalistic certain processes that were previously handled in easy informality. The foregoing analysis is not to be interpreted as a lamentation, nor as a chastisement of either the university or its publics. Hindsight is 20–20, and few university officials even in the 1950s, no matter how forward-looking, could have foreseen the changes in store. Moreover, the other organizations in the university's organization set (state legislature, federal government, economic organizations, and others) had *their* own environments to respond to. Our point has been to show how changes in the university's environment have, for better or for worse, made life within the university vastly different from what it was a decade or two ago.

DIMENSIONS OF THE ENVIRONMENT

Rate of change

Although the environments of all organizations in modern societies change at some pace, environments differ both in their rates of change and in the importance of such change to the operations of specific organizations. A company in the plastics industry, for example, faces an environment in which technological innovations cause extremely short product life cycles, frequent changes in production processes, constant revision of customers' product specifications, and numerous opportunities to induce the exit of a mobile professional and scientific work force. The pharmaceutical, electronics, and aerospace industries provide some of these same environmental characteristics. On the other hand, a firm in the container industry operates in a relatively placid technological and economic environment. Because of the consumer market orientation of the packaged food industry, its rate of change is perhaps greater than that of the container industry, but it is not as great as that of the plastics industry (Lawrence & Lorsch, 1964).

Burns and Stalker (1961) argue that the rate of environmental change determines the type of organizational structure which is most effective for organizational functioning. They suggest that the more traditional or *mechanistic* organization form is best suited to stable environments. The mechanistic form manifests itself in such features as:

1. A highly specialized division of labor.
2. A centralized or hierarchical basis of authority and influence.
3. A preponderance of vertical, as opposed to lateral, communication patterns.
4. Detailed policies, procedures, and rules for each participant, which are not to be deviated from.

The logic underlying such features is primarily one of *maximizing the efficiency of internal production processes.* The need for slack and flexibility are not imperative, since adaptation requirements are few and insignificant.

An organization which faces a dynamic, unstable environment, however, must place a premium on the ability to adapt to change; inefficiencies in the short run can be tolerated if they are essential to maintaining the resiliency necessary for quick adaptation. This calls for an *organic* organization form, which takes on the following attributes:

1. Continual revision of participants' role responsibilities and prerogatives, which change informally as a function of interaction with others.
2. Decentralized patterns of influence and authority, which inhere primarily in the expertise relevant to a problem rather than in office or rank.
3. A preponderance of lateral rather than vertical communication patterns, which convey expertise and advice as opposed to commands or decisions.
4. Reliance on judgment rather than detailed rules.

Burns and Stalker stress that neither form is innately superior to the other, but that "the beginning of administrative wisdom is the awareness that there is no one optimum type of management system" (Tosi & Hamner, 1974, p. 44).

Warren Bennis (1964) has argued that time is on the side of the organic structure, which will supersede the bureaucratic organization as the dominant form of human organization. Although he credits the organizational bureaucracy for many of the achievements of modern industrial societies, he has nevertheless suggested that its long suit is the efficient execution of the routine in a stable environment. Bennis foresaw the increasing rate of change in knowledge, technology, population, and social-political constraints on the firm as mandating a new kind of organization. This new structural form—already glimpsed in the aerospace industry and the Apollo project—would consist of rapidly changing *temporary systems,* whose participants have no fixed role or office but rotate from one task force to another as their specialized expertise is needed. "Linking pin" personnel will coordinate the diverse task groups, managing not so much by authority as by their ability to mediate and translate the needs and jargon of the different groups to each other. One suspects that the activities carried out in such *organic-adaptive* organizations would appear messy, wasteful of effort, and grossly inefficient to some observer viewing these goings-on from a suitable vantage point. But that might be the inevitable price for the capacity to adapt to dynamic environments.

There is a counterargument to Bennis' thesis, although it seems to receive little attention. Bureaucracies might be more than equal to the challenge of environmental change when they are governed in an authoritarian manner. In the 1930s, as the United States and the European democracies wallowed in the mire of an economic depression, some observers looked at Hitler's Germany and Mussolini's Italy with envy, and concluded that such regimes could at least "make the trains run on time." In our own era, some commentators see the Soviet Union as having a competitive edge over the Western world in cleaning up the physical environment, by virtue of the Soviet Union's power to conscript social action without time-consuming deliberation. Such a solution sounds unappealing to us, and many would regard it in any case as an unviable alternative in the face of Western trends toward the leveling of authority, but history has taught us that people view authoritarian organizations with a less jaundiced eye when other forms of social collectivity prove inadequate to deal with recurring crises.

In fact, Bennis himself has more recently backed away from his earlier prediction that bureaucracies were on the way out. His reflections (see W. F. Dowling, "Conversation with Warren Bennis," *Organizational Dynamics,* Winter 1974) have led him to conclude that a precondition for the organic form of organization is a certain degree of consensus concerning basic issues among the constituents and publics of the organization. However, it appears to him that the pluralism of our culture—the amazing variety of blocs and organized interest groups whose aims are often at cross-purposes—rules out the development of any such consensus, at least for organizations in the public sector (for example, universities, state and local governments, and hospitals). Bennis now believes that the turbulence of an organization's environment, particularly in the form of increased pressures from the organization's diverse publics, acts to make organizations more—not less—hierarchical, because pressure groups insist on dealing personally with the head of the organization. Pressures exerted upon the top of the organization are then necessarily transmitted downward as constraints on the organization's members, not as matters subject to leisurely deliberation by all organization participants.

Aside from opting for a particular structural form, organizations attempt to handle environmental change in a proactive manner by "researching the future." To the extent that environmental forces can be diagnosed and their logical development predicted, organizations can plan ahead in order to meet the challenges posed by the environment. Kelly (1974) identifies four methods used to research the future:

1. The *delphi method*, which offers a means of pooling and refining the collective subjective judgments of experts by a process of successive polling and feedback.

2. The *scenario*, which represents essentially the narration of a fictitious sequence of future events in order to bring to light the repercussions of one phenomenon upon others and to identify critical branch points beyond which certain options are precluded.

3. *Computer simulation*, which starts with a simplified mathematical or statistical model of real-world relationships, and processes past or current data in the model to predict the parameters of the future.

4. *Technological forecasting*, which may combine any of the first three methods along with more intuitive or informal clinical insights in order to assess the ultimate ripple effects of technological innovations, looming resource shortages, or changing trends in resource usage. Utterback and Brown (1972) argue that there is a sound basis for technological forecasting, since technological change is "a relatively continuous process which casts shadows far ahead." As an exercise in technological forecasting, they trace the impact of a developing shortage of silver on photography (to date, photographic film has been based on silver compounds).

Uncertainty

Correlated with rate of change, but distinguishable from it as a dimension of organizational environments, is the uncertainty (about both the present and the future) created by complex interdependence and interaction among environmental forces. Lawrence and Lorsch (1969) identify three components of uncertainty: (1) lack of clear information about the existing state of crucial environmental variables; (2) lack of knowledge about cause-and-effect relationships among organizational actions and environmental responses; and (3) the time span of definitive feedback—the length of time that must pass before an organization can ascertain the adequacy or effectiveness of its decisions.

The more uncertain the environment of the organization, the greater the premium placed on organizational flexibility and "slack," and the riskier it becomes to invest all of the organization's eggs in one strategy or process basket. At the extreme, environmental uncertainty may render long-range planning a farcical form of soothsaying, since forecasting will probably be based on scarcely tenable assumptions. In 1963, *Dun's Review* ("Long-Range Planning and Cloudy Horizons," 1963) questioned the utility of long-range planning after surveying the track records of the planners themselves. The alternative, it seems, is simply to avoid like the plague any organizational overcommitment to a single product, market, technology, area of expertise, or philosophy. This posture (or lack of one) encourages diversity and even conflict within the organization's boundaries in order to maximize the array of options needed at any given time. As Karl Weick (1969) puts it, evolution favors those social organisms whose equivocality of retention and operating processes matches the equivocality of environmental inputs.

Beneficence

Environments vary considerably in the degree of generosity and leniency they grant to organizations. Of course, no organization enjoys unlimited or unqualified support from all of its publics, but some enjoy easier access to important inputs (dollars, personnel, scarce resources) or greater autonomy in functioning than do others. Some organizations are allowed to perish when not able to hack it on their own, whereas others are bailed out of recurring crises even when these crises are of their own making.

The beneficence of the environment is probably a function that consists mainly of two related but separate factors: (1) the perceived contributions that the organization makes to the environment by means of its output, and (2) the perceptions of the organization's publics that its dominant goals, values, and ideals are consonant rather than dissonant with the prevailing cultural ethos. The two factors are not necessarily the same for the simple reason that the organization may dispose of its output to environmental sectors that are totally distinct from the sectors that have the potential to reward, harass, or exert constraints upon the organization. One consequence of this is that organizational leaders, quite understandably, sometimes seem to expend more effort in shaping the "image" of their institution than they do in actually trying to improve its product or service. The major oil companies, for example, have recently invested heavily in "institutional advertising" designed to combat the widespread view that their refineries and tankers are systematically despoiling nature or that they are artificially restricting the supply of gasoline in order to gouge the consumer. In the 1950s, arguments for government support of agricultural commodity prices rested not so much on the economic contributions of small farms (which were alleged to be negligible by some economists), but rather on the assertion that the life-style of the small farm helped perpetuate some of the finest ideals and attributes of the American national character. On the other hand, the major firms in a number of industries whose contribution to the economy and affluence of modern America is undeniable, find themselves increasingly hamstrung by constraints because of allegations that they are callous, authoritarian, insensitive to the aesthetics of our physical surroundings, or use their size unfairly in competition against the "underdogs."

Ironically, it is when organizations fail to make their contributions that image problems become less troublesome, suggesting that one Machiavellian strategy an organization might use in fighting a bad public image is to deliberately give clients a taste of what life can be like when the organization is so hemmed in that it cannot cope with its primary mission effectively. Presumably, that could have the effect of making active allies out of those who depend on the organization's product or service.

SUBSYSTEM ENVIRONMENTS

Although it makes some sense to think in terms of the environment of the total organization, it is also useful to consider the different sectors of the environment which affect the functioning and decision making of various subsystems of the organization. The different sectors of the environment generally will vary in the three dimensions discussed in the preceding section—rate of change, uncertainty, and beneficence. Even though the aggregate environment of the organization may tend toward placidity, the research and development subsystem may confront volatility and uncertainty in its relevant subenvironment. On the other hand, though a company may have to contend with a hostile environment on most fronts, its purchasing department may be enjoying a state of fond cordiality with the outside agents on whom it depends.

The work of Lorsch and Lawrence (1965) cogently illustrates the importance of recognizing the differential environments of organizational subsystems. Lorsch and Lawrence began their research with the study of innovation in the plastics industry. Effective innovation in an enterprise requires the collaboration of its production, sales, and research subsystems: the final product must satisfy the contraints set by production costs and scheduling; it must meet a consumer need and the other tests of marketability; and, of course, it must draw upon the latest advances in scientific knowledge. However, the production, sales, and research subsystems are attuned to vastly differing environments. Production typically deals with an environment marked by a high degree of certainty and stability and operates on a very short, almost immediate, time cycle of feedback. Sales grapples with an environment manifesting somewhat less certainty, frequent change (a function of fickle consumer preferences and aggressive competitors), and a time cycle that is measured in weeks or months as compared to the hours or days of the production time cycle. Research gazes outward to an environment which is quintessentially unstructured and uncertain, sometimes changing markedly with the latest research report and sometimes requiring years before relevant cause-and-effect relationships crystallize.

The differing environments of these subsystems dictate drastic differences in the structure and internal work orientation of the three areas. Production departments tend toward a high degree of structure and formalization, managed by a rather directive and controlling leadership style. Research activities are quite unstructured, marked by collegial rather than authority-based relationships, and research people do their work in a "play it by ear" style, guided by undetailed rules and procedures. Sales departments exhibit a level of structure and formalization intermediate between that of production and research, a somewhat permissive and casual tone of interpersonal relationships, but disciplined by a cycle of reasonably quick and unequivocal performance feedback.

All very well, and as it should be; as Lorsch and Lawrence note, "Specialized orientations and structures (appropriate for the environmental sector confronted) facilitate a unit's task performance." Furthermore, of the two plastics firms studied by Lorsch and Lawrence, the more innovative one showed the *greater* differences in the internal structure, orientation, and style of its departments. But given such differences, how does an enterprise achieve the integration and coordination necessary to make an abstract model on the drawing board into a marketable product which also satisfies the binding constraints set by production tools and efficiency considerations? Paradoxically, the company that achieved the more effective integration for product innovation was the company with greater differences in orientation among the three subsystems. Both companies had official coordinating departments, comprising representatives from the different functions. However, the less successful firm had a coordinating department which was overconcerned with immediate market considerations, whereas its counterpart in the more innovative organization dealt with a balance of issues posed by all three orientations. Furthermore, the latter group freely encouraged open conflict and disagreement (as a natural consequence of differences in environmental perspective), but having once arrived at a consensus, the group's decisions were final and were upheld by higher management. A by-product of this give-and-take was that representatives of each subsystem acquired an understanding and appreciation of the problems faced by the other subsystems.

ORGANIZATION BOUNDARIES

Organizations, like all living systems, are demarcated from their environments by *boundaries*. The boundary includes, but is not limited to, physical barriers between internal activities and outside forces; it entails, in addition, differences in lingo, norms, and intensity of interaction. Furthermore, there are degrees of "boundariness"—boundariness is not an all-or-nothing phenomenon. Although the elusive concept of organization boundary is difficult to capture in a crisp definition, the presence of such a boundary is manifested by a quantum jump in the amount of force or effort necessary to sustain a flow of movement, communication, or activity. It is easy, for example, to carry all manner of personal belongings in your car as you drive from city to city in the United States; but when you reach the Canadian border, a slight increase in effort (stopping your car and checking with a customs official) is needed. If you wish to carry those same belongings to Soviet Russia, you will require an enormous increment in effort to accommodate a much stricter search and inquiry about what you are bringing along. The boundary between the United States and the USSR is much more rigid and less permeable—in psychological, sociological, and political terms—than is the boundary between the United States and Canada. Similarly, I easily converse with my immediate friends and colleagues in the School of Business, but find that I have to be more selective, deliberate, and formal when circumstances require me to call upon a faculty member in another area of the university. Furthermore, my increase in effort is greater when I communicate with someone in classics or chemistry rather than with someone in economics or social psychology, and greater still when I communicate with a municipal official outside the university.

Boundaries serve important functions for organizations. James Thompson has developed a fascinating book-length theory of organizational action from the single premise that organizations seek to protect their technological core from environmental disturbances (Thompson, 1967). Boundaries, then, *buffer* the organization's internal operations from outside irritants. They do this in part by smoothing or balancing the flow of input and output transactions. Boundaries also serve a *filtering and coding* function, by which inappropriate inputs are either screened out or, in the case of human inputs, are socialized in some fashion in order to fit organizational needs. In addition, boundaries code information so that communication systems are not choked by excessive "noise," but rather flow like rivulets. Finally, boundaries *protect the integrity* of the organizational system, preventing it from being absorbed by the environment or from losing the distinctive character that distinguishes it from other systems.

To say that boundaries serve these functions is not to suggest that they serve them in any optimal or promotive fashion. Boundaries, like the organizations they surround, are not "natural" in any spontaneous or automatic sense; they are contrived, and they require deliberate human actions to ensure their maintenance and viability. An organization may lose sight of its distinctive missions by being too receptive to distracting goals urged on it by the environment. Some critics of present-day universities suggest that, in their well-intentioned efforts to help solve a broad spectrum of society's social and political problems, they have lost their systemic uniqueness as educational institutions. Moreover, organizations may be so hard pressed to find participants that they admit into their fold persons with values and motives incongruent with organizational purposes and processes.

However, the most perplexing dilemma in boundary management arises from the fact that boundaries must ideally strike a balance between permeability to appropriate inputs and impenetrability to irrelevant or disturbing inputs. An organization cannot hermetically seal itself off from its surroundings; it must interact with the environment to import needed energy, information, and other inputs, to maintain legitimacy in the larger social system, and to maintain relationships with the sectors toward which its output is disposed. The more uncertain, turbulent, or hostile an organization's environment, the greater its problem of striking the appropriate balance between boundary permeability and rigidity. Consider the case of the firm that produces a homeogeneous, standardized product for a well-defined and stable target market. The purchasing personnel may confidently shoo away all vendors except those few who supply its traditional materials. The production and sales managers can restrict their business reading to a few specialized trade journals. The company president need not devote much time to outsiders, confining his attention to a few large customers and perhaps to informal or ceremonial activities involving local community leaders. On the other hand, the presidency of the United States must take into account a heterogeneous, unstable, and highly uncertain domestic and foreign environment. On the one hand, the president must be protected from trivia that would consume the time he needs for serious thought on important policy matters; on the other hand, he must not lose touch with the publics he serves. Yet how can anyone know just what is trivial? In this instance, there are no ready-made formulas for programming boundary coding and filtering functions. Every anecdotal account of a chief executive who failed because of excessive attention to detail can probably be countered with an example of one who failed because he isolated himself from the events of the day.

BOUNDARY ROLES

Except in a metaphoric sense, organizations do not, of course, actually interact with the environment. People interact, and they interact with other people. Relationships among organizations ultimately boil down to relationships among people. People perform the boundary functions of the organization; they do the purchasing, selling, lobbying, "impression management," negotiating, recruiting, and dispatching; and to an increasing extent in formal organizations, they do so in officially designated *boundary roles.*

A boundary role, like the boundary itself, is not an all-or-nothing matter; roles differ in *boundary relevance* as a function of the amount of time their occupants engage in boundary-spanning interactions or as a function of the importance of such interactions for role performance. However, we may simplify the discussion by speaking of boundary roles as those which are higher than average in boundary relevance, and of *internal roles* as those which are less than average in boundary relevance.

Figure 18–2 illustrates the boundary transaction system which links one organization to another in its environment. Let us take organization A as the focal organization and organization B as a member of its organization set—organization B could be a federal regulatory agency, a supplier of essential raw materials, an important customer, or a community civic organization. The boundary role person (BRP), representing his *constituents* (C) or his internal colleagues, engages in interaction with a counterpart BRP who also represents a constituency.

The nature of this transaction system makes the social psychology of boundary roles quite distinctive in comparison to the psychological dynamics of internal roles. The theory elaborating the psychology of boundary role behavior is found in the work of Kahn, Wolfe, Quinn, Snoek, and Rosenthal (1964) at the University of Michigan's Institute for Social Research, in the theory of labor negotiations advanced by Walton and McKersie (1965), and in the writing of Adams (1976). These

Figure 18–2
Boundary transaction system

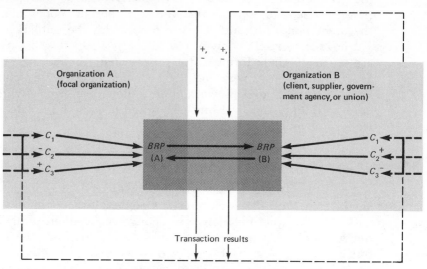

Solid arrows represent influence attempts; broken arrows represent effects of transaction results.
Source: Adopted from J. S. Adams, "The Structure and Dynamics of Behavior in Organization
Boundary Roles," in M. Dunnette (Ed.), *Handbook of Industrial and Organizational Psychology*
(Chicago: Rand McNally, 1976), p. 1180.

authors clearly document, first of all, the fact that people in boundary
roles experience *a high degree of role conflict.* The BRP must take
into account not only the expectations and influence pressures of constituents, but also the demands of his counterpart BRP. The BRP, then,
must grapple with two different—sometimes contradictory—sets of
goals, values, and beliefs.

The BRP's task is made even more difficult by the inconsistent prescriptions of his own constituents. The latter tend to have biased conceptions of the BRP's job. For example, Strauss (1962) found in his
study of purchasing agents that different departments (engineering,
manufacturing, production scheduling, quality control) tried to impose
their own criteria on the purchasing agent's evaluation of suppliers
and parts. When specialized departments have their own narrowly
defined goals or are evaluated by one-dimensional performance
measures, they will exert pressure on the BRP to secure agreements
with outsiders favorable to their particular interests.

The BRP, by virtue of the fact that his interactions occur with outsiders, cannot use authority to accomplish his ends. His counterpart owes
no allegiance to the norms and rules of the BRP's organization. Consequently, the BRP must use other methods of influence in the recurring
social exchange cycle (Organ & Wall, 1974). These methods may take

the form of overt bargaining or negotiation, in which the BRP tempers his own demands and makes the concessions necessary to effect a reasonable settlement. This bargaining process, of course, holds considerable interest for the BRP's constituents, who may pressure the BRP to "hang tough" and "drive a hard bargain." Any deviation from such an aggressive posture could cause the BRP to look weak or disloyal, and thus make him vulnerable to punishment from powerful constituents (Wall, 1975). To the extent that the BRP's constituents urge him to assume a competitive and aggressive bargaining stance—to maximize rather than optimize settlements with outsiders—the BRP is compelled to maneuver within a very restricted set of options. If he is unable to maintain a working relationship with the environment, he fails altogether; yet he must maintain that relationship in a fashion that leaves his image in the eyes of constituents untainted by signs of weakness or lack of commitment to his organization's values.

In the absency of authority, the BRP may seek to influence outsiders by using friendship or ingratiation techniques. A favorite device seems to be picking up the jargon and verbal symbols of his counterpart. Walton and McKersie (1965) encountered a labor union spokesman who won the favor of management representatives by using business-like language, such as "the policy of our organization" and "the decisions of our executive board." (A BRP does this with some risk if his constituents know about it, since the latter may wonder whether their representative has been "brainwashed.") The BRP may also use expertise as influence, as in the case of industrial sales representatives who apply engineering and technical know-how to servicing their clients.

Due to his exposure to the environment, the BRP often senses trends and developments which dictate changes in organizational policies and procedures. Hearing the complaints and criticisms of outsiders or recognizing new dependence relationships between his organization and environmental sectors, he tends to feel the inadequacy of present organizational arrangements more keenly than do his constituents. This knowledge makes it necessary for the BRP to become an agent of change. His advocacy of change, however, may simply fall on deaf ears or may initiate protracted conflict with his constituents, who do not and cannot see the organization from the BRP's perspective. Nevertheless, the boundary role person must represent the environment to his organization, as well as vice versa, becoming an activist broker between the viewpoints of constituents and outsiders. In so doing, he has to influence his own tribe, more often by persuasion and bargaining than by unilateral decision.

An article in the April 1974 issue of *Fortune* magazine ("New Kind of Challenge for Salesmen," 1974) describes some of the BRP's dilemmas and strategies for coping with them. The article dealt with the "new kind of challenge" presented to salesmen by temporary shortages in basic industrial materials—such as steel, aluminum, plastics, and synthetic fibers—which their companies sold to other manufacturing firms. Suddenly these salesmen faced the problem, not of acquiring new orders, but of filling old ones to traditional clients. One salesman had a fight with his own production department after it began to book orders for other accounts from inventory being held in reserve for a customer of his. Another observed that his most important task during that period was to keep customers from blaming his company for the shortage. His method of managing this task was to stay "in close touch with purchasing agents, carefully explaining the causes of the shortage, . . . and keeping informed of his customers' own production and marketing plans" so that he could foresee changes in their needs. On the other hand, he felt compelled to keep "a close watch on his customers' inventories in order to prevent hoarding." This same BRP, who sold aluminum to manufacturers and distributors, had to haggle with his own product offices because they were allotting a customer $\frac{1}{12}$ of his annual volume of purchases each month, in disregard of the cyclical fluctuations of the customer's needs. In the end he compromised, "and we got two-thirds of what we asked for." In order to get cooperation from his production personnel, he had to reciprocate by persuading customers to help reduce costs by ordering in large lot sizes. An industrial chemicals representative found that by coming through in the pinch for deliveries to purchasing agents, he could induce them to return the favor by providing intelligence about what his competitors were up to.

Organ (1971) has suggested that the distinctive demands made by boundary roles call for a particular mix of aptitudes and personality attributes. Sensitivity to semantics looms as a critical skill, since the BRP must avoid words that alienate outsiders, and needs to translate external viewpoints into the language of his constituency. A good memory for details serves the BRP well, since the more he can show that he remembers about outside clients, the more impressed they are with his sympathetic posture. The BRP must be capable of a measured degree of flexibility in his opinions and attitudes, not getting hung up on an obsession with ideological consistency or symbolic issues devoid of substantive stakes; this flexibility, however, must not appear as "wishy-washiness" to constituents, who sometimes prefer to see rock-ribbed resistance in the BRP's moral commitment. The BRP must not be averse to occasionally switching between two faces: one of benign reasonableness to external agents and one of corporate zeal to his constituents. If he cannot achieve the latter, he will probably be denied the latitude and discretion essential to accomplishing the former. The effective BRP values pragmatism above aesthetics, since viable solutions to conflict may not be symmetrical, elegant, or beautiful. A political instinct is essential to the BRP in order to manage the shifting coalitions through which he gets things done.

CONCLUSION

Important as the external environment is to the psychology of organizational behavior, we possess only a meager fund of empirical knowledge about it. This disappointing disparity results from several factors. First, the systematic incorporation of the environment into organization theory dates from quite recent times. As noted at the outset of the chapter, only in the late 1950s did even the sketchiest conceptual frameworks and taxonomies of environments emerge. Even today, as the reader may have already concluded, the concepts and terminology employed are less precise than one would hope. Second, empirical study of the organization vis-à-vis its environment presents severe practical and methodological problems. The result is that much of our knowledge about organizational-environmental linkages comes from in-depth case studies of single organizations. Such studies often provide a wealth of clinical insight and perspectives, but they seldom permit confident conclusions. When studies of this kind work backward in historical hindsight fashion, they can instill dangerous overconfidence in ability to assess cause-effect relationships (consult Fischoff and Beyth, 1975, on the "I knew it would happen" syndrome).

Nevertheless, informed speculation about the environment is a managerial imperative which cannot be put off until precise answers are available. It is hoped that this chapter has offered the reader a usable set of conceptual maps with which to raise the appropriate questions, even if those maps fail to disclose a clear passage to the answers.

SUMMARY

The organization, as an open system, depends upon its environment for the acquisition of inputs, the disposal of outputs, and the legitimation of its existence. The organization set is a useful conceptual tool for understanding the structure and dynamics of relationships between the organization and its environment. One important characteristic of the organization's relevant environment is its rate of change, which determines whether organic or mechanistic organization structure is appropriate. Uncertainty and beneficence are also crucial parameters of the environment. Different parts of the total organization may face out upon environmental sectors that vary substantially in these characteristics, suggesting that subsystems within a single organization should logically vary in structure.

Organizations are adjoined to their environments by boundaries, which may be both physical and psychological in nature. Boundaries buffer the organization's core technologies from environmental disturbances, serve filtering and coding functions, and protect the political, sociological, and psychological integrity of the organization. Boundary functions are ultimately managed, for better or worse, by persons acting in boundary role capacities. Boundary role persons are highly susceptible to conflict between the expectations of their constituents and the demands of external agents; the distinctive stresses endemic to such roles appear to call for incumbents who possess a rare blend of skills, traits, and values.

CONCEPTS TO REMEMBER

organization environment	computer simulation
organization set	technological forecasting
mechanistic structures	subsystem environment
organic structures	organization boundary
temporary systems	boundary role
delphi method	constituents
scenario	

QUESTIONS FOR DISCUSSION

1. Choose an organization with which you are familiar and map out its organization set. What conflicts are apparent? How does the organization cope with these conflicts?

2. What are the costs associated with an organic-adaptive form? Consider not only economic, but social and psychological costs for organization members.

3. *U.S. News & World Report* (September 6, 1976) reported the results of a survey in which people were asked to rate 20 major industries on a scale from 1 (poor) to 7 (excellent). The top five were airlines, banks, trucking, department stores, and tire manufacturers; the bottom five were appliance repair services, automobile manufacturers, oil and gas companies, automobile dealers, and railroads. What are likely to be the effects (in the near future) of such differences in perceptions by the public?

4. If subsystems within the organization must be structured differently in order to adapt to their respective environments, how is coordination or integration of the various subsystems achieved?

5. Are boundary roles inherently or inevitably stressful? What conditions sometimes alleviate the stress?

REFERENCES

Adams, J. S. The structure and dynamics of behavior in organization boundary roles. In M. Dunnette (Ed.), *Handbook of industrial and organizational psychology.* Chicago: Rand-McNally, 1975, in press.

Bennis, W. G. *Organizational developments and the fate of bureaucracy.* Invited address delivered at meetings of American Psychological Association, Washington, D.C., September 5, 1964.

Burns, T., & Stalker, G. M. *The management of innovation.* London: Tavistock, 1961. Abridged and reproduced in part in H. L. Tosi & W. C. Hamner, (Eds.), *Organizational behavior and management: A contingency approach.* Chicago: St Clair Press, 1974.

Churchman, C. W. *The systems approach.* New York: Dell Publishing, 1968.

Evan, W. E. The organization set: Toward a theory of interorganizational relations. In J. D. Thompson (Ed.), *Approaches to organizational design.* Pittsburgh: University of Pittsburgh Press, 1966.

Fischoff, B., & Beyth, R. I knew it would happen: Remembered probabilities of once-future things. *Organizational Behavior and Human Performance,* 1975, *13,* 1–16.

Hall, R. H. *Organizations: Structure and process.* Englewood Cliffs, N.J.: Prentice-Hall, 1972.

Kahn, R. L., Wolfe, D., Quinn, R., Snoek, J. D., & Rosenthal, R. *Organizational stress.* New York: Wiley, 1964.

Katz, D., & Kahn, R. L. *The social psychology of organizations.* New York: Wiley, 1966.

Kelly, J. *Organizational behavior* (Rev. ed.). Homewood, Ill.: Irwin, 1974.

Lawrence, P. R., & Lorsch, J. W. *Organization and environment.* Homewood, Ill.: Irwin, 1964.

Long-range planning and cloudy horizons. *Dun's Review,* 1963, *18.*

Lorsch, J. W., & Lawrence, P. R. Organizing for product innovation. *Harvard Business Review,* 1965, *43,* 109–120.

Merton, R. K. *Social theory and social structure* (Rev. ed.). Glencoe, Ill.: Free Press, 1957.

A new kind of challenge for salesmen. *Fortune,* April 1974, pp. 156–166.

Organ, D. W. Linking pins between organizations and environment. *Business Horizons,* 1971, *14,* 73–80.

Organ, D. W., & Wall, J. A. Decision-making behavior in organization boundary exchanges. *Proceedings,* Midwest Academy of Management, Kent, Ohio, 1974.

Parsons, T. *Structure and process in modern societies.* New York: Free Press, 1960.

Strauss, G. Tactics of lateral relationship: The purchasing agent. *Administrative Science Quarterly,* 1962, *7,* 161–186.

Thompson, J. D. *Organizations in action.* New York: McGraw-Hill, 1967.

Thompson, J. D., & McEwen, W. J. Organization goals and environment: Goal-setting as an interaction process. *American Sociological Review,* 1958, *23,* 23–31.

Utterback, J. M., & Brown, J. W. Monitoring for technological opportunities. *Business Horizons,* 1972, *15,* 5–15.

Tosi, H. L., & Hamner, W. C. (Eds.). *Organizational behavior and management: A contingency approach.* Chicago: St. Clair Press, 1974.

Wall, J. A. Effects of constituent trust and representative bargaining orientation on intergroup bargaining. *Journal of Personality and Social Psychology,* 1975, *31,* 1004–1012.

Walton, R. E., & McKersie, R. B. *A behavioral theory of labor negotiations.* New York: McGraw-Hill, 1965.

Weick, K. E. *The social psychology of organizing.* Reading, Mass.: Addison-Wesley, 1969.

Author index

Subject index

A

Activation theory, 137, 141, 173–74, 322–23
Aggression, 198–201
  displacement of, 200–201
Anxiety, 74, 77, 168–72, 178, 201–3
Attitude change, 122–27
  and persuasion, 126–27
Attitudes, 107–22
  components of, 109–10
  functional bases of, 118–20
  and interpersonal attraction, 302
  and prejudice, 120–22
  relationship to behavior, 110–12
  sources of, 112–14
  structure and consistency, 114–15
Attribution theory, 100–101, 151–53
Authority, 370–73
  limitations of, 372–73
Autocratic-democratic dimension, 15, 331–32, 394
Avoidance learning, 46–47

B

Bargaining, 356
Boundary roles, 345–46, 421–24
Bureaucracy, 414–15

C

Career stages, 139–41
Case studies, 18–21
Classical conditioning, 39–40, 74–75
Cognitive dissonance, 115–18
Cognitive processes, 107
Communication patterns, 310–11
Competition, 204–5, 332–34
Computer simulation, 415
Conflict, 341–58
  between-group, 344–49

Conflict—*Cont.*
  functional and dysfunctional, 351–52
  between organizations, 349–51
  within-group, 342–44
Conflict resolution, 353–57
Consideration, 386, 392
Contingencies of reinforcement, 41–49, 107
Contingency Model of Leadership Effectiveness, 397–400
Contingency-shaped behavior, 58
Control in organizations, 363–66
Coping, 194–95
Correlational studies, 23–27
Critical incident method, 154–55

D

Delphi technique, 327–29, 415
Depression, 195, 198
Discipline, 73–85
  a case study of, 81–83
  styles of, 83
Discriminative stimulus, 45
Distributive justice, 366–67

E

Ecological control, 377
Emotionality, 168–72, 176
Equity-inequity, 83, 260–61
Equity theory, 148–50, 323–24, 367–68
Escape learning, 46
Ethics (in research), 31, 84
Ethnocentrism, 347–48
Exchange theory of attraction, 301
Expectancy theory of motivation, 12, 142–46, 391
Expert power, 373–75
Extinction, 47–48, 76, 198, 371, 374
Extraversion-introversion, 172, 176